MW01094980

Fight Pictures

The publisher gratefully acknowledges the generous support of Eric Papenfuse and Catherine Lawrence as members of the Publisher's Circle of the University of California Press Foundation.

Fight Pictures

A History of Boxing and Early Cinema

DAN STREIBLE

University of California Press

BERKELEY   LOS ANGELES   LONDON

University of California Press, one of the most distinguished university presses in the United States, enriches lives around the world by advancing scholarship in the humanities, social sciences, and natural sciences. Its activities are supported by the UC Press Foundation and by philanthropic contributions from individuals and institutions. For more information, visit www.ucpress.edu.

University of California Press
Berkeley and Los Angeles, California

University of California Press, Ltd.
London, England

Library of Congress Cataloging-in-Publication Data

Streible, Dan.
    Fight pictures : a history of boxing and early cinema / Dan Streible.
        p.   cm.
    Includes bibliographical references and index
    ISBN 978-0-520-25074-1 (cloth : alk. paper)—ISBN 978-0-520-25075-8 (pbk. : alk. paper)
        1. Boxing films—United States—History and criticism.   I. Title.

PN1995.9.B69S77   2008
791.43'6579—dc22   2007043788

Manufactured in the United States of America

17   16   15   14   13   12   11   10   09   08
10   9   8   7   6   5   4   3   2   1

This book is printed on Natures Book, which contains 50% post-consumer waste and meets the minimum requirements of ANSI/NISO Z39.48-1992 (R 1997) (*Permanence of Paper*).

For my parents, Mama Joan & Papa Jim

Contents

Illustrations

Foreword

If one wanted to make a case for American exceptionalism, there would be no more compelling instance than the arrival of cinema in the United States. Its impact on every day life in the 1890s and 1900s was immediate, powerful and multifaceted, lacking equivalents in other Western nations. From the outset, cinema transformed American theater, religion, print journalism, photography, politics, visual arts, and sports. Culturally, socially, and (eventually) economically, motion pictures were a powerful disruptive force that played with fundamental contractions in the cultural gestalt. In the fall of 1896, presidential candidate William McKinley insisted on conducting his electoral campaign from his front porch but his virtual self appeared in many American theaters, where his lifelike appearance rallied the Republican faithful. Baptists and other Protestant groups forbade their congregations to attend the theater—but they often brought in traveling showmen who screened filmed extracts of forbidden theatrical performances in their churches as a way to raise money. Live performances of the Passion play were systematically banned in the United States, but Protestant clergy quickly endorsed Passion play films and soon used them as a tool for proselytizing.

And, of course, film had an impact outside the church as well. It benefited John C. Rice, a balding comedian with a supporting role in the musical comedy *The Widow Jones*, which starred May Irwin. As the 1895–96 theatrical season came to an end, Irwin's management, feeling he made her seem old, announced a more youthful replacement. Two weeks later, a short film made of the musical's final scene, in which Rice kissed Miss Irwin, was screened for the first time. Soon the scene was playing in theaters across the country, and *Picture of a Kiss* (also known as *The John C. Rice–May Irwin Kiss*) quickly turned Rice into a kissing star—an American Don Juan. Irwin's management ate crow and was eventually forced to dismiss his replacement and rehire the comedian with a number of new perks.

Fight films played with many of the same contradictions and reverberations. Prizefighting was illegal in every state of the union but, barely a year after the debut of cinema, a lifelike simulacrum of a brutal heavyweight championship prizefight was being shown in high-toned theaters across the country. The boxers (and their promoters) were making big money from their virtual performances. Even more shockingly (and, for many, more puzzling), young American women were flocking to theaters to see Robert Fitzsimmons clobber previously undefeated heavyweight champion James J. Corbett. As this instance might suggest, fight films were at the very heart of cinema's transformation of American entertainment and culture.

Nonetheless, as Dan Streible's *Fight Pictures* reveals, circumstances surrounding prizefighting were different from other areas of cinematic transformation. Prizefighting was the arena where the impact of this new technology was most avidly embraced *and* contested. The wild nature of this struggle remains simultaneously riveting and revealing of America's divisive cultural landscape—then and now (the culture wars of the 1990s, the ongoing fights over gay marriage and the role of religion). When the charismatic Jack Johnson, an uncompromising black man, became heavyweight champion in 1908 and subsequently defeated a number of white men in the ring while openly bedding (and marrying) white women outside it, politically powerful forces enabled conservative values to prevail. Fifteen years after the *Corbett-Fitzsimmons Fight* unspooled in the nation's leading theaters, the United States government banned the interstate transportation of fight films, effectively undermining their economic value. These visual simulacra—though not boxing itself—were reduced to a quasi-legal status.

The joint victory of moralizing and racist forces was again only temporary. As Streible details, in the 1920s and 1930s fight films flourished in an underground economy while the nation was riveted to the radio, listening to fights such as the championship bout between Joe Louis and Max Schmeling. The ban on this form of entertainment had failed as miserably as Prohibition's ban on liquor. Fight films were again legalized in 1940. It was in the United States that the motion picture industry and the boxing fraternity worked together to transform a blood sport and move it out of the shadows and into the mainstream cultural arena. Fight films were shown in Europe, generating significant income but not the same degree of controversy.

There is another saga that should be told here, and that is the story behind Dan Streible's much-awaited book. Indeed, this important and revealing tale says much about the field of film and media studies and where it has been going for more than two decades. At the outset Dan and I shared a serious interest in early fight films. In the mid-1980s I had submitted a chapter-by-chapter breakdown for my book *The Emergence of Cinema: The American Screen to 1907*, in which I devote half a chapter to film-related aspects of the Corbett-Fitzsimmons Fight. As it turned out, this was the one topic in my proposal that received strenuous objections from the series editor and several members of the editorial board of the ten-volume "History of American Cinema." Such criticism, of course, only confirmed my conviction that fight films were an essential subject for inclusion. Meanwhile, as a graduate student at the University of Texas at Austin, Dan had become interested in early feature films and was soon investigating one aspect of this topic—the output of fight pictures. His article "A History of the Boxing Film, 1894–1915: Social Concern and Social Control in the Progressive Era" appeared in an 1989 issue of the journal *Film History* and outlined a complex and extended history of this topic. Instantly, he was recognized as the scholarly authority on a topic that was of immediate interest to film scholars, boxing enthusiasts, cultural historians and so on. Certainly this publication was one reason why my chapter on the subject sailed through a skeptical editorial committee as my book went to press.

In a time-honored academic tradition, Streible's article on boxing films became the foundation for his dissertation, "A History of the Prizefight Film, 1894–1915," which he completed in August 1994. By this stage, he was recognized as prominent member of a second wave of scholars researching and writing on American early cinema that includes people such as Greg Waller, Roberta Pearson, William Uricchio, Richard Abel, Lynne Kirby, Shelly Stamp Lindsay, Lee Grieveson, Jacqueline Stewart. Numerous presses were vying for the opportunity to publish Dan's manuscript, which meshed scholarship with a rich panoply of colorful figures. Book prizes seemed assured. So why did we have to wait another fourteen years for it to appear?!

Dan Streible may have been one of a second wave of scholars working on important aspects of early cinema, but his study of fight films led him to pioneer and lead what has become widely known as the orphan film movement. Because of their lowly status and apparent lack of aesthetic value, fight films were of little interest to film archives in museums—or to nonprofit funders who sought to preserve films of recognized artistic and cultural value. Not just fight films but industrials, local views, improvised story films made by traveling showmen, educational subjects, fiction films lacking obvious commercial value (for example, regional productions), and home movies were all outside the purview of these established cultural institutions. Fight films became Dan's entrée to a new, much broader agenda. In September 1999, he held a conference (the first of a series), "Orphans of the Storm: Saving 'Orphan Films' in the Digital Age." Over the course of that event—and the subsequent biannual conferences on orphaned films, which he organized with unforgettable ingenuity and flair, I and many other hardened conference goers became part of this newly constituted community of scholars, archivists, collectors and lab technicians, who (following Dan's lead) happily refer to themselves as "orphanistas." As a result of Dan's leadership, the orphan film movement has expanded and transformed the way we approach film and media studies. It has reaffirmed the radically democratic and egalitarian side of our field, generating new energy and a revitalized philosophy at a moment when film studies was becoming more integrated into academia and in danger of falling prey to elitist tendencies.

Dan has been an inspiration to many of us in film studies. There may have been a time when I could (perhaps idly) think of Dan as a kind of protégé, but for many years now I have happily and humbly thought of myself as his student and disciple. If this book had a gestation period of fourteen years, it was because its author was on a mission of the utmost urgency. *Fight Pictures* certainly became a richer, more thorough book during the intervening years. Bearing the insights of the orphan film movement as much as the older "early cinema" paradigm, *Fight Pictures* is the result of some twenty years of intellectual ferment. It is a long-awaited work from someone recognized by many of us as one of America's national treasures.

Charles Musser
Yale University

Acknowledgments

This book could not have been completed without institutional support and the encouragement and advice of many generous colleagues and friends.

At the University of Texas at Austin, where this project began as a dissertation, I was fortunate to have encouraging mentors and a hearty cohort in the Department of Radio-Television-Film. Janet Staiger gave me scholarly guidance, detailed critiques, and constant support. Other teachers enriched my experience and education, particularly Tom Schatz, Charles Ramírez Berg, Joli Jensen, John Downing, Terry Todd, Lewis Gould, Horace Newcomb, Sharon Strover, Jan Todd, George C. Wright, and Bob Davis. I offer special thanks to my classmate, officemate, co-teacher, and rent-sharer Eric Schaefer for making the work lighter. Fellow UT RTF comrades who brightened the path include Mark Miller, Jim Wehmeyer, Eithne Johnson, Phil Riley, Tinky Weisblat, Lucila Vargas, Judi Hoffman, and Alison Macor.

A faculty-development research grant from the University of Wisconsin–Oshkosh allowed me to begin this book project. My gratitude to Jeff Lipschutz, Jeff Sconce, Karla Berry, and Michael Zimmerman.

The University of South Carolina's College of Liberal Arts summer stipend helped me continue the work. I also benefited enormously from the supportive intellectual community of the USC Film Studies Program. Susan Courtney took a deep interest in my manuscript and was a vital booster. I am grateful for years of inspiration from Laura Kissel, as well as our fellow *orphanista* Julie Hubbert. Other great Carolina colleagues and friends deserve thanks, including Karl Heider, Ina Hark, Steve Marsh, Craig Kridel, Greg Forter, Nicholas Vazsonyi, Agnes Mueller, Rebecca Stern, Davis Baird, Deanna Leamon, and Brad Collins. The title "student assistant" fails to convey the dedication and talent with which Michael Conklin, Elizabeth Miller, Matt Sefick, and factotum David Burch rewarded me.

xviii / *Acknowledgments*

Among colleagues studying early cinema, Charles Musser stood out as a most excellent editor and critic, a generous scholar, and a faithful advocate. In short, he made this book possible. Others who bolstered my research include Tom Gunning, Miriam Hansen, Jacqueline Stewart, Aaron Baker, Todd Boyd, Daniel Bernardi, Ben Singer, Richard Abel, André Gaudreault, Richard Koszarski, Chris Horak, Patrick Myler, Mark Williams, Mary Desjardins, Anna McCarthy, Pat Loughney, Antonia Lant, Vanessa Toulmin, Greg Waller, Geoffrey C. Ward, Jane Gaines, Matthew Bernstein, Eli Savada, Rob Nanovic, George Willeman, Don Crafton, and Domitor *confrères*.

The inspirational archivists Nico de Klerk, Bill O'Farrell, and Rick Prelinger deserve praise for their generosity and invaluable knowledge. At the Library of Congress, the gifted and gracious staff in the Motion Picture and Television Reading Room gave (as always) expert research support. Rosemary Hanes, Madeline Matz, Zoran Sinobad, and Josie Walters-Johnston led me to much of the material at the core of this book. The magnificent Mike Mashon in the Moving Image Section extended more favors than a reasonable researcher should expect. He also kept affably reminding me to finish.

At the University of California Press, Mary Francis shepherded the manuscript with aplomb and made the process a pleasure, as did Kalicia Pivirotto, Mary Severance, and Erika Büky.

Finally, I have had the indispensable and loving support of my family in Louisville, Kentucky (hometown of Muhammad Ali and D. W. Griffith, who bookend the story of *Fight Pictures*). In addition to my parents, to whom this book is dedicated, my brother Tom and sister Amy kept the faith. Most especially, I could not have written this book without the caring support and advice of my beloved, brilliant cowgirl polymath, Teri Tynes.

Permission has been granted to publish portions of this book that originally appeared in Daniel Bernardi, ed., *The Birth of Whiteness: Race and the Emergence of U.S. Cinema* (Rutgers University Press, 1996); Claire Dupré La Tour, André Gaudrealt, and Roberta Pearson, eds., *Le cinéma au tournant du siècle* (Éditions Nota Bene, 1999); Aaron Baker and Todd Boyd, eds., *Out of Bounds: Sports, Media and the Politics of Identity* (Indiana University Press, 1997), 16–47; *Arachne* 2, no. 2 (1995); and *Film History* 3, no. 3 (1989).

Chronology

Preliminaries

History, Prizefighting, Early Cinema

Late on the night of July 19, 1996, the opening ceremonies for the centennial Olympic games in Atlanta culminated with a stunning moment. A series of famous athletes relayed the Olympic flame to the enormous torch atop the stadium. The identity of the final torchbearer had been kept secret. When television cameras revealed it to be Muhammad Ali, humbled by the palsy of Parkinson's disease, onlookers first gasped, then cheered and wept at the sight. The most celebrated athlete of his era, the irrepressible "Louisville Lip" had fallen silent, his famous powers of speech stolen by disease and the apparent ravages of dementia pugilistica. His appearance in Atlanta was a glorious comeback, offering the sight of a fallen fighter bravely and stoically overcoming his infirmity. Ali ignited the Olympic flame with a steady right hand, while his left shook uncontrollably. The sense of physical decline was made all the more apparent by the ceremony's earlier celebration of the body beautiful, highlighted by a giant tableau vivant of silhouettes replicating the statuesque physiques of the athletes of classical Greece. Although Ali's athletic skills had gone, he had come to represent the transcendental values of courage, determination, and international goodwill.

That the world would embrace a prizefighter as a legitimate representative of sport, much less a sporting icon, would have been unimaginable a century before. Perhaps, indeed, only a figure as storied and exceptional as Muhammad Ali could confer prestige on a sport as inglorious as prizefighting. Yet his appearance at the Olympic centennial invites comparison to the image of the boxer a hundred years earlier. How did the nineteenth-century criminal act of prizefighting, attended by only a small constituency, become the mainstream modern sport that draws millions of spectators and created twentieth-century legends such as Ali, Joe Louis, Jack Dempsey, and Jack

Johnson? What transformed the fight game from an illegal blood sport to an accepted part of popular culture?

To answer these questions, we should consider another anniversary observed circa 1996: the centennial of cinema. Just as the modern Olympic Games and the phenomenal growth of professional sports would not have been possible without broadcast media, the invention and early practices of moving pictures greatly changed prizefighting. Whereas other sports were irregularly captured on film in the two decades cinema that preceded Hollywood and newsreels, boxing had an intimate relationship with motion pictures from the beginning..

This book is a cultural and social history of the relationship between prizefighting and early cinema. During the first twenty years of cinema, films of boxers and prizefights constituted one of the medium's most conspicuous genres. Several recordings of title bouts garnered huge profits for both the early motion-picture trade and the promoters of pugilism. Their success helped transform, modernize, and legitimate the stigmatized practice of prizefighting. But the stigma also made fight pictures highly problematic products for the film industry. From 1894 to 1915, the genre remained a much-debated phenomenon. Yet despite this long and lively public discourse about prizefight films, historians have not adequately studied this significant period. *Fight Pictures* redresses that omission.

Early cinema has been a fertile area of research, but relatively little has been published about boxing films. This is surprising given the number of productions undertaken. More than one hundred such films were produced by 1907, and more than two hundred by 1915. However, only a few dozen survive, and many only in private collections, Disney/ESPN having purchased the nearly monopolistic Big Fights, Inc., library in 1998.[1] Historical writing about these films was also hindered by their initial suppression. Like prizefighting itself, motion-picture recordings were heavily policed and sometimes forbidden in Progressive Era America. From 1912 to 1940, federal law in fact banned interstate transportation of fight films, even as the sport itself gained in popularity. Although scholars have written extensively about other censored genres, the boxing picture remained neglected. An exception to this is a chapter in Lee Grieveson's *Policing Cinema: Movies and Censorship in Early Twentieth-Century America* (2004), although it focuses on the regulatory strictures in effect from 1910 to 1912.

The movies themselves are seldom compelling viewing. Most are observational recordings framed in extreme long shot, with little editing. Their rather artless use of the medium has put them outside the historiography of cinema's aesthetic development. A revisionist interest in "primitive cinema," however, has emerged in the past two decades. Recognizing that, in Tom Gunning's words, "the history of the early cinema" had been "written and theorized under the hegemony of narrative films," scholars have sought to understand the first moving pictures by studying the contexts of their original production, exhibition, and reception.[2] Gunning's rubric of a "cinema of attractions" encouraged a reassessment of the period and the understanding that it was misleading to look at more than a decade of films as simply "preclassical." Researchers looked not just at the surviving films but also at the documentation (legal records, trade journals, newspapers, business files) of the conditions under which the medium emerged. My own work is indebted to these historians, who recognized that boxing films were an important yet understudied part of the history of cinema in these years.

No single work has examined fight pictures in depth. However, both early and recent historians have noted their significance. The first widely circulated history of movies, Terry Ramsaye's *A Million and One Nights* (1926), takes boxing as one of its motifs. Prominent throughout are the Latham brothers (best known for their father's patented "Latham loop," which facilitated the mechanical projection of celluloid film). Ramsaye imagines a conversation of 1894 in which Gray Latham, after seeing Thomas Edison's new kinetoscope, prophesies, "Everybody's crazy about prize fights, and all we have to do is to get Edison to photograph a fight for this machine and we can take it out and make a fortune on it." For Ramsaye, this "made the prize ring and pugilism the major influence in the technical evolution of the motion picture for the entire decade of the art." He offers other connections between boxing and the movies, making grand, if dubious, claims. The decision to re-create boxing matches for the camera, for example, constituted "the birth of production policy for the motion picture." The "star contract" was born when the champion James J. Corbett was paid to appear before the Edison camera. The American Mutoscope & Biograph Company developed artificial lighting to shoot the 1899 Jim Jeffries–Tom Sharkey fight indoors. Ramsaye concludes, however, that this incident "was destined to be the last service of the prize ring to the motion picture. All the fight pictures which have followed in these twenty-odd years have exerted a detrimental influence on the social status of the screen." With this dismissal, *A Million and One Nights* sweeps away a history of "all the fight pictures" that proliferated in the first two decades of cinema.[3]

Sixty-odd years passed before cinema scholars delved into the primary sources and reexamined the fight pictures the pioneer generation knew well. Charles Musser's authoritative *Emergence of Cinema* (1990) was the first book since Ramsaye's to give attention to fight films. It demonstrates that feature-length fight-picture presentations, though intended primarily for the "all-male world of blood sports," helped boxing gain wider acceptance.[4] His brief account focuses only on the years 1897 to 1900 but yields suggestive details: numerous films, big profits, prominent exhibition, public controversies, and historic shifts in spectatorship. Miriam Hansen's *Babel and Babylon* (1991) argues that the reception of the first prizefight film in 1897 was a watershed event in the history of screen spectatorship, one which brought the issue of gender into the public sphere in a significant way.

Fight Pictures explores these issues but expands the period of time and subjects under examination. Three types of literature inform this book: cinema studies, sports history, and social history.

THE HISTORIOGRAPHY OF EARLY CINEMA

Studies of early motion pictures emphasize that cinema in its first two decades was fundamentally different from the institution that existed afterward. From the teens onward, "classical" cinema predominated: feature-length narrative fiction, produced by a studio system. Companies institutionalized this form of production, eclipsing or driving out alternative practices. Yet, rather than conclude that the history of the medium must be written as a triumphalist evolution or a tragedy, we can envision alternatives by looking at pre-Hollywood motion pictures. Exploring the varieties of film experience that existed before classical cinema curbs a historical blindness that makes it difficult to imagine movies as being anything other than the form we now know. Histories of early cinema, as Hansen has said, ought to help create a "usable past."[5]

Toward this end, I structure this account of the fight picture as a social history, one that elucidates how commercial cinema and professional sport were part of social and cultural experience. What were the historical conditions of production and reception for fight films between 1894 and 1915? What was it like to see these images when movies were new and prizefights taboo? *Fight Pictures* focuses on the convergence of the screen and the ring as social institutions. It examines the experiences of people who encountered fight pictures, describing the concrete realities shaping the lives of filmmakers, fighters, and spectators.

Treating the years 1894 to 1915 as a distinct era in cinema history follows conventional film historiography. From the invention of motion pictures in the 1890s until about 1906, motion pictures took many forms and appeared in diverse venues. In the "transitional" decade that followed, movies were transformed, developing a stable venue (the "permanent-movie-house" period, in Ben Brewster's term), an organized production and distribution industry, and a recognized narrative form. By the early teens the American and European film industries had adopted the feature-length film as the stock-in-trade, even as one-reel shorts continued to be important and a narrative style predominant.[6] Whatever year one might contend "early cinema" or the "transitional" era ended, 1915 marks a clear break in the history of fight pictures. In that year, U.S. authorities quashed one last attempt to exploit a film of a big bout, *Willard-Johnson Boxing Match.* Production all but ceased as distribution was barred.

However, the fight film also provided a continuity across these years of rapid change in motion pictures. Its principal form—observational recording of a prizefight—changed little between 1897 and 1915, even as cinematic style was evolving rapidly. Its format—the feature-length presentation—also persisted from 1897 on, even though films of such length would not become conventional until after the ban on fight pictures. Finally, prizefight films were anomalies, albeit constant and important ones, in early cinema. Theirs is a parallel history that runs alongside the story of the development of mainstream commercial cinema.

In *Film History: Theory and Practice* (1985), Robert C. Allen and Douglas Gomery suggest that social film historians investigate five categories: film production, moviegoing, the form and content of movies on the screen, discourses on motion pictures, and cinema's relationship to other social institutions.[7] A synthesis of these areas of inquiry creates an understanding of film as part of a larger social process. Posing questions in each of these five areas generates a useful preview of my project.

Who made fight films? All the major film manufacturers of the period worked with boxing subjects, including the most powerful rivals—Edison, Biograph, and Vitagraph. A fourth leader, Lubin, cornered the market in "fake" fight reproductions. Even after combining to form their monopoly-minded Patents Company, these producers continued to exploit fight films as a sideline. However, because of the nature of prizefighting—socially censured and controlled by its own high-stakes promoters—other film outfits also operated alongside the mainstream. Specialists like Miles Bros. and one-time incorporations such as the Veriscope Company, American Sportagraph, and the Pantomimic Corporation coexisted with the dominant producers.

What did fight pictures show? The genre consisted of several variations—shots of men sparring for the camera, celebrity pugilists enacting a bout, boxing burlesques, reenactments of popular fights, and films of

Figure 1.   Detail from a cartoon in the British humor magazine *Pick-Me-Up*, April 25, 1896 (supplied by Stephen Bottomore). One of many indications of the close association between boxing and the earliest moving pictures.

real prizefights. Genre lines often blurred, especially in the 1890s, when there was no coherent set of expectations about what made a fight or a film "authentic."

Who saw these pictures? Initially, they attracted much of the same audience as the boxing matches themselves, a male sporting subculture that included a mix of working-class and slumming upper- and middle-class patrons. Affluent men attended the big bouts, which commanded steep ticket prices and were held in remote spots, such as Nevada, the Texas-Mexico border, New Mexico, and Cuba. However, working men from the city predominated at most ringsides, where they cheered for boxers of like backgrounds. Often criminalized, prizefighting was part of an underworld connected to gambling and other vice trades. Professional boxing retained a social stigma because of the men who ran and patronized it.

Cinema, however, proved a mediating institution. Spectators could see fights without entering the dubious cultural milieu of the ring. Movie shows gave access to a wider general audience of men who could not afford to attend the big bouts sponsored by clubs. They also granted unexpected access to women. Under limited and controlled conditions, a female audience became prizefight spectators for the first time. With exhibitions in legitimate theaters and opera houses, then, the 1897 *Corbett-Fitzsimmons Fight* gained the sport a new, more legitimated clientele. However, regardless of the venue, strict racial segregation remained the law of the land in the United States. African American audiences, who especially sought out the Jack Johnson pictures of 1908 through 1915, engaged in separate spheres of exhibition and reception.

What was said about the films? Plenty. Progressive Era reform groups, government officials, religious leaders, and newspapers clanged their criticism of motion pictures that reproduced the morally dubious practice of pugilism. During publicized bouts, they waged opposition campaigns. Public discourse about fight pictures became most strident when issues of race came to the fore. When Jack Johnson defeated "white hope" Jim Jeffries in 1910, the film of the event was censored in many locations, and debates raged. Many whites argued the need for social control and the suppression of Johnson's image, while most black journalists pointed to the bans as further evidence of race-based double standards. Amid this controversy, bastions of yellow journalism (particularly William Hearst's papers) and sporting tabloids (led by the *National Police Gazette*) sensationalized and promoted prizefights as well as their filmed replays.

What relationship did this form of cinema have with other social institutions? Early filmmakers shared an affiliation with organizers of professional boxing. These were not simply disparate groups that came together for mutual financial benefit. Rather, the picture trade and the ring world were both part of what their members called the "sporting and theatrical syndicate," a close-knit association of male entrepreneurs who mixed in many aspects of the show business. They were also closely linked to the press, another institution that promoted both prizefights and films.

The evidence provided by such multifaceted investigation helps overcome the post hoc designation *primitive*, sometimes used to describe early cinema's lack of artistic polish. Although images of ring combat tend to reinforce this notion, the fight picture's simple, observational aesthetic did not inhibit audience engagement. Scholars have embraced Gunning's term "cinema of attractions" to explain that, for the first audiences, films were not defined by a lack of narrativity. Rather, they were seen as extensions of traditions—such as circus, burlesque, and variety theater—that emphasized display and spectacle rather than story. Because boxing films were often incorporated into these performance traditions, Gunning's model is an apt one.

Historians now acknowledge what Allen called in 1990 "the previously unacknowledged variety of exhibition practices . . . in the first two decades of the commercial exploitation of the movies."[8] Inspired by studies of the intriguing social dynamics uncovered in case histories—such as Kathryn H. Fuller's study of the small-town picture show, Jacqueline Najuma Stewart's portrait of black Chicago venues for silent movies, and Gregory A. Waller's research on exhibition in Kentucky—*Fight Pictures* explores how prizefight screenings were exhibited differently in particular locations. Only with the examination of specific presentations does the vitality of these films become apparent.

Fight films were presented in atypical fashion, employing special feature presentations, live celebrity appearances, extra promotion, longer than average runs, higher admission prices, larger facilities, and professional announcers (although they were seldom accompanied by music). Before the nickelodeon, their backers introduced feature-film displays to high-class environs like the Academy of Music in New York City, as well as to burlesque halls from Philadelphia to Louisville and San Francisco. Fight pictures were also presented in places where boxing news was discussed. Some were shown privately at "stag" smokers. On at least one conspicuous occasion, in 1900, thousands of Philadelphians gathered outside a telegraph office to hear the results of one prizefight while they viewed reenactments of another projected onto the side of a building. During the age of nickelodeons, fight films continued to be shown in multiple venues. Amusement parks, fairs, circuses, and carnivals showed them to their eclectic audiences. In other contexts, segregated spaces were constructed for patrons of different races. Black-oriented theaters sometimes pitched screenings of Johnson films as celebrations of African American solidarity, while white houses often excluded nonwhite patrons under the pretext of avoiding race riots.

As these examples suggest, studies of exhibition investigate the composition of movie audiences. Identifying the patrons of fight pictures presents complex, sometimes contradictory, insights. Boxing's history is firmly tied to working-class culture. Ring heroes rose out of the laboring class, from John L. Sullivan to Jack Dempsey, from Bob the "Fighting Blacksmith" Fitzsimmons to Jim the "Boilermaker" Jeffries. The rationale for censoring the films came from genteel and middle-class reformers who judged the sight of fisticuffs brutalizing. But many in the middle class patronized the fights and films. The sport developed bourgeois icons: "Gentleman Jim" Corbett, Georges the "Orchid Man" Carpentier, and the athletic-club bout. Ultimately, regardless of their interclass appeal, fight pictures were subject to the control of upper- and middle-class interests: exhibitors, aware of the class stigma of boxing, often priced working-class patrons out of the audience.

Conflict over race remains central to the history of the prizefight film. With African American champions at the center of several key productions, a significant alternative cinema experience existed in black-only variety theaters and movie houses. Fight pictures, particularly those "starring" Jack Johnson, were the only widely circulated cinematic representations of powerful black individuals. These films elicited popular celebration in African American theaters while inciting fear among a white society that used censorship and segregation to exert social control over black America.

The case of boxing films also offers important evidence about the role of gender in audiences for early cinema. Women constituted much of the general movie audience, and their patronage was welcomed as a stamp of social acceptability. However, the explanation of the role of women in the history of the movies has been somewhat reductionist: to woo a female audience, it is argued, the trade promoted supposedly feminine genres—fiction in general and domestic melodramas specifically. By implication, fight pictures went against the grain of a popular entertainment form that sought to appeal to both sexes: their nonfictional and male-oriented content would exclude them from the cinematic mainstream. Yet this was not entirely the case. Although some fight-film exhibitors preferred to deal with "stag houses," from the beginning many boxing pictures drew significant audiences of women. From 1897 and perhaps even earlier, presentations were successfully organized "especially for ladies." Fight-film interests recruited women for the purposes of legitimation and found a receptive audience.

SPORTS HISTORY

Three types of writing on boxing aid this book. The first might be called boxiana (after Pierce Egan's 1812 book on pugilism): anecdotal histories, fan

literature, ephemera, record books, popular biographies, and sports periodicals, especially the *National Police Gazette*. Second, critical reflections on
boxing by later essayists—among them Gerald Early, Joyce Carol Oates,
A. J. Liebling, Norman Mailer, George Plimpton, Dick Schaap, and Ralph
Wiley —bridge the gap between popular and academic discourses. As Early
has said, these are partisans writing about a sport that fascinates them. Yet
Oates, Liebling, Plimpton, Schaap, and others acknowledge seeing the moving pictures of early twentieth-century prizefighters. Their interpretive
turns emphasize racial, national, and class conflicts, as well as gender
identity, in boxing as a cultural phenomenon.

The third type of source is the work of sports historians. As Elliott Gorn
and Warren Goldstein note in *A Brief History of American Sports* (1993),
the academic study of American sports boomed over the past generation,
much of it driven by the "new social history."[9] Several works historicizing
prizefighting have been crucial to my understanding of the fight film. All
conclude that in nineteenth-century America and Britain, boxing began as
a blood sport favored by a violent working-class subculture but developed
into an organized, publicized sport that many middle- and upper-class men
patronized. Despite its outlaw status, professional boxing spread under the
influence of urbanization and mass-circulation newspapers. Criticism of
prizefighting never went away, but the sport became sanctioned as it served
the disparate purposes of nationalist, military, racial, religious, and philo-
sophical discourses.

In *America's Sporting Heritage, 1850–1950* (1974), John Rickards Betts
documents the role that sporting journals (the *Spirit of the Times, New York
Clipper*, and *Police Gazette*) and the tabloid press played in popularizing
prizefighting and other sports. He recognizes that the constituency that attended fights was a problematic social mix of the "leisure class" and the
"dangerous classes" from "saloons, pool rooms, and the gambling fraternity." Betts also identifies a "technological revolution," including the inventions of photography and cinematography, as spurring the growth of
sports and celebrity athletes.[10]

Subsequent histories delve deeper into the rise of sports, including *Sport
in Industrial America, 1850–1920* (1995) and *The American Sporting Experience* (1984) by Steven A. Riess, as well as Allen Guttmann's *A Whole
New Ball Game: An Interpretation of American Sports* (1988). Each shows
how the growth of modern sport was tied to large social shifts, especially
industrialization and urbanization, which created masses of workers seeking structured leisure. Guttmann argues that the rubric of "modernization"
is key to understanding how sports developed. In agrarian antebellum

America, sports were relegated to what Riess describes as "a traditionally oriented male bachelor sub-culture." During the Gilded Age, they grew into a mass phenomenon with the hallmarks of modernization: corporate control, commercial sponsorship, formal rules, bureaucratic regulation, profit orientation, national competition and promotion, mass-mediated publicity, and mass spectatorship. Boxing and baseball were the two earliest and most conspicuous examples.[11]

These histories consistently point out how athletics altered conceptions of class and gender. In "Sport and the Redefinition of American Middle-Class Masculinity," Riess shows how the sporting subculture was transformed by a social movement that expanded "clean" sports to the middle class. Riess and others attribute this change to several causes: the "muscular Christianity" philosophy that brought physical culture into religion via the YMCA; a revivalist sports creed that put athletic fitness into schools; businesses that sponsored athletic teams to make for better workers; and an increased "martial spirit" that saw combat sports as training for war. In sum, Riess argues, the middle class encouraged sports that cultivated "manly" qualities. Proponents of the "strenuous life," led by boxing enthusiast Theodore Roosevelt, feared national weakness, excessive "feminization" of society, and the "race suicide" of Anglo-Americans in the face of mass immigration. Sports prospered, according to Riess, because they were thought to create "self-controlled, disciplined men of action who were team players in the work-place, bearers of the white man's burden, who would protect the race against inferior immigrant strains and surmount the feminization of American culture."[12]

Boxing's history has been closely chronicled, especially by fans and the trade press. However, the strongest scholarship on prizefighting has focused on the periods prior to the invention of cinema and after the advent of electronic media. Dennis Brailsford's *Bareknuckles: A Social History of Prize Fighting* (1988) examines early British fisticuffs, and Gorn's *The Manly Art: Bare-Knuckle Prize Fighting in America* (1986) looks at the U.S. equivalent. Michael T. Isenberg's excellent *John L. Sullivan and His America* (1988) does the same. Of the major historical works on boxing, only Jeffrey T. Sammons's *Beyond the Ring: The Role of Boxing in American Society* (1988) covers the Progressive Era, and it concentrates on boxing after 1930. Scholars examining the ring careers of Jack Dempsey, Joe Louis, or Muhammad Ali, for example, neglect the emergence of fight pictures.

Nevertheless, research on the earlier period profiles the milieu of prizefighting that early cinema entered. Gorn paints a vivid picture of the changes in the audiences for and organizers of big fights. He points out that the original constituency for boxing was a unique social group identified by the now-archaic term *fancy* —a "sporting fraternity that . . . lived beyond the pale of respectable society." The fancy was a "motley crowd," of "rich and poor, well-born and debased, resplendent and ragged." As in America, men from subjugated ethnic groups—"Irishmen, blacks, and Jews"—came to the ring in Britain, where they could complete with Englishmen on equal terms. Prizefighting, Gorn writes, was "part of a hybrid culture that appealed to the highest and lowest."[13]

As the sport became popular in the United States, a similar subculture developed to support professional fighters. Timothy J. Gilfoyle has shown how prizefighting in New York City was part of a larger "sporting life" for "sporting men." This "underground" linked the individuals who indulged in blood sports, prostitution, theatrical entertainment, gambling, alcohol, and ward politics. In *City of Eros* (1992), Gilfoyle documents how this sporting life brought men of varying classes together and asserted values of heterosexual "urban masculinity." Howard P. Chudacoff's *The Age of the Bachelor* (1999) more broadly characterizes the late nineteenth century as an era when urban American life developed a culture in which prizefighting could flourish.[14]

By the 1890s, new and bigger forces controlled the ring. Backers of the game waged a continuing battle against legal suppression. They gradually achieved legitimacy by reforming to appease the genteel ruling class, and by heavily promoting big fights to a new mass audience. Isenberg shows how John L. Sullivan, the working-class Irish American who became the first internationally famous champion, succeeded in the latter undertaking. With Barnumesque promoters and a tabloid media buildup by the *Police Gazette,* Sullivan became a celebrity, known even by those who had never seen a prizefight or followed the sport. Although Sullivan fought for most of his career in the bare-knuckle style, he joined the move to reform his trade by converting to the Marquess of Queensberry rules. The new rules, said Sullivan, allowed the game to be "conducted for the benefit of gentlemen, not rowdies." He lost his title to James J. Corbett in 1892 wearing padded boxing gloves.

The Sullivan-Corbett bout of September 7, 1892, is considered a historical watershed for prizefighting. Rather than a clandestine, bare-knuckle combat on the turf, the match was part of a three-day boxing festival at the Olympic Club in New Orleans. Without fear of the usual police interference, ten thousand fans from across the country saw the young, "scientific" boxer, "Gentleman Jim," defeat the veteran brawler inside a well-appointed, electrically lighted indoor arena. Pulling off big fights remained a problem under antipugilism laws, but this sanctioned event set a precedent. Mass media attention lent the sport further validation. A national information network of telegraph, telephone, and newspaper communication instantly disseminated results of the fight to audiences assembled at theaters, saloons, clubs, and news offices.[15] Boxing had become a modern business and a prominent social practice, albeit still a highly criticized one.

It is here that my investigation begins. Motion-picture coverage added to this trend to modernize, popularize, and legitimize professional boxing. Conversely, early filmmakers were connected to the "sporting and theatrical syndicate" that constituted the sociological realm of prizefighting, a connection they would eventually break in their move to become more autonomous and respectable. Yet in its first two decades cinema played an important role in the ring. These years were marked by a struggle by boxing organizers to find a legal safe haven. New York became its first headquarters, when the state legalized bouts between 1896 and 1900. San Francisco, the home of Corbett and his manager William A. Brady, hosted many major fights thereafter. When political and legal wrangling pushed prizefights out of these locales, the unregulated West—especially Nevada—welcomed promoters. The sport became governed by referees enforcing the Queensberry rules. A "fair stand-up boxing match" had to be contested in a ring, with padded gloves; timed three-minute rounds and one-minute rest periods; punches only above the waist; and no wrestling, kicking, or gouging. Matches were restricted to opponents of equal weight classes. Each weight division had a sanctioned champion.[16]

Under these conditions, boxing's entry into the modern era coincided with the rise of the motion picture. Cameras followed the champions, especially the heavyweight titleholders: Corbett (1892–97), Bob Fitzsimmons (1897–99), Jim Jeffries (1899–1905), Tommy Burns (1906–8), Jack Johnson (1908–1915), and Jess Willard. With the exception of Burns, who rose after Jeffries' retirement, each successor won his title by knocking out the defending champion in front of motion-picture cameras. Other champions also figured prominently in the fight-picture marketplace, including lightweights Joe Gans (1902–8), Battling Nelson (1908–10), and Ad Wolgast (1910–12); middleweights Kid McCoy (1897–98), Stanley Ketchel, and Billy Papke (1908–11); and George Dixon (1898–1900) and Terry McGovern (1899–1901), who both held featherweight and bantamweight crowns.

Despite the wealth of anecdotal boxiana from this period, few scholarly works have supplemented that of Sammons. Biographies of Jack Johnson by Randy Roberts (1983) and Geoffrey C. Ward (2003) and Steven A. Riess's 1985 essay "In the Ring and Out: Professional Boxing in New York,

Figure 2. Frame from a 35 mm film, "Unid. Atkinson No. 41," ca. 1890s. (AFI/Dennis Atkinson Collection, Library of Congress, Motion Picture, Broadcasting and Recorded Sound Division.) Fewer than one-quarter of pre-1916 fight films survive, many only in fragments. So many were produced that some extant films are not identifiable.

1896–1920" are exceptions, although none highlight the enormous role of motion pictures. Roberts and Ward thoroughly document the professional and personal activities of Johnson, including his rise and fall as a boxer and his theatrical tours, personal life, and legal battles. They also analyze the larger discourse on race that dominated the public reception of the black champion's image. I extend this analysis to Johnson's appearances on film.[17]

Riess details the social and political forces affecting New York boxing at the time of the fight film's appearance. While emphasizing the sport's troubled quest for legality, he shows the intricacies of how bouts were organized, promoted, exploited, and often prevented by competing fraternal, commercial, and political groups. My research expands on two themes of these findings. First, neither boxing nor film production was an autonomous entity. Both were tied to other practices and institutions. Riess notes that the men involved played multiple roles: as boxers and actors, saloon keepers and machine politicians, theater managers and gambling organizers, elected officials and club owners, lobbyists and newspapermen, promoters and—sometimes—motion-picture entrepreneurs. Second, because fight pictures came out of the sociological sphere of sporting and theatrical men, they had a stigma attached to them. Prizefights and movies came under attack throughout the Progressive Era, along with trusts, Tammany Hall, gambling, and alcohol.

However, the raucous world of live prizefights differed from the conditions under which fight pictures were exhibited and received. Motion pictures of fights—silent, black-and-white, edited, and narrated—mediated the experience of watching bouts in which men sweated and bled before shouting partisans. Transplanted into a variety of venues, prizefights were seen by new audiences, who often made different sense of them. The social stigma remained, but the sport and the spectators' experience of it were transformed.

SOCIAL HISTORY

How should a social history of these twin phenomena be written? How might it contribute to what Gunning calls "the immense task of placing films within the horizons of social history"?[18] Two perspectives have converged in recent scholarship: "social film history" as practiced within film studies and the revisionist "new social history" that emerged in the second half of the twentieth century. As Mary Beth Haralovich noted in her 1985 essay "Film and Social History," cinema historians tended not to "journey far enough outside of the film text and the film industry." Since that time, investigations of early cinema have begun to answer her call "to strike a middle ground between Allen and Gomery's presentation of social film history and the goals and procedures of social history."[19]

Social history emerged in its "new" phase with the publication of E. P. Thompson's *Making of the English Working Class* (1964) and the marxisant works of his British cohort, followed by the work of a new generation of American revisionist historians. They decentered events and "great men" of the past, giving more weight to economics, demographics, and the material conditions of everyday life. This social history of the making of the fight pictures sympathizes with these aims: rescuing the lost and suppressed history of a censored cultural product and practice, valuing the ordinary experiences of marginalized as well as mainstream groups, and focusing on local events.[20]

Figure 3. Cartoon from the *Chicago Tribune,* July 7, 1910. Published with the comment: "Suppose the fight pictures are barred! Will attendance at a clandestine presentation of them become as zestful as the old time custom of stealing off to the countryside to see a pair of pugs belt each other in some farmer's barn? Instead of the secret 'mill' will it be the secret 'film show'?" The cartoon encapsulates subjects key to early fight films: working-class male audiences, interracial conflict, legal bans, and clandestine exhibition.

As Peter N. Stearns has written, this "history from the bottom up" measures its success by how adequately it "conveys the experiences of the people being characterized."[21] Arising from a sense that "too much of the human experience was being left out" when history privileged political leaders and wars, revisionist-minded scholars turned to histories of the working class, women, slaves, and ethnic groups. Like the *Annales* school historians who pioneered these methods in France before World War II, they focused on ordinary activities—work, leisure, sexual behavior, domestic life—that would reveal as much about human history as the study of politics and war did. Moviegoing surely belongs on the list of experiences of everyday life.

In American life during the rise of motion pictures and professional sports, the conflicts between and among many groups—particularly conflicts demarcated by race and class—were immediate, profound, and unmasked. My analysis, therefore, often highlights class and racial conflict as the source of social friction and change. Following the work of previous social historians, particularly those who have studied the Progressive Era, I adopt the framework of "social control" that others have used "as a means of cutting through the complexities in this nexus of relationships" that constitute social life. In explaining, for example, how prizefight films came to be censored by a racist society during the reign of a black champion, the social control model allows one, in Stearns's words, to "get behind the facade of upper-class rhetoric and assumptions of social homogeneity."[22] However, the social-control framework in no way proposes total control from the top; rather, it insists that resistance and opposition exist at all levels of social life. Struggle over materials and meanings continued during the implementation of control mechanisms. The banning of Jack Johnson films by a white-run state is one instance of an assertion of social control of a feared and suppressed African American community. Yet the history of opposition (evidence that many blacks and some whites resisted the ban, celebrated Johnson victories, and attended clandestine showings) is of equal or greater value to later generations in search of a usable past.

PREVIEW

What was the history of prizefight films before 1915? What were the conditions of their production and reception? *Fight Pictures* shows the significant shifts in the genre during its first two decades. Fight films generated conflict and underwent rapid changes. Throughout, they remained a genre that served an important economic and social function.

Historicizing the social conditions in which these films appeared, in chapter 1 I explain how and why the very earliest generation of moving-picture photography developed such an immediate and pronounced affinity for boxing subjects. Sparring scenes and posing prize fighters were commonly represented in precinematic serial photography, inventors' prototype motion pictures, commercial kinetoscopes, and early projected films. Boxing, with its brief rounds confined to a single setting, was highly compatible with early filmmaking, with its limited lengths of celluloid and restricted camera movement. Early producers competed for boxing subjects. However, this was much more than a neat marriage of form and function. The popularity of Edison's *Corbett and Courtney before the Kinetograph* indicated the value of using celebrity pugilists. Boxing and boxers had specific cultural meanings derived from concrete social formations. I examine the social status and practices of professional boxing in the United States during the 1890s. Both films and fights constituted parts of the "sporting and theatrical" community. Men interested in exploiting these two commodities forged an affiliation that allowed each to promote the other.

Chapter 2 chronicles the most important product of the early marriage of film and fights: the Veriscope Company's recording and exploitation of the much-hyped Corbett-Fitzsimmons heavyweight title bout of 1897. The eleven-reel motion picture was the first genuine prizefight film. It remained early cinema's most lucrative property, touring as a theatrical feature for several years. Its success proved a watershed for professional boxing. Promoters could thereafter hope to rake in extensive profits from a big fight without relying on gate receipts. The most salient aspect of the *Corbett-Fitzsimmons Fight* was not how it played to the audience of sporting men, but how the veriscope expanded the audience for prizefight spectatorship. Cinema changed the nature of the fight game and the social experience of watching a disreputable sport. Women, surprisingly, became fight-picture viewers, and in turn the subject of discourse about the gender dynamics of spectatorship.

In the wake of the huge financial success of the Veriscope pictures, all of the major American motion picture manufacturers joined boxing promoters in trying to produce big fight films. The results were inconsistent, ranging from Biograph's lucrative feature production of *Jeffries-Sharkey Fight* in 1899 to the disappointing *Jeffries-Ruhlin Fight* shot by Edison in 1901. Although the heavyweight champion Jim Jeffries remained fairly popular throughout his reign (1899–1904), interest in both prizefights and motion pictures temporarily declined thereafter. Chapter 3 chronicles the ways in which the chaotic and competitive film industry entered into the battle for potentially lucrative fight footage. I chart the successes, problems, and vagaries of fight film production and exhibition. In so doing, I demonstrate why the genre remained an important sideline for the industry but too unpredictable for filmmakers to build their fortunes on it.

During the same period, the idiomatic genre of fake, or reenacted, fight films proved more sustainable than boxing actualities. Several companies engaged in the practice, although it was never massively profitable. Siegmund Lubin's film company in Philadelphia specialized in this hybrid form, producing dozens of "reproductions," principally between 1897 and 1901. Chapter 4 explains not only the Lubin production methods but also the social origins and cultural interpretations of the art of the fake. Faking was a craft used and abused by both boxers and filmmakers. Journalistic and show-business traditions of ballyhoo, publicity, and fakery infected boxing promotion and motion-picture exploitation. During this period, when theatrical traditions of reenactment blended with new expectations about photographic reproduction, both sellers and exhibitors of fake fight films capitalized on this ambiguity. The genre was a historically limited one, however. As more authentic prizefight films arrived in the nickelodeon period, it soon faded away.

Chapter 5 documents the continuing changes in the production and reception of the genre from 1905 to 1915, a boom period in cinema and in social reform. Industrially, the fight picture had two distinct phases. From 1905 to 1908, a San Francisco-based firm, Miles Bros., took advantage of its proximity to the fight syndicate's headquarters and specialized in well-photographed prizefights. Despite Miles's financial success with fight pictures, the company was shut out of the Motion Picture Patents Company cartel that dominated the industry after 1908. New film-company combinations allowed a place for fight pictures in the interstices of the industry. Commerce in motion pictures was dominated by short, fictional works. But a single topical fight film could produce thousands of dollars in profits. Both dominant companies and short-lived incorporations continued to market feature-length fight pictures on an occasional basis. However, the film industry was facing mounting criticism for its association with prizefighting. The class, race, gender, and age of audiences for movies in general and fight films in particular remained a concern. Reform rhetoric and censorship forced the trade to finesse ways to profit from fight pictures while espousing the goals of their critics.

Debates and conflicts over racial matters escalated dramatically when Jack Johnson held the heavyweight crown from 1908 to 1915. The racial division of American society led to distinct, race-based interpretations of the films of Johnson's bouts. African American audiences saw them as a cause for celebration; white society reacted mainly in fear and dismay. With Jack London and other white critics leading a public campaign to prove blacks inferior by having a white boxer defeat Johnson, the continued success of the black champion only heightened the conflict. After allowing the Johnson fight films a degree of liberty for several years, the white majority's ultimate reaction was one of suppression.

I divide this apex of the fight-picture phenomenon into two parts. Chapter 6 focuses on Johnson's first three fight films in the years 1908 to 1910, climaxing with the *Johnson-Jeffries Fight.* An examination of these movies provides a window on the underresearched existence of a vital and vigorous history of early film exhibition in African American communities. The African American reception of the Johnson fight films was connected to the establishment of a black-only exhibition circuit and an important, albeit unsuccessful, early integration campaign often aimed at white-owned theaters and nickelodeons. Johnson's larger-than-life, heroic screen image spurred black audiences' demands for access.

The Johnson fight pictures, showing a formidable champion's complete dominance over several white hopes, made for uncomfortable contradictions to the white ruling class's ideology of racial superiority. In chapter 7, I examine the second half of Johnson's reign and his final fight pictures. The decline in the boxer's reputation encouraged the total suppression of his films. The federal criminalization of interstate traffic in fight films in 1912 was largely motivated by racist fears of Johnson's persona.

Fight Pictures concludes with a chapter explaining how fight pictures were forced underground after the 1915 enforcement of their ban. Although they could not be commercially exploited in full until decriminalized in 1940, prizefight films continued to be made. At first, they often traveled clandestinely to a smaller audience of fans. By the late 1920s, bootleg and contraband copies were brazenly exhibited again. Later, prizefighting figured prominently in the development of early radio and television. With the instantaneous broadcast of fight results through these new media, the role of filmed replays of the fights greatly diminished.

SOURCES

In addition to reading contemporary sources and a wide range of historical accounts of the period, I have viewed as many prints of fight films as I could. These fall into three categories: scenes of boxers sparring, reenactments of topical bouts, and recordings of actual prizefights. Copyright records, photographs, and surviving still frames supplement descriptions of these motion pictures. In investigating the production, exhibition, and audiences of prizefight films, I rely on a variety of primary sources, including trade journals (*Variety, New York Clipper, New York Dramatic Mirror, Moving Picture*

World, Moving Picture News, the *Nickelodeon,* and the British *Bioscope*), periodicals, and advertisements; producer and distributor catalogs; business records; congressional, regulatory, and legal documentation; memoirs, letters, and diaries; and secondary historical literature on the Progressive Era, motion pictures, and boxing. Even the era's literary production is sometimes revealing, as in Rudyard Kipling's story "Mrs. Bathurst" (1904). "Were you in Cape Town last December when Phyllis's Circus came?" one British soldier in South Africa inquires of another. "I ask because they had a new turn of a scientific nature," he says. "Oh, you mean the cinematograph—the pictures of prize-fights and steamers. I've seen 'em up-country," the other answers. "Biograph or cinematograph was what I was alludin' to," replies the first.[23] Though fictional, the story reiterates how closely early cinema was associated with prizefights.

Many primary sources are journalistic and must be read with great skepticism. The era's yellow press drove sales by inflating, coloring, and fabricating news items. Papers like William Randolph Hearst's *San Francisco Examiner* had a vested interest in many big fights. Show-business trade papers, too, were of course notorious for their hype. Sports journals, fed by shameless ring promoters, are also filled with unverifiable reports and gossip. The most notorious of all, the *Police Gazette,* was a scandal sheet that sensationalized and illustrated tales of crime, sex, and blood sports. It also organized and promoted big prizefights.[24] However, to explain the conditions of reception for contemporary spectators, it is important to account for the readings of the films prompted by the content of these mass-circulation papers.

As this history of the fight picture reveals, early cinema remains a fascinating object of study. *Fight Pictures* aims to expand the body of historical knowledge about film and to dispel vague and stereotypical assumptions about "primitive" cinema. More important, it amplifies broader, crucial issues of American culture and social life.

1 The Sporting and Theatrical Syndicate

Boxing Pictures and the Origins of Cinema, 1891–1896

> To the sporting fraternity I can say that before long it will be possible to apply this system to prize fights and boxing exhibitions. The whole scene with the comments of the spectators, the talk of the seconds, the noise of the blows, and so on will be faithfully transferred.
>
> THOMAS EDISON, quoted in "The Kinetograph,"
> *New York Sun*, May 28, 1891

Thomas Edison's direct address to "the sporting fraternity" as a prime audience for his forthcoming invention was not an idle remark. As moving-picture technologies developed over the next five years, boxing remained an important part of the earliest productions. Press and professional discourses often coupled them. When Edison introduced this general connection in 1891, the *New York Sun* concluded with a specific one. "With out-of-door athletic exhibitions and prize fights," the paper said of the kinetograph, "its work will be just as perfect, and Luther Carey's stride will be measured as carefully and reproduced as distinctly as the terrible blows by which Fitzsimmons disposed of Dempsey." These topical references presumed an insider's knowledge—of Carey, the record holder in the hundred-yard dash, and of the pugilist Robert Fitzsimmons, who had recently won the middleweight championship.[1] In the era before cinema, such arcana had limited circulation. Movie coverage changed that. Of all the sports, boxing became the most closely affiliated with early cinema.

Fight pictures did not become a matter of substantial public commentary until sporting, theatrical, and motion-picture interests collectively capitalized on the cinematic representation of newsworthy bouts—usually heavyweight title contests such as Corbett-Fitzsimmons (1897), Jeffries-Sharkey (1899), or Johnson-Jeffries (1910). Yet the producers of motion pictures, particularly in the United States, linked their technology with boxing from the beginning. Fight titles constituted only a small percentage of the several thousand subjects listed for sale in early film catalogs. However, the frequent appearance of pugilists before the cameras of pioneer manufacturers was more than incidental. During the months between regular production for the Edison kinetoscope in 1894 and the international conversion to projected screenings in 1895–96, fight pictures emerged as the first genre of moving pictures to be distinguished by special forms of production and presentation. Commentators on the technology often associated it with this genre. The connection between motion pictures and boxing became one that, over the next two decades, both institutions sought to exploit, even as each tried to shed the other's sometimes tainting influence.

Why did boxing and cinema develop this interrelationship? Most apparent was the match of two practices that relied on brief, segmented units of performance. Recognizing this, makers of motion pictures competed for the best boxing subjects. Commercial competition existed between the Edison company and its rivals, but also among Edison's subcontractors—the Kinetoscope Company (also called Raff & Gammon), the Kinetoscope Exhibiting Company (Latham, Rector and Tilden), and the Continental Commerce Company (Maguire & Baucus). The most important determinant, however, was sociological. In the 1890s, prizefighting and filmmaking shared a milieu: an urban, male community known to its contemporaries as the "sporting and theatrical" world.

INITIAL EXPERIMENTS: "MEN IN MOTION"

Evidence of cinema's affinity for pugilism comes from the very earliest recordings: W. K. L. Dickson's 1891–92 experiments at the Edison laboratory (see figure 4) and the 1894–95 kinetoscope pictures staged in Edison's "Black Maria" studio (see figures 5 and 6). Amateur and professional fighters of varying degrees of fame came to the New Jersey laboratory and sparred while technicians recorded their actions in installments lasting little more than a minute. By the end of their first year in the "Kinetographic Theatre," the Dickson team had filmed *Leonard-Cushing Fight, Corbett and Courtney Before the Kinetograph, Hornbacker-Murphy Fight, Billy Edwards and Warwick,* and others. There were also "burlesque boxing bouts," vaudeville turns of knockabout comedy stunts performed by stage veterans. The first catalogs also included numbers of athletic display or combat: *Wrestling Match, Gladiatorial Combat, Cock Fight, Boxing Cats, Wrestling Dogs, Lady Fencers, Mexican Duel,* and films of contortionists, gymnasts, and (foremost) female dancers.

Figure 4. [*Men Boxing*] (1891), experiment with the Edison-Dickson horizontal-feed kinetograph. This prototype recorded circularly matted images on ¾-inch-gauge celluloid, just over half the width of the 35 mm standard that followed. (Library of Congress, Motion Picture, Broadcasting and Recorded Sound Division.)

Figure 5. R. F. Outcault's drawing of Edison's Black Maria, imagining a sparring match with synchronous sound recording. *The Electrical World,* June 16, 1894.

Similar impressions about the kinetic nature of this imagery are apparent in Dickson's illustrations for his book *History of the Kinetograph, Kineto-scope, and Kineto-phonograph* (1895). His drawing of the Corbett-Courtney fight appears on the cover alongside wrestlers, fencers, strongmen, dancers, and boxing animals. Such subject matter suited the kinetoscope's brief

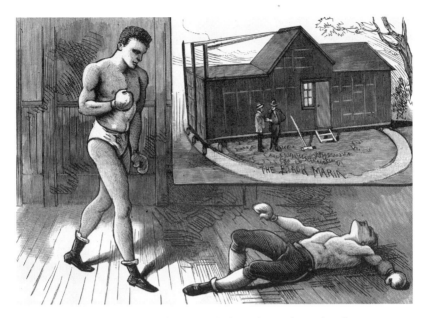

Figure 6. Fanciful illustration for "Knocked Out by Corbett: The Champion Cleverly Defeats Peter Courtney in Six Rounds for the Edison Kinetoscope," *Police Gazette*, September 22, 1894.

running time and the kinetograph's immobility. Boxing films were iterations of the corporeal and visual dynamism animating peep shows. The fighters' shuffling feet and flailing arms were on a par with Annabelle's serpentine dance and Professor Tschernoff's trained-dog act.

The early filmmakers' fascination with capturing the human physique in motion added to the prevalence of boxers in films. Recordings of what a Kinetoscope Company bulletin called the "scienced and skillful . . . exhibition of sparring"[2] could be classed with the series of poses by the celebrity strongman Eugen Sandow (1894), the widely viewed scene of May Irwin and John C. Rice in *The Kiss* (1896), or even *Edison Kinetoscopic Record of a Sneeze, January 7, 1894*. In a coincidence worth noting, on that same January 7 a press item about Edison's latest inventions suggested that his kinetoscope could be used to record the upcoming heavyweight title bout. "It is claimed that by the use of this machine all the rounds of a boxing contest, every blow in a prize-fight or other contest, can be reproduced, and the whole placed on exhibition at a nickel a head. By this means the hundreds of thousands who would wish to see the meeting between [Jim] Corbett and [Charlie] Mitchell can witness the encounter, counterfeited by the

Figure 7.   Eadweard Muybridge, *Athletes Boxing* (1893),
zoopraxiscope disc. Muybridge projected 12-inch spinning glass
discs onto a screen, creating a looping animation at the end of his
lantern lectures. (Library of Congress, Prints and Photographs
Division.)

kinetograph, on every street corner within a week after the gladiators
meet."[3]

Such subjects had precinematic antecedents. Dickson's films of boxers
continued the work expected of moving pictures. Commentaries on the development of the cinematic apparatus envisioned motion pictures as the
fruition of work by the photographer-scientists Eadweard Muybridge and
Étienne-Jules Marey. Their serial photography and chronophotography of
the 1870s and 1880s studied animal and human locomotion. Muybridge's
Athletes Boxing (1879) stood out for some who saw the series. In 1882, when
the photographer gave his first London presentation, *Photographic News* reported that the Prince of Wales greeted him with the words, "I should like to
see your boxing pictures." In 1888, Edison received Muybridge in his new
West Orange lab, while Muybridge was on a lecture tour with lantern slides.
Edison took an interest in his colleague's zoopraxiscope, which projected still

Figure 8.   The San Francisco fight between Dal Hawkins and
George Dixon was not filmed, but the local press chose to illustrate it with a "kinetoscopic" image (which might have been more
properly called "zoopraxiscopic"). *San Francisco Examiner*, July
24, 1897.

images in rapid succession from a rotating glass disc, approximating continuous motion. Muybridge used it at the end of his New Jersey presentation
for "projecting animated versions of boxing and dancing."[4]

Edison recordings drew on these precursors. As early as spring 1891,
Dickson used a prototype camera to record a fleeting sequence of two men
standing toe to toe and circling their mitts. A rope in the foreground suggested a boxing ring. By autumn 1892, Dickson's crew had shot a similar
test. *The Phonogram* magazine printed frames from *Boxing*, alongside examples from *Fencing* and *Wrestling*. Restating Edison's promise to "reproduce motion and sound simultaneously," the accompanying article concluded: "The kinetograph will also record with fidelity all that takes place at
prize fights, baseball contests and the noise, stir and progress of games."[5]

These test pictures, however, are more reminiscent of Muybridge's motion studies than of later sound movies. The 1892 experiments even include

Figure 9.   *Eadweard Muybridge, Nude Male Athletes Boxing,* plate 336, *Animal Locomotion* (1887). (Library of Congress, Prints and Photographs Division.)

a gridded backdrop similar to that used in Muybridge's *Animal Locomotion* series. Dickson's 1894 pictures of men in boxing trunks also resemble Muybridge's mostly nude athletic models walking, jumping, running, wrestling, and boxing. *Harper's Weekly* made the connection in June 1891. In "Edison's Kinetograph," the author George Parsons Lathrop discussed experiments in motion photography. The object of the cameras of Marey, Muybridge and Edison, he wrote, was to record "men in motion." The "great possibilities" of the kinetograph included the ability "to repeat in life-like shadow-play" all manner of human activities, including "prize-fights, athletic games, [etc.]"[6] Given moving pictures envisioned by this generation of inventors, and the degree to which interest in the "science" of boxing comported with their science, it is not surprising that fight pictures headed the list of preferred subjects when Dickson wrote in 1894 that kinetoscopic "records embrace pugilistic encounters."[7]

    Although they shared the kineticism and foregrounding of bodies visible in other recordings, fight pictures immediately distinguished themselves. They used different production methods, technologies, and personnel. The genre was also exhibited, publicized, and received in a manner distinct from other film subjects.

THE KINETOSCOPE EXHIBITING COMPANY

The production of fight pictures diverged from the Edison company's other early motion-picture activities. The firm collaborated with independent entrepreneurs who sought to exploit its technologies. Edison began selling kinetoscope viewing devices and film loops to amusement operators in April 1894. Marketing proved disorganized until Norman C. Raff and Frank R. Gammon received "exclusive American marketing" rights by September 1. For two years their Kinetoscope Company sold territorial rights for the use of the machines and sold owners prints of the fifty-foot "photographic strips" produced in the Black Maria. The coin-in-the-slot novelty device— which appeared in arcades, hotels, amusement parks, and phonograph parlors—did only middling business even at its peak.

However, Raff and Gammon were not the only ones to contract for use of Edison's motion-picture technology. Before the Kinetoscope Company's "exclusive" agreement was finalized, a group of speculators lobbied Edison for the right to build a camera and viewer capable of holding longer strips of celluloid. The group consisted of the brothers Otway and Gray Latham, their father Woodville (a scientist and inventor), the engineer Enoch J. Rector (the brothers' college classmate), and financial partners Samuel J. Tilden Jr. (heir of the former New York governor) and J. Harry Cox (of the Tilden Company, America's oldest pharmaceutical manufacturer). Their stated purpose was to profit from recording and commercially exhibiting prize-fight pictures.

Edison's business manager, William E. Gilmore, granted the Latham application in May 1894 after interviewing Otway, who offered as references Tilden and the attorney John Dos Passos. On May 15, Latham ordered "ten Kenetiscopes." Rector began working alongside Dickson in the previously secret research labs. By June they had tripled the kinetograph's film capacity to 150 feet. Their company made good on its promise to use the improved equipment for the production of fight pictures. Although Latham recorded only a handful of bouts during the company's brief existence, each production made an impact.[8]

THE LEONARD-CUSHING FIGHT

After negotiations and technical alterations to convert the Black Maria into a makeshift boxing ring, the Latham partnership made its first film, the *Leonard-Cushing Fight,* on June 14, 1894. Historian Gordon Hendricks describes the incident as "the first big Black Maria event" (apart from the Sandow visit in March) and "the last of comparable notoriety until the next Latham production—the Corbett-Courtney fight" in September.[9] The Lathams' drive to record a prizefight expedited Dickson's achievement of better photographic results. The crew waited through several days of clouds for ideal sunlight, meanwhile conducting experiments (apparently unsuccessful) with "auxiliary lighting." They also arranged the boxers' exhibition to comport with the new camera's capacity: it consisted of six one-minute rounds and culminated in a knockout by the favorite.

To a large extent, boxing succeeded as moving-picture fare because it could be structured around the kinetoscope's formal constraints. Kinetoscope parlors generally placed machines in rows of five or six. By putting a film of one round in each machine and setting up a knockout climax, the serialized presentation encouraged exhibitors to buy all six films and the customers to watch the entire sequence. A *New York World* journalist who saw the fight being recorded made the strategy explicit: "The theory is that when in the first round he [the customer paying ten cents per view] sees Mr. Leonard, to use his own language, "pushing Mr. Cushing in the face," he will want to see the next round and the next four. Thus he will pay sixty cents for the complete kinetograph of this strange and unheard of fight."[10]

The Lathams banked on this strategy to such a degree that by August, now incorporated as the Kinetoscope Exhibiting Company, they opened their own Manhattan storefront (see figure 10). The *Leonard-Cushing Fight* was the sole attraction, viewable on six new-model kinetoscopes. The monothematic presentation proved feasible for a short time, with seventy-two more machines ordered on August 23. Additional kinetoscope operators in Brooklyn (whence both lightweights hailed) were already marketing the films.[11]

Selling rounds as separate films proved viable for several years, even as projectors replaced peep shows and cameras became capable of filming longer events. The *Leonard-Cushing Fight* remained in the Edison catalogs into the 1900s, still "sold by rounds." Other companies still used this packaging practice as late as 1907.[12] An exhibitor whose venue might not allow projection of a full-length fight could purchase a condensation of the best rounds, or even the knockout alone. As Charles Musser points out, this opportunity for the exhibitor to choose parts of a film series and reassemble them for particular screenings functioned as the modus operandi for motion-picture entertainment until about 1903, when single-film, multi-shot narratives became the stock-in-trade.[13]

The *Leonard-Cushing Fight* and subsequent films matched boxing's short units of performance with the modular production and exhibition

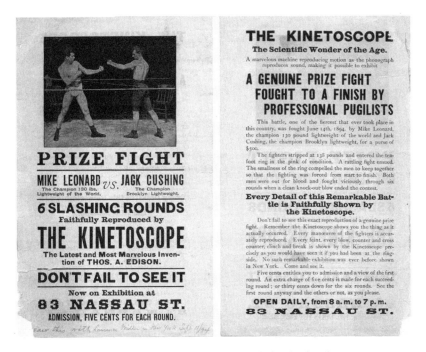

Figure 10. Handbill (6 by 9.5 inches, double-sided) for the first boxing pictures, the *Leonard-Cushing Fight* (1894). The Kinetoscope Exhibiting Company showed the six films in August, during the opening of its storefront in New York's financial district. An unknown customer kept this souvenir and wrote on it: "I saw this with Laurence Miller in New York Sept 11/94." (From the author's collection.)

needs of cinema. But their significance is better explained by the meanings attached to prizefighting. Such images were not neutral to those who made or watched them. The general appeal of physical movement and the aptness of running times were secondary grounds for the genre's proliferation compared to more conspicuous variables, such as the reputations of individual boxers, the promotional efforts of ring-friendly showmen, and the cultural controversies embedded in prizefighting.

Although of only minor importance compared to later boxing films, even the *Leonard-Cushing Fight* suggests how social context influenced a film's production, exhibition, and reception. For example, why Leonard and Cushing? That the participants are named is itself significant. Early British and French producers, occasionally using boxers as subjects in a medley of *actualités*, often used generic titles: *Boxeurs* (Lumière, 1895), *Boxing Match* (Robert Paul, 1895), *Glove Contest* (Birt Acres, 1896), *Magnificent Glove*

Fight (1897), *Fight* (G. A. Smith, 1898), and *Great Glove Fight* (James Williamson, 1900). The Lathams, conversely, engaged in the marketing of filmed prizefights in which matching big-name athletes against each other increased publicity and receipts. The brothers spent considerable time creating a notable match-up for their debut. They considered pitting the undefeated Australian boxer Young Griffo against the popular George "Kid" Levigne (the pair had recently fought in New York) or the unbeaten lightweight champion Jack McAuliffe.[14] When negotiations with these top-rank figures fell through, two Brooklyn lightweights were selected to enact the first bout before a motion-picture camera. Mike Leonard was a regional celebrity and a legitimate contender; Jack Cushing was an overmatched unknown.

Leonard versus Cushing, therefore, signified more of a set-up than a set-to: an opportunity for the celebrity favorite to exhibit his form while dispatching a credible fall guy. In retrospect, the extant portion of the film is notable for how little it resembles an actual contest. It appears an iconic, minimalist representation of a pugilistic scene. The gloved participants pose toe to toe in a half-sized ring. Behind them, against a black backdrop, kneel four men in white shirts holding towels. A referee stands immobile beside a bucket and stool in the right corner. This bare mise-en-scène, suggesting the likeness of a prize ring, shows Leonard to advantage. Cushing appears in the style of the deposed bare-knuckle champ John L. Sullivan: bare-chested, with dark, high-waisted, knee-length pants, sporting a crew cut and handlebar mustache, and displaying a slow, flat-footed boxing form. In contrast, the pompadoured Leonard (billed as "the Beau Brummel of pugilism") wears only cheeky white briefs, supported by a traditional American-flag belt.[15] The limited Black Maria lighting and dark background make him the more visible figure. He is far more active and is allowed to land his punches unanswered.

Although the event was a staged presentation, confusion ensued about the nature of "this very strange and unusual fight." Newspapers described the bout in contradictory terms. Some reported a bout conducted with "real, solemn, bloody earnest" that was "satisfactory to the spectators." Yet they simultaneously acknowledged the manipulation of the contest: "The rules of the ring were remodeled to suit the kinetograph;" the boxers were "compelled to pose until the lights were adjusted;" or, as Jack Cushing was quoted as saying, "Fighting in front of a photographing machine was no fight."[16]

Perhaps exhibitors or sports fans were disgruntled by the false promise of "an actual six-round contest" full of "hard fighting."[17] Perhaps disinterested viewers watched the brief scenes with momentary curiosity. But the problem of distinguishing genuine contests from ones set up for the camera plagued both the early film industry and the sport of boxing. The cry of "Fake!" was heard both from ringside and screenside once boxing promoters and film companies joined hands. The equivocal reception of the Latham debut embodied the problematic nature of fight pictures.

The ambiguous nature of the fisticuffs between Leonard and Cushing also led to legal problems. Before the films had even been exhibited, a judge in Essex County, New Jersey, announced that a grand jury would investigate Edison and his associates for sponsoring an illegal act: a prizefight, or at least "something which was certainly meant to appear to be a fight to a finish."[18] Following a denial of involvement by Thomas Edison himself, no legal action ensued. Nevertheless, the implications of legal scrutiny of fight film production were ominous. No state censorship resulted from the minor kinetoscope productions of Latham, Rector, and Tilden, but their subsequent exhibition as feature films in 1897 elicited some of the first legislative controls on motion pictures in the United States. This alliance with the illegal sport of prizefighting compromised cinema throughout its early history. Both exhibitors and viewers of the "living pictures of the great prize fight" between Leonard and Cushing would have recognized that they were party to an illicit venture.[19] Less clear is the degree to which viewers thought themselves onlookers to a crime in progress or saw the films as fanciful recreations of a newsworthy event (much as they would have received theatrical reenactments, newspaper illustrations of crimes, or even the later filmed restagings of sensational murders or robberies).

In either case, the acceptance of the fight genre by a portion of the public and filmmakers' willingness to associate with pugilism both demonstrate that prizefighting, though illegal in most states, received a considerable degree of social acceptance. Historians of the sport have established that professional boxing at this time built a significant following even as it was suppressed.[20] Prizefighting was considered more like alcohol consumption or gambling than robbery or assault. Its status as sport or crime, amusement or vice, remained in flux. Like these other activities, prizefighting had its abolitionists and prohibitionists as well as its reformers, advocates, and practitioners. By choosing to film prizefighters, Edison, Latham, and subsequent producers knowingly entered this public fray.

The producers' attitude toward prizefighting was complex, one of neither straightforward advocacy nor sheer clandestine profiteering. The privileged status of Thomas Edison gave early film producers an advantage. For example, when the *New York World* noted of the Leonard-Cushing pictures that "Thomas A. Edison photographed them with his machine," the association granted publicity and legitimacy to the films. Not only was the great inventor in attendance with "six scientific friends," but he was also greatly caught up in the heat of the contest, "imitat[ing] every movement of the fighters." Furthermore, the *World* reported, "Mr. Edison was well fitted to supervise a prize-fight," having been a frequenter of contests at Harry Hill's famous boxing establishment and thereby connected with his fellow Gilded Age hero John L. Sullivan. The *New York Journal* made light of the cultural contradiction, beginning its report on the first fight picture with the words: "Prize-fight in the interest of electrical science, Thomas A. Edison, inventor, philosopher, master of ceremonies." At the same time, the *New York Sun*, detailing the grand jury investigation of the bout, could claim that "Wizard Edison" "did not see it, as he was up in the mountains" instead, they noted, "W. K. L. Dickson has charge" of the kinetoscope works. A Boston writer defended Edison as "a human and gentle man, who never saw a prize fight, nor would he permit one to be fought on his premises." Thus, the films could simultaneously use the Edison brand for advantage and protect Thomas Edison's personal reputation for integrity.[21]

The subcontracted production system used to make these fight pictures also allowed a less risky form of exploitation. While the Kinetoscope Exhibiting Company arranged to record conspicuous prizefights, the official Edison Manufacturing Company turned out a variety of subjects that allowed Edison and Dickson (and their public-relations staff) to write about the educational, scientific, and morally edifying possibilities of their pictures. This segregation deflected adverse publicity surrounding boxing pictures and simultaneously left the parent company with legal control over the films, patents, and, of course, profits.

CORBETT AND COURTNEY BEFORE THE KINETOGRAPH

Profits were not substantial for the *Leonard-Cushing Fight*. The modest number of kinetoscopes on the market and the limited fame of the two principals minimized the returns. But Latham, Rector, and Tilden negotiated further match-ups. Although business at their Manhattan kinetoscope parlor dwindled after only a few weeks, the Lathams soon secured a far more lucrative subject, featuring the world heavyweight champion, James J. Corbett. These pictures, Musser's definitive study concludes, "generated the most income of any motion picture subject made during the kinetoscope era."[22]

Copyrighted as *Corbett and Courtney before the Kinetograph*, the production followed the pattern of its predecessor: one-minute films of six

SAM'L J. TILDEN, Pres't.
ENOCH J. RECTOR, Vice-Pres't
J. H. COX, Sec'y and Treas.

SOLE OWNERS OF
JAMES J. CORBETT'S
KINETOSCOPIC EXHIBITIONS

The Kinetoscope Exhibiting Co.

NEW LEBANON, N. Y.

Figure 11. Kinetoscope Exhibiting Company letterhead, 1896.
(Thomas A. Edison Papers.)

rounds of sparring, culminating in a prearranged knockout by the favorite. The Dickson-Latham crew made only minor alterations in preparation for the appearance of the champion: a slightly wider ring, a larger on-screen audience to authenticate the performance, and, judging from extant prints, better illumination of the subjects. These niceties aside, the production was virtually indistinguishable from *Leonard-Cushing,* save for the identity of the boxers.

Yet the reception of this second fight picture was remarkably different. The Leonard-Cushing films had received brief and limited attention, but *Corbett and Courtney* became the most widely seen kinetoscope attraction, its popularity continuing into 1896 and 1897. The films' near ubiquity is evident in contemporary photographs and illustrations of kinetoscope parlors and arcades.[23] Hendricks's *The Kinetoscope* concludes that *Corbett-Courtney* was "the most conspicuous motion picture to date, and it exceeded in notoriety all others for some time"; it "served to focus, as no other event had yet done, national attention on the Kinetoscope and the motion picture."[24]

This unprecedented reception resulted from orchestrated publicity maneuvers involving newspaper, theatrical, sporting, and motion-picture interests. Some sources indicate that the filmmakers first attempted to induce the retired but extraordinarily popular John L. Sullivan to box for the camera, but there is no evidence that he had dealings with Edison or the Lathams.[25] Instead, they engaged Corbett, who had dethroned Sullivan in 1892. So central was he to the Kinetoscope Exhibiting Company's success that the firm later had his visage engraved on its letterhead (see figure 11).

Regardless of the choice of opponent, in 1894 "Gentleman Jim" was the central attraction, a figure of rising and multifaceted celebrity. Corbett had risen quickly to the position of contender by employing a new, "scientific" method of boxing that used quick, agile, score-and-retreat tactics to outpoint slugging and gouging bruisers. On February 18, 1890, the up-and-coming Corbett beat Sullivan's rival, Jake Kilrain, in New Orleans. On May 21, 1891, he came to national prominence by fighting a remarkable sixty-one-round draw with the storied heavyweight Peter Jackson in San Francisco. A veteran black West Indian fighter and the Australian champion, Jackson was ranked among the best of his era, but he could not get a title match because Sullivan refused to take on any nonwhite challengers. [26] When he "drew the color line" against Jackson, he was hardly alone in maintaining the segregationist order of the day. But others in the fight game were staging interracial bouts. (For his fellow Irish American, however, the champ consented to a joint appearance. In June, Sullivan and Corbett sparred briefly at a charitable event, wearing evening clothes with their boxing gloves.)

Corbett's performance against Jackson yielded larger opportunities. Accepting an offer from the showman (and fellow San Franciscan) William A. Brady, Corbett became a popular touring stage actor. During the theatrical season of 1891–92, he first appeared in a sparring scene from the oft-produced Boucicault melodrama *After Dark* (1868).[27] Brady obtained backing for a title bout against Sullivan in September 1892. The "Great John L." had himself been capitalizing on his status through theatrical appearances such as onstage sparring exhibitions and a touring melodrama, *Honest Hearts and Willing Hands*. In fact, Sullivan had not defended his title in more than three years.[28] When the challenger Corbett defeated the aging champion, Brady immediately placed him in *Gentleman Jack*, a loosely biographical play commissioned for the star. For three seasons, he toured as Jack Royden, a Princeton man and bank clerk who, at the behest of his sweetheart, reluctantly enters the ring and defeats a prizefighter who is in cahoots with the villain.[29]

Unlike other professional boxers, the heavyweight titleholder seldom actually engaged in prizefights. Instead he cashed in on the belt through public appearances. For Corbett these included making speeches, sparring in theaters, syndicating press columns, accepting or dismissing challenges from contenders, publishing ghostwritten books, and giving shows—at the World's Fair, the Folies Bergère, Drury Lane, and other prominent spots throughout Europe and North America. But his principal vehicle remained his lead role as Gentleman Jack in the melodrama that reinforced his public persona. Brady later wrote that "the Sullivan fight and winning the championship was just a publicity stunt for Corbett's forthcoming play."[30] For both Corbett and Brady, prizefighting was as much a promotional endeavor as a sporting competition. The championship was not the end but the means to exploiting other lucrative opportunities.

Figure 12. James J. Corbett in fighting attitude and in costume for the play *A Naval Cadet* (1896). (Library of Congress, Prints and Photographs Division.)

Corbett's appearance before the kinetograph constituted another such opportunity. He did not defend his title in 1893 and fought only a short bout with the British champion Charlie Mitchell in January 1894. The prospect of Corbett's taking on a new opponent therefore sparked anticipation of the film production. His presence alone guaranteed advance publicity. Speculation about the identity of his opponent only raised expectations.

The prospect of a terrific pairing, while not fulfilled by the little-known Peter Courtney, generated gossip and press releases. The Latham brothers attempted to strike a rematch between Corbett and Peter Jackson, offering $15,000 for a contest "in a ten-foot ring before the kinetoscope." Otway's press release, written as a letter to the fighters' managers from the "Photo-Electric Exhibition Co.," suggested "this would be the best way to settle the match," because "everyone who would desire would ultimately, through the Edison invention, see the affair." Brady replied in kind. For a purse of $25,000, he wrote, "we should be glad to have it come off under your direction before the kinetoscope, as Mr. Corbett would be delighted to have his motions and actions in the ring preserved for future generations."[31] But Corbett's stated determination to reinforce Sullivan's "color line" precluded a confrontation with Jackson. A title fight with the top contender Robert

Fitzsimmons, who had a string of knockout victories, was deemed more probable.

The Kinetoscope Exhibiting Company made concerted efforts to land a Corbett-Fitzsimmons bout but failed to clinch a deal (though Enoch Rector would film the match in 1897). Disappointed at Corbett's unwillingness to share the spotlight with "Fitz," the Lathams substituted Courtney, a New Jersey heavyweight selected because he was said to have "stood up against" Fitzsimmons earlier that year.[32]

Production of the Corbett-Courtney films again brought promotional opportunities not afforded other motion pictures. The meeting was staged on September 7, the second anniversary of Corbett's victory over Sullivan.[33] Thomas Edison put in a rare personal appearance at the Black Maria to greet the champion and his entourage, who were performing *Gentleman Jack* in Manhattan that week. And of course both the Corbett and Edison organizations encouraged press coverage. The following day many New York and New Jersey newspapers published accounts and illustrations of both the moving-picture apparatus and the boxers' performance.

What is striking about these reports is their consistent, almost conspiratorial, misrepresentation of the match as a real fight. Journalists offered colorful descriptions that supported the Edison company's attempt to sell "an actual contest," even though the sparring was prearranged and tame.[34] Surviving portions of the film show a smiling and laughing Corbett playfully slapping away Courtney's exaggerated swats. Although this improvised performance belies Brady's claim that "careful rehearsal" was done, it also illustrates his contention that Corbett, Courtney, and the filmmakers were complicit in "staging this phony battle."[35] As in *Leonard-Cushing*, mismatched contestants and an optimally timed knockout further signify an obvious setup. But those reading about the curious Black Maria bout were told instead of a "genuine fight" and presented with illustrations titled "The Champion Cleverly Defeat[ing] Peter Courtney."[36] The Corbett knockout even entered some ring record books. Later boxing histories and Edison biographies perpetuate the story with so much embellishment that Hendricks complains there is "more error recorded concerning this subject than any other."[37]

The point of recounting these muddled chronicles is not to set some record straight, but to illustrate the polysemic nature of the reception of early motion pictures. Issues of representation and realism, recording and re-creating, fact and facsimile were inchoate in early film exhibition. Were these photographic documents from Edison the Man of Science, or lifelike reproductions (illusions? tricks?) created by the Wizard of Menlo Park? The answer was both. As Tom Gunning expresses it, the later "Manichean division" between fact and fiction was not part of "the horizon of expectations in which films originally appeared. . . . The reception of the cinematic image" in 1894 readily fused *actualité* and fantasy, spectacles of popular science and magic.[38]

This double perception coalesced in the Corbett films. Press accounts willfully created one colorful version of the event that conditioned public reception of the pictures themselves. Responses to the filmed bout were further complicated by boxing's tradition of ambiguous performance: even ring habitués could not always distinguish an honest prizefight from a bogus one. Finally, the mise-en-scène before the kinetograph paled in comparison to the stagecraft that concluded *Gentleman Jack*. Reviewers of the play remarked on the highly realistic reconstruction of the New Orleans Olympic Club, site of Corbett's 1892 victory over Sullivan. The climactic set piece proved an audience favorite, prompting Brady to enhance it with "a twenty-four-foot ring in the center of the stage, a referee, timekeeper, seconds, and bottle holders," plus three hundred extras cheering the champion's boxing prowess.[39] The Black Maria films restaged that restaging (casting Brady as timekeeper), but in much less detail. The Corbett-Courtney production was the cinematic twin of the *Leonard-Cushing Fight*, save for the vastly greater celebrity of its lead performer.

These layers of meaning and perception explain why the pictures were not denounced as fakes. Without expectations that a Corbett appearance had to be an earnest fight to the finish or presumptions that moving pictures needed to be "genuine," audiences could encounter *Corbett and Courtney before the Kinetograph* on several levels: as fans of an idol, partisans of boxing, curiosity seekers drawn by the novel technology, or gossips intrigued by publicity over the event. Unconfined by a fixed form of presentation, the films developed broad appeal beyond a select sporting constituency.

The outcome of another legal controversy supplied further evidence that the multifaceted nature of the filmed bout worked to its advantage. The day Corbett's activities were reported in the press, a judge ordered a second grand-jury investigation of Edison's alleged prizefight scheme. Although both Edison and Dickson had been accurately identified as producers of the affair, their subpoenas were waved away by a bald-faced public denial from Edison (with help, no doubt, from his formidable legal staff). Attempts to indict the boxers and spectators also failed.[40] To an even greater degree than in the Leonard-Cushing case, the hint of scandal attracted the public to the Corbett films, while the certainty of exoneration prevented any setbacks for the producers.

THE AFTERMATH OF THE CORBETT-COURTNEY FIGHT PICTURE

The coup of an exclusive contract with the heavyweight champion, especially when validated by the financial success of *Corbett-Courtney,* prompted two changes at Edison Manufacturing: a further subdivision of production interests between the competing parties of the Kinetoscope Co. (Raff & Gammon), the Kinetoscope Exhibiting Co. (Latham, Rector, and Tilden), and the Continental Commerce Co. (Maguire & Baucus); and an increase in the production of boxing pictures.

The first change altered the traditional characterization of Edison, Inc., as a monolithic industrial giant. Rather than a single firm pursuing one line of production, in September 1894 the company became a manufacturing corporation whose creative work was subcontracted to other parties. While Dickson supervised activities in the Kinetographic Theatre and produced subjects directly for the Edison Manufacturing Company, he also facilitated productions by licensees. "Edison films" included subjects that originated not only with Dickson but also with Raff & Gammon, the Latham outfit, and Maguire & Baucus (agents for the kinetoscope abroad). Although the parent corporation profited, the smaller outfits considered themselves competitors. Each bore its own production costs, including the hiring of talent. Each urged Edison to pursue policies that would be to its own advantage.

One result of this competition was the immediate increase in boxing-film production that followed the *Corbett-Courtney* triumph. Although the Lathams had been granted use of equipment solely for the recording of prizefights, Raff & Gammon also began shooting fight pictures when their contract took effect in September 1894. With a schedule far more active and varied than the Lathams', Raff & Gammon recorded both conventional and burlesque boxing subjects, along with a variety of vaudeville acts. The first performers to follow Corbett's turn in the Black Maria were the Glenroy Brothers, comic boxers who appeared four times for the Kinetoscope Company. *Walton and Slavin,* a short-and-tall duo from Broadway, followed in October, days after *Hornbacker and Murphy, Five Round Glove Contest to a Finish* (see figure 13), for which actual prizefighters were hired. These early films remained restricted to rounds of twenty seconds, as the Kinetoscope Company still sold fifty-foot film loops for the original Edison machine, rather than film for the Lathams' expanded model. Raff & Gammon never landed ring celebrities to compete with Latham, either. In its final months, struggling to sell Edison's vitascope projectors, the firm was still making its own fight pictures. But *Boxing Contest between Tommy White and Solly Smith* (1896), with its

Figure 13. Edison's *Hornbacker and Murphy, Five Round Glove Contest to a Finish* (August 1894), featured little-known professional pugilists in five abbreviated rounds. The letter *R* at lower left brands it as a Raff & Gammon production. Only one round was known to survive until an additional one was discovered in England in 2005. These three nonconsecutive frames are taken from that print. (University of Sheffield National Fairground Archive.)

featherweights, remained obscure, and the return of Mike Leonard to the Black Maria for *Bag Punching* (October 1896) was lost in the mix of variety.[41]

Adding to the competition between Edison's main franchisees, other producers of motion pictures entered the market from 1894 through 1896. They too offered boxing scenes among their first efforts. In the United States. these included Maguire & Baucus, the inventor Charles E. Chinnock, and the American Mutoscope Company.

Maguire & Baucus produced films to supplement the prints they purchased from Raff & Gammon and the Latham firm.[42] The operators branded the Black Maria film *Billy Edwards Boxing* as their own by placing a placard with their "MB" logo in the foreground.[43] They planned fight pictures on a larger scale to compete with the Kinetoscope Exhibiting Co. Ramsaye's 1926 account mentions that in September 1894, Maguire & Baucus attempted to sign a contract with Raff & Gammon in which "one Hugh Behan was employed at a contingent $3,000 a year to frame a fight between 'such first class fighters as Corbett, Jackson, Fitzsimmons, M'Auliffe, Griffo, Dixon, or Maher, and a suitable opponent.' " Ramsaye ends by saying merely, "The project produced no picture fights and was soon forgotten"—although not by Behan, who managed the popular Young Griffo when the boxer appeared in a Latham film, one of the first publicly projected motion pictures, in May 1895.[44]

Charles Chinnock, a former vice president of the Edison United Manufacturing Company, offered early competition to Edison by building and selling a kinetoscope-like viewing machine of his own design. He filmed several subjects between November 1894 and August 1895 and sold them to supply his machines, which circulated in saloons, hotels, and amusement centers from New York to Philadelphia (at such venues as Coney Island, Huber's Museum, and the Eden Musée) and in England and France. Chinnock's first pictures recorded a boxing match between his nephew Robert T. Moore and James W. Lahey. A production schedule began in January 1895 with a second fight (between a man identified only as "McDermott" and an unnamed opponent) and other films imitative of Black Maria subjects (such as a cockfight and female dancers).[45]

A more lasting Edison competitor, American Mutoscope, also found boxing a suitable subject for its first test pictures.[46] Ramsaye's *A Million and One Nights* and Hendricks's *Beginnings of the Biograph* agree that the venture originated with a letter written by Dickson to Harry N. Marvin concerning "the possibility of some small simple device which could be made to show cheaply the final punch and knockout of a prize fight."[47] This flip-card peep show, dubbed the mutoscope, was placed on the market in 1897, but boxing and other subjects were being recorded by the biograph camera in 1895 and 1896. In Syracuse, New York, during June 1895, the company first tested its technology by photographing the cofounders, Herman Casler and Harry Marvin, sparring against a white backdrop.[48] That their initial impulse in front of a moving-picture camera was to stage a fisticuff caricature underscores the strength of the association between boxing and the year-old medium. Another reason for the choice, however, was probably that Dickson, the photographer of the Black Maria fighters, had left Edison's employ to become a founding partner in the company.

On August 5, when the camera was tested more extensively at the company's workshop in Canastota, New York, Dickson acted as cinematographer, filming two local "experts" in a sparring exhibition. The local paper identified the participants as "Prof. Al. Leonard and his pupil Bert Hosley," who "went at each other" for "more than one minute."[49] Although American Mutoscope moved on to a variety of other genres, the company continued to incorporate fight pictures into its schedule, even recording the heavyweight title bout in 1899. The first four subjects listed for sale in the 1903 American Mutoscope and Biograph catalog were sparring contests.[50]

As more makes of cameras and projectors became available throughout 1896, other entrepreneurs contributed to the welter of fight pictures in both Europe and America. In Germany, the Skladanowsky Bioskop's earliest projected shows (of November 1895) included a film of a man sparring with a boxing kangaroo. In England, where the sport had long been popular, some motion-picture pioneers engaged active British pugilists. Birt Acres shot *A Prize Fight by Jem Mace and Burke,* and Robert Paul made *Boxing Match between Toff Wall and Dido Plum.* In the United States, even local productions began to appear. In Pittsburgh, the theater owner Harry Davis filmed *Maher-Choynski Glove Contest.* In New Orleans, a now-unknown filmmaker made *Prize Fight by Skelly and Murphy* for local exhibition.[51]

Of course, even after big-screen projection became dominant, a peepshow market endured. The machines remained so closely associated with boxing iconography that American Mutoscope could offer its own meta-movie in 1899. *The Automatic Prize Fight* showed two boys who "rig up a fake" mutoscope and induce an old farmer to take a peek at what he supposes to be a fight picture, only to be the recipient of a real punch in the face.[52]

FRAMING REAL FIGHTS IN THE AGE OF PROJECTED FILM

Although the Latham, Rector, and Tilden enterprise manufactured only two sets of films in 1894, the more productive Kinetoscope Co. and Maguire & Baucus failed to outmaneuver them for future big fights. Through Rector and the Latham brothers, the Kinetoscope Exhibiting Co. maintained influential ties to sporting circles that businessmen like Raff and the Wall Street lawyers Maguire and Baucus lacked. The Lathams' ability to recruit recognizable talent was sufficient for Edison to continue favoring their contract, even when it meant waiting months for a single film.

Immediately following Corbett's film debut, the Lathams began negotiating for a fight picture that would surpass *Corbett-Courtney* in length, authenticity, and marketability. The optimal scenario would be an on-location recording of a championship fight between Corbett and Fitzsimmons. The pair's public feuding led to the signing of a grudge-match agreement in October. Hoping to capture the event on film, the Lathams pushed Rector and the Edison engineers to expand the capacity of their camera—at least to the limits of the three-minute rounds of genuine prizefights.

By November 1894 the technology had progressed sufficiently for Gray Latham to intervene in plans to hold the Corbett-Fitzsimmons fight in Jacksonville, Florida. The theatrical and sporting journal the *New York Clipper*, which became a national vehicle for early motion-picture advertisements, published Latham's "startling proposition":

> [Since the fight will likely not be allowed in Florida] we propose to make you an offer, which will certainly demand consideration. This offer would have been made at the time the several clubs were bidding for the championship contest, but for the fact that . . . the experiments at three minute subjects with the kinetograph had not proved entirely successful. Now, however, we shall not only be able to take each three minute round of the fight, but also the action of the seconds, etc., during the one minute rest between rounds. . . .
>
> Our offer is a plain one. The fight must be held in the morning, and, in case the date selected should prove a cloudy day, we will ask for a postponement until a clear day comes round. . . . We want the fight before November 1, 1895, and will give $50,000 for it. . . . We are enabled to offer this amount of money without depending upon the gate receipts, because, while a good many tickets will be sold, that is an entirely after consideration with us.

Both principals replied that, should the Florida Athletic Club deal fall through, the Kinetoscope Exhibiting Company "would have as good an opportunity to secure the fight as any other organization."[53] The Corbett-Fitzsimmons duel eventually materialized in grand fashion, but not until 1897. By then, significant changes in the motion pictures had occurred, and amid the shifting powers, the Latham interests failed. However, their partner, Rector, survived to become the principal broker of the next two major fight-picture productions.

Relations between the Lathams, their partners, and their competitors were changing by the end of 1894. With the Corbett-Fitzsimmons fight on hold, Woodville Latham pursued technological challenges rather than film production. Like inventors elsewhere, he realized that Edison was not expediting research in a projection system that could displace the kinetoscope. In order to develop a projector technology, which would place his firm in competition against Edison, the Lathams diversified their interests. Retaining the Kinetoscope Exhibiting Company subcontract, they incorporated the Lambda Company for the purposes of inventing and exploiting a motion-picture projector.

The Latham-Lambda project set up shop in Manhattan. Having established a working relationship with Edison Manufacturing employees during the development of the "prizefight kinetoscope," Woodville Latham induced the technician Eugene Lauste to join his staff. Together they developed the simple "Latham loop," which enabled projectors and cameras to handle longer films. (The loop became essential in nearly all motion-picture mechanisms, although Latham failed to patent it until 1902.) Further expertise came occasionally from Dickson, who was loosening his ties with Edison before joining American Mutoscope in the spring of 1895. By that time, the Lambda team had completed work on its "pantoptikon," a wide-film-format camera and projector, which they demonstrated to the press on April 21.[54]

Again the inventors of a new film technology first promoted their product with a film of a short boxing bout. And again the Latham connections succeeded in enlisting a well-known professional to appear in it. Young Griffo, the popular Australian who had nearly posed for the first set of Latham pictures, performed for the new camera in early May. The performance, however, differed from the ones that had gone before. Leonard and Cushing, Corbett and Courtney, and the other pugilists had merely sparred for the kinetograph. Griffo and his opponent, "Battling" [Charlie] Barnett, replayed a match they had just fought (on May 4) in Madison Square Garden.[55] Shortly after their bout, an abbreviated version took place under the supervision of Latham, Lauste, and (perhaps) Dickson on the Garden roof.[56] The film offered topicality that previous productions had not. If such reenactments could be marketed quickly, their commercial value could exceed that of unofficial match-ups created solely for the movies. *Young Griffo–Battling Barnett* may have benefited from public knowledge of the Madison Square Garden fight, but it was a minor event. However, as film and boxing became big businesses over the next decade, filmed "reproductions" of famous fights became standard fare.

Although Thomas Edison already had been quoted denouncing the Lathams' projection efforts as a legal infringement on his kinetoscope,[57] the firm rushed *Griffo-Barnett* to market in New York. On May 20, 1895, the pantopticon, renamed the "eidoloscope," debuted in a Broadway store front, showing the prizefight film to the world's first commercial viewers of a projected moving picture.[58] The projection of longer films had been accomplished by the addition of the simple Latham loop, although the running time was still only about four minutes. The wide-screen image offered a full view of the ring and, judging from press descriptions, an entire three-minute round of boxing with preliminary and concluding action to frame the event.[59] (The Corbett rounds, by contrast, ended in medias res when film ran out.) The machine functioned imperfectly at times, yet public response was reportedly good: Lauste ran the Griffo film in a tent show on Coney Island's Surf Avenue throughout the summer of 1895, encouraging the production of several other subjects on the rooftop film stage, including a scene of the professional wrestlers Ross and Roeber.[60] The early exhibitor George K. Spoor also recollected the machine's success, reporting that the operator Gilbert P. Hamilton ran one of Chicago's first projected movie shows in the summer of 1896. According to Spoor, Hamilton ran "a prize fight or a boxing contest, about one hundred feet in length" on an eidoloscope located in an old church. Its reception was favorable enough for managers at the Schiller theater to engage the pictures as entr'acte material for a stage production of *Robinson Crusoe*.[61]

Further alienating and upstaging Edison, the Lathams' Eidoloscope Company sold territorial rights to its projector and supplied subjects to shows across the United States in 1895 and 1896. Film historians have documented the circulation of Eidoloscope exhibitions: from New York City and Coney Island to a Chicago variety theater and dime museum (August–September 1895); to the Cotton States Exposition, Atlanta, and a stop in Indiana (September–October); Virginia screenings by a third Latham brother; Keith's Bijou in Philadelphia (December); Rochester's Wonderland (January 1896); a Syracuse storefront (March); a successful Manhattan reappearance at Hammerstein's Olympia and the St. James Hotel (May); a long run in the Detroit Opera House, followed by a summer park show (May–June); and in a Boston theater (June). The projector did service in a touring production of *Carmen* (November–December 1896), showing a ten-minute film of a bullfight that Lauste and Gray Latham had shot in Mexico.[62] Distribution was wide, but not strong enough to mount a threat to Edison's business. Even if the machine's technical performance had been better, without the resources to manufacture more machines and films, or the reputation to sell them, the Lathams' influence on a national entertainment market remained limited. The eidoloscope offered poor competition to Edison's vitascope (introduced in April 1896) and other superior projection machines. The Latham projector dwindled from sight early the following year. By 1898, the Eidoloscope Company was in receivership, having been taken over by a partner in the Vitascope Company of New Jersey.[63]

Despite having challenged Edison directly, the Lathams were able to retain ties to his company because of the financial prospects of the Corbett-Fitzsimmons bout. Although they had angered their powerful partner by using his own employees to build their projector, Rector "maintained diplomatic relations" with Edison.[64] The Kinetoscope Exhibiting Co., which Rector directed after the Latham split, still held its exclusive contract with Corbett. The proposed ringside films looked increasingly lucrative as anticipation for the bout mounted. With Rector pressing this advantage as reason to overlook the Latham misdealings, in September 1895 Edison specially built "four prize fight machines" (with an elaborate battery system) that would allow for location filming.

With its prizefight contract, the Kinetoscope Exhibiting Co. was allowed to remain in business despite the fact that it had produced only two sets of pictures and that its original contractors had attempted to undermine Edison. The Lathams' original rivals, Raff & Gammon, attempted to exploit this tension when their kinetoscope sales continued to wane. The public increasingly anticipated large-screen exhibitions, and the closest thing to a bona fide hit, *Corbett and Courtney before the Kinetograph*, was denied to the Kinetoscope Co. by the Lathams.

In an effort to bolster business, Raff & Gammon wrote to Thomas Edison on August 19, 1895 with an obsequious appeal for Edison to rescind his arrangements with "the Latham people" and grant the Corbett-Fitzsimmons picture rights to them, "the men who are really pushing the business of Kinetoscope sales." Airing their resentment of the competition's success with fight pictures, Raff & Gammon itemized their grievances: the Corbett-Courtney fight and the machines made for it violated the "exclusive" Kinetoscope Company contract; the Lathams had "sacrificed" Edison for their own gain by bringing out a "Screen Machine," "an imitation Kinetoscope," and original films; and, most reprehensibly, the letter alleged, the Latham people had attempted to go behind Edison's back by asking "the biggest amusement firm in America (viz: Jefferson, Klaw and Erlanger)," to capitalize the Eidoloscope Company.[65] The last item is especially telling, indicating the type of collusion and tendency to monopoly that characterized both the sporting and theatrical sectors (and indeed most American industry) in this era of trusts. In 1895, Klaw and Erlanger, a leading theatrical booking agency, arranged a "secret meeting" with other impresarios that gave rise to the Theatrical Syndicate, a cartel monopolizing playhouse bookings across the United States.[66] The syndicate (which included the star actor Joseph Jefferson) considered incorporating motion pictures into their road companies, and the Lathams aspired to become part of that monopoly rather than Edison's. However, Raff & Gammon convinced "Jefferson, Klaw and Erlanger" to consider Edison technologies instead. By informing on the Lathams, Raff believed he had demonstrated loyalty that Edison should reward with a prize-fight contract.[67]

Latham participation, however, had become moot. With Eidoloscope pursuing its independent goals, Enoch Rector (with Samuel Tilden's financial backing) now controlled the Kinetoscope Exhibiting Co. He dealt directly with both the film and prizefight interests. Rector eventually proved willing to negotiate exhibition plans with Raff & Gammon, but their firm proved to be of too little consequence. Raff & Gammon expedited Edison's entrance into the projection business by investing in the C. Francis Jenkins–Thomas Armat system, which Edison successfully marketed as the vitascope. Their own Vitascope Company failed even more quickly than their Kinetoscope Company. Edison developed a different project of his own and promoted it over the vitascope, forcing Raff & Gammon out of the film business altogether by the end of 1896..[68] On the strength of a single fight-picture guarantee, however, Rector preserved a strategic position in the sporting and theatrical business. The lasting power of the Corbett-Fitzsimmons fight pictures proved worth the wait.

The role of prizefight and boxing subjects in the history of cinema's kinetoscope and early projection period was significant for several reasons, not all of them considered by earlier historians. Although Ramsaye and Hendricks correctly devote more than passing attention to the phenomenon, their interpretations of the significance of fight films should not be overemphasized. Ramsaye's essentialist notion of pugilism and the "destiny for the motion picture" should be anathema to any historian, though his specific references to events and individuals have proved useful. Hendricks's monographs emphasize mechanical accomplishments. Still, both authors demonstrate conclusively that the brief, contained, recognizable, kinetic action of a round of boxing was well suited to the technical limitations of the first motion pictures.

The prevalence of fight pictures in the earliest cinema has other significant implications. The conspicuous nature of prizefight films (derived from their length, the reputations of the participants, and their cultural status)—or perhaps even the *Corbett-Courtney* pictures alone—caused early producers and audiences to associate film presentation with boxing. Pursuit of profit was an obvious motivation as well.

Further telling evidence of the significance of fight films comes by way of contrast with the concurrent Lumière *cinématographe* productions. Among the Lumière subjects of the 1890s, numbering more than one thousand, only one, *Pedlar Palmer v. Donovan*, shot in England, was a fight picture; two were fistic burlesques done by clowns.[69] In 1896, Charles Webster, a Raff & Gammon agent scouting *cinématographe* presentations in London, wrote to his employers (who had become desperate in their attempt to acquire fight films) that the Lumière pictures "are all local and cost a mere nothing in comparison to ours. They have no colors, prize fights or dancers, yet are received with cheers nightly for the past two month."[70]

Webster's surprise at finding a successful film show without a prizefight attraction underscores the common association between cinema and boxing. It might seem appropriate to conclude that this was in part a national or cultural bias: American firms sought boxing events, and Europeans succeeded well without them. However, even Lumière's own posters advertised boxing alongside its signature images of *actualité* (such as train stations) and the famous gag from *L'arroseur arose* (1895).[71] Illustrations of the *Projektionsgerät* developed by the German manufacturer Oskar Messter depict the machine casting an image of two fighters on a screen.[72] Cinema regularly evoked the image of prizefighters. Many contemporary characterizations of moving pictures accorded with Henry Tyrell's 1896 description in *The Illustrated America*, noting that typical exhibitions consisted of "street scenes, railway-trains in motion, boxing-bouts, bull-fights and military eventualities."[73]

The affiliation between boxing and moving pictures was not, however, merely the result of filmmakers deciding to record boxers because they were simple to frame. When historicizing nineteenth-century cinema, it is a fallacy to think of the film industry, boxing world, and theatrical business as autonomous entities. In the 1890s, they inhabited a common sociological world, where men (almost always) involved in all manner of amusement, entertainment, promotion, and popular presentation operated within and saw themselves as part of a shared endeavor. The cinema of the 1890s presented itself to fellow professionals not in film trade papers but in places such as the *New York Clipper,* which billed itself as "the oldest American theatrical and sporting journal." There the theater, circus, vaudeville, music, drama, minstrelsy, sports, games, magic, dance, mechanical amusements, novelties, and moving pictures, all commingled. The editor Frank Queen made the *Clipper* the leading advocate of professional boxing in the pre-Sullivan era. His efforts were surpassed by Richard K. Fox, the audacious Irish sporting man who in 1876 bought the failing *National Police Gazette* and turned it into a mass-circulation "sporting and theatrical" tabloid that hyped prizefights to excess. It was in the *Gazette* that Americans read the richest and most widely circulated account of the Corbett-Courtney fight. Each issue included pinup posters of two sorts—prizefighters and theater soubrettes.[74]

The men making and showing fight pictures saw themselves as part of this theatrical and sporting syndicate. Jim Corbett was not merely a professional boxer but also a stage idol, picture personality, lecturer, fight promoter, columnist, and raconteur. The title of his autobiography, *The Roar of the Crowd,* connotes these diverse roles. William Brady moved easily from the roles of fight manager and promoter to those of actor, agent, theater owner, Hale's Tours operator, and, later, Hollywood producer (he was the founder of World Pictures and the first president of the National Association of the Motion Picture Industry, from 1915 to 1920). The titles of his two autobiographies, *Showman* and *The Fighting Man,* are also indicative. Brady was no doubt the main inspiration for the theater historian Albert McCleery's characterization of turn-of-the-century show impresarios. They were "dignified gentlemen, those producers, astute and elderly, with derby hats, silky black moustaches, fur coats and large diamonds in rings on their fat fingers and in pins in their cravats. Some of them had been prize fight promoters."[75] Finally, Terry Ramsaye draws a similar portrait of the Latham brothers as Broadway gallants with interests in all aspects of the show and sporting world.

In New York, the de facto national headquarters of boxing, the men who created fight pictures shared a common social milieu. Its center was Harry Hill's concert saloon, a Lower East Side establishment that was Gotham's most popular men's entertainment venue between 1870 and 1895. Boxing was showcased along with variety shows, accompanied by dining, drinking, dancing, and sexual assignations. Harry Hill was himself a former boxer and a matchmaker. As Timothy J. Gilfoyle and others have chronicled, John L. Sullivan made his New York ring debut there. P. T. Barnum was Hill's landlord. Richard Fox and Frank Queen made fight deals in the club. Thomas Edison, a regular client, made it one of the first public buildings to have electric light. Fighters, promoters, backers, gamblers, politicos, editors, writers, and fans all passed through Hill's and similar establishments.[76]

In 1896, a new institution emerged that changed the ring business in New York. From 1896 to 1900, state law permitted boxing matches, but only in regulated, incorporated clubs. Hence, as commercial cinema was being born, those who wanted to profit from fight pictures had to deal with the peculiarities of these policed and politicized venues. The athletic club became a place to see professional fights, rather than a space for amateurs to play and exercise. Men could pay to become members of the club on fight night. The recording of prizefights and star boxers was subject to delicate negotiations among interested parties, local power brokers, and the police. In New York, this most often meant dealing with Democratic loyalists, whose party had authored the 1896 legislation.[77] It no doubt helped the Lathams that the financial backer of their Kinetoscope Exhibiting Co. was party stalwart

Samuel J. Tilden. His namesake uncle, a Democratic governor of New York, had won the nationwide popular vote for the presidency of the United States in 1876.

The connection between motion pictures and prizefights, then, was not merely technical or incidental. The social network of self-described sporting and theatrical professionals made the link a consistent and rationalized one. Specific practitioners and promoters forged the affiliation between boxing and cinema, relying on the two practices to publicize each other. This they did, with mixed results, for the next two decades.

2 The Corbett-Fitzsimmons Fight
Women at the Veriscope, 1897

Almost everybody of the male sex has at some time experienced a
mild desire to see an actual prizefight, and this desire will with many
be strengthened by the chance of seeing a prizefight without the
more revolting incidents of the actual contest. Of course, the
connoisseur misses the sight of blood and the sound of profane
language, but many a Quaker must acknowledge a temptation to see
a fight that has already been fought and which his patronage will
therefore not encourage.

"The 'Veriscope,'" New York Times, May 26, 1897

On St. Patrick's Day 1897, after three years' anticipation, delay, and hype,
James John Corbett and Robert Prometheus Fitzsimmons fought their
heavyweight championship contest in Carson City, Nevada. The underdog
Fitzsimmons dethroned the popular champion with a much-discussed
"solar plexus punch" in the fourteenth round. Under the direction of Enoch
J. Rector and the promotion of Texas gambler Dan A. Stuart, motion pictures of the entire event were successfully filmed and prominently exhibited across the United States and abroad. As the first feature-length film, the
Corbett-Fitzsimmons Fight was a cinematic landmark. Yet (its temptation
of Quakers aside) its more important, and surprising, consequence was its
unprecedented ability to bring women into the audience for prizefighting.

The eleven thousand feet of film taken by Rector's cameras became a
one-hundred-minute presentation when projected by his "veriscope." With
prominent screenings worldwide, the *Corbett-Fitzsimmons Fight* was one
of the earliest individual productions to generate and sustain public commentary on the cinema. From the time of its proposed creation in 1894 until
its release two months after the fight, the recording was widely discussed by
the public and press. Its lengthy run and rerun—a new exhibition
experience—invited commentary on the quality of cinematic reproduction,
the results of the contest, the social effects of the fight picture, and the nature of its audience. Yet in histories of cinema the *Corbett-Fitzsimmons
Fight* has been but a footnote, characterized as an atypically long actuality
that anticipated feature-length motion pictures. Paul Rotha's passing

comment typifies its treatment: "Exceptionally dull as this enormous length of film must have been, its novelty was probably astounding."[1]

The *Corbett-Fitzsimmons Fight* offers a rich case study of early cinema. First, the film was in one sense not an aberration, but an anticipated installment in the series of fight pictures that were already de rigueur for film producers. Second, even though its manner of exhibition was new, the *Corbett-Fitzsimmons Fight* was for many viewers their first memorable contact with cinematic presentation. Finally, the film was not dismissed as dull by its contemporaries: rather, the Veriscope pictures received attention precisely because they were longer, bigger, and more auspicious. Nineteenth-century archival sources that are usually mute on the subject of motion pictures are rife with details about Corbett and Fitzsimmons before the veriscope.

I examine the case of the *Corbett-Fitzsimmons Fight* on three levels: the story of its making, both the manufacturing of a grudge-match scenario and the openly reported difficulties of taking good pictures; its exhibition as a feature attraction and the complications resulting from cheap imitations; and its reception, including debates about censorship and attempts to offset censure by highlighting female patronage.

THE BUILDUP

Interest in the recording of the Corbett-Fitzsimmons fight was piqued by long-running press accounts of the vicissitudes of pulling off the bout as well as by growing interest in how motion pictures were made and by the curious episodes surrounding attempts to film the heavyweight championship. The Latham brothers proposed the idea of recording the champion Corbett battling the up-and-coming Fitzsimmons as soon as Edison had licensed their Kinetoscope Exhibiting Company. With the success of *Corbett and Courtney before the Kinetograph* (1894) and an exclusive film contract with the champion, the Lathams continued pressing for a Corbett-Fitzsimmons film. As Gray Latham's "startling proposition" in the *New York Clipper* made clear, by November 1894 his company held both the unique technological capacity for filming a bona fide contest and a purse large enough to attract the participants. The well-established Gentleman Jim, however, was less willing to risk the championship belt. He was drawing a sizable income from public appearances and from his second stage vehicle, *A Naval Cadet* (1895–98).[2] Moreover, Corbett and William Brady were still getting easy money from the kinetograph pictures.

Nevertheless, the Florida Athletic Club managed to arrange terms for a Corbett-Fitzsimmons battle. Despite threats from the governor, the group had hosted Corbett's title defense against Charlie Mitchell in Jacksonville in January 1894. That October, the club brokered a deal in which the champion agreed to take on Fitzsimmons, the top-ranked contender. In November, however, Fitzsimmons inflicted fatal injuries on his sparring partner during a public exhibition. Although cleared of criminal charges, Fitzsimmons assumed a low profile, and the promoters postponed the bout indefinitely.[3]

The president of the Florida Athletic Club, Dan A. Stuart, a prominent Dallas entrepreneur and sporting man, purchased the fight contract for himself and his fellow Dallasites Joseph Vendig and William K. Wheelock. Their syndicate engineered the event others had been unable to realize. It also managed its motion-picture coverage very successfully.

Stuart and his organization calculated that demand, coupled with their political influence, would enable them to pull off the contest in Texas despite opposition. Wheelock, a former Dallas alderman, operated the hotel and railroad businesses needed to bring sporting men to the fight. Stuart was active in national sporting and gambling circles, and operated saloons, pool halls, and a theater in Dallas. His holdings in cattle and cotton also gave him influence with the interests that controlled the state. With these favorable conditions, both boxers signed to fight for the title at the Texas State Fair and Dallas Exposition on October 31, 1895. Stuart began construction on an outdoor arena seating fifty thousand. Corbett's exclusive contract with Rector's company remained in effect, with neither Stuart nor Fitzsimmons yet party to the picture deal.

The Texas governor, Charles A. Culberson, campaigned to prevent the fight, declaring that "the consensus of modern opinion is that prizefighting is brutal and degrading." Culberson had both moral and political motives. According to his biographer, the "young Christian governor" was ostensibly acting in concert with the "earnest demand" of civic and religious groups who besieged him, asking him to ban the "disgraceful orgies" of prizefighting.[4] Culberson's ulterior motive, however, was his long-standing feud with Dan Stuart. Unable to curb Stuart's carpetbagging ventures in the past, as governor Culberson now took extraordinary measures. When advised that existing statutes were unenforceable, he ordered a special "prizefight" session of the legislature "to denounce prizefighting . . . and prohibit the same." On October 1, the lawmakers convened, and the next day prizefighting became a felony in Texas. A grand jury investigated Stuart's "conspiracy" to circumvent the new law. When the managers, trainers, and Dallas organizers were summoned to testify, they complained it was clear "the Governor

Figure 14.   At left, Dan A. Stuart (1846–1909), pictured in the *Galveston News*, February 22, 1896; at right, William A. Brady (1863–1950), the influential show-man who managed Corbett and then Jeffries while promoting major theatrical enterprises. (Library of Congress, Prints and Photographs Division.)

and the Attorney-General are not so fiercely after the prize fighters as they are after Dan Stuart, whom they have determined to crush."[5]

The Stuart syndicate investigated an alternative location in the resort town of Hot Springs, Arkansas, which was willing to host the event for the sake of publicity. The Arkansas governor intervened, arresting Corbett and Fitzsimmons when they entered the state. Both again delayed their match-up indefinitely.[6]

To make matters worse for Stuart and the Kinetoscope Exhibiting Com-pany, Corbett announced his "retirement" from the ring. In November 1895, he unofficially resigned his championship to the Irish heavyweight Peter Maher. The move was a dig at Fitzsimmons, who had bettered Maher three years earlier. Attention focused on Maher's title defense. The Rector-Tilden group again scrambled for a share of the publicity.

THE FITZSIMMONS-MAHER BOUT:
FIGHT PICTURES AND THE WILD WEST

On February 21, 1896, Peter Maher's fight on a Rio Grande sandbar with the top-ranked contender Bob Fitzsimmons entered the realm of folklore. The participation of "moving picture men" contributed to the conspicuous events.

Well before the contest, the quest for a championship battle was again thrust into the national spotlight. As state after state legislated against prizefighting, Capitol Hill prevented the Fitzsimmons-Maher fight from occurring on federal land. When Maher began training in New Mexico, the territory's congressional delegate introduced a bill prohibiting pugilism in the federal territories and the District of Columbia. After revisions by Rep. David Browning Culberson, the father of the Texas governor, the bill passed unanimously.[7]

Although rebuffed by the highest authorities, Stuart sought to recoup his investment in the deferred Corbett fight by handling the Fitzsimmons-Maher affair. In December 1895, he got the parties to sign agreements on a boat in the Gulf of Mexico. Already known as a "master of bombast" (for promoting ideas such as holding the bout in a hot-air balloon), Stuart proposed a "fistic carnival" of amusements and athletic events to take place in February 1896 in or near the border community of El Paso–Ciudad de Juarez. Although the promoter seemed to be promising the impossible—that the fight would take place on neither Texan nor Mexican soil—both boxers went into training near El Paso. While planning the Dallas fight, Stuart had secured an agreement with the Kinetoscope Exhibiting Company. Enoch Rector, still in favor with the Edison Manufacturing Company, possessed four cameras that would enable him to do ringside photography for exhibition on kinetoscopes.[8]

But the film crew performed services beyond that of photographic bystanders. The exotic location—a sandbar in the Rio Grande river bed—stemmed from Gray Latham's reference to an unnamed "Mexican agent" in his November 1894 proposal. He claimed to be able to guarantee a safe location for the Corbett-Fitzsimmons fight. The "agent" was probably Gray's brother Otway, who had filmed a bullfight in Mexico City with Eugène Lauste just after the Maher fight, operating under the aegis of their new Eidoloscope Company. Even if their presence in Mexico suggests that the Lathams attended the Maher bout, it was Rector who coordinated the fight pictures.

When Stuart's plans for a week-long carnival were endangered by the Texas Rangers' orders to enforce the new prizefight ban, the filmmakers helped the promoter fulfill his promise to hold the Maher-Fitzsimmons contest. To avoid Texas lawmen and threats from the Mexican government, Rector journeyed to the frontier town of Langtry. There he secured a secret location on a sandbar across the border. According to one account, "Ranger

Ed Aten received orders to watch the kinetoscope and lumber which would be used to build the ring." On February 17, he and a fellow Ranger "saw the machine and lumber loaded on a flatcar," riding with it from El Paso to Langtry.[9] With the legendary character Judge Roy Bean, who presided over the town, Rector clandestinely employed locals to construct an elevated boxing platform. They also fashioned a ringside "frame compartment" to house the Edison-built cameras.[10] To keep out gatecrashers, they put up a canvas enclosure sixteen feet high and two hundred feet in circumference. Two hundred ticket holders from around the country boarded a chartered train in El Paso on February 20 and arrived in Langtry the following afternoon. With supervision by another Western lawman and gambler (and sportswriter), Bat Masterson, the entourage trekked across the Rio Grande on a pontoon bridge, finally arriving at the designated site.

Promoters considered postponement when a light rain and overcast sky blocked the sunlight needed for sure exposure of their film, but logistics precluded further delay. Whether Rector rolled his cameras or not is undocumented.[11] The ensuing fight proved an anticlimax, as Fitzsimmons knocked out the Irish champion in a mere ninety-five seconds. (The Langtry lore includes versions in which Fitz, denied picture rights, scored the quick knockout so that there would be "damn little film for anyone to enjoy the rights to.")[12]

Rector did not give up on pictures of a Fitzsimmons-Maher bout. "Immediately after the fight," the *Clipper*'s man on the scene reported, "Mr. Rector, on behalf of the kinetoscope people, offered Fitzsimmons and Maher a purse of $5,000 to be battled for next day." The proposal was not conceived of as a second title bout but as a choreographed exhibition in the style of *Corbett-Courtney*. When asked to redo the bout for the camera, Fitzsimmons reportedly agreed "to put Maher out in six rounds," though the real fight lasted but one. The *Galveston News* reported that "Rector, the kinetoscope man, came to him with a proposition to fight Maher six rounds in front of his machine, which would not work to-day because of the dark weather." The victor at first agreed, but grew contentious and canceled. "I don't care about fighting before the kinetoscope," said Fitzsimmons. "Every time they want me to do anything they want to give the other fellow all the money and I want some of it. I will fight Maher again, of course, if the money is put up, but I don't fight before that machine unless I get $5000 cash and 50 per cent of the receipts."[13]

After his victory, Fitzsimmons toured in vaudeville. But the boxing world awaited his match against Corbett before recognizing either as champion. Corbett attempted to relegitimize his claim to the title with a match against the contender "Sailor" Tom Sharkey in June 1896, but he managed only a draw. In December, Fitzsimmons took on Sharkey as well. The referee, legendary lawman Wyatt Earp, surprised observers by calling a foul and awarding the decision to Sharkey. Like the Texas-Mexico border fight, this San Francisco event perpetuated the image of prizefighting as an outlaw's game at home in the Wild West.[14]

THE EXPANDING PRESENCE OF CINEMA

As cinema grew in reach and popularity in 1896 and 1897, it included boxing in its projected programs, from the premiere of the Edison Vitascope onward. Some were generic parts of traveling shows, such as that run by the tent-show exhibitor William Swanson, who toured the Midwest in 1897 with prints of *The Kiss*, a cockfight, and "a one-round prize fight." Others fed publicity for the Fitzsimmons-Corbett championship. In particular, the *Corbett-Courtney Fight* remained popular for both kinetoscopes and projectors. "The Great Corbett Fight" was a key attraction for the earliest moving-picture operations. Patrons were invited to "get pointers [for the Carson bout] by seeing Corbett fight."[15] Other shows republicized the "Great Corbett Fight" after his loss to Fitzsimmons, hoping customers would pay to see what they assumed was a replay of the Carson City fight.[16]

Simultaneously, wider coverage of the fight game became possible because of the rapid proliferation of film technologies. In the year between Enoch Rector's mishap in February 1896 and his *Corbett-Fitzsimmons Fight*, the phenomenon of moving pictures expanded into projection experiments.

In the theatrical season of 1896–97, a flood of new projectors appeared, led by the 68 mm biograph, which was followed by many lesser "graphs" and "scopes." Theatrical trade ads show an amazing and amusing variety of gadgetry: the animatoscope, vitascope, vidiscope, viascope, bioscope, cinagraph, cineograph, cinographoscope, kineoptoscope, kineopticon, kinodrome, magniscope, electroscope, projectograph, eragraph, zooscope, ad infinitum.[17] By season's end these became the subject of satire. Days after Rector shot the *Corbett-Fitzsimmons Fight*, Weber & Fields's Broadway Music Hall presented "The Lobsterscope," a sketch billed as "a burlesque of all animated picture machines (patent protected!)." The turn featured performers before a black curtain illuminated by a strobe light and included "a burlesque of the Corbett-Fitzsimmons prize fight."[18]

Veriscope's film appeared amid this confusion of moving-picture machines. Industrial competition had changed so rapidly that by the time the
Corbett-Fitzsimmons contest was fought, none of the companies originally
deemed likely to record remained. Only the Rector-Tilden partnership existed when Corbett finally signed to meet Fitzsimmons, and it no longer operated under the aegis of the Kinetoscope Exhibiting Co. or with the aid of
specially built Edison cameras. After the failure of the modified kine-
tographs at the Fitzsimmons-Maher fight, Rector engineered his own
camera-projector system. Improving on the Edison "prizefight machine,"
Rector built a smaller, lighter, hand-cranked model that employed a large-
format film stock and required less light. His "veriscope" tested well. It projected images with an aspect ratio of nearly 1.7 to 1, better framing the width
of a boxing ring.[19]

PRODUCING THE CARSON CITY FIGHT

With the technical possibilities of the new veriscope, Dan Stuart's contract
and Rector's film deal with Corbett took on greater value. Gentleman Jim
and Ruby Robert maintained an almost daily presence in the American
press, publicly taunting one another. Meanwhile, the indefatigable Stuart
continued to negotiate a legal venue for his contest. Lobbying finally succeeded in Nevada, which agreed to legalize the sport again in hopes of gaining publicity and capital.[20] Then, as now, the place constituted a morally lim-
inal region. The "Nevada Disgrace," denounced by congressmen as "little
more than a mining camp" for this embrace of pugilism, augmented its reputation by promoting prizefighting as it had gambling and alcohol.[21] The
arena Stuart had intended for Dallas was constructed in Carson City for the
March 17 battle.

Stuart again engaged Rector's photographic services. Corbett and
Fitzsimmons agreed to fight under Stuart's supervision, but they wanted a
new picture agreement. In the previous contract, all revenues from kinetoscope film sales were to go to Corbett and his manager, William Brady. According to Brady, the monopoly on film rights was conceded "as a bonus for
condescending to sign."[22] But Fitzsimmons now had an equal claim on the
title, and both ring stars were dependent on Stuart. More important, the
new moving-picture technology significantly raised the value of a recording of the fight. The majority of the revenues were signed over to the promoters (30 percent to Stuart, 40 percent to Rector) and the balance divided
between the contestants.[23]

As Musser points out, this negotiation marked a turning point in the development of prizefighting. Previously, even high-profile matches could not rely on ticket sales to cover the large purses put up for the fighters. Side bets and theatrical tours provided the profit margin. With the prospect of a projectable motion-picture record, promoters could now make good on the suggestion made by Gray Latham in November 1894, that fight film companies could offer large amounts of money to boxers "without depending on gate receipts."[24] Motion pictures proved the key to larger profits. After the *Corbett-Fitzsimmons Fight*, film rights played a central role in major fight negotiations over the next two decades.

Motion-picture reproduction also altered boxing performance. The production of the film became as crucial as the athletic display itself. The promoters weighed everything about the event—time, duration, location, and spectator seating—with the goal of creating the best possible pictures. To many onlookers, the event became as much the making of a movie as a legitimate boxing contest. As a Boston headline put it, "The Kinetoscope will dominate wholly the arrangements for the holding of the battle."[25]

Again Rector and Stuart constructed a wooden house at ringside for film equipment, this time consisting of three Veriscope cameras and thousands of feet of their proprietary gauge of celluloid. They stenciled "Copyrighted the Veriscope Company" in large letters along the side of the ring facing the cameras. "Enoch Rector took another turn at his multikinetoscope this morning," the *Chicago Tribune* noted on the eve of the battle, as he rehearsed "the big photographing machine." Just before the opening bell, Stuart delayed events "for the kinetoscope."[26] The *San Francisco Examiner*, itself a heavy promoter of the fight, noted the incident: "The kinetoscope man emerged from his doll house and proceeded to make sighting shots through a camera. . . . The sun [was] a bit too bright for best photographic work, and it was a moral certainty that Dan Stuart was going to be repaid for the $100,000 he had advanced in the promotion of pugilism by securing through the kinetoscope all the pictures he wanted."[27] When photographic conditions were deemed acceptable, the preliminaries commenced in the ring and were directed toward the camera: the introduction of John L. Sullivan, his manager Billy Madden, and the referee, George Siler; and the entrance, posing, and disrobing of the fighters.[28] Each camera shot up to six minutes of footage before reloading, and all three recorded continuously through the fourteen rounds.

Other production decisions by Veriscope impinged on the rules of boxing. The night before the bout, Stuart had carpenters reduce the width of the ring from twenty-four feet to twenty-two at the request of the cinematographers.

Figure 15. Cutaway illustration of Enoch Rector's
Veriscope camera. "One of Three Kinetoscopes that
Will Preserve on Film Every Movement of the Great
Fight," *San Francisco Chronicle*, March 16, 1897.
(Supplied by Richard Abel.)

When Siler discovered the violation, he ordered the ring restored to its
proper dimensions.[29] Stuart's fear that the Veriscope camera would not be
able to film the action in the corners proved justified. When Fitzsimmons
knocked Corbett down for the final count in the fourteenth round, Corbett
appeared to be aware enough to steal to the corner, out of camera range. Or
so a reporter suggested: "The field of the camera, which took the final kine-
tographs did not include the space near the ropes into which Corbett
crawled. . . . The pictures show him painfully crawling out of the camera's
field, and at the end his head, arms, and shoulders are out of the picture, only
his legs and trunk showing."[30]

The fight came off without overt interference from the cameramen. Once the bell sounded, Veriscope captured all of the rounds and rest periods, as well as pre- and post-fight action. Eleven thousand feet of film, running nearly two hours, was exposed without interruption. In the weeks between the taking of the pictures in Carson City and the processing of the negatives, rumors circulated that the duration of the fight had been predetermined to match the needs of film exhibition.[31]

The Veriscope Company planned full-length, projected exhibitions to theater audiences. A prediction made by Tom Sharkey represented the promoters' worst fears: "The kinetoscope people won't need much tape for this fight. The men will go at each other like tigers and it will all be over in less than twenty minutes." However, a clerk for Dan Stuart reported that "Corbett and Fitzsimmons had contracted with the kinetoscope people to make the fight last ten rounds" (though he later denounced the rumor).[32] Another report suggested that, because Corbett failed to press his advantage after knocking Fitzsimmons to the canvas in the sixth round, "there must have been some agreement to keep the fight going over ten rounds for the benefit of the kinetoscope people." The *San Francisco Chronicle* quoted the architect of the Carson City arena saying that a U.S. attorney extorted money by "threatening to make known that Corbett and Fitzsimmons had agreed with the kinetoscope people to allow their contest to last ten rounds." He then denied the rumor.[33]

ANTICIPATION OF THE FIGHT PICTURES: CENSORSHIP AND "NEGATIVE" PUBLICITY

With eleven thousand feet of film in the can, the production of the *Corbett-Fitzsimmons Fight* pictures had in a sense only just begun. The long-awaited picture remained engulfed in controversy during the two months before its premiere. Threats of censorship, rumors of photographic failure, and exploitative imitations generated daily publicity.

In February 1897, the U.S. Congress, which one year earlier had enacted preemptive legislation against the prizefight, debated regulating depictions of it. The chair of the House Commerce Committee, J. Frank Aldrich, proposed a bill "to forbid the transmission by mail or interstate commerce of any picture or description of any prize fight."[34] Aldrich and Sen. George Hoar presented petitions from a coalition of religious and civic groups who rallied in Washington on February 28. As part of a larger Purity Crusade, organizations such as the National Reform League, the YMCA, the United

Society for Christian Endeavor, and, most prominently, the 300,000-member Women's Christian Temperance Union (WCTU), pressed for stronger anti-prizefight legislation.

On March 1 the bill went to the House floor. Aldrich described the legislation as an extension of Congress's previous ban on pugilism, arguing that pictures were "only a little less harmful than the degrading sport" itself. Further, he contended that the bill was consistent with existing statutes "prohibiting the interstate transportation of obscene pictures," since "pictures of the brutality of pugilism are hardly less harmful to our youth." The consensus in the House was that the "degrading, brutal, and disgusting business" of prizefighting had "no place in a Christian and civilized community." But the bill was written too broadly. While some argued it was "right to establish a censorship of the press in the interest of public morals," Rep. Amos Cummings charged that the "very dangerous legislation" would prohibit newspapers from reporting on any criminal activity. Another dissenter argued that an onerous government censorship bureau would have to be set up. The Aldrich bill failed to pass.[35]

After the March 17 bout, a new Congress turned its attention to the motion pictures taken in Carson City. On March 19, the House reintroduced the Aldrich bill. The Senate offered legislation "to prohibit the reproduction in the District of Columbia and the Territories, by kinetoscope or kindred devices, of such pugilistic encounters and fights as are forbidden" by law.[36] In April, a group of prominent public men issued a memorial titled "Against Prizefight Pictures." With signatories who included a U.S. Supreme Court justice, three governors, and religious leaders, their petition condemned the "brutal encounter" between Corbett and Fitzsimmons, as well as the press exploitation of "the disgraceful event." The congressional measures never came to a vote, however.[37]

State and local actions offset federal inaction. The *New York Tribune* editorialized: "If a prizefight is a brutal and degrading performance, properly forbidden by law the pictorial reproduction of it by kinetoscope can scarcely be edifying or elevating and may properly also be forbidden by law. Some States, it is pleasant to observe, are enacting special laws against such exhibitions. The existing laws in this state ought to be sufficient to prevent them. If not, it ought not to take long to make them so."[38] Ten state legislatures (and Canada) introduced bans. Municipal governments considered motions to suppress screenings of the fight.[39]

Few acted on the initial furor of bills and apocalyptic rhetoric. Several factors accounted for the defeat of legislation against fight pictures. First, prizefighting still had a tremendous popular following. Through press agents, theater, popular press, athletic clubs, and *Police Gazette* posters, Gentleman Jim, Ruby Robert, and other fighters became celebrities. Second, in 1897, there was no commonly held notion of what cinema was. It was not one technology or practice, but dozens. The manner and place in which moving pictures might appear were varied. The theme of censorship debates, which would become familiar in the twentieth century—the question of whether the harmful effects of mass media require regulation—were barely beginning to be articulated. Finally, prohibition of the *Corbett-Fitzsimmons Fight* was countered by an effective publicity campaign. Veriscope first waited for activists' ardor to cool and then co-opted the very female constituency that partly threatened the venture.

The significance of the unrealized legislation bears consideration. For the first time in American history, citizens lobbied for government censorship of motion pictures. Arguments about fight pictures in 1897 addressed the specific qualities of the genre as well as rationales for regulating motion pictures in general. Fight pictures were deemed unique. The activity recorded threatened the national well-being. The Corbett-Fitzsimmons contest drew condemnation from clergy who saw pugilism as "not the manly art, but the art of the devil," and regarded the uproar as evidence of America's "moral degeneracy." Secular voices such as the *New York Times* argued that "it is not very creditable to our civilization perhaps that that achievement of what is now called the 'veriscope' that has attracted and will attract the widest attention should be the representation of a prizefight."[40] Spectatorship could be limited to a few thousand fans if "broadcast" cinematic reproductions could be prevented. A ban on fight pictures would extend laws keeping boxing's brutality outside the borders of advanced civilization.

Yet even at this early point in cinema history, the movies' supposed "capacity for evil" and influence over susceptible minds—officially articulated by the Supreme Court in 1915 to justify state censorship—were being suggested in the discourse surrounding the *Corbett-Fitzsimmons Fight*. Moving pictures were held by some to threaten an even greater harm than prizefighting. As Gregory A. Waller points out, opponents of the *Corbett-Fitzsimmons Fight* were among the first to question the "insidious influence of this new mechanical means of 'life-like' reproduction." Protesters feared that the Veriscope pictures would reach "every village and hamlet with this spectacular performance." The "life like representations of these degrading spectacles" could only "brutalize" spectators, "especially the youth." Others warned against the potency of the "hypnotic exhibition."[41]

Aware that opponents of the fight were mobilizing to suppress his recording of it, Dan Stuart released misleading stories. While legislators debated bans, the Veriscope Company suggested they would be irrelevant because its precious negatives had not been exposed properly.

Hearst's *San Francisco Examiner* chronicled the fortunes of the Veriscope negatives. In a March 27 item, Stuart was asked "How about the pictures?" His initial response from Dallas was, "They are all right. An agent of the Varioscope company will sail from New York for Liverpool tomorrow to copyright the photographs."[42] However, the following week the *Examiner* headline ran: "Kinetoscope Scheme is a Failure— Negatives of Great Fight Show Many Defects—Big Venture that Promised Great Returns Will Be Profitless—Efforts to Restore the Films to Usefulness May Prove Futile—Projector of the Enterprise has Given Up All Hope of Success." This wire story from New York included an interchange with Enoch Rector, the figure so central to the Veriscope and Kinetoscope Exhibiting companies, but so noticeably absent from most documentation.

> E. J. Rector [reports a] dark future—or no future—ahead for the kinetoscope views of the recent fistic encounter in Carson. And that means a great deal of those who "paid the freight" for the photographic enterprise. . . .
>
> Rector avers that he is not worried about the prospect of legislation that will cripple the business of giving profitable exhibitions of the prizefight. . . .
>
> It was this Rector who secured the exclusive kinetoscope privileges. . . . He had visions of millions from a photographic reproduction. . . . He spared no expense to get pictures of every move made by the fistic kings. When Corbett gave up the ghost in the fourteenth round there was no end of hustling among the men who were aiming the big lenses at the gory combatants. All the agony depicted in the features of the fallen prize fighters was studiously wrought out in plates [sic], so Rector believed.
>
> Rector says the whole lot of snapshots look like the first efforts of a novice. When the plates were developed every defect known to photography made its unwelcome appearance. The negatives were sent to the Edison laboratory, in Orange, N.J., to be developed. Frank Gammon of Rabb [sic] & Gammon, managers of the vitascope, under whose direction the negatives were being developed, confirms Rector's statement. He says they are not panning out. Rector is not losing any sleep over what various legislative bodies may do to "knock out" his pictorial prizefight enterprize, so he says. . . . [W]hile those negatives are being put through a course in chemistry out in Orange, the Legislature of this

State, Maine, Massachusetts, Illinois, Indiana, Wisconsin, and the
United States Senate for the District of Columbia have been industri-
ously trying to fix a penalty for kinetoscope exhibitions of the fight by
rounds. . . .

Rector says bids for the right to make kinetoscope views of the fight
were received from England, France, Australia, South Africa, and the
Sandwich Islands, but that the defective negatives render useless the
making of such contracts.[43]

Although papers reported "announcements from New York that the kinetoscope pictures of the Corbett-Fitzsimmons fight are not what had been
expected," some recognized the story for what it was. The veteran ring
announcer Billy Jordan made it clear: "I do not believe that the films are
spoiled. Those photographers are very acute. They want to ward off suspicion and call off the Legislatures and Congress for a while, that's all. If the
impression goes abroad that the kinetoscope pictures are failures the various legislatures will not make laws against them." A cartoon captioned
"When They Heard That the Kinetoscope Pictures Were a Failure" illustrated how the ex- and new champions might have reacted.

As threats of censorship subsided, favorable evaluations replaced stories of
ruined negatives. Peter Bacigalupi of San Francisco, a pioneer kinetoscope parlor operator, stated on April 5: "It is a pity that the kinetoscope did not work
well, but rest assured that they will be able to use some of the films showing
at least one or two of the rounds." Corbett's camp then reported surprise over
the rumor of Rector's failure. The following week, Stuart himself denied the
story as he embarked for Europe "to push the interest of the pictures of the
Carson Fight." On April 18, his company said the views were "good in spots."
The *Examiner* announced the pictures were "now ready for printing, and in
a few days a small company of capitalists will know the extent of their sorrow
or the measure of their fortune. The pictures are not all bad."[44]

By May, it was clear that the complete fight had been recorded safely.
Having used three cameras, Rector had duplicate coverage to compensate
for any malfunctions or poor exposures. His pioneering challenge was to
edit three sets of negatives into one release version. The company first offered screenings to the press in New York. Papers carried illustrations based
on the Veriscope frames.

By any measure, the strategy to publicize the Corbett-Fitzsimmons pictures was successful. The boxers continued to roast each other in the press,
spurring more gossip about the filmed fight. But the press releases managed
by Stuart and the athletes' agents, William Brady and Martin Julian,
avoided direct combat with the moralists who sought to quash the pictures.

By the eve of the Veriscope premiere, the new heavyweight champion was on Capitol Hill hobnobbing with the solons of the Senate, who tabled their bill against fight pictures.[45]

"FIGHT PICTURES THAT ARE FAKES"

Veriscope's calculated delay created an opportunity for competitors to fill the two-month void with filmed reenactments. The fake-prizefight film genre born in the spring of 1897 survived for more than a decade.

Traditions of reenactment predated cinema. For the Corbett-Fitzsimmons championship, some theaters paid for newswire transmissions and provided patrons with onstage reenactments performed by boxing experts. On New York stages, for example, Mike Donovan offered a "mimic show" as descriptions came in, while another venue offered a shadowgraph of the bout, with boxers performing behind a scrim.[46]

The unprecedented publicity for the "fight of the century" brought forth well-circulated fake fight films. Before either Veriscope or Lubin's cineograph reached the market with their versions of *Corbett-Fitzsimmons*, ads appeared for the "New Magniscope" and films of the "Corbett-Fitzsimmons fight reproduced life size." Sold in Chicago by agents of the Western Phonograph Company, the film was "an exact reproduction of the encounter" as staged by a small company in Illinois. The invention of Edward Hill Amet, the Magniscope projector had been developed in 1896 with the aid of the theater manager George Spoor. With distribution provided by George Kleine, a dealer in optical equipment, the machine sold well; but only in March 1897 did Amet devise a camera and venture into producing original films. The reenactment of the Carson City bout was one of his first efforts. No prints or descriptions of it survive, but Amet's early photographic results may well have been disappointing. Subsequent Magniscope ads omitted mention of the film.[47]

Amet benefited from the ambiguity implied in describing a moving picture as a "reproduction." Prospective buyers needed to read the fine print to realize that it showed a reenacted bout rather the original event. A year later, Amet intermixed his authentic footage of the Spanish-American War with re-creations he shot using miniatures.[48]

A second imitation of the fight received greater attention. Siegmund Lubin, an optical manufacturer who had been successfully marketing his cineograph, began an ad campaign for his "Corbett and Fitzsimmons Films, in counterpart of the great fight," on April 17.[49] The Philadelphia producer promoted his "great fac simile" over the hundreds of other short films he had manufactured.

The following week Stuart arrived in his Manhattan office and responded to the threat posed by the imitators to his exploitation plans. Stuart told the press that his negatives were in perfect shape, three-fourths of them already developed. He also countered the fakes in the trade press with an ad authenticating his product and threatening legal reprisal. His April 24 response to Lubin laid claim to the sole rights to both production and exhibition of the *Corbett-Fitzsimmons Fight*.

> The [original] films will be copyrighted in every country in the world, and in every instance the laws distinctly state that "ANY COLORABLE IMITATION OF A COPYRIGHT IS AN INFRINGEMENT," and is punishable by a heavy fine (IN THE UNITED STATES BY FINE AND IMPRISONMENT). As this picture will be given throughout the country in theatres as a dramatic representation, unprincipled parties are advertising that they have films for sale in imitation of this great contest. Warning is given to persons contemplating the purchase of these bogus films that they will not be permitted to exhibit them. A word to the wise is sufficient. WE WILL PROSECUTE ALL INFRINGEMENTS.[50]

Stuart pushed back the delivery date for the Veriscope film to May 15, saying, "The delay in placing it before the public is caused by making the necessary deposits in the copyright offices of the world, which gives protection against fakirs, counterfeiters and colorable imitators."[51]

Legal threats, however, presented no real obstacle to imitators. Motion pictures of reenactments were products demonstrably distinct from actuality footage. Furthermore, U.S. copyright law made no provision for motion pictures in 1897. Even those films which producers printed frame by frame to copyright as photographs were protected only against duplication, not imitation.

Lubin responded by imitating Stuart's tactics. On May 15 (with Veriscope suffering mechanical problems and still not ready for its promised release), "S. Lubin, Optician, Manufacturer of the Cineograph," tried to legitimize his version by assuring buyers that he was "in receipt of Certificates of Copyright from the Librarian of Congress of the United States of my films, of the great fac simile of the 14 Round Fight of 1897 Reproduced by Counterparts of Corbett and Fitzsimmons."[52]

By getting his films to market ahead of Stuart and advertising boldly, Lubin seized a share of the demand for pictures that others had labored three years to create. When Veriscope finally released its pictures, Lubin increased the prominence of his ads. Weekly promotions for Lubin's

Figure 16.   Frame from Lubin's first fake, *Corbett and Fitzsimmons, Films in Counterpart of The Great Fight* (1897), cataloged as "Unidentified. LACMNH #9. Early Boxing Film." (Library of Congress, Motion Picture, Broadcasting and Recorded Sound Division.)

cineograph hyped *Corbett and Fitzsimmons* above all other offerings. Posters and stills of the Carson City arena were added to the package sold to fight film buyers.[53]

Such sales tactics were the only way Lubin could have turned a profit on what was a comically unconvincing fake. Secondary accounts describe how Lubin hired "two freight handlers from the Pennsylvania railroad" to reenact the newspaper accounts of the fight for his camera.[54] None of these descriptions reveal the maladroit fakery of Lubin's first fight picture. A portion of this film survives as a previously unidentified print in the Library of Congress (see figure 16).[55] Shot from a low camera angle, the film consists of two boxers standing in a tiny roped square, some six feet wide, against a white sheet. As they randomly spar, their ersatz identities become clear: Corbett's counterpart wears a pompadour wig, while the other, in imitation of the balding Fitzsimmons, sports a hairnet. The third recognizable ring figure, the referee George Siler, is portrayed by a stand-in with a fake handlebar mustache. The only other details added to this minimal representation are a pair of seconds who mind the bucket and stool in Fitz's corner.

Confirmation that this odd snippet is the Lubin production comes from a May 22 item in the *San Francisco Examiner.* Hearst newspapers had "acquired a monopoly of 'inside' information"[56] on the Corbett-Fitzsimmons fight. Accounts of Veriscope's ups and downs, followed by sensational descriptions of the pictures, indicate that the paper had a vested interest in Stuart's motion picture. The *Examiner* story disparages the Lubin reenactment while promoting the forthcoming Veriscope pictures. Nevertheless, the report offers a rare and detailed characterization of how Lubin's fight films were made, promoted, exhibited, and received in 1897.

FIGHT PICTURES THAT ARE FAKES.

CLEVER SCHEMERS WORKING SAN FRANCISCO WITH A
COUNTERFEIT KINETOSCOPE.

. . . [T]roubles of another kind menace the kinetoscope proprietors and in this particular case the profits are more likely to be decreased than fattened. There is a fake "masheen" in the field. . . .

The worst of it is that the formulators of the fake photos are unloading their shadowy wares on the San Francisco public. The concern would have been in full blast several days ago only that something went wrong with the electrical appliances. It might have been better for the promoters had they got their verascope or animatoscope or whatever it is called going sooner, for even now Dan A. Stuart of Dallas, Tex., is keeping the wires between New York and this point tingling in his frantic efforts to expose the fraud.

"The Examiner" received one of Stuart's telegrams, and Alf Ellinghouse, the well-known theatrical man, received another. In both wires the urgent request is made that the San Francisco public be warned of the attempt to foist "fake imitations" of the championship fight pictures on it. The assurance is also given that the bona fide kinetoscope views will be in this city shortly, and that they will be introduced in such a manner as to leave no doubt as to their genuineness.

The method of counterfeiting the battle of the champions is simple enough when it is explained. According to Ellinghouse some enterprising Eastern schemers made a careful search through the ranks of the unemployed pugilists until two men bearing reasonable resemblance to Fitzsimmons and Corbett were found. The rest was comparatively easy. One of the impersonators was fitted out with "a bald wig," the other with a pompadour, and their faces were made up so as to give them as near the appearance of the originals as possible.

Ring costumes tallying with those worn by the rival heavyweights on St. Patrick's Day were supplied the mimic champions and they were extensively rehearsed on all the prominent features of the fight. When the make-believe Fitzsimmons had perfected himself in the solar plexus punch and the bogus Corbett had schooled himself in the gradual fall and the look of agony until you couldn't tell them from the real thing, the fakers went through their lifelike imitation before a 'scope of some kind and the pictures were secured.

The show is in progress on Market street, opposite the Phelan building. The window notices describe it as "The new cincograph [cineograph], reproducing in counterpart (counterfeit would have been more correct) Corbett vs. Fitzsimmons at Carson. Fourteen rounds and a knock out. Life size."

The affair played to big houses last night, and those who paid and saw declared the imitation a wretched one. The big mustache with which the schemers have fitted the bogus referee Siler is said to be a libel of the worst kind. Corbett's wig is a fizzle, and the flimsiness of the entire fake is palpable.

Whether or not viewers responded as negatively as this account would have it, the proliferation of fake fight films threatened to pollute the Veriscope market. In New Orleans, for example, the Vitascope exhibitor William T. Rock added Lubin's *Fac Simile of the Great Fight* to his program in June. Across town the Lumière *cinématographe* also advertised *The Great Fight*. Likewise, in Rochester, New York, a 35 mm imitation of *Corbett-Fitzsimmons* preceded the Veriscope show by a month. A beer garden presented the fake pictures on a "kinematograph," accompanied by loud, mechanical music produced by an orchestrion. In August, the Opera House played the actual Carson City fight pictures.[57]

Other cinematic presentations also capitalized on the vogue for prizefight material throughout the spring of 1897. Projection prints of Edison's 1894 Corbett-Courtney pictures were selling "in large quantities" (leading Corbett to sue for ownership of them). Lubin used them when installing a cineograph service at a Philadelphia dime museum in late March. In other places, advertisements promised pictures of "the Great Corbett Fight" during the week of Veriscope's debut but actually projected the Edison film.[58]

None of these offered more competition to Veriscope than Lubin's facsimile did. Unlike the carefully controlled Veriscope enterprise, this counterpart was adaptable to a variety of exhibition forms. Lubin sold prints of the fourteen one-round films in any combination. Buyers could purchase an individual round (as Rock did), select a few for inclusion in a variety program, or obtain the entire set to run as a freestanding presentation. Lubin also sold with "no bonus for territory," allowing multiple exhibitors to compete within the same locales.[59] Owners of the faked Corbett-Fitzsimmons films, therefore, included itinerant showmen with 35 mm projectors, as well as variety-theater owners. Itinerants either provided their own exhibition space (as the Ringling Brothers circus did when it featured Lubin's film)[60] or played short engagements in any venue available. Theater owners ran the films they purchased until demand was exhausted, then resold them.

Established theaters subscribing to the Lubin exhibition service received regular supplies of fresh titles. Huber's dime museum in New York, Bradenburgh's Museum in Philadelphia, the Bijou Theatre in Louisville, and others received Lubin's imitation *Corbett and Fitzsimmons Fight* in their regular shipment of moving pictures. Additionally, Lubin sent his own cineograph units on the road with his prizefight reproduction. Operators such as Arthur Hotaling toured the country, either giving feature presentations of their own or attaching themselves to vaudeville or burlesque troupes. Advertisements announcing "The New York Burlesquers and The Great Cineograph, reproducing the Corbett-Fitzsimmons Fight by counterparts," appeared, for example, in Washington, DC, more than two months ahead of the Veriscope show.[61]

Audience reactions to the fabricated Corbett-Fitzsimmons film varied. As Musser documents, spectators expecting to see a record of the actual fight had been known to rush the box office in a fury; patrons accustomed to the reenactment tradition, or who saw the films in the circuslike environs of a midway, fairground, boardwalk, or dime museum, were more tolerant.[62]

However, Lubin's fake could not compete directly with the large-format, wide-screen, complete, and well-publicized Veriscope recording. When the Veriscope pictures finally reached the American market that summer, references to Lubin's version all but disappeared.

VERISCOPE EXHIBITIONS

The first complete public presentation of the *Corbett-Fitzsimmons Fight* by Veriscope occurred before 2,100 spectators on a Saturday evening, May 22, 1897, at the sold-out Academy of Music in New York City. Within weeks, several Veriscope projectors with prints of the film were traversing the United States and nations abroad. Traveling Veriscope units reproduced the bout for audiences paying as much as one dollar. Stuart's primary targets were prestige venues like the academies of music, opera houses, and high-class vaudeville halls. The mass popularity of the pictures soon led to their

Figure 17.   Frame from a 63 mm Veriscope print of the *Corbett-Fitzsimmons Fight* (1897). (George Eastman House.)

exhibition in other amusement places as well—fairgrounds, storefronts, and parks—where they reached a broader and less affluent audience. By creating an international distribution plan, sustaining publicity, and elevating admission prices, Stuart's enterprise garnered the first fortune in motion-picture history: an estimated gross of $750,000 and well over $100,000 in net profits.[63]

"THE CARSON BATTLE REPRODUCED FOR THE BENEFIT OF THE LOCAL PRESS"

The first screenings of the *Corbett-Fitzsimmons Fight* were New York press shows in advance of the theatrical premiere. Other motion-picture entrepreneurs had offered displays for journalists. Edison welcomed reporters to the Black Maria. The Lathams did likewise with their eidoloscope demonstration in 1895. But these showcased machinery rather than subject matter. Stuart and Rector had created a film whose content drew intense attention.

Vested interests—those promoting the fight, its pictures, and the career of the fallen idol—tried to color audience perceptions of what the films revealed. Had Fitzsimmons been down for the count in round six? Did Fitzsimmons not foul Corbett at the end of the fight? For the first time, a full photographic replay could examine such questions. But these queries encouraged a particular reading of the film. Suggesting that the Veriscope could prove the ex-champion had been slighted, Stuart benefited from the

heightened interest, and Corbett and his fans held onto a claim of his superiority. The *San Francisco Examiner,* as the chief organ for Veriscope publicity, served three hometown figures: Corbett, Brady and Hearst. The paper
boosted its gossip-driven circulation by perpetuating stories about the controversy.

As early as May 12, the Veriscope office in New York leaked stories to the
press about what "the camera seems to prove . . . beyond peradventure."
"Fitz Fouled Jim Corbett" became a front-page headline in the *Examiner,*
which reported those "who will see the vatascope [sic] pictures of the recent
Carson mill at the exhibition to be given [in New York] Saturday night will
see the foul that Manager Brady has always insisted occurred." Brady and
other fight men repeated the claim after previewing the films.[64]

Another respondent to these press screenings questioned the veracity
and reliability of moving pictures. W. W. Naughton pointed to a motif in
public and critical discourse on the *Corbett-Fitzsimmons Fight* and early
cinema (and even much of subsequent film theory): Could the camera
record and reveal objective, scientific truth, particularly facts not discernible
to the human eye? Naughton touched on two key moments in American
culture that cultivated this notion: Dion Boucicault's popular melodrama
The Octoroon (written in 1859 and produced continuously throughout the
nineteenth century) and Eadweard Muybridge's serial photography of
horses in motion.

His first report on "the secrets laid bare by the kinetoscope" quoted a well-
known line from Boucicault's play: "The apparatus can't lie." Others interpreting the fight picture also used this catchphrase.[65] In *The Octoroon* the
line is spoken by Salem Scudder (a character made popular by Joseph Jefferson), a plantation overseer and amateur photographer whose camera acci-
dentally snaps a picture of a murder in progress. A kangaroo court sees the
photographic plate and condemns the murderer. " 'Tis false!" the guilty man
shouts. " 'Tis true!" replies Scudder. "The apparatus can't lie."[66] The motion-
picture camera, like the still camera before it, was perceived as an instrument
that would produce the evidence needed to render a verdict in the case of
Corbett versus Fitzsimmons. Only the foolish would argue against the camera's "proof." On hearing the Veriscope story from New York, Naughton
wrote that Fitzsimmons "will probably admit that he violated the ethics of
the ring when he peeps into the 'masheen' and sees himself swatting Corbett on the chin, although it is quite within the bounds of probability that the
garrulous [manager Martin] Julian will contend that it is all a conspiracy, and
that 'the kinetoscope was fixed. . . . The camera, if it gives all the details distinctly, will verify Corbett's words and convince any reasonable person."[67]

The *Corbett-Fitzsimmons Fight* was not the first occasion when photography was used to settle sporting disputes. Later, commenting on newspaper reproductions of frames from the Veriscope motion pictures, Naughton noted his "wonderful respect for the camera as a catcher of details. . . . This respect dates back to the time he first saw a snapshot of a racehorse in action. Prior to that he believed, in common with many famous artists, apparently, that a thoroughbred's movements were the poetry of motion: but when the camera showed the nag with . . . his four hoofs so gathered together beneath him that a bucket would have held them all it was time to admit that the human eye misses a good many things."[68]

The reference was to the work of Muybridge (yet another San Franciscan). His serial photographs had gained prominence in sporting circles when used to support the wager of the former governor of California, Leland Stanford, that all four of a horse's hooves left the ground in mid-gallop. Naughton no doubt saw Muybridge's illustrated lecture on this subject in San Francisco in 1878 and may have seen the photographer's later presentations of human motion studies that included boxers and other athletes.[69] Like other commentators, therefore, Naughton addressed the veriscope as a quasi-scientific display whose images would "have to be scrutinized" and compared to descriptions of the fight. The pictures would tell the truth.

Others watched Veriscope presentations and argued the reverse: the apparatus could indeed lie, or at least misrepresent events. The silent, colorless, flickering, and sometimes snowy images of the fight remained shadowy reproductions of reality. Viewers were aware that photography could employ tricks of perspective. What the veriscope disclosed was open to question. By the time the press screening came to San Francisco in July, it was obvious that the New York reporters' interpretation of the films was a matter of selective perception. "One thing the press men who saw the exhibition last night could not understand was how the New York writers could describe Corbett's look of agony in such harrowing terms. They must have had clearer films across the Rockies than were shown here, for any one who could detect a 'look of agony' on the Corbett face exhibited last night could discover a look of suffering on a bladder of lard." The *Examiner*'s illustration was captioned: "Was this a foul punch, or does the Veriscope libel Fitzsimmons?" (figure 18).[70]

William Brady claimed credit for a more blatant, Barnumesque attempt to make the cinematic apparatus lie. His second memoir, *Showman* (1937), relates how he manipulated an early Veriscope screening, hoping to mislead the audience into believing Corbett had been robbed by a long count in the sixth round.

WAS THIS A FOUL PUNCH, OR DOES THE VERISCOPE LIBEL FITZSIMMONS?

Figure 18. Illustration of the Corbett-Fitzsimmons fight, based on Veriscope film frames, *San Francisco Examiner*, July 13, 1897.

When the picture opened at the Academy of Music in New York . . . it was Bill Brady who gave the accompanying descriptive lecture from the stage. . . . The fellow who ran the projection-machine was a Corbett fan, so I didn't even have to bribe him to help me put on my act. . . . [T]his was one of the early hand-cranked machines and we could slow down the film at will without anybody's being the wiser.

"Now, ladies and gentlemen," I said, "here is where I shall prove to you that James J. Corbett is by rights still champion of the world. I want you to see this with your own eyes instead of taking my word for it. This is the round where Corbett knocked Fitzsimmons down. As he goes down, the referee will begin to count. I'll count too, watch in hand. I want you all to count with me. Fitz will get up as the referee counts nine, presumably nine seconds, ladies and gentlemen—but, if you check with your own watches, you'll see it was a lot longer than that."

Then my confederate in the projection-booth started the film again—Fitz went down—the film was slowed—and it was a full thirteen seconds on the screen, with me dramatically counting off each second, before he got up again.

. . . At that point a huge figure reared up in the audience beneath me and roared:

"Brady, you're a liar!"

I looked close in the gloom and made out that it was the late William Muldoon, the famous Solid Man, who had been timekeeper at the Carson City fight. There was no denying that I was a liar. Fitz put up such a kick about my oration that I was never again allowed to repeat the performance. But it didn't matter. The newspapers picked up the argument, as I knew they would, and there was a long and violent controversy in print about this question of a long count. . . . Liar or not, I'd succeeded in raising an issue in the public mind.[71]

Stuart supplied reporters with technical details (for example, statistics on projection speed and the physical length of the film were repeated in reviews across the nation) but he also used preliminary screenings to suggest enticing descriptions and interpretive scenarios that might be used by newspapers describing the *Corbett-Fitzsimmons Fight*. He provided written copy for journalists. In reviews of the Veriscope film, descriptions of key scenes were nearly identical across time and region.[72] Press previews set public expectations about the *Corbett-Fitzsimmons Fight*.

ACADEMIES, OPERA HOUSES, AND FAIRGROUNDS

With the cooperation of the press, Veriscope began its far-flung and lengthy tour. For the first time in the short history of motion pictures, a commercial venture was taking its apparatus on the road with a single film subject. Its success was unprecedented: it played for several years in a variety of venues. Veriscope exhibitions reached a wide and diverse audience in arenas of high, middle, and low social status. Employing protean exhibition and promotional strategies, the *Corbett-Fitzsimmons* film reached from the sublime to the pedestrian, playing academies of music and opera houses, fairgrounds and circuses.

Stuart sought to capture the high ground first. On April 24, his first trade advertisement informed theatrical proprietors that "this picture will be given throughout this country in theatres as a dramatic representation."[73] In a bold and innovative marketing ploy, Stuart distributed the entire *Corbett-Fitzsimmons Fight* as a hundred-minute feature that would constitute a complete theatrical attraction. The film's 63 mm gauge made it incompatible with 35 mm projectors, heightening the exclusivity. Operators, each armed with a projector and a print of the film, were miniature road shows.

Requests for the long-awaited *Corbett-Fitzsimmons Fight* flooded into the Manhattan office. They needed no further trade advertising. "The demand for the pictures has caused the employes of the company to frequently work overtime," noted the *New York Times*. Two weeks after Veriscope's debut, the company suffered a tragic setback: its accountant fell down an elevator shaft while leaving the office on a Sunday afternoon. Further limited by the number of projectors built, few agents obtained contracts. Veriscope outfits were manufactured on the premises and sold (as the vitascope, kinetoscope, and phonograph had been) on a "states' rights" basis, selling franchises to a given territory. Brady, for example, paid Stuart for the right to exploit Veriscope's film in the South. "The intention of the owners is to have the pictures exhibited in thirty-five different places on the opening night," Stuart originally claimed. However, because of technical difficulties in the production of prints and projectors, only eleven outfits were on tour in the United States when the theatrical season began. Later, up to twenty projection units were in action.[74]

The innovative presentation offered theaters a lucrative show during summer weeks that might otherwise have been dark. Simultaneously, exhibitions were given in other amusement venues: parks, summer resorts, fairgrounds, boardwalks, and a few storefronts. In Dayton, the Ohio rights holder Billy Thompson presented the Veriscope pictures at both a summer park and the Grand Opera House. The Fairview Park debut on July 4 was cut short when the projectionist received an electric shock during the first reel change. Only July 6, the Grand Opera House offered its first-ever moving picture display, with Thompson narrating the complete film.[75] For four years, the *Corbett-Fitzsimmons Fight* remained a perennial and reliable draw in a variety of social contexts.

The Veriscope film traversed regional, class, gender, ethnic, and age boundaries. This appeal was all the more remarkable given the shortcomings of the equipment. "The machine," complained the *New York Times*, "leaves a good deal to be desired." Its "constant quiver" "destroys the illusion" and operates "unpleasantly on the nerves of the spectator." Despite technical improvements to the projectors and better prints being struck in June, most reviews complained that "continued vibration and coruscation," "sudden jumps," "flickering," and "too much blur" were "trying on the eyes." The films often broke in mid-reel, some prints being "chipped and cracked, or worn so as to present many flaws and imperfection."[76] Yet, even with superior motion-picture machines on the market in 1897–98, Veriscope presentations remained cinema's premier attraction.

Veriscope's initial and most lucrative runs were in the large, prominent theaters of urban centers. The gala premiere at New York's Academy of Music resembled many screenings that followed. The Academy typically hosted refined cultural events (though it had also hosted "boxing entertainments").[77] The rowdy connotation of *fight* was avoided for this presentation, which was billed instead as "the Veriscope Pictures of the Corbett-Fitzsimmons Sparring Contest." With reserved seats priced from twenty-five cents to one dollar, middle- and upper-class patrons predominated. Theatrical papers took note of the "enormous crowd" at Veriscope shows, including a " 'goodly sprinkling of ladies,' who appeared as much interested in the exhibition as those made of stronger stuff." Although the hour-and-a-half program "was suspended at frequent intervals" for reel changes and breakdowns, the audience reaction was lively. At times the pictures "provoked enthusiasm as wild and demonstrative as might have been bought out by the fight itself." The opening night crowd showed its familiarity with newspaper claims about the knockout. The "house rang with shouts of 'Where's the foul?' 'Where's the foul?' " and "loud requests for the last round to be shown over again."[78]

Another noteworthy aspect of the *Corbett-Fitzsimmons Fight*'s mode of exhibition was the use of an onstage narrator or lecturer. The commentary varied in content and quality from place to place, but it usually included a description of the key moments in the match, the identification of ringside celebrities, and details of the veriscope's technological capabilities. The narrator's presence connected fight-picture exhibition to the tradition of the illustrated lecture. As Musser has shown, the practice of narrating stereopticon programs was a precedent for full-length programs of fight pictures and passion-play films. Specializing in the travelogue genre (which in its own way the Nevada fight film resembled), touring lecturers such as Alexander Black, E. Burton Holmes, and Dwight Elemendorf began incorporating motion pictures into lantern slide shows in 1897 and 1898.[79] An explanatory boxing lecture, therefore, helped downplay the unsavory, blood-and-guts aspect of the exhibition by suggesting the genteel style of presentation used in illustrated lectures on the bourgeois lyceum circuit.

Spoken narration of prizefight films also stands out because it lacked musical accompaniment, an otherwise standard element of motion-picture and illustrated-lecture presentations. Silent films were seldom truly silent. Music (live or recorded) was de rigueur for motion-picture exhibitions from the time of even the earliest projections. Even shows with lecturers, whether they were explaining the technology or reading scripture for *The Passion Play*, included background music. The noticeable silence between and behind the fight announcer's words invited the film audience to become part of the re-creation of the event, cheering, shouting, and playing the part of the ringside crowd, and the young "sports" who frequented these shows readily cooperated. The *Washington Post* noted that Veriscope's "silent show" at the new National Theater featured one of the liveliest audiences in town. While a sometimes blundering lecturer told "how many feet of 'fillum' " had been used, there was much "side talk" and "horseplay." The "howling gallery" included shouting men, "imitators of blows," and "intensely excited" youngsters.[80] More than a year after the fight, the veriscope continued to elicit such reactions. When the *Corbett-Fitzsimmons Fight* played the New Orleans Grand Opera House in 1898, a reviewer wrote: "Every man and woman who watched the life pictures felt themselves at the open ringside, and from the moment the picture battle began until . . . the last excited spectator moved out of the ring, the interest was at fever heat."[81] Spirited audience reaction may not have been unique to the *Corbett-Fitzsimmons Fight*, but its sui generis mode of exhibition demonstrated the sociality of early filmgoing.

Dozens of cities hosted Veriscope shows with similar results. The longest run was in Chicago, where it broke attendance records for the Grand Opera House. Prestige and profits remained high. Admissions continued at one dollar for matinee and evening performances. Similar treatment was accorded the *Corbett-Fitzsimmons Fight* abroad. In London, the film attracted prominent members of society at the Little Theatre, adjoining Westminster Aquarium.[82] In each venue, however, the exhibition took a different form. Because of malfunctions and regular reel changes, some exhibitors scheduled variety acts to supplement the lecturer.

Americans residing in smaller towns saw the Veriscope show in more modest circumstances. As local histories of early film exhibition have increased in number, one of the emerging constants has been the late-nineteenth-century institution of the opera house in small cities and towns. Distinct from the "grand opera house" in the metropolis, the provincial opera (or "opry") house often served as the center for all major commercial entertainment. It booked a variety of performances, from star vehicles to minstrel shows; passion plays and battles royal; *Uncle Tom* troupes and lectures by Booker T. Washington. The opera house of the 1890s was also where small-town America often saw its first moving-picture demonstration. Sometimes that was the *Corbett-Fitzsimmons Fight*.

Gregory A. Waller documents a Veriscope unit's appearance in Kentucky's Lexington Opera House, a three-story structure with 1,250 seats. It introduced moving pictures to the city of twenty-six thousand in December 1896, with an entr'acte display of a "cineomatragraph." Vitascope, phantoscope, and magniscope shows passed through in the following year. By the time of the Corbett-Fitzsimmons controversy, Lexington was familiar enough with motion pictures for a local church to ask the board of aldermen to pass "an ordinance prohibiting the exhibition in our city of any picture, however made, or representation of such fights." The effort failed: Lexington received the *Corbett-Fitzsimmons Fight* favorably when it played that fall.

Drawing from less populated areas, opera-house exhibitions were scheduled for short runs, typically three days. Ticket prices, however, were as high as for the New York premiere, with reserved box seats still costing one dollar. Evening and matinee shows were also maintained, with "larger and more enthusiastic" crowds reported at night. Afternoon presentations, conspicuously, were "largely made up of ladies." Although press accounts made no mention of a lecturer, sound effects included "a bell behind the scenes," which rang whenever the time keeper was "seen to clang the gong in the pictures." As Waller notes, the exhibitor had to take special pains to construct the event as "perfectly proper" for genteel audiences. Lexington's manager, therefore, reported that "thousands of ladies and gentlemen" were taking an interest in the veriscope.[83]

If proprietors of opera houses and urban theaters were careful to structure Veriscope shows to attract a more bourgeois clientele (and to segregate them from the raucous fight fans in the cheap seats), a third line of exhibition offered freer access to the *Corbett-Fitzsimmons Fight*. Fairgrounds and amusement parks set up Veriscope displays. Here the film shed any trappings of exclusivity, allowing crowds of different classes, ages, and racial and ethnic groups to see and comment on the reproduction together. In some areas this was the predominant form of veriscope exhibition. In Rhode Island, for example, the WCTU protested the "debasing influence" "exerted by the side shows of many of our fair grounds," taking particular note of "the vitascopic exhibition of prize fights" that fair associations sponsored in 1897. In other settings, such as the summer picture shows at New Orleans Athletic Park in June 1898, the *Corbett-Fitzsimmons Fight* was exhibited in open-air venues or large tents.[84]

The most conspicuous of all such Veriscope installations occurred at the Texas State Fair and Dallas Exposition in October 1897. For two weeks "the Carson fight pictures [were] reproduced to large audiences" that came to Stuart's hometown. The "Fitzsimmons-Corbett Fight Shown by the Veriscope" was heralded as a central attraction. The pictures again reinvented themselves to match the milieu. Ads and news coverage turned the Veriscope pictures simultaneously into a midway attraction for the State

Fair's "Amusement Row"; "the greatest electrical invention" for the Exposition's display of technology; and a political symbol of Stuart's victory over his nemesis, Governor Culberson.

Taking its place alongside the embalmed 80,000-pound whale, marionette plays, menageries, a Venetian carnival, French paintings, Oriental acrobats, and "the largest married couple in the world," the *Corbett-Fitzsimmons Fight* became the fairground sideshow the WCTU deplored. On the "midway plaisance" the "verascope people" built a makeshift theater for screenings held every two hours during the day and once each evening. The fair attracted diverse elements of society. Farmers and businessmen, students and soldiers, men, women and children, upper-, middle-, and lower-classes, Shriners, Elks, and Pythians mixed more freely in this holiday atmosphere than in daily life. Normally segregated groups were encouraged to attend the fair (on "Colored People's Day"). At the midway, fairgoers could drop in on the film and offer their running commentary. The *Dallas Morning News* found it "amusing to hear the comments of the crowd while the exhibition is going on and the fight by rounds is being reproduced on canvas."

The Texas fair emphasized the "operational aesthetic" of veriscope technology. The previous year's gathering had presented movie technology (the phantoscope and animatographe), but 1897 emphasized "more Machinery" than ever. The "great progress in science" included a host of moving picture apparatuses. "Prof. Rock's cinematograph," the mutoscope, Edison's vitascope, and others surrounded the veriscope. Promoting the veriscope projector as a technical marvel, fair ads invoked the name of "Edison, the Wizard of Menlo Park," as a universal signifier of invention. Of the Wizard's many advancements, the ads inaccurately claimed, "perhaps the most wonderful of all is the verascope."

Dallas audiences, however, associated the *Corbett-Fitzsimmons Fight* with Dan A. Stuart, not Edison. Promotion for the fight pictures reminded fairgoers of Stuart's struggle to pull off the bout. Since the fight had been planned for the 1895 State Fair, the anticipation of finally seeing Corbett and Fitzsimmons in the ring was especially keen. Stuart, Wheelock, and the other Dallas entrepreneurs who had invested in the fight contract played up their triumphant return with the famous pictures in hand.

The local press did not lose sight of the political irony of Governor Culberson, who had called the "prize-fight session" of the legislature, opening a state fair which featured the *Corbett-Fitzsimmons Fight*. The *Dallas Morning News* lampooned the incumbent. In its review of the Veriscope show, the paper detailed the comings and goings of political figures. With "many well known people being in attendance," the *Morning News* said, "every politician of note and all the little fellows . . . witnessed the reproduction." Although the former governor John Reagan, rival candidates for governor, and legislators had "taken in the show" and "were delighted," Culberson "religiously refrained from venturing close to the building where the verascope exhibitions [took] place. The members of the governor's staff . . . however, have patronized the Corbett-Fitzsimmons show."[85]

The *Corbett-Fitzsimmons Fight*'s ability to adapt to varied forms of exhibition made it a long-lived moneymaker. The elements of circus and carnival sustained its popularity after the bout lost its topicality. The Veriscope version of *Corbett-Fitzsimmons* became a circus property, just as Lubin's reenactment had. At least one "circus minister" even built a career on the *Corbett-Fitzsimmons Fight*. Doc Waddell, an agent for Ringling Brothers, Barnum & Bailey, and others circuses, toured the United States with the pictures.[86]

Two other reconstitutions of the films are noted in Musser's research. When playing return engagements, the films were often revised. The Bob Fitzsimmons Vaudeville Company, for example, used the pictures (with some 1,400 feet of added postfight footage) as advance publicity for its 1898 stage show. The film continued to run on its own merits until 1901. Records from an early storefront theater in Tacoma, Washington, for instance, indicate that when *Corbett-Fitzsimmons* was booked in November 1901, it yielded bigger receipts than most other programs.[87]

THE QUESTION OF RECEPTION:
FEMALE SPECTATORS AT THE VERISCOPE

Amid all of the publicity, the variety of exhibition forms, and the mixed reception of the film, one historically surprising motif recurs in documentation about the Veriscope shows: women in apparently unexpected numbers patronized the *Corbett-Fitzsimmons Fight*. Miriam Hansen has described this as an "exemplary moment of crisis" in the history of spectatorship. Understanding the historical role of the "spectatrix" begins with the Veriscope.[88]

Again, it was Charles Musser's research that first brought attention to the female clientele for *Corbett-Fitzsimmons*. "Although men of sporting blood were the veriscope's intended audience," he notes, quite a different response arose. Not only were men of the upper crust and nonsporting public turning out for the fight pictures, but women were, too. "In Boston, women were reported to form 'a considerable portion of the audience,' and according to at least one source, women constituted fully 60 percent of Chicago's patronage. In many other cities and towns, a similar pattern emerged. To male reporters, it was a puzzle."[89]

Other local accounts support this observation. In San Francisco, the *Examiner* mentioned that "women as well as men watch the changing pictures of the veriscope with eagerness." A Dallas report pointed out that "Hundreds of ladies have witnessed these exhibitions," while the New Orleans press noted that women attended evening shows as well as ladies' matinees.[90]

Certainly women did see Veriscope's fight pictures, but the reports of their turnout are suspect and were probably suggested to the press by the Veriscope Company. Accounts of responses to the *Corbett-Fitzsimmons Fight* were often colored by or derived from material distributed by promoters. Many Veriscope write-ups have a great degree of sameness about them, down to particular phrases and facts. Repeated mention is made, for example, that the film was "one and a half miles" long, that it consisted of "189,000 exposures," and so on.

Both Stuart and Brady exploited newspaper connections to keep stories about their boxers and pictures almost constantly in print. Among the methods employed were wiring press releases directly to news offices, spreading rumors to gossip columns, and syndicating ghostwritten pieces signed by their boxers. Brady emulated Joseph H. Tooker, the theatrical showman who stirred up publicity, pro and con, by fabricating outlandish letters, sermons, fan mail, and news items.[91]

The company probably distributed press sheets with items prepared for newspapers to reprint. It also provided advance screenings, "press nights," in which Veriscope viewings were held for local journalists. The lecturer and operator who traveled with the films had the motive, means, and opportunity to supply reporters with angles for stories on the public response to the fight reproduction.

The Hearst press syndicate also poured resources into publicizing the fight, buying exclusive interviews, sending celebrity reporters and artists to Carson City, and chartering express trains. Although they had no share in picture profits, Hearst papers and other yellow papers had a vested interest in milking the story. The idea that genteel ladies were flocking to see this slugfest contains all the elements of classic yellow journalism. Like so many fabricated stories of the era, it alluded to crime, sexual transgression, exotic locale, social taboo, sporting life, and popular science—all with the veneer of factual reporting.

Substantiating how much of this story of women's attendance was orchestrated is difficult. Isolating one local Veriscope exhibition, however, strengthens the case. Looking at Lexington, Kentucky, Waller offers a skeptical view of claims about female patronage. He notes that Charles Scott, who booked the *Corbett-Fitzsimmons Fight* for his opera house, provided Lexington newspapers with a "promotional article a week before the fight films" arrived. The piece claimed "one of the most remarkable features of the veriscope pictures of the contest is the great interest shown in the exhibition by women." Waller concludes: "True or false, this 'fact' established a precedent, and Scott provided a 'perfectly proper' opportunity for taking in the fight films by scheduling matinee showings 'especially for ladies.'"[92]

Waller also provides evidence as to why Veriscope would have benefited from publicity about a female audience. The Lexington press covered the debate on fight-film censorship in March 1897. Because that campaign was spearheaded by the WCTU (who ranked it second only to suffrage on their annual agenda),[93] press accounts represented the film as a "stag" venture meeting feminine opposition. Stuart's management waylaid censorship measures threatened by all-male legislatures (stories abounded about congressmen's desires to see the big fight). Overcoming female resistance to his enterprise would help assuage moralist antipathy.

To channel the film's reception, Veriscope sought higher-class exhibition venues and, rather than protect women and children from exposure, encouraged "ladies" to come and see this "illustration" of a boxing contest. The result for women was a socially problematic conjunction of two cultural practices: attending the theater and becoming a spectator in the male domain of prizefighting.

Prizefighting was an almost entirely male purview. Whether at club contests, mining-camp mills, or clandestine bouts, women were excluded from this rowdy social setting. Although some women might have read the emerging sports pages of the day, such material was aimed at male readers. But by the 1890s, mass-circulation dailies also solicited female readers by featuring women reporters. In 1892, when the Hearst papers titillated readers by sending their star female writer, "Annie Laurie," to cover a prizefight, she wrote: "Men have a world into which women cannot enter."[94]

Female spectatorship at fights was represented as a transgression. Annie Laurie could only watch "from behind a curtained booth." The figure of the lone, disguised woman at ringside recurred in tabloid stories of the 1890s; some were comical, others sensationalist. In the Corbett era, such anecdotes peppered the widely read *Police Gazette.* Colorful items such as "How a Female Sport Saw a Fight," in which a cigarette-smoking blonde sat near ringside dressed in a man's suit, drew on boxing lore dating to the days of John L. Sullivan, whose girlfriend, Ann Livingston, reportedly attended the 1888 Sullivan-Charlie Mitchell fight "dressed as a boy."[95] The *Gazette* also published stories about female pugilists. These were done as comic inversions, emphasizing the distance between boxing and perceptions of femininity and masculinity. By suggesting that the "manly art" was being usurped, they also revealed a male perception of female threat. As Steven Riess has shown, American men of this period saw boxing as an activity that countered a perceived "feminization" of social life.[96]

The lone woman at ringside took on a particular identity when Rose Julian Fitzsimmons became noted for sitting in her husband's corner. Like Annie Laurie, she initially watched bouts from a peep hole. At Carson City she broke with decorum by making herself conspicuous in the first row. Her "boisterous and Amazonian action" was widely reported and even sermonized against.[97]

As a public figure, the wife of the champion was granted some license, but other women at the Nevada fight were not. One sports writer remarked: "The most curious members of the spectators were a few women who had braved public opinion for the new sensation. They were mostly of the peroxide blonde order." This veiled reference to prostitutes bolsters Hansen's argument that in considering women's participation in any public activity, we must remember that the "public sphere was gendered from the start," that it began as "an arena of civic action for the 'public man,' " at a time when the idea of a "public woman" was synonymous with prostitution.[98]

Yet the spectacle of pugilism was not completely closed to women in 1897. As Timothy J. Gilfoyle documents in his history of prostitution, "public women" of the urban "underground" certainly had contact with the male sporting life.[99] "Respectable" ladies had limited exposure as well. Through theatrical performances—sparring exhibitions, physical culture shows, living pictures, illustrated lectures, and melodramas starring prizefighters—women had access to a controlled form of the sport, its celebrities, and their displayed bodies. Corbett and Fitzsimmons attracted a female following during their tours.[100] Through their theatrical presentation, the Veriscope shows invited women to experience what was then their closest contact with an authentic prizefight.

The regulated public space of the theater was a problematic one for American women of the Gilded Age. As Robert C. Allen argues, the nineteenth century was a period of "cultural reorientation" for the American theater. Before the Civil War, commercial theaters and concert saloons catered to working-class men. Unescorted women who attended were often known or reputed to be prostitutes. Theater managers tacitly condoned this association, allowing a notorious "third tier" where prostitutes rendezvoused with clients.

Allen charts the reconstruction of American theatrical institutions as a process of gentrification, in which working-class audiences and forms were put into separate spheres (burlesque, minstrelsy, and others) by managers seeking the patronage of an ascending middle class. They began to recruit women and families, creating a self-reinforcing process in which female presence became a marker of social acceptability, "sanctifying" and feminizing theatergoing. Following the leads of the cagey showmen P. T. Barnum and Moses Kimball, New York theaters in 1865 began scheduling Saturday matinees for women. Proprietors transformed the male-dominated "pit" (main floor) into the "parquette," creating seating for women beyond the conspicuous loge. Finally, the valorization of a female audience was consolidated by the showman Tony Pastor in the 1880s and by the institutionalization of "polite" vaudeville by B. F. Keith and other theater owners in the 1890s. The "house and the entertainment [should] directly appeal to the support of ladies and children," Keith wrote in 1898. Vaudeville became, Allen says, the "first form of commercial theatrical entertainment to draw unescorted, middle-class women in significant numbers."[101] At the time of the *Corbett-Fitzsimmons Fight*, therefore, many women had only just begun to find the theater to be a receptive, legitimated social space.

The Matinee Girl

The majority of women who ventured into the opera houses of America to see the Veriscope pictures attended the "ladies' matinee." From the *Boston Herald* to the *Lexington Herald*, publicity announced the fight films not as a transgression but as the "proper" thing for ladies to see. The *San Francisco Chronicle* insisted "the women folk exhibit even more enthusiasm than the sterner sex."[102] But how did they react to the flickering black and white images of Fitzsimmons knocking out Corbett? What did their attendance mean? Musser and Hansen suggest that the *Corbett-Fitzsimmons Fight* was a utopian moment in the history of female spectatorship, one in which middle-class women were temporarily free to indulge in the pleasure of "perusing . . . well-trained male bodies in semi-nudity."[103] Commentary by female reporters reveals a more complicated reception.

The "Matinee Girl," a columnist for the *New York Dramatic Mirror*, wrote a notice of the *Corbett-Fitzsimmons Fight*'s debut:

> I saw the prize fight at the Academy. . . . Of course I mean the
> Veriscope. I saw lots of girls I knew there, but I didn't pretend to notice
> they were there. I felt just as much ashamed of it as they were!

It is a pity Corbett doesn't win. He is a great favorite with us, but he's been knocked out of our hearts by his recent defeat.

Mr. Brady will have to give away some very expensive souvenirs if he ever expects to have his star regain his popularity with the Saturday afternoon audiences. Fitzsimmons isn't pretty—but oh, my![104]

The ladies' matinee served to draw matinee girls to the theater (where they were treated to gifts and "souvenirs") even in the somewhat embarrassing circumstances of a prizefight exhibition. Because the writer was an insider reporting to other trade members, her account may be read as yet another item driven more by publicity than reportage. Yet her representation of the motives and reactions of her constituency is consistent with Hansen's interpretation. The female spectator of fight pictures is lured by the sight of a "pretty" athlete. Hansen compares the display of boxers to the baring of Rudolph Valentino's torso two decades later. She describes the Veriscope phenomenon, however, as an "accident" in which women were allowed a pleasurable glimpse at the athletes' bodies. Whether their pleasure involved a general sexual desire or an attraction to a specific individual remains uncertain. As the Matinee Girl notes, they came to see their "great favorite" Gentleman Jim. Other pugs would not have elicited the same response.

Although journalists never mention the point, nobody seeing either the *Corbett-Fitzsimmons* or *Corbett-Courtney* films could fail to notice the Gentleman's prominently displayed gluteus maximus. The revealing trunks he sports in the filmed bouts were not often worn by other fighters. His daring choice of costume played to his image as a ladies' man. If word of mouth had not gotten around after Corbett's cheeky kinetoscope appearance, the motion pictures showing him literally disrobing in Carson City must have provoked comment, however sotto voce. The matinee girls' feeling "much ashamed" suggests a blushing at the explicit physical display—what Hansen calls the "forbidden sight"—of Corbett as they had never before seen him.[105]

Whether watching fight pictures of Corbett and Fitzsimmons was indeed an erotic experience for women, akin to the Valentino cult, is impossible to ascertain. The Matinee Girl's claim that Corbett was a "great favorite . . . knocked out of our hearts" is as close as any journalist came to mentioning female desire. However, an intriguing postscript adds weight to the notion that fight pictures served as a projection of such desire. In the theatrical seasons of 1900 through 1902, Bob and Rose Fitzsimmons toured together in *The Honest Blacksmith,* a comic melodrama commissioned from the Broadway playwright William B. Gill in which the couple impersonated themselves.

Before the tour began, it was announced that the show would incorporate "cinematograph fight pictures." Rose, a show-business veteran, told the *New York World* the production would climax with a "great 'vision' scene." She would faint on hearing an incorrect report that Fitz had lost a prizefight. "But, recovering, I have a vision, which is to be represented by moving pictures at the back of the stage, of the fight itself and I see Fitz winning. I forget my grief and grow prouder of him every minute."[106] That a woman's dream of her sweetheart could be represented by a Fitzsimmons fight picture confirms the effect of Veriscope's marketing.

The images used in *The Honest Blacksmith* were actually from Bob Fitzsimmons's second celluloid appearance. Lubin's *Life Motion Photographs of the Fitzsimmons and Ruhlin Fight* (1900) combined footage of the boxers training with the later reenactment of Fitz's victory for the cineograph in Philadelphia. These fight pictures were sometimes specially advertised as an element of the show, though not acknowledged as a reenactment. "In the last act," the *Washington Post* erroneously stated, "the moving pictures of the Fitzsimmons-Ruhlin fight at Madison Square Garden are nicely worked in as a part of a vision of Mrs. Fitzsimmons."

Rose Fitzsimmons's admission was an exception, of course. Even assuming that women were indeed attracted to the boxer's body, the potential eroticism of the moment was tempered by the violence of the bout, the knockout of the star, and the spotty quality of the reproduction—as well as the unprecedented public nature of such an experience. (And in the case of the Fitzsimmonses, the eroticism of boxing was diminished when, in 1901, Bob was arrested for punching Rose during a backstage argument. They reconciled, but he added jokes about his wife beating to the play.)[107]

Alice Rix, Spectatrix

The complicating factors which question the premise that women flocked to the Veriscope are raised directly in a feature story written by a newspaperwoman attending the San Francisco debut of the *Corbett-Fitzsimmons Fight*. "Alice Rix at the Veriscope," an exposé of the film's exhibition at the Olympia vaudeville palace in July 1897, appeared in the Sunday magazine of Hearst's *Examiner*.[108] This document contains layers of evidence absent in other sources. Written by a woman and illustrated by a woman, primarily for women readers, on the subject of female audiences, it offers a rare description of a Veriscope exhibition and an audience's responses.

Alice Rix was a sixtyish society woman from a prominent family of Bay Area settlers.[109] Her byline appeared regularly in the Sunday supplement.

Among the "women's features" in the magazine were floridly written, dramatic stories by female reporters. Hearst editors exploited the conspicuousness of women in journalism, giving them prominent bylines and assigning them to sensational stories. Often, as Barbara Belford points out, they were placed in taboo or "dangerous situations to titillate readers." "Sob sister" journalists, such as Alice Rix (and her better-known pseudonymous counterparts Nellie Bly, Dorothy Dix, and Annie Laurie), sought the "secret" story which "only a woman could extract."[110] In 1897, Rix's Veriscope report was one in a series of her exposés of such subjects as the "girl slaves" of Chinatown, "women tramps" of Oakland, exploited migrant workers, and the interior of San Quentin Prison.

Interestingly, Rix begins by insinuating that the story about women clamoring to see the fight pictures was a fabricated male fantasy perpetuated by newspapers like her own:

> Where is she?
> Where is woman at the prize fight?
> Where is that fierce, primitive savage thing, that harpy, that bird of prey, that worse-than-man who was expected to sit six rows deep before the Veriscope at the Olympia and gloat over the bloody sport of the ring? Where is the brute?
> I do not see her on Monday night. But, then, as somebody reminds me, Monday is Press night.
> It is on Tuesday then that I may expect her?
> Yes, certainly. She will be there on Tuesday.
> Various simple ostriches [i.e., women] of my acquaintance assure me there will be a crush of women at the Olympia every night and a bigger crush still at the matinees. That is woman's first opportunity, you know, to see a prize fight with the blessing of the world upon her head and she would rather lose the head than miss it. Why? Look at her in New York where the Veriscope was running at the Academy of Music. I saw her at the Veriscope in New York, of course, sitting fierce-eyed and dry-mouthed before the screen with her thumbs down? No? I read about her, then? And saw the pictures in the papers?
> I see [cheap, sporting men] at the entrance to the Olympia. They are waiting there, as one of them remarks, to watch the women pour in. . . . A short line forms before the box office. There is not a woman in it.

Eventually, Rix reports, only sixty women in a crowd of about a thousand people made their way into the theater. She notes the social typology of the crowd. The gallery, as usual, was occupied by boisterous, working-class spectators, while the middle-class "sporting men incline[d] to the boxes." The dress circle, where one might expect to find the proper ladies, was empty.

Instead, women at the Olympia sat in the main parquette section and "dressed down." Rix describes them as demure wives and mothers with their families, and well-bred society girls escorted by young sports.

Few women were in earnest to see the boxers; nor were they particularly captivated by the pictures. Despite elements enhancing the exhibition—a musical overture, a screen-side announcer—most of the audience failed to respond with enthusiasm. Men familiar with prizefighting found the silent, monochromatic reproduction lacking.

> But the women said nothing. During the next intermission they yawned and moved about restlessly in their chairs. . . . The Veriscope is a blood-less battle, fought on canvas by the wraiths and shades of men. . . .
> The San Francisco woman sat calmly before the Veriscope.
> So did the San Francisco man.

San Francisco audiences, seeing their hometown hero dethroned, might have been more subdued than others. But, as Rix reports it, she and her fellow viewers failed to warm to the medium of cinema itself. Rather than marveling at their technical or magical qualities, she found moving pictures "awful."

> I am reminded suddenly of a long-forgotten childish terror of the Magic Lantern show. The drawing-room in darkness, the ghastly white plain stretching away into the unknown world of shadows. It was all very well to call it a linen sheet, to say it was stretched between inno-cent familiar folding doors, it nevertheless divided the known and safe from the mysterious beyond where awful shadows lived and moved with a frightful rapidity and made no sounds at all.
> And they were always awful, no matter how grotesquely amusing the shape they took, and they followed me to the nursery in after hours and sat on my heart and soul the black night through. And sometimes even morning light could not drive them quite away, and now forsooth, it seems they have withstood the years.
> I would not go to see the Veriscope often. It is, as one of the girls in front of me said, "A little too leery for me."

Although this evocative description reinforces the discursive connection be-tween cinema and dreams, it is a far cry from the stereotype that soon de-veloped of the enchanted, movie-mad female spectator.

Further complexities concerning the figure of the female viewer accom-pany Rix's essay in the form of an illustration, signed by Mary Harrison (figure 19). Her drawing, "The Interested and the Disinterested," depicts opposing reactions by two women at the Veriscope. The "interested" party, a smiling woman, leans forward in her box seat, enjoying her view of the

Figure 19.   "The Interested and the Disinterested," illustration for "Alice Rix at the Veriscope," *San Francisco Examiner,* July 18, 1897.

shadow Corbett. Behind her stands the "disinterested" companion, looking away, her back to the screen.

The figures parallel two modes of female reception. The first is represented by the Matinee Girl, an unmarried theater habitué and adoring Corbett fan. The second is that of Alice Rix, the society matron and arbiter of taste who denied that anything untoward was occurring among those few San Francisco women who saw fight pictures. Looking over the shoulder of the seated, younger woman, we follow her line of sight to the movie screen, on which the silhouette of Corbett's famous figure appears. Although the directness of her gaze is attenuated by a veil and a fan, she takes not only interest but pleasure in the experience. She delights in the transgression of looking as well as in the image itself. Her counterpart appears not merely disinterested but slightly dismayed at the other's keen interest. This Rix-like figure also holds a lorgnette. She does not use it, but it is a reminder that opera glasses were the era's instrument allowing the *longneuse* to magnify her view of performers, to be a spectatrix. However one reads these figures and their expressions, the artist's rendering of female spectators at the Veriscope suggests a more intriguing dynamic of reception than Rix's essay of disinterest does.

This illustration holds even greater significance for an assessment of female spectatorship during this period given its similarity to the genre of Paris Opera paintings and prints in circulation a few years earlier. Antonia Lant points out that impressionist artists produced a series of works—including Mary Cassatt's *At the Opera* (1880) and August Renoir's *La loge* (1880)—representing women (and some men) in the "activity of looking out of and into an elevated opera box." In these depictions, for the nineteenth-century spectatrix, the very activity of looking and of being allowed to "overtly scrutinize her surroundings" was at least as important as what she was looking at.[111] So it was for Veriscope audiences. However, the sketch of the San Francisco loge also differs from the Parisian artists' renderings. The women in the *Examiner* illustration react differently to the motion-picture spectacle. While one looks away from the image with a chaperone's sense of propriety, the other leans forward to secure a more concerted view. This latter gesture suggests two things: first, that cinema encouraged viewers to attend less to activity within the theater and more to the presentation itself; and, second, that women found something intriguing in the reproductions of Corbett and Fitzsimmons. They were there to focus on screen content rather than on seeing and being seen by others in the theater.

Such representations, as Lant puts it, hint at "the social and psychic conditions of the nineteenth-century female's public life." Because primary sources are scarce, hints sometimes must suffice. The lack of documentation also makes it difficult to evaluate modes of male spectatorship and reception. If the boxers' dress and display had erotic connotations for some women, male spectatorship also involved a sexual dynamic. Whether hetero- or homosexual, the audience was one of men watching men. Thomas Waugh offers a historical understanding of this phenomenon. He speculates on how the 1894 kinetoscope of Strongman Sandow's muscle flexing and other artifacts, like the Corbett-Courtney pictures, may have "accommodated the homoerotic gaze."

To what degree was there a gay male audience for *Corbett-Fitzsimmons* or its successors? As Waugh shows, "many emerging cultural forms" at the time—academic nude photography, sports photographs, *Police Gazette* illustrations, physical culture magazines, and postcards, as well as some early motion pictures—made the male athlete a spectatorial object. A century later, he argues that these appear to represent "the first stirrings of the homoerotic construction of the male body." Just as we know that the constituency for prizefighting was men, for these related practices "the institution of looking at the male body was overwhelmingly male." But it is difficult to reliably say more. Much as discourse about female desire was repressed in the discussion of women attending fight films, the same was true in the writings of men on physical culture. Waugh concludes: "Specific documentation of the homoerotic articulation and appropriation of the strongman image is as scanty as a fig leaf." At most we can "presume that the homosocial [i.e., all-male] infrastructure" and "sexual atmosphere" of the physical culture movement "legitimized the pleasure of looking at male beauty" and "sheltered an important (if superficially invisible) gay constituency."[112]

The aesthetics of physical culture also set it apart from turn-of-the-century prizefighting. The sleek, clean, statuesque poses of Sandow differ markedly from the stereotypical "pug-ugly" prizefighter. Corbett aside, the boxer of the period was seldom represented by his beauty but rather by his disfigurements—broken nose, black eyes, cauliflower ears—and his ability to maul. Physical culture was a still-life display of idealized bodies; prizefighting was blood sport, a spectacle of men damaging one another's bodies. If it was male beauty that attracted gay men, as well as heterosexual women, to Sandow and Corbett, the dynamics and aesthetics of prizefighting worked against that. Gilfoyle's *City of Eros* even documents how the sporting press was particularly homophobic in its presentation of boxing as a symbol of "manliness." The world of boxing was more likely to comport with the traditional patriarchal culture of masculinity than with a gay subculture. Homosexual or bisexual men may been motivated to watch the sport for the same reason heterosexuals did, but its erotic attractions were tempered.[113]

Even if claims about a veritable craze by women to see the *Corbett-Fitzsimmons Fight* were exaggerated, a female audience of some size saw the films. Women's contact with these widely circulated prizefight pictures constituted an important moment, one which gave women access to the male domain of the prize ring and to the sight of boxers in action. Yet that access was always limited, mediated, and controlled, and the moment was indeed ephemeral. More than in any other sport, the participants and spectators of boxing remained predominantly male. Subsequent fight pictures, even those showing Jim Corbett, did not attract female patrons in significant numbers. The few reports of women at later boxing films treated the event as a mere oddity.[114] Though an invited "ladies' " audience helped legitimize the Veriscope enterprise, throughout the ensuing Progressive Era, fight-film promoters often had to pledge to bar women and children.

The *Corbett-Fitzsimmons Fight* remains an atypical example of early cinema. Its format, fame, controversy, longevity, and profitability distinguished it from other motion pictures in 1897. Despite its enormous financial success, however, Veriscope did not establish a paradigm for cinema form or practice. Yet its film's nonpareil status suggests a rethinking of film historiography. The public discourse that surrounded a motion picture of so little aesthetic or formal interest testifies to the need to pay more attention to the social conditions of exhibition and reception when evaluating a film's place in the history of cinema.

More important, the question of this film's reception by women calls into question conceptions of the historical development of cinematic form and movie audiences. The argument made for classical Hollywood cinema has often been applied to early film as well: that cinema was constructed for a heuristic male viewer, with women as the object of the gaze. Given the voyeuristic, peep-show aesthetic of so many early cinema subjects—dancing girls, disrobing acts, and the like—this conception holds. But with the male boxer (especially the exhibitionistic Corbett) as the screen subject and the female viewer as the audience, the dynamic shifted. Although ring events were mostly male entertainment, women on occasion sought pleasure from them. If some women made Corbett's physique the object of their gaze, they may well have enjoyed other stag displays, too. Contemporaneous representations of young women peering into mutoscope peep shows (looking at striptease scenes) supplement the evidence offered by Veriscope's female audience. Images such as John Sloan's lithograph *Fun 1¢* (1905), or any of several photographs taken at turn-of-the-century Coney Island depicting similar scenes, bolster the notion of a female audience for male-oriented entertainment.

Even though the women who took pleasure in seeing the Veriscope pictures did so for only a moment in the history of cinema, their presence signaled a significant rupture in the expected course of events. That the fight picture evoked such simultaneous pleasure and alarm makes the *Corbett-Fitzsimmons Fight* among the most intriguing artifacts of early cinema.

3   Under the Lights

Filming Ringside in the Jim Jeffries Era,
1899–1904

> The machinery for taking the moving pictures attracted much
> attention. . . . It was a picturesque scene, this twentieth-century
> arena, this machine-age gladiatorial contest. The house in darkness
> and the ring a white blaze of light . . . and under the clustered arc
> lamps, in the blinding glare, the two battling elemental males.
>
> Jack London, "Gladiators of the Machine Age,"
> *San Francisco Examiner*, November 16, 1901

After the bonanza of the *Corbett-Fitzsimmons Fight*, boxing promoters and
motion-picture manufacturers continued to record important bouts. For
filmmakers, the pursuit of a fight picture with six-figure profits remained an
important sideline. For matchmakers, the role of motion pictures became
prominent. Realizing that recordings could mine huge veins of profit, ring
managers made extra efforts to accommodate movie cameras. Boxers tolerated the intrusion, as they stood to rake in a large share of the receipts.

In the decade following *Corbett-Fitzsimmons*, both stars were eclipsed
by another figure glimpsed in that film: James Jackson Jeffries. He had been
Corbett's sparring partner before winning the heavyweight title by defeating Fitzsimmons on June 9, 1899. Jeffries retained his crown for six years,
undefeated in six title defenses, before retiring. When his title bouts were
not recorded, reenactments were. And Jeffries himself was the subject of
other early-century actualities filmed outside the ring. More than twenty
movie titles featured his name during this period. His cinema-aided
celebrity continued after he vacated the title. Other fight pictures captured
him in his role as a referee of high-profile bouts. Later, the film of his return to the ring and ignominious defeat at the hands of Jack Johnson in 1910
became more widely discussed than any motion picture of its era.

The Corbett-Fitzsimmons pictures remained in circulation for more
than three years, and new productions continually joined them on the market. Competing interests recorded dozens of boxing and prizefight subjects
between 1897 and 1904, when motion-picture entertainment became a regular feature of commercial amusements. For the chaotic film-production

industry, this period was one of cutthroat competition. All of the leading American manufacturers—Edison, Biograph, Vitagraph, Lubin, and Selig— entered the battle for lucrative fight footage. British producers and small U.S. firms did likewise.

The quality of productions was inconsistent. Photographic and financial results were disappointing more often than not. This lack of success helped mute moralist protests, as did a reversal of fortune for boxing in New York. Under the Horton law, Tammany Democrats profited from the thousands of legalized bouts held between 1896 and 1900. However, with the support of Republican governor Theodore Roosevelt, legislators recriminalized prize-fighting in 1900.[1] Professional boxing moved west again. This interval of less conspicuous fight pictures coincided with Jim Jeffries' reign as heavy-weight champion. A study of the production and exhibition of these films, from the exceptionally profitable *Jeffries-Sharkey Fight* (1899) to the lack-luster *Jeffries and Ruhlin Sparring Contest* (1901) and others, reveals the vagaries of the genre.

More than fifty boxing movies circulated between 1897 and 1904. These continued to fall into three categories: sparring scenes staged for cameras, reenactments of prizefights, and recordings of professional bouts. Compa-nies seeking to turn out a steady supply of new films preferred the first two, in which performance could be controlled. Prominent film manufacturers seldom recorded professional bouts on their own. Instead, ring promoters hired camera operators ad hoc and exploited the films themselves or in tan-dem with motion-picture brands.

By 1900, filmed reenactments outstripped the production of bona fide fight pictures. About half of all fight films during this period were "reproductions," most of them manufactured by the Lubin Company of Philadelphia.

Nearly as common were short boxing rounds, like those that had been sta-ples of the kinetoscope era. Many were nondescript scenes for peep shows and early projected displays. Like their American counterparts, British fair-ground exhibitors used them in variety programs. British producers favored generic titles such as Warwick Trading Company's *A Boxing Match* (1898), G. A Smith's *Fight* (1898), and James Williamson's *Great Glove Fight* (ca. 1900). Only occasionally did these make it to the United States.[2]

American sellers tried to milk the success of the Corbett films. Produc-ers valued name fighters and knockout finishes. The International Film Company's description of the *Downey-Paterson Fight* (1897) exemplified this: "This fast and furious six round fight is conceded to be the best ever offered to the public. There is more punching and hitting in any one round than in six rounds of the many tame fights now on the market. Paterson scores a clean knock-down in the third, while Downey scores a knock-down in the fifth, and knock-down and knock-out in the sixth, winning the fight with the same heart blow that Bob Fitzsimmons delivered to J. J. Corbett in their famous fight at Carson City, Nev."[3]

Comic treatments joined the "tame fights" on the market: Edison's *Comedy Set-To* (1898), *Gordon Sisters Boxing* (1901), and *A Scrap in Black and White* (1903); Biograph's *Chuck Connors vs. Chin Ong* (1899), *The Last Round Ended in a Free Fight* (1903), *A Couple of Lightweights at Coney Island* (1904), and others. Some merely used boxing as a pretext for knockabout humor, as in Lubin's *Boxing in Barrels* (1901) and *Prof. Langtry's Boxing School* (1903). One film used the ring as political metaphor. During the Boer War, the satirical *Glove Fight between John Bull and President Kruger* (1900, Anglo-American Exchange) caricatured the president of South Africa being knocked out by the British icon.

More often, gags substituted a presumed characteristic of the prizefighter with its opposite or a variation. The ostensible humor provides a basis for understanding fight pictures and the sport itself. Instead of athletic young prizefighters squaring off, these films depicted men versus women, women versus women, children versus children, and so on. The fact that *A Scrap in Black in White* and *Chuck Connors vs. Chin Ong* found humor in interracial fisticuffs underscores the significance of racial difference. Consistent with the era's crude stereotyping, movies that presented black boxers used them as the butts of cruel jokes. Selig's *Barrel Fighters* and *Prize Fight in Coon Town* (1903) attempted cinematic equivalents of the "coon song" then prevalent in musical theater.[4]

INITIAL FAILURES FOLLOWING THE VERISCOPE MODEL

Starting in 1899, companies replicated the Veriscope model, recording contests for theatrical exploitation. But cinematographers found it difficult to repeat Enoch Rector's achievement. Several efforts to record big bouts met with conspicuous failure. Not until November 3, 1899, when Biograph cameras captured the Jim Jeffries–Tom Sharkey slugfest at the Coney Island Athletic Club, was Veriscope's feat duplicated. The events that intervened between Carson City and Coney Island illustrate how risky the business of filming prizefights could be. The technology proved as unpredictable as ring results.

Circumstances within the prizefight syndicate precluded immediate follow-ups to the *Corbett-Fitzsimmons Fight*. As lucrative as fight pictures could be, traditional methods of exploiting a championship belt still held sway. Fitzsimmons toured internationally with his own vaudeville company and did not fight during the first year and half that Veriscope outfits were on the road.

In 1898, no prizefights were filmed. Pictures of the Spanish-American War diverted attention from other topical films, but ring events also contributed to this lull. The move to indoor venues interfered with cinematography. By law, New York bouts had to be sponsored by athletic clubs, which held fights indoors and at night. There were even traditionalist arguments for confining bouts to these dimly lit boxing dens. The *Police Gazette* noted that clubhouse fights were "more satisfactory to the sporting fraternity" because "there is a picturesqueness loaned to these affairs under the glare of the electric and gas lights." Aesthetics aside, decisions to hold some big fights indoors were political. Tammany controlled the Lenox and Broadway athletic clubs, while another Democratic faction ran the Coney Island Athletic Club (owned by Martin Julian and William Brady). The three clubs agreed to alternate the hosting of contests.[5]

In July 1899, however, Sam Austin reported in the *Gazette* that clubs would either have to provide motion picture facilities or pay much bigger purses to compete.

> To a club which has the facilities for making a photographic reproduction of the battle, $50,000 would not be too much for the fighters to expect, but any club not possessing such facilities would be taking an extremely hazardous chance. The kinetoscopic exhibition of fistic contests has passed beyond the experimental stages. When Fitzsimmons and Corbett were shown, the films were indistinct and unsatisfactory, yet how much money was made by exhibiting them in every country on the globe will never be known. To such an extent has the photographing of movable objects been perfected since then that a wholly satisfactory result may be obtained, and considering the amount of interest that is now being taken in pugilistic affairs an exhibition of a genuine championship fight, such as the one forthcoming [Jeffries-Sharkey], ought to profit its promoters to the extent of several hundred thousand dollars.[6]

Austin's pronouncement that fight pictures had "passed beyond the experimental stages" contradicted his own recent experience. A month earlier, he had witnessed Vitagraph's failed attempt to record Fitzsimmons' title defense against Jim Jeffries.

American Vitagraph's Failure: The Fitzsimmons-Jeffries Fight

The primary instigator of the Fitzsimmons-Jeffries fight was William Brady, the promoter of the Corbett films. No longer associated with the fallen idol, he signed the Californian James J. Jeffries, a bruising behemoth and rising challenger. Brady convinced his partner (and sometime rival) Martin Julian to accept the Jeffries challenge to Fitz's title. Tammany boss Big Tim Sullivan helped Brady obtain a license to host the heavyweight championship bout in New York, the first ever held there. Brady pursued the lucrative possibilities of a cinematic recording. In May 1899 he commissioned Albert E. Smith of American Vitagraph to build facilities for taking indoor pictures of the fight.

Although Brady had worked with Edison for Corbett's Black Maria bout, legal troubles between the two (a lawsuit over royalties on *Corbett-Courtney* and Edison's claim of patent infringement by Veriscope) put distance between them. Vitagraph had a partnership with Edison. Smith's was also the only production firm other than Biograph directly involved in exhibition, with a national network of units projecting 35 mm films in vaudeville houses. Specializing in topical pictures, his company suited the needs of the fight-film enterprise.[7]

According to Smith's autobiography, which begins with this incident, Brady put up $5,000 and "agreed to furnish a theater and two fighters and pay all the costs of the experiment" to accomplish cinematography using only artificial light. In the Manhattan Theater, Smith and his partner, J. Stuart Blackton, took test pictures of a sparring match using "special arc lights big enough to carry . . . jumbo-sized carbons."[8] Results were promising enough to warrant a contract to record the actual fight. The press noted that, "contrary to expectations," the Fitzsimmons-Jeffries contest would not have to be moved into the daylight, thanks to the "offer of a prominent firm to make pictures of the fight by the use of electric lights."[9] Sporting papers gave the historic plan further attention, reporting that "a new machine has been invented especially for this event." Due to "the assurance of a photographic concern" "using carefully adjusted electrical lights," the sponsoring club scheduled the bout to proceed at the customary late-night hour.[10]

This decision assuaged some suspicions about the contest's legitimacy. The recent Corbett-Sharkey match had been largely dismissed as a fake, and insiders remembered accusations that Corbett-Fitzsimmons had been played out for the sake of cameras. Not wanting to appear in conspiracy with "the kinetoscope picture business," the *Police Gazette* said, the Coney Island club "made no secret of its intentions to have a photographic reproduction of the fight made for exhibition purposes."[11] The principals scuttled rumors of performances prearranged to suit the filmmakers. Jeffries told the press: "You bet your life the kinetoscope won't hold us back once we begin. . . . There will be no posing to give the picture machine a chance."[12] In fact, reports that the fight was to be filmed might have inhibited a fix. W. W. Naughton wrote on the eve of the fight that Tammany Hall had its "monopoly on the prize-fighting business" broken by failing to control this bout. Yet his fears of politically motivated police interference were diminishing: "Chief of Police Devery is still on the rampage, but chances are he'll cool down before the picture machine begins buzzing at the Coney Island Club on Friday night."[13]

The Fitzsimmons-Jeffries encounter proceeded as scheduled on June 9. Jeffries, only twenty-four years old, took the championship with an eleven-round knockout. But Vitagraph failed on two counts. In the lesser offense, "the vitagraph stand, . . . raised ten feet above the flooring" for the cameras and crew, obstructed the view of patrons in $15 seats. A *San Francisco Examiner* reporter quipped: "The most satisfactory thing connected with the fight was the vitagraph. By its benevolent performance several thousand men who attended the fight will be able to learn what happened." The author Julian Hawthorne, hired by the Hearst papers, could report only that his view had been blocked by "the vitascope."[14]

That inconvenience paled beside the failure of Vitagraph's elaborate lighting setup. Journalists noted the conspicuous "platform from which huge cylinders like bottomless hot tubes glowered down" and "the devices from which came the electric glare that was to aid the taking of the pictures." The *Philadelphia Ledger* described the "great beam of blinding white light" as "like a thousand calciums," showing the fighters' "great white bodies in strange relief." Smith recollected "The first round had not been under way more than a minute when suddenly half of the arc lights blacked out. Blackton and I . . . photographed the entire fight . . . but it was wasted effort; the print was dark and useless."[15] The *Police Gazette* had actually predicted failure: "The management continues to announce, in a rather lukewarm manner, however, that the fight will be reproduced by a special photographic machine which may be depended upon to get results from electric or other artificial light quite as satisfactory as those obtained in the glare of sunshine. This is not so, and the results will prove it."[16]

Initially, the press did not report the electrical fiasco. Blow-by-blow descriptions failed to mention the malfunction, which would have been obvious to all witnesses. In its initial coverage, the *New York Times* referred only to "the vitascope, which took photographs of the fight and will reproduce them indefinitely."[17] But two weeks later a *Times* editorial took glee in revealing that the hyped prizefight "did not get itself indelibly fixed on a long photographic film, and consequently will not give unholy delight in the future to the patrons of the variety theatres." The paper jeered at the "the

Coney Island scientists" and their "rude devices": "[A] wobbly old engine and beer barrel rheostats brought the cinematographers confusion—and heavy loss. . . . They spent something like $5,000 on their machines, but only 12 of their 24 lamps would burn, and the twelve burned so badly that when the expensive roll of gelatine was 'developed' it showed—nothing at all. . . . This particular fight will never get upon the illuminated screens of any theatre."[18]

The press otherwise ignored the calamity. Yet when a poor imitation, Lubin's *Reproduction of the Fitzsimmons-Jeffries Fight,* went into circulation in July 1899, the *Police Gazette* also informed sports fans about the fate of the authentic version. Sam Austin related that "Fitzsimmons, Jeffries, Julian, Brady and others who were interested in the success of the enterprise subsequently admitted that the picture taking effort was a failure and lamented the loss of several hundred thousand dollars which they might have profited through a splendid scheme which had been perfected to exhibit the photographs all over the world."[19]

Austin complained about the poor quality of the reproduction, yet it attracted steady business. Smith and Blackton even added it to Vitagraph's film service. Siegmund Lubin in turn advertised that "the American Vitagraph Co. of New York City are showing our fight films . . . with wonderful success." The re-creation proved popular enough that a "well-patronized" storefront operation—Vitagraph Hall, on Pennsylvania Avenue in Washington, DC—opened to showcase the *Fitzsimmons-Jeffries Fight* exclusively.[20]

In August, Edison Manufacturing also began selling prints of a "faithfully reproduced" *Jeffries-Fitzsimmons Fight.* Its six- and eleven-round versions of the Coney Island fight appear to have been a new reenactment. Unverified secondary accounts suggest that Edison and/or Vitagraph filmed this version, enticing both Jeffries and Fitzsimmons to perform the restaging.[21]

Although its master plan to record the big fight failed, the sporting and theatrical syndicate deployed reels of actuality footage to capitalize on Jeffries' celebrity. Brady arranged for the new champ to appear at New York's Casino Roof Garden after his victory. Jeffries and his sparring partner Jim Daly staged a demonstration of blows that felled Fitzsimmons. Introducing the live appearance, Vitagraph projected moving pictures of Jeffries training with Daly in New Jersey. Blackton and Smith shot the series on June 7 in Asbury Park. Despite their June 9 fiasco, by June 17 the pair at least had these views—*Jeffries Skipping Rope, Throwing Medicine Ball,* and others—on exhibition.[22] For more than a decade, touring pugilists commonly incorporated such short films into their variety-theater presentations.

American Sportagraph's Failure: The Palmer-McGovern Fight

Failure to secure footage of the hyped title bout cost filmmakers and promoters greatly. Yet, for some entrepreneurs, the potential money to be made with another Veriscope-like success outweighed the risk of a Vitagraph-like debacle. Plans were made to try again with the next Jeffries contest. In the hiatus between heavyweight title matches, another notable venture fizzled, though in quite a different way different from the Coney Island brownout. Motion pictures, superior in technical quality to any previous fight films, were taken of the dramatic world bantamweight championship between the English titleholder "Pedlar" Palmer and the popular American champ Terry McGovern. To the promoters' chagrin, McGovern knocked Palmer out in the first round, leaving them with a perfectly photographed but unexploitable film.

Their extensive planning, however, indicated that fight films remained the most coveted properties in the motion-picture business. Foreseeing long-term operations, members of the boxing and film fraternity incorporated the American Sportagraph Company in the summer of 1899. Led by the Westchester Athletic Club, they considered arranging a Fitzsimmons–Kid McCoy fight "before a kinetoscope machine" as early as June.[23] Instead the organization waited until the signing of the contest between the U.S. and British champions. While touring with the newly crowned Jeffries in England, William Brady encouraged British fighters to come to America. The Westchester club had an outdoor facility in Tuckahoe (a fifteen-minute train ride north of Manhattan), and therefore a better chance at cinematic success. By August, a deal to film a Palmer-McGovern contest had been signed.[24]

The American Sportagraph Company commissioned special equipment—cameras, printers, and projectors using a unique, wide-gauge film stock. Edwin S. Porter designed and built the proprietary machinery.[25] American Sportagraph offered advance sales of its films and projectors, promising "No Fakes, No Fac-Similes, or Fraudulent Reproductions." Sportagraph made explicit its intentions to use Veriscope's method of exhibition, but adding extra attractions. The *Palmer-McGovern Fight* would tour opera houses under the direction of buyers of territorial rights. The projector was billed as flexible (running on either AC or DC power), lightweight (weighing thirty pounds), and easy to set up. Ads promised an elaborate showcase: "In conjunction with the Palmer-McGovern pictures, we will show photographs, reproductions of noted Horse, Bicycle, Foot and Yacht Races, Sculling Matches, Wrestling Contests, and other outdoor exercises and amusements,

with the stars of the sporting world as contestants. Between the various pictures high class vaudeville acts will be given, making one of the strongest
two and one half hour shows on the road."[26]

The ads also gave directions on train transport. On a weekday afternoon,
ten thousand men made the trip to Tuckahoe. Many must have realized,
as the *Police Gazette* reported, that "the making of pictures" was to be "the
most important adjunct of this battle," because when the club proprietor decided there were too many clouds to guarantee good cinematography, he
asked them to return the following day! The crowd, which included digni-
taries and out-of-town visitors, obliged.[27]

The presence of the local favorite McGovern (the "Brooklyn Terror")
helped ensure attendance. Weather conditions were ideal for the conspicuous "picture machine, sheathed in funereal-black tar paper, with two little
glass windows." Sam Austin described the cinematic anticlimax: "So far as
the picture taking went it was successful. The machine was started when
Palmer entered the ring and all the incidental details for preparing for the
battle, the toss for corners, donning the gloves, introduction of the referee
and principals were all accurately reproduced, but as the fight itself lasted
less than three minutes it is a question if the series of pictures can be made
valuable for exhibition purposes."[28]

American Sportagraph thought not. Discussion of the film ceased. No
screenings were forthcoming. Neither the ad hoc film group nor the
Westchester Athletic Club got involved in the picture game again. Most independent promoters learned their lesson: even superior quality control was
no guarantee of a marketable product. Increasingly, boxing organizers chose
not to acquire motion-picture equipment themselves. They turned filming
over to experienced film manufacturers.

AMERICAN BIOGRAPH'S SUCCESS:
THE JEFFRIES-SHARKEY CONTEST

William Brady hired a contingent of experts from American Mutoscope &
Biograph to record Jim Jeffries' first title defense, fought against Tom
Sharkey on the night of November 3, 1899. Although its setup resembled
the Vitagraph effort of June, Biograph's exceptional crew succeeded in capturing almost all of the twenty-five-round Jeffries victory on their large-
format film. The slugfest entered boxing lore, with the presence of Biograph's
intense arc lights and rival film companies' piracy figuring prominently in
anecdotes about that night at Coney Island. The success of the *Jeffries-Sharkey*

Figure 20. American Mutoscope & Biograph technicians setting up to record the Jeffries-Sharkey bout at the Coney Island Athletic Club, November 3, 1899. (Library of Congress, Prints and Photographs Division.)

Contest was important to the survival of its genre. Producers at last had a recording of undisputed quality. The production and exploitation of the Jeffries-Sharkey fight pictures characterize the competitive, sometimes unprincipled nature of the early motion-picture industry.

Unlike his predecessors, Jeffries quickly agreed to take on the leading contender. By September, Brady and Sharkey's manager, Thomas O'Rourke, had hired American Mutoscope & Biograph to film the contest. The partners considered removing the roof on the Coney Island pavilion, but gambled on another indoor affair under the lights.

They invested heavily in electrical equipment. Biograph advertised its technological expertise and outlay: 11 electricians to operate the "400 specially built arc lights," reflectors, and "special feed wires from the central station" to dynamos in the club house; 12 skilled operators for the four cameras; $6,300 for carpenters, current, wiring, and lighting; and "7¼ miles of film" taken on the largest film stock "ever made" (2 by 2.75 inches). Press accounts repeated the technical information.[29]

Biograph also photographed two sets of test pictures weeks before the fight. In September, Austin reported in the *Police Gazette:*

I have already seen an excellent specimen of what can be done with a machine which has been recently invented for the purpose. An experimental picture was taken of the recent fight between George Dixon and "Sam" Bolan, and exhibited the other day to a few privileged spectators, and I can truthfully say that it was the best continuous pictures of a fistic battle that I have ever seen. The detail was marvelous, every action of the fighters was reproduced with astonishing exactness, and the blinding effect so noticeable after looking at continuous pictures was absolutely lacking. If the operators succeed in making as satisfactory a reproduction of the Jeffries-Sharkey fight as they did of the experimental trial a great feat will have been accomplished and a great money-making enterprise inaugurated, for $200,000 will hardly approximate the net profits from the exhibitions which will be given all over the world.[30]

Biograph catalogs included a second set of pictures, titled *Test: Coney Island Athletic Club.* A different pair of boxers was filmed by cameras placed on the same platform used on the night of the fight.[31]

The installation of electric lights for cameras had a greater effect on this bout than on any prior to it. The harsh glare of the arcs added something new, unusual, and historic to the event. But, as many descriptions and later histories relate, the heat from Biograph's intense lighting affected the fighters. Scorched scalps, massive perspiration, and weight loss caused by the low-hanging lamps combined with the rib-crushing beating suffered by both gladiators to make the match memorable but brutal.

Biograph's success was nearly usurped by pirate cameramen from Edison and Vitagraph, allies against the bigger Biograph. The Edison Manufacturing Company actually touted its scheme. At least seven clandestine cinematographers, including James H. White (head of Edison's production facilities), Albert Smith and James B. French (of Vitagraph), and Joe Howard and Ida Emerson (exhibitors and vaudevillians who used motion pictures in their act) smuggled two portable "hand machine" cameras into the crowd. They formed two groups and stood on opposite sides of the arena. From the mezzanine, each filmed several minutes of action. Pinkerton security, hired to detect just such an infringement, spotted but failed to apprehend them. James White took two sets of films to Washington, DC, the following day, where he copyrighted them under the titles *The Battle of Jeffries and Sharkey for Championship of the World* and *The Jeffries-Sharkey Contest.* Although folklore has Edison employee White spiriting the negatives away from Vitagraph in the dead of night (after using its cameras and developers), Charles Musser points out that under the existing alliance between Vitagraph and Edison, the latter controlled ownership of any negatives.[32]

Edison, Vitagraph, Lubin, and Biograph battled for legal and market position to exploit the various versions of the big fight. Brady and O'Rourke fired the first shot with a warning notice in the *New York Clipper.* They asserted Biograph's exclusive picture rights, warning that "certain fake film

Figure 21. Frames of the Jeffries-Sharkey fight: left, a surviving Biograph muto-scope card; right, Vitagraph's poached footage of the same event. (Library of Congress, Motion Picture, Broadcasting and Recorded Sound Division.)

manufacturers of Philadelphia and other places are preparing to spring counterfeits to be announced as reproductions of the great fight, as was done in the case of . . . Jeffries and Fitzsimmons, of which fight no pictures were ever taken."[33] Lubin had copyrighted two titles (*Reproduction of the Sharkey and Jeffries Fight* and *Reproduction of the Jeffries and Sharkey Fight*) as far back as September 9, and he proceeded with his usual sales tactics immediately after the real event.

The Edison company, however, made a more concerted effort to preempt Biograph. Its pirated pictures were abbreviated and inferior. Extant prints reveal hats and pillars partially blocking the view of distant ring action (see figure 21). Yet Edison's legal staff used their earlier copyright date to seek "an injunction prohibiting the Biograph Company from exhibiting its pictures." American Mutoscope & Biograph did not obtain copyright for *Jeffries-Sharkey Contest* and its four camera negatives until November 10, 11, 13, and 15. Brady countered by crashing a private screening of the bootlegged footage in New York on November 8. He paraded through the Theatre Comique burlesque house shouting, "These pictures are fake!" and "I'll get an injunction to stop them." Advertisements sought to legitimize Edison's claim to the "Sharkey-Jeffries films." An audacious notice on November 11 claimed to have "the real thing" taken by "Our Special Photographers, . . . Messrs. Howard and Emerson." The following week, agents in New York were selling the *Jeffries-Sharkey Contest*. These included regular Edison agents—Maguire & Baucus and the Kinetograph Co.—as well as an independent jobber, James J. Armstrong. Joe Howard peddled prints himself, showing portions to theater managers to secure bookings.[34] The scheme faired poorly, with spectators catching on to the fact that the film was "looped": that is, the recorded action was shown multiple times and mis-represented as successive rounds. With the exception of novelty presenta-tions at Huber's dime museum, the pirated *Jeffries-Sharkey Contest* played to unreceptive audiences in few places. Small-town audiences attacked the padded films as well.[35]

Biograph won some legal protection against its rivals. On December 23, the New York Supreme Court enjoined Edison Manufacturing from "ex-hibiting any copy, real or otherwise, of the Sharkey-Jeffries fight." In Con-necticut, when the New Britain Opera House tried to show the pirated ver-sion, police seized the print. (The manager replaced it with a fake version of the *Fitzsimmons-Jeffries Fight* he had on hand.)[36]

Biograph had less success in preventing the exhibition of reenactments. Lubin fakes were becoming regular installations on the motion-picture cir-cuit. In this case they also had the advantage of far better cinematography than the Edison-Vitagraph prints. Brady and O'Rourke, the *Clipper* re-ported, proposed "to make an active warfare on all imitations and repro-ductions," engaging Lubin in retaliatory trade ads. When Biograph declared a challenge of "$5,000 to S. Lubin of Philadelphia, if he [could] demonstrate that his alleged reproduction of the Jeffries-Sharkey Fight" was anything more than a bogus fake, Lubin countered with a challenge of $10,000 to anyone who could prove that his film was not copyrighted!

With pirated footage off the market, Lubin's reenactment was the only version of the Jeffries-Sharkey fight available to operators with standard 35 mm projectors. Biograph stuck to its proprietary large format. Even those in on the Edison scheme bought Lubin prints. Lubin's ads presented en-dorsements from Vitagraph and Howard & Emerson, both of which switched to exhibiting the Lubin version. F. M. Prescott, a former Edison licensee, issued a supplemental catalog solely to advertise the reproduction.[37]

Meanwhile, Biograph kept the public informed about the authenticity and superiority of its product. The *Police Gazette* championed the produc-tion. Although Sam Austin mistakenly speculated that the "story about a second and unauthorized set of pictures" was false, he condemned the maker of "fake pictures of Jeffries and Fitzsimmons" for repeating its act with *Jeffries-Sharkey*. Nevertheless, Austin concluded that despite the money that would be lost to fakers, up to a half million dollars would be made from the genuine recording. The *Gazette* also reprinted frames from the Biograph film in place of its usual woodcuts and posed photographs. The Hearst and Pulitzer papers did likewise. After a press screening, the *Gazette* devoted special attention to the films, congratulating the Biograph crew by name (Arthur E. Johnstone, Wallace McCutcheon, and F. J. Marion) and

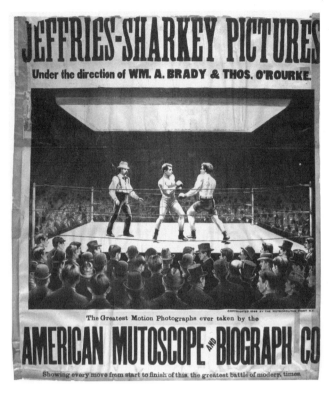

Figure 22. Lithographic poster for *Jeffries-Sharkey Pictures* (1899). (Library of Congress, Prints and Photographs Division.)

saying their pictures were "as near perfect as the photographer's science can make it."[38] It also repeated the details stressed in Biograph advertising, noting the films' physical length ("seven and a half miles") and unprecedented running time ("122 minutes").

The exhibition life of *Jeffries-Sharkey* closely followed that of *Corbett-Fitzsimmons*. Both used a unique gauge of celluloid that other makes of projector could not show. Though this second major fight-picture tour met with financial success, it also ran its course more quickly.

Notably, the release of Biograph's *Jeffries-Sharkey Contest* elicited few calls for censorship. The fight lacked the extensive buildup and legal wrangling of the Nevada match. Furthermore, Veriscope's skillful exploitation had defused early antagonisms. The status of prizefighting had been raised by showing the pictures in legitimate environs. Finding the *Corbett-Fitzsimmons Fight* less graphic than might have been imagined, the public

Figure 23.   "Spectators Applaud Sharkey. Visitors at the New York Theatre Carried Away with His Work as Shown by the Biograph," *Police Gazette*, December 9, 1899.

suspended protests against *Jeffries-Sharkey*, even though it featured a harsher display of pugilism. Screen re-presentation was helping professional boxing gain acceptance.

Dressed up as a theatrical feature and photographic marvel, a well-presented fight picture encouraged acceptance of the sport in a way that more playful forms could not. Events in New York City after the bout illustrated this trend. William Brady had become managing director of Koster and Bial's Music Hall and was showcasing his champ in a new burlesque, *Round New York in 80 Minutes*. On November 6, while Jim Jeffries sparred on stage, he was arrested for violating the anti-prizefight law. Two weeks later Biograph's *Jeffries-Sharkey Contest* debuted at the New York Theatre as a gala event (see figure 23).[39]

Round New York in 80 Minutes was a high point for the Gotham-centered sporting and theatrical world. It was also representative of the use of motion pictures in multimedia entertainment of the period. Brady hired writers to hash together a topical revue for several hundred performers. Its "tales about gay life in New York" unfolded in ten set pieces, concluding with a re-creation of the Coney Island Athletic Club on the night of the fight. Jim Corbett commented from ringside as Sharkey and Jeffries sparred. "Vitagraph views" were added in the second week. At the same time, the Biograph fight pictures played ten blocks up Broadway, and Edison's bootleg version continued at Huber's Museum downtown. In December, Jeffries and Sharkey added their "living picture" poses of Roman gladiators to the three-hour *80 Minutes* show.[40]

Brady and O'Rourke inaugurated Biograph's Jeffries-Sharkey exhibition in a big-time vaudeville setting. Reels of Biograph's motion pictures were interspersed with acrobats, high-wire acts, music, dancing, and singing. The capacity audience cheered the game Tom Sharkey, who was in attendance.[41] The pictures ran for several weeks, as they did in other big cities (sans variety acts), accompanied by large posters made especially for the film. Smaller cities and towns booked Biograph road companies for three-day runs and drew modest crowds.[42]

The female audience for the *Corbett-Fitzsimmons Fight* failed to return to the *Jeffries-Sharkey* shows. Ladies' matinees were seldom advertised. Organized protest by women's groups all but disappeared. Lillie Devereux Blake (figure 24), a prominent suffragist and writer, was one of the few voices raised in opposition. She editorialized in the *New York World* against the brutality of the pictures and urged their ban. Blake was joined by a group of Methodist ministers who lamented that the "motley crowd" who patronized the Jeffries-Sharkey fight had made "the night hideous with a saturnalia of vice and crime," an immorality perpetuated because the "latest triumphs of modern invention have been seized by greedy purveyors of amusement to repeat daily before promiscuous audiences scenes of that prize fight."[43]

However, Brady, O'Rourke, and Biograph felt little pressure to seek female patronage. Some women turned out for the Biograph program, but their attendance provoked little discussion. Without Corbett as a drawing card, far fewer matinee girls attended. In San Francisco, which had drawn one of the largest audiences for *Jeffries-Sharkey Contest*, demand for tickets was so great that the Alhambra Theatre warned against scalpers. Even so, women were such a small, but still desirable, part of the clientele that management offered them free admission.[44]

With *Jeffries-Sharkey* and the fight pictures that followed, promoters appealed to boxing aficionados rather than to the general public. The hundreds of thousands who flocked to the grand spectacle of the Veriscope display and Biograph's *Jeffries-Sharkey Contest* seldom returned to the routine releases aimed at the male sporting public. For insiders like Sam Austin,

Figure 24.   Lillie Devereux Blake (1833–1913), author, feminist, and suffragist. "Brutality, Says Mrs. Blake, in Prize Fight Pictures: She Sees the Sharkey-Jeffries Biograph Exhibition and Couldn't Stand the 'Hideous Brutality,'" *New York World,* November 21, 1899.

the replay was an opportunity to make a "careful study of the fight and an analysis of everything that happened in the ring at Coney Island." To such viewers, he contended, it was apparent that Sharkey's performance had been underrated. "Strangely enough there is a unanimity of sentiment on this point among people who did not actually see the fight, but who have only witnessed the reproduction and are forced to draw their own conclusions from the phantom battle so cleverly shown upon the screen."[45]

There was more cleverness in the phantom battle than Biograph advertised. The real Jeffries-Sharkey pictures were lauded for their ability to capture the events with photographic exactitude, making reenactments superfluous. Promotional material insisted the pictures showed "Every Movement from Start to Finish."[46] However, though the fact was seldom mentioned, Biograph's cameras broke down just before the bout was completed. The malfunction coincided with the confused moment in the twenty-fifth round when Jeffries' glove came off and the referee, Siler, paused to tie it back on. As Sharkey tried to take advantage, the bell sounded, and Siler raised Jeffries' arm in victory. The press incorrectly reported that "not a single incident of the fight was lost" by the cinematographers.[47]

Brady described the camera breakdown in his memoirs, noting that "the end of the fight had to be taken over again some time later." At a Rochester screening, the "traveling narrator," in a rare bit of candor, explained "one of the fuses blowed out and the critical moment was lost."[48] Some postfight footage was taken and used to conclude the film. But when and how were retakes shot? By whom? Was a jump cut left between the last half-round and the postfight scene? Was an earlier round substituted for the botched one? Was a reenacted twenty-fifth spliced in to replace the incomplete original?

The only surviving answer is the nostalgic, anecdotal, secondhand piece "Some Unwritten Fight History" (1934), by journalist Dan Parker:

> Sharkey was hauled out of bed two months after the bout, and he and Jeff stripped for action again in the old Coney Island A.C. It was late in January [1900] now and Coney Island was practically deserted. Scouts were sent out into the highways and byways to dig up enough "supers" to furnish a crowd background. . . .
>
> Ringside conditions of the original fight were reproduced. How to bring Referee George Siler back from the West was a problem until Bill Brady offered to impersonate him. Borrowing a black slouch hat from a man at ringside and donning a false mustache, Brady made an acceptable Siler and refereed the second screening [*sic*] of the 25th round.[49]

Reviews ignored the altered last round, or glossed over it, as when the *New York World* noted: "Only in the twenty-fifth round is there a hitch in the pictures, and this has been well smoothed over."[50] Although Biograph pulled off the switch, the fact that cameras could still fail signaled again the risks of such projects. The completed *Jeffries-Sharkey Contest* proved a huge hit, but the brush with disaster inhibited coverage of some later prizefights. American Mutoscope & Biograph chose not to film bouts on location again, preferring to shoot fight reproductions in its Manhattan studio.

EDISON'S LAST FIGHT PICTURE:
JEFFRIES AND RUHLIN SPARRING CONTEST

Between 1900 and 1904, when he prematurely announced his retirement, Jeffries defended his crown annually. Cameras recorded only one of these defenses. Jeffries' flagging popularity was less to blame than circumstantial difficulties within the motion-picture industry and the ring syndicate.

The success of touring Biograph units in 1899 and 1900 afforded the champ some easy money—one-third of the picture profits—and respite from competition and training. Jeffries did theatrical work, but he had neither the talent nor the yen for stage performance, preferring simple sparring demonstrations. After his November defense, papers speculated that he would "take a long rest—possibly a year—to give the pictures a chance." Brady soon signed his man to a fight against Corbett, but stipulated "We want to give the pictures of the Jeffries-Sharkey fight a chance to be shown."[51]

The run of *Jeffries-Sharkey Contest* was extraordinarily successful for its time, but in March 1900 Biograph began distributing the feature film in ancillary markets. Brady and O'Rourke sold territorial rights (aimed at "managers of summer resorts and parks") for "nickel-in-the-slot" muto-scope scenes of the fight (see figure 25).[52]

Also in March, New York repealed its 1896 Horton law. Led by the political boss "Big Tim" Sullivan, Tammanyites had legalized prizefighting, but then the corruption of "the pugilism syndicate" too obviously controlled the sport and gambling activities related to it. A new ban on prize-fights began on August 31, 1900.[53] To beat this deadline, several major heavyweight matches were lined up in the spring and summer, including the last of the important Coney Island club fights: Jeffries versus Corbett, on May 11.

As that contest approached, motion pictures of the champion regained topical value. Vitagraph began selling a new series: the "only authentic pictures of James J. Jeffries" in his training camp. The only other genuine prizefight picture available was the *McGovern-Dixon Championship Fight*, but its release was delayed for three months.[54] The Lubin Company intensified its making of re-creations, issuing eight "Reproductions of" fight pictures in the six months between Jeffries title fights.

Any high-quality recording of a good prizefight between notable figures promised substantial profits. But by 1900 cinematographers had a dubious ring record. Commitments for picture exploitation wavered. The contract between Fitzsimmons and Sharkey signed in March, for example, stated that

Figure 25. Mutoscope card from *Jeffries-Sharkey Contest* (1899). All that survive from the feature-length motion picture are a few cards from the mutoscope version. The original was shot on 68 mm film stock. (Library of Congress, Motion Picture, Broadcasting and Recorded Sound Division.)

the winner would divide any film receipts with "the company taking the pictures . . . *if* it can be arranged to have pictures of the fight taken."[55] Jeffries-Corbett, an exciting contest (in which Corbett outboxed his heftier opponent until he was suddenly knocked out in the twenty-third), went unfilmed.

On November 15, 1901, Edison cameras took a stab at the fight-picture challenge, shooting the title bout between Jim Jeffries and Gus Ruhlin. Like its predecessors, the enterprise suffered a troubled production and distribution history.

San Francisco, and particularly its Mechanics' Pavilion, had become a mecca for the sport and would be the site of all of Jeffries' remaining defenses.[56] With the picture manufacturers based mainly in the East, San Francisco bouts lacked proximity to filmmaking facilities. But by 1901 that issue had become moot. Legal maneuvers by motion-picture companies took a sharp turn that reduced production everywhere. A court held that Thomas Edison's claims to key camera patents were justified, giving him (temporarily) a near monopoly on U.S. picture production. The boxing film market came almost to a standstill when Siegmund Lubin fled to Europe to escape legal troubles.

As Musser documents, the Edison Manufacturing Company did not rush into new production. In November, its recently built New York film studio sat idle because resources were diverted to recording the Jeffries-Ruhlin fight. James White, of the Edison-licensed Kinetoscope Company, directed a dozen electricians in the installation of eighty arc lights and navy search lamps (used as follow spots on the boxers) to illuminate the pavilion ring. "The fierce heat which was experienced in fights at New York was removed," said the *Gazette*, by leaving open the top of the lighting rig. As White filmed the event, Ruhlin and Jeffries fought beneath a banner proclaiming "Moving Pictures Made by the Edison Manufacturing Co., Orange, N.J."[57]

"The machinery for taking the moving pictures attracted much attention. It is new here," San Francisco's *Examiner* said. The budding local writer Jack London took note of the technology's encroaching presence, describing the motion-picture apparatus as changing the face of a primitive ritual in a modern age. Witnessing Jeffries and Ruhlin from press row and under the bright movie lights, he wrote: "It was a picturesque scene, this twentieth-century arena, this machine-age gladiatorial contest. The house in darkness and the ring a white blaze of light; the tick-tick of the telegraph keys, the monotonous dictation of the stenographers . . . and under the clustered arc lamps, in the blinding glare, the two battling elemental males, and around all the sea of faces . . . a vast crowd [was] eager to see two men beat and batter each other into pulp."[58]

What the crowd saw and the cameras recorded, however, observers declared disappointing "from a spectator's point of view." After five rounds of uneventful punching, Ruhlin's corner threw in the towel, eliciting cries of "Fake!" from several thousand fans.[59] Once again a fight-film project had gone sour. The cross-continental trek yielded White and Edison only footage of a brief, slow-footed ring performance.

Further damaging the profit potential of the *Jeffries and Ruhlin Sparring Contest* was its substandard cinematography. The *Examiner* obligingly printed the company line: "Messrs. White and [J. F.] Byrne, after examining the films last night, said that they believed a fine set of pictures had been

Figure 26. Frame from Edison's *Jeffries and Ruhlin Sparring Contest at San Francisco, Cal., November 15, 1901—Five Rounds.* (Library of Congress, Motion Picture, Broadcasting and Recorded Sound Division.)

obtained."[60] In truth, the negatives had not yet been developed. A surviving copy indicates that the pictures were less than fine. Poor contrast, jump cuts, and a clouded finish in the paper-print version at the Library of Congress may or may not have been present in the original, but the off-center framing and extremely long camera distance certainly were. Unlike the sharp images in Biograph's *Jeffries-Sharkey Contest,* the figures in White's *Jeffries and Ruhlin* are barely identifiable. The images are not much better than those in the shadowy pirate version of *Jeffries-Sharkey* that White helped shoot in 1899, confirming his reputation as a second-rate cameraman (see figure 26).[61]

Although the technical expenses incurred in shooting this fight ($457) were much lower than for past setups, return on the investment was not great. Its mid-length running time (about twenty minutes) precluded both of the usual forms of exhibition. *Jeffries and Ruhlin Sparring Contest,* White later testified, was "not long enough . . . to form a complete exhibition, and therefore had to be put in vaudeville as a short act."[62] White sold only one print of the film while in California. His Kinetoscope Company's exhibition service ran the pictures for two weeks in December at a Manhattan theater, along with scenes of Ruhlin and Jeffries in training. But the film otherwise received few headline showings.

The Edison catalog soon offered single rounds of *Jeffries and Ruhlin*. Rather than restrict sales within territories, it sold the subject freely and by the foot, just as thousands of other films were sold. This approach required reframing the fight picture for a general audience. Catalogs softened the hard-hitting rhetoric used for marketing a whole fight picture to sporting men and represented it as a "sparring contest" of interest to all. "Once in the ring the opposing factions showed the best of good nature," the sales blurb reassured readers. "Jeffries and Ruhlin shook hands pleasantly." The accompanying *Jeffries-Ruhlin Training* series even billed as "a little piece of comedy."[63] With prizefighting approaching the nadir of its legitimacy, a heavyweight championship fight picture was relegated to the status of an interesting topical view rather than a special event. Nevertheless the screen presence of the heavyweight champion gave even this tame motion picture some drawing power. Both Edison and the Kleine Optical Company (an important early distributor) sold the Jeffries and Ruhlin pictures for several years. On occasion the entire fight was revived in variety settings. The New Orleans Trocadero Theatre, for example, billed the *Jeffries-Ruhlin Prize Fight* in tandem with Edison's *Great Spanish Bull Fight* (1901) for a week in February 1903. Trocadero also soft-pedaled the violence, calling the exhibition "a refined entertainment for ladies, gentlemen and children."[64]

Continuing production troubles, coupled with a decline in the popularity of prizefighting, precipitated a crisis in 1902. No film manufacturers traveled to San Francisco to record the rematch between Jim Jeffries and Bob Fitzsimmons that July (although some bid for the option).[65] Patent litigation, piracy, and a lack of exhibition outlets curtailed American film production across the board. What profit motive still existed for pursuing elusive fight-picture jackpots was all but cut off by the demands of the high-stakes showmen who controlled boxing. The ban on prizefighting in New York had been blamed on the pugilism syndicate's avarice and insistence on "manipulating the game to their advantage."[66] In San Francisco, similar forces made picture producers' efforts unrewarding. The articles of agreement signed for the 1902 Jeffries-Fitzsimmons contest provided terms for a possible "contract between the contestants, the club, and any parties which may take the moving pictures." But the ring syndicate insisted on retaining all potential movie profits.[67] Despite the degree of skill needed to secure ringside pictures, camera operators were treated as hired hands. None accepted such terms, even for a world championship.

After disposing of the forty-year-old Fitz in eight rounds, Jeffries defeated Jim Corbett in similar fashion on August 14, 1903, when they too met in a rematch in San Francisco. Despite a crowd of ten thousand, no film was made at Mechanics' Pavilion of Gentleman Jim, in his final ring appearance, being pummeled for ten rounds. On August 26, 1904, Jeffries' final title defense against an obscure Montana miner received still less publicity. The ignominious mismatch against Jack Munroe ended in two rounds. Having twice disposed of most of the nineteenth-century heavyweight legends, Jeffries retired to his California ranch in May 1905.[68]

The final years of the Jeffries reign saw fight-picture production all but cease. In 1902, no prizefights were filmed. Lubin, just returned from his exile, produced only a single reenactment, *Jeffries-Fitzsimmons Reproduction Prize Fight Films*. In 1903, only one authentic recording was made, Selig Polyscope's *Light Heavyweight Championship Contest between Root and Gardner*. By 1904, production had reached a standstill. Neither authentic nor fake fight films were produced anywhere.[69]

Professional boxing and commercial cinema reached a simultaneous nadir. The fight game declined for several reasons: legislative reforms, the disrepute of fakery and fixes, and the fading celebrity of aging heavyweight stars. The decline in fight pictures was inseparable from the entire American film industry's "period of commercial crisis" (as Musser labels the years 1900 to1903). Legal entanglements, unregulated copying of prints, and other problems affected many fight pictures in particular. The displacement of fight pictures, however, was only a small part of the sea change in cinema. As American filmmaking revived after 1903, producers emphasized constructed narratives over actualities. Nonfiction works such as the *Corbett-Fitzsimmons Fight* and *Jeffries-Sharkey Contest* were remarkably popular, but attempts to replicate their success failed because of vagaries in technical or athletic performance. No motion-picture enterprise could sustain itself on fight pictures alone. Lubin was the sole company to capitalize regularly on boxing subjects. Its production method—staged direction of performers on a set—became standard procedure in the mass manufacture of narrative films after 1903.

FIGHT-PICTURE OPTIONS, CIRCA 1900

Motion pictures of a heavyweight championship tilt served as the ultimate commodity, but alternatives existed to these promoter-controlled enterprises. A 1903 catalog from Selig Polyscope, under the heading "Prize

Fights," articulated the models under which such films were conceptualized. Promoting its *Gans-McGovern Fight* (1900), Selig's copy began: "With the exception of this film there are absolutely no genuine moving picture films representing genuine prize fights on the market. The prize fight films, so-called, are either taken by the fight promoters and retained by them for exhibition, not on sale and cannot be procured, or else they are the boldest fake reproductions put up the day following the fight."[70] These were the three options for rationalizing production. The "boldest" was that of the organizer of timely reproductions: a company [that is, Lubin] could plan and control its representations, then release its product according to a set schedule.

Recordings made by boxing promoters constituted a second model, in which independent entrepreneurs controlled individual films. As demonstrated by the Corbett-Fitzsimmons and Jeffries-Sharkey pictures, groups with no stake in moving pictures per se could incorporate for the purposes of exploiting a single property. Such operations hired a cinematographer, took ownership of the negatives, and handled their own advertising, publicity, distribution, exhibition, legal work, and bookkeeping. For self-promoting businessmen like Dan Stuart, William Brady, Martin Julian, Sam Harris, and Thomas O'Rourke, arranging for and exploiting a single motion picture was little different from promoting a fight, a horse race, or a theatrical tour. These fight-picture entrepreneurs—all of whom were also theater managers and showmen—resembled the U.S. movie industry's second generation of exhibitors turned producers, such as William Fox, the Warner brothers, Adolph Zukor, and Marcus Loew rather than the first inventor-producers (such as Edison and Lubin). Film manufacturers were glad to leave the financial risks to such gamblers, although they gained little more than some brand-name publicity when ring sponsors demanded most of the picture profits. If owners of cameras and projectors were to stay in business, another mode of production was necessary.

Selig presented this third option. By filming matches of lesser renown, the Chicago-based company retained autonomy over sales and profits without confining itself to staged reproductions. Such arrangements allowed a stable production firm to make an occasional foray into prizefight actualities, diversifying its catalog without disrupting its output. Although Selig Polyscope filmed only a few bouts (*McGovern-Gans*, 1900; *Root-Gardner*, 1903; *Nelson-Gans Fight Pictures*, 1908), its "profitable sideline" example was adopted by Miles Brothers of San Francisco, which dominated fight-picture production in the nickelodeon era of 1905 through 1912.

The protean movie business used all of these strategies in negotiating fight pictures. On the heels of the Brady and O'Rourke presentation of the 1899 *Jeffries-Sharkey Contest,* other independent ventures followed. The most immediate was a second production showcasing Terry McGovern. Although plans for the one-minute McGovern-Palmer film had gone awry, the undefeated "Brooklyn Terror" remained the most watched of the lesser-weight pugilists and the most popular boxing celebrity in New York. His manager, Sam H. Harris, proved to be one of the most gifted producer-promoters in American popular culture.[71] Harris created a partnership with Thomas O'Rourke, head of the Lenox Athletic Club, who managed the veteran champion George Dixon as well as Tom Sharkey. The two contracted with the Broadway Athletic Club in Manhattan to have lights and cameras installed for McGovern's fight against Dixon for the featherweight championship. On the night of January 9, 1900, Biograph's feat was duplicated: cinematographers captured McGovern's eight-round bout on film.

Few details about the filming of the McGovern-Dixon fight were reported. The identity of the crew is unknown. That the films were sold broadly indicates that 35 mm equipment was used (as opposed to Biograph's), but advertisements mentioned no brand name. With O'Rourke and Harris acting as "the sole managers and proprietors," the McGovern-Dixon film defined the category of "independent" production better than any other of its era. A new company was not incorporated (as with Veriscope or American Sportagraph). The entrepreneurs merely advertised prints for sale and handled orders from their room in a Manhattan hotel.[72]

Working outside the established film-handling process created problems. Technical difficulties evidently arose during the development of negatives and prints. Announcements of the films did not appear until a month after the bout, when O'Rourke and Harris solicited bids for territorial rights to exploit pictures that would "be ready in two weeks." (Lubin's *Reproduction of the McGovern-Dixon Fight,* of course, was released the week after the actual contest.) To keep interest alive, the boxers staged a live exhibition in New York on February 21. Belatedly the film was shown as a special feature at scattered theaters, such as the Buckingham in Louisville, in late March. The only *Clipper* ad for "the genuine pictures of the McGovern-Dixon Championship Fight" appeared on April 7. The three-month marketing delay necessitated a rethinking of exhibition strategy. Instead of a theatrical tour, O'Rourke and Harris suggested that "these pictures can be engaged as a Special Feature for Parks, Summer Resorts, and to Strengthen Road Companies." Interest was low, however, in the amusement trade. The usual *Police Gazette* endorsement never came, and by June the promoters were forced to pair their fighters against one another for the third time in six months—this time without cameras.[73]

The abandonment of the independent use of motion pictures by boxing promoters was complete by the end of the year, as evidenced by two other projects. The first, the Fitzsimmons-Ruhlin fight, was held in Madison Square Garden on August 10, 1900, just before the New York ban on prize-fights took effect. For the first time, motion-picture equipment was installed inside the famous facility, which had become "consecrated as the home of prize fighting."[74] That the *Police Gazette* made only passing reference to the "blazing" electric lights implies that such setups had become routine, as fight films now had a regular theatrical clientele: "At one end of the building a picture machine had been erected and it was generally understood that an attempt was to be made to reproduce the fight for the benefit of the out-of-town contingent who like to look at noiseless, shadowy battles from a theatre seat." The "man with a red shirt and panama hat" who operated the camera for the fight promoters remained anonymous—and disappointed his contractors. Although the leading vaudeville agent, William Morris, and major exhibitors such as Oscar Hammerstein booked the *Fitzsimmons and Ruhlin Fight Pictures* for several weeks in August and September, the fight in the Garden was not what their pictures showed. Instead, the supposedly authentic film was actually taken by Lubin. The difference with this "re-production," however, was that the original participants traveled to Philadelphia immediately after the bout and reenacted their six-round contest themselves. The screen presence of the real Fitzsimmons and Ruhlin allowed Lubin's fake to pass as legitimate.[75]

The other fight picture that signaled an end to extraindustrial production was another recording of a Terry McGovern title fight. To capture the McGovern-Gans fight in December 1900, Harris turned to the recently incorporated Selig Polyscope Company. Harris's coproducer, Lou Houseman, added to the list of men in the sporting and theatrical fraternity responsible for integrating fight and film interests. Houseman worked for Chicago newspapers while also managing boxers. His fighter, Joe Gans, was a formidable challenger and would later costar in some of the most popular prizefight films of the nickelodeon era.[76]

In the match against McGovern, the evidence suggests that Gans, like many other black boxers at the time, was ordered to take a dive. In front of movie cameras and seventeen thousand fans at Tattersall's arena in Chicago, the challenger offered little resistance to McGovern's attack. The surviving film shows that in the second round, Gans went to the canvas six times, apparently without being decisively struck. Did McGovern even throw a

Figure 27.   Poster supplements to the *Police Gazette*. Left, Terry McGovern, the bantamweight champion of 1899, made into a celebrity by showman Sam H. Harris (October 22, 1898); right, Joe Gans, lightweight champion, 1902–8 (September 3, 1898). (Library of Congress, Prints and Photographs Division.)

punch when Gans was supposedly knocked out? Spectators and journalists labeled the contest a fake. The mayor and aldermen immediately reinforced a longstanding ban on prizefighting in the city, which had been attempting to move into the boxing market left open by the New York ban.[77]

The controversy gave the *McGovern-Gans Fight* publicity that resulted in greater sales and wider exhibition than the previous McGovern films. Selig technicians succeeded where others had failed, using "600 arc lights and four enormous electric reflectors" to light up the arena. The brevity of the event left Selig with motion pictures that, even with "all the preliminaries," ran only six hundred feet in length (no more than ten minutes).[78] The catalog omitted mention of the bout's disrepute, emphasizing instead its authenticity and action. "This is not only a genuine picture taken while the fight was in actual progress, but the only picture of the kind which can be procured. . . . All of our patrons do not approve of prize fights, but all must admit that no subject shows such wonderful spirit, motion, life and action as a genuine prize fight, and the enormous popularity which these films have enjoyed justifies our patrons in investing in a set of them."[79]

Press discussion, however, centered on the fix. Houseman, the individual most deeply implicated in the fraud, argued that his investment in the films proved that he did not order a setup. "Those fight pictures," he said in the *Police Gazette*, "will show a great deal and go a long way toward proving that the fight wasn't a fake. Just consider it would have been worth $50,000 to me to have the fight go the limit for the sake of the pictures alone. If there was a fake, why couldn't they have faked longer and gone long enough to make the pictures good?"[80] In subsequent *Gazette* stories, the referee, George Siler, and former Gans opponents agreed with Sam Austin that "the pictures have failed to clear up the mystery of Gans' poor showing." Yet, Austin said, "when the pictures are circulated about the country many persons who did not see the fight will have an opportunity to pass upon it."[81]

Despite Austin's speculation, the film's audience was restricted primarily to those who took a specific interest in prizefighting. The lone *Clipper* ad placed by Houseman and Harris targeted "Burlesque and Vaudeville Managers" who wanted to strengthen their bill with a turn that was "just the length of a fifteen minute act." Some sales were made to touring vaudeville companies. But the emphasis on burlesque was a telling signal that the fight picture, especially one like *McGovern-Gans* that showed the seamiest side of the sport, had moved from the opera-house venue that encouraged female patronage to the homosocial world of theatrical amusement.

By 1900 the term *burlesque,* which had once connoted broad-based light entertainment, signified risqué shows for men. Some burlesque houses, such as Hurtig and Seamon's Music Hall in Chicago, which did good business with the debut of the Selig film, played to audiences of mixed gender. But the entertainment was clearly aimed at male patrons. The Hurtig and Seamon's show used the *McGovern-Gans Fight Pictures* as an "extra attraction" to enhance its troupe of "beautiful women," the Bowery Burlesquers. They performed sketches with such suggestive titles as "The Sheik Slave." The phrase "Smoking Permitted" in advertisements made it clear that the house's reserved seating and free refreshments were intended for sporting gentlemen. That all of this activity took place across the street from the Chicago City Hall, which had banned fights because of the Gans scandal, was an irony that spoke to the social contradictions inherent in the fight picture phenomenon.[82]

The association between ring promoters and film manufacturers continued into the early 1900s, and the presence of cameras significantly affected the sport. Sometimes cinematographic intrusion directly altered athletes' performances, as when Jeffries and Sharkey had to suffer the heat of arc lights and also secretly restage their final round for cameras. Organizers had to ensure that the details of mounting a major prizefight jibed with the needs of film crews. With huge profit potential in motion-picture replays, the pugilistic syndicate cooperatively arranged locations, times, and durations of fights to accommodate cinematography. Star boxers also changed their show-business and promotional schedules in accord with film exhibition. Boxing insiders saw that fight films broadened the presence and accessibility of their sport, expanding and legitimizing their trade. Motion pictures also sanitized prizefighting's image, replaying the combat without the sight of blood, the smell of sweat, or the sound of punches.

In moving from short, staged sparring pictures to location shoots, however, filmmakers encountered frustrations. Both boxers and cameras gave unpredictable performances, resulting in bottom lines that ranged from thousands of dollars in losses to six-digit profits. Still, the pursuit of big payoffs kept the major film manufacturers involved in fight-film productions for some years. By 1900, however, these were only sidelines. The motion-picture business was seeking stability and autonomy even as the ring enterprise was looking to keep picture profits to itself.

The often-lackluster fight films of the Jeffries and McGovern era never fell to the level of "chaser" (a vaudeville term for acts appearing at the end of a bill, supposedly boring enough to chase audiences out of the theater). They could be counted on to outdraw most other individual films, but their moments of success proved too unreliable for motion-picture manufacturers to build an industry on them. The only company that consistently profited from the fight game was Lubin, with its regular reenactments. That model of controlled production worked against the filming of authentic prizefights. However, the Lubin method comported with the successful practices of the American film industry as it entered into the mass production of story films. These two aspects of fight-picture history—the art of the fake and the place of genuine fight films in the nickelodeon era—are taken up in the next two chapters.

4   Fake Fight Films
S. Lubin of Philadelphia, 1897–1908

> It is instructive to observe that in this beautiful city whenever two
> prize-fighters dare to fight they are "pulled," while out in the great
> untrammeled West whenever the fighters in the "fake" scopes fail
> to fight the scopists are scooped.
>
> *New York Dramatic Mirror*, June 26, 1897

In *The Great Cat Massacre*, the historian Robert Darnton writes: "We constantly need to be shaken out of a false sense of familiarity with the past, to
be administered doses of culture shock." The best way to accomplish this,
he says, is "to wander through the archives." "When we cannot get a
proverb, or a joke, or a ritual, or a poem," he continues, "we know we are on
to something. By picking at the document where it is most opaque, we may
be able to unravel an alien system of meaning." Darnton unravels an enig-
matic anecdote about Parisians slaughtering house cats to understand life
under France's Old Regime.[1]

Similarly, the surviving film fragments of fight reenactments and commentary on them (including the epigraph) are an opaque, alien system of
meaning. Understanding the idiomatic genre of fake fight films requires an
examination of its production practices, exhibition contexts, and reception
tendencies. As with the earliest boxing pictures and the *Corbett-Fitzsimmons
Fight*, distinctions between genuine and imitation are not easily drawn.
Reenactments were often accepted, while deceptive fakes received criticism.
By considering how the art of the fake was used and abused by boxers and
filmmakers, we can unravel what the genre meant to its contemporaries.

Prizefight reenactments constituted a significant portion of early boxing
films. Between 1897 and 1910, the number of reproductions exceeded the
number of films shot at ringside. American companies manufactured at least
thirty-two re-creations during this period (and none thereafter), while
shooting about thirty prizefights on location (although British imports
added to that number). Until 1906, fakes outnumbered actualities in every
year. From 1897 to 1904, they predominated by nearly three to one (twenty-
three reproductions, compared to only nine authentic films). Doubtless the
number of faked films would have been greater had Siegmund Lubin not

been forced out of production during the 1901–2 season. His method of fight reproduction peaked at a half dozen per year in the 1899–1900 season. Works such as *Reproduction of the Fitzsimmons-Jeffries Fight* (1899) and *Reproduction of the Jeffries and Corbett Fight* (1900) sometimes stood out among the thousands of brief motion pictures made at the time. Reenactments of heavyweight title bouts received prominent advertisement. Their longer running times also made these films objects of special presentation. S. Lubin, as both the producer and his company were known, was the genre's chief practitioner.

THE TRADITION OF THE FAKE

The fake fight films that sprang up after the Corbett-Fitzsimmons bout had antecedents in cinema, theater, photography, and print. American popular culture before the invention of cinema was distinguished by a fascination with hoaxes, trickery, deception, hoopla, dodges, and flimflams. The nineteenth-century art of "humbug"—putting on a slightly (though not entirely) deceptive exhibition for a curious, paying audience—did not meet with particular condemnation. The era's best known purveyor of amusements, P. T. Barnum, demonstrated that calculated, good-natured imposture could be incorporated into entertainment. The fact that Barnum's claims about his curios—such George Washington's 160-year-old nurse or the Fiji mermaid—were exposed as untrue did not lessen their popularity. As Neil Harris put it: "American audiences did not mind cries of trickery, in fact, they delighted in debate" about it. Many attractions proved that "amusement and deceit could coexist." That spectators came to commercial entertainment with "expectations of exaggeration or masquerade" explains the acceptance of Lubin's motion-picture fakes. As Jane Gaines argues, the "tradition of hucksterism" infected much of early cinema exploitation.[2] Lubin's trade-paper puffery and palpably cheap fight pictures played on this show tradition.

Prizefighting in America had long had a reputation for performances of ambiguous authenticity. Compounding this was the suspect manner in which the press represented bouts to the public. Not only did spectators cry "fake" when they suspected results had been prearranged to satisfy gambling interests, but the public also read the sensational tabloid coverage of these events. Even before the dawn of yellow journalism, the dubious nature of this tradition had been established. In 1863, for example, Samuel L. Clemens satirized prizefighting and its press. In "The Only True and Reliable Account of the Great Prize Fight," Clemens added a postscript "revealing" his story was a hoax. "I had been swindled," he said, "with a detailed account of a fight which had never occurred. . . . I wrote it out (as other reporters have done before me) in language calculated to deceive the public into the conclusion that I was present at it myself, and to embellish it with a string of falsehoods intended to render that deception as plausible as possible."[3] In this context, the selling of crudely reenacted fight pictures was almost conventional.

EXTRACINEMATIC ANTECEDENTS OF COUNTERFEIT PRESENTMENTS

Fake fight films met with a mixed reaction because they derived from conflicting practices: accepted forms of re-presentation that predated motion pictures, and misrepresentations contrived to deceive. Examples of the first type were the living pictures, dramatizations, and recitations used to present historical or newsworthy events in theaters. To illustrate noted fights, boxers offered sparring performances in imitation of a bout. The original contestants would often walk through their rounds again on stage.

Other acceptable reportage relied on illustrations. Although photography was commonplace decades before cinema, newspapers did not publish action photos of boxing bouts until well after the institutionalization of fight films. During the transition from artist renderings to photojournalism, various forms of illustration coexisted. From the 1850s to the early 1900s, illustrators produced engravings and lithographs based on photographs. After 1890, halftone and rotogravure processes enabled photographs to be reprinted en masse. However, only the illustrated weeklies regularly published photos. Poor image quality on newsprint prevented dailies from converting to photographic illustration until after 1900.[4]

In the interim, the press created hybrids. The commercial rivalry between the Hearst and Pulitzer news organizations began to peak in 1897, leading to the splashy use of images, fabricated interviews, and "composite" photos.[5] Hearst's flagship, trying to scoop others with fight news, implemented new forms of illustration with each major fight. The *San Francisco Examiner*, which still relied on line drawings in 1897, published several images derived from veriscope frames. News artists played on the vogue for illustrative series inspired by the veriscope, providing such images as "Kinetoscopic Glimpses of the Hawkins-Dixon Glove Contest" (a bout that was not filmed). For the Jeffries-Sharkey contest in 1899, the paper set up a photo session to illustrate the match. The morning after, the *Examiner* provided "life-like camera representations of the most effective blows." As telegraphed descriptions came in from Coney Island, two California boxers struck studio poses for "flashlight" photographs.[6] The system mirrored Lubin's. Dailies added posed photographs, but not until 1902 did Hearst introduce "action photos." And only with the 1903 Jeffries-Corbett rematch did the *Examiner* lay claim to a "first-time accomplishment in modern journalism" by printing "Flashlights Taken at Ringside"—six years after Corbett-Fitzsimmons had been recorded in motion pictures.[7]

In other ways, motion pictures pushed ahead of press coverage. Although the *Police Gazette* published studio photographs of boxers, at the turn of the century it still relied on stylized lithographs and woodcuts to illustrate action sequences. But the moving-picture industry's ties to boxing provided the *Gazette* with occasional photodocumentation. Biograph stills from its *Jeffries-Sharkey Contest* appeared in 1899, and copyrighted Lubin frames from the Ruhlin-Fitzsimmons reenactment were published in 1900.[8] Other periodicals also ran such images.

The concept of motion pictures "in counterpart," therefore, was hardly alien. Fight pictures contributed to the notion of early cinema as an illustrated newspaper. Nonfiction subjects predominated, and images of the Spanish-American conflict of 1898 raised flagging interest in motion pictures. Other sensational events—the assassination of President William McKinley, the Boer War, the Galveston flood—received moving picture coverage. Like the print press, the "visual newspaper" of cinema mixed authentic pictures and staged reenactments with little discrimination. As Miriam Hansen argues, complaints about "fake pictures" were not directed at reconstructions per se. "Fakes" could include works of inferior photographic or dramatic qualities.[9] By contrast, other forms of imitation developed pejorative reputations. Dishonorable precedents existed for film reproductions as well. Reception of fakery varied depending on quality, circumstances, and degree of deception. Fakers who defrauded audiences (but lacked Barnum's savvy) met condemnation.

Attacks on film fakery occurred at the beginning and the end of the era of fight reproduction. In January 1895 the *Dramatic Mirror* linked motion pictures to prior forms of fakery. In "An Invention Disgraced," the journal warned: "Rumors of reprehensible exhibitions in the invention called the kinetoscope are already abroad," as were "complaints of a brutal misrepresentation that affects the theatrical profession." A "pretended reproduction" of the late actor John Edward McCullough was circulating in phonograph-kinetoscope parlors. The popular McCullough had spent most of his last months in an insane asylum, a fact exploited by an anonymous "phonographer" who sold bogus recordings of the thespian's mad recita-tions.[10] Two years later, the *San Francisco Examiner* saw the incident as a forerunner of fight reproductions. When Lubin's sham *Corbett-Fitzsimmons* appeared, the paper observed: "The idea of having a counterfeit presentment of the great Carson battle is not as thoroughly original as would appear at first blush. This because it is well known that for years past professional mimics have been furnishing phonograph manufacturers with all kinds of voice products, from the ravings of John McCullough to the Bowery songs of Maggie Cline. And if ears are to be deceived why not eyes?"[11]

As late as 1908 (the year Lubin made his final fight reproduction), one photography journal blamed the "degradation of the motion-picture" on fake films that were a "misrepresentation of life." *Photo-Era* wanted to ban "another class of fake-pictures." Referring to those "artistically-simulated scenes which are so near real life that they can be distinguished only by the expert," it complained of a depiction of the Russo-Japanese War that was a "joined film—the first part real, the second part faked, and the artfulness of it comes from the fact that the general public cannot say where the real leaves off and the fake commences."[12] Reenactment itself was not objec-tionable. Only artful dodgers were attacked.

The amusement trade recognized that competition generated such scams. As the *Dramatic Mirror* put it, "the commercial spirit that seized upon the products of an ingenuity like that of Edison stops at nothing." The fake film phenomenon was part of early cinema's many unregulated practices.

Fake fight films pitched as the real thing contributed to early commer-cial cinema's shady reputation. Motion pictures came with "caveat emptor" warnings. Weber and Field's 1897 satire of the Lobsterscope not only pointed up the plague of defective "graphs and scopes" but also suggested picture patrons might be "lobsters"—that is, easily duped victims. Two incidents involving Lubin's debut film, *Reproduction of the Corbett and Fitzsimmons Fight*, illustrate the industry's complacency toward fakes. When customers of the " 'fake' veriscope" in a Chicago storefront com-plained of the film's duplicity, the exhibitor informed them that they were "lobsters" who had gotten their ten-cent look at the "facsimile."[13] Arthur Hotaling ran a Lubin concession in 1897. When the manager of the venue failed to pay him, Hotaling threatened to turn the aura of fakery that sur-rounded such exhibitions against him.

> I told the manager that, as a sort of farewell offering, we would let him
> have a print of the reproduction of the Corbett-Fitzsimmons fight free
> of extra cost for one night. I even threw in several dollars' worth of
> paper to post the boards, and about the whole town packed onto the

pier. It came time for the show. . . . The manager urged me to hurry in [with the film print], but I waited until the audience got good and impatient and some had begun to cry fake. When they were all wrought up I showed him the bad checks and demanded that they be made good before I took the film to the booth.[14]

Such a carnival atmosphere pervaded many early moving-picture shows. Crowds assembled at the barker's call, but they were suspicious, even when they accepted the license of reproductions.

Over their decade of sporadic existence, fight reproductions met increasing resistance. Attempts to deceive fans harmed the presenters' reputation, and, as camera technology improved, routine filming from ringside displaced reenactments. Yet for several years, these impersonations had a niche in the motion-picture market. Lubin's distinctive production, exhibition, and exploitation strategies merit special attention. The company's tactics were simultaneously primitive and innovative, borrowing from nineteenth-century traditions while also emphasizing a studio-controlled economy of production. Lubin's fake fight pictures pushed the limits of cinematic exploitation as aggressively as any early film product.

LUBIN'S "REPRODUCTIONS"

The Lubin company staked out the fake-fight genre as its own. Like many others, Siegmund Lubin sold his own line of Corbett-Fitzsimmons products in the 1897–98 season. His clumsy counterpart pictures were a sideshow to those of the grand Veriscope, but Lubin developed a reputation as a specialist in "reproductions" of topical events. Nearly two years passed before Lubin followed up and improved on his boxing debut. In November 1898, his success enabled him to dominate the fight-picture market for the full year leading up to Biograph's spectacular *Jeffries-Sharkey* hit. Beginning with the *Corbett and Sharkey Fight* (1898) and continuing with reenactments of the Sharkey-McCoy, Fitzsimmons-Jeffries and McGovern-Palmer bouts, Lubin honed his system of production, copyright, and exploitation. From 1897 to 1908, his company shot reenactments of more than two dozen topical bouts.

A German immigrant to the United States, Siegmund Lubin had earned a degree from the University of Heidelberg. In 1882, Lubin established an optician's shop in Philadelphia. He added stereopticon slides to his line and by 1894 had expanded into photographic interests. Eadweard Muybridge (at the University of Pennsylvania), inventor C. Francis Jenkins, and vitascope exhibitor William T. Rock introduced him to motion pictures. In 1896, working with Jenkins, Lubin built a high-quality camera and projector. Ads for his "cineograph" appeared weekly beginning in January 1897. Of the many films Lubin sold during his first two years, only one had boxing as its subject. Nevertheless, biographers characterize him as making "his first fortune from recreated fight films" and as a boxing fan who "was at the ringside at every important contest."[15]

Secondary sources also mischaracterize Lubin as a cut-rate entrepreneur whose modus operandi was piracy (that is, duplicating prints of some works produced by rivals and remaking others shot for shot) and shooting reenactments of real events. But such practices were the norm by the time Lubin entered motion pictures. To single him out, or to reduce him to a peddler of secondhand goods, verges on anti-Semitic stereotyping. In fact, Lubin's company produced many types of original films of excellent photographic quality and became an industrial leader within a decade.[16] Even the "S. Lubin" trade advertisements of the 1890s reveal its business practices as creative, not simply aggressive or derivative.

The Lubin motion picture "in imitation of Corbett and Fitzsimmons" was typical of neither previous boxing films nor the company's later work. From 1894 through 1897, boxing films featured named pugilists reconstructing a recent match or mixing it up for the camera. By using a pair of "ringers," Lubin initiated a cheaper, quicker method of exploiting the notoriety of prizefighting, one which slipstreamed behind its promoters' hype but was not obligated to its stars. Still in an experimental stage, Lubin shot brief subjects in his backyard. In the fourteen rounds of the Corbett-Fitzsimmons facsimile, actors gestured on a small platform with a white sheet for backdrop.[17]

Lubin did not shy from circulating this obvious fake. Preceding the Veriscope debut, he spurred sales by confusing buyers about its authenticity. Ads mentioned the "fac simile" nature of the films but proclaimed the legitimacy of copyright. Adding to the smokescreen, the film service provided its buyers with posters and photographs showing the actual Carson City arena. Further confusing the issue, the trade review of the Veriscope premiere was headlined "The Championship Fight Reproduced" and mentioned Lubin's films alongside Stuart's "reproduction." Perhaps in deference to a buyer of much advertising space, the *New York Clipper* reported in a non sequitur: "We have received from S. Lubin, manufacturing optician, of Philadelphia, Pennsylvania, the manufacturer of the cineograph, three excellent photographic views of the ring at Carson City, Nevada. . . . Snapshots taken in the inclosure . . . show the principals, attendants and spectators."[18]

Lubin's backyard burlesque paled when the authentic *Corbett-Fitzsimmons Fight* gained circulation in the theatrical season. The company suspended fight-picture promotion and emphasized sales of its optically superior cineograph and the diversity of its catalog. Nearly all manufacturers duplicated competitors' prints, but Lubin himself brazenly advertised his copying of Edison, Lumière, and Méliès films. When others cautioned buyers against frauds and "trick artists," their ads were directed against "S. Lubin."[19]

FAKING PASSION PLAYS, WAR FILMS, AND PRIZEFIGHTS

Cagily playing his reputation for imitation against more legitimate subject matter, Lubin shifted emphasis in 1898. The year's vogue for passion plays and war films began in February. Both genres contributed to a confusion in reception as new forms of representation and re-representation developed during this historical transition into "the age of mechanical reproduction." Like other motion-picture manufacturers, Lubin highlighted his passion-play and Spanish-American War films, though he again blurred the line between authenticity and imitation.

Dramatic renderings of Christ's passion had existed for centuries; the decennial performance of the passion play at Oberammergau, in Bavaria, became particularly revered. A lavish stage production based on this pageant had been prepared in New York in 1880 but banned as sacrilegious. Magic-lantern shows of such dramatizations had been presented as well. In 1898 competing motion pictures were exhibited in the United States. One, *Passion Play of Horitz*, was filmed in Austria in 1897 by the International Film Company (as an ersatz Oberammergau, which would not be staged again until 1900); another, *Passion Play of Ober Ammergau (Salmi Morse Version)*, used costumes from the banned stage show and was photographed on a Manhattan rooftop; a third, produced earlier in France, debuted in America in February. All three were exhibited in multiple forms. Commentators debated the propriety of the new medium, but none of these moving pictures was censored. Having passed through so many layers of textual representation and reproduction (a film of a performance of a play based on a pageant adapted from a biblical narrative), copies of the cinematic passion plays of 1898 traveled freely, without censure. Unlike the theatrical performance with live actors banned in New York, film presentations were usually welcomed as a continuation of a pictorial tradition.

Given such license, the Lubin company issued its own rendition in May, *The Passion Play of Oberammergau:* "NOT copies, but original subjects."

The claim was true enough, but it was another backyard affair produced cheaply.[20] With so many life-of-Christ films on the market, these less expensive fifty- and one hundred-foot scenes passed as part of the mix. Despite advertisements from competitors warning buyers about "the genuine vs. the counterfeit," "Lubin's Passion Play Films" (the deceptive "Oberammergau" was dropped) were the featured product in the company's ads for the rest of the year.

Lubin continued labeling reproductions with misleading descriptions in his 1898 Cuban war pictures. Again he was neither the sole producer of fakes nor the lone duper of others' films. American manufacturers shot hundreds of individual subjects, both actual and staged. The multiplicity of pictures made the mixing of genres more prevalent, but there was little worry about counterfeiting so long as exhibitors had topical illustrations of war news. Although Lubin lacked the resources of Edison and Biograph (which had cameramen in Cuba), the company benefited from the nationwide interest in war and military subjects. In addition to actualities of parades and naval scenes, Lubin filmed battle reenactments, selling them as documentary. In this regard Lubin was not out of step with the "wargraph" suppliers Edison, Vitagraph, Biograph, Magniscope and others who practiced topical reproduction.[21]

By the end of 1898, with the war over and passion plays a drug on the market, Lubin returned with vigor to prizefight reenactments. In December, Lubin announced the sale of *Fac-simile of the Corbett and Sharkey Fight.* The actual Corbett-Sharkey match of November 22 had ended in controversy. When it was reported that Corbett's handlers threw the fight for gamblers, a police investigation ensued, and the bout became a hot topic. But inside the gaslit Lenox Athletic Club, it had gone unfilmed. Lubin exploited the topicality, placing ads in the same issue of the *Clipper* that featured a report of the fight itself.[22] He added testimonials for his nine-round reproduction. Connie McVey, who as Corbett's trainer allegedly had thrown the fight by jumping into the ring and causing a disqualification, helped Lubin cloud the issue of the film's veracity. McVey's mock telegram to Lubin pronounced: "I had the pleasure of seeing your Life Motion Pictures of the late Corbett and Sharkey fight, and judge of my surprise when I recognized myself jumping into the ring just as it occurred. I have seen many Life Motion Pictures of Prize Fighting in my time, but yours, without exception, is the greatest, liveliest and most true that I have ever witnessed. I cannot imagine for one moment how you procured so true a picture in every detail, which, to say the least, is an exact reproduction, and can only attribute it to your indomitable energy and pluck."[23] *Pluck* was indeed the appropriate word, suggesting both chutzpah and swindle. The taint surrounding the actual match, however, overpowered interest in Lubin's reproduction. With few takers, ads for the *Corbett and Sharkey Fight* were dropped.

Before consigning his cameras to reenactments, however, Lubin made a plucky bid for exclusive access to ring stars. In December 1898, supplied with $20,000 from a "party of well-known capitalists," S. Lubin headed to New York to sign two top heavyweights to box a genuine fight to the finish. "The only stipulation made by Mr. Lubin," the *Chicago Tribune* reported, "is that the battle shall be in private" at an undisclosed location.[24] He failed to break into New York's high-stakes sporting and theatrical community, but by 1900 Lubin had gained standing in the ring world with his reenactments.

REPRODUCTION OF THE SHARKEY-McCOY FIGHT

The third Lubin fight picture, a reenactment of the ten-round bout between Tom Sharkey and Kid McCoy, proved successful just a month after the second had failed. On January 10, 1899, Sharkey engaged in another Lenox Avenue club fight, knocking out McCoy. Lubin again hired actors to replicate the contest. Two weeks later the cineograph offered *Re-enactment of Sharkey-McCoy Fight* "reproduced in life motion, in 10 rounds, each round 100 feet long."[25]

Lubin also copyrighted this work as separate photographs. This had not been done for the previous film and had only been partially done with his *Corbett-Fitzsimmons* reproduction (for which Lubin claimed two copyright registration numbers, though the Library of Congress has no record of them). Copyright became central to Lubin's strategy—and to the development of the entire moving-picture industry. The ten copyright stills that are preserved from *Re-enactment of Sharkey-McCoy Fight* show generic scenes of two gloved boxers (who bear little resemblance to their supposed counterparts) being watched by a referee, corner men, and five formally dressed male spectators standing below the ring. Only the first and last pictures indicate specifically posed pieces of action, beginning with a ritual handshake and ending with one pugilist down on the canvas.

Filmed on the platform used throughout 1897 and 1898, the stills reveal changes from Lubin's first effort. A wider ring was built and the camera set back to reveal the entire scene. The backdrop was changed from white to black for better contrast. Figures wearing outlandish wigs and makeup were replaced by athletic actors. In short, the pictures reveal an increased realism in the representation. This trend persisted, although in this first 1899 effort, Lubin's boxing scene resembles the first experiments in the Edison studio.

Although the Sharkey and McCoy bout received little press, as it was not a title fight, the Lubin films enjoyed wide circulation. The cincograph had become an installation at Philadelphia's "largest amusement resort," Bradenburgh's Museum. This guaranteed the top-billed picture a prominent display and newspaper write-ups. Other regional amusement centers featured the film. Lubin played up their endorsements. The burlesque promoters Howard and Emerson claimed advance sales for tickets at their opera house in Newark. A Massachusetts showman reported sellouts for his theater and road-show outfits. Lubin opened a screening room in his office, and by February he could boast of sales of the *Sharkey-McCoy* pictures to variety, vaudeville, burlesque, dime museum, and opera house venues throughout the East and South.[26]

Other exhibitors began using purchased and duped prints of Lubin's original. Biograph's film service at the People's Theatre of Philadelphia added the fight, along with Lubin's faked *Battle of San Juan Hill* (1899), in March. In April the fight pictures were used by George Spoor's "kinodrome" as entr'acte material for a stock company playing the palatial St. Charles Theatre in New Orleans. Spuriously billed as having been "taken in the Lenox A.C.," the same films played simultaneously in the Crescent City's Academy of Music, where Tom Sharkey sparred as part of a vaudeville show. The following August, the new champion, Jim Jeffries, used copies of the "Sharkey v. M'Coy" films during his European theatrical tour. In anticipation of his title defense against Sharkey, Jeffries gave stage exhibitions at the Royal Aquarium theater in London (where the Veriscope *Corbett-Fitzsimmons Fight* had screened two years earlier). The event, promoted by William Brady, led to a two-month run of Lubin's pictures showing "the Whole of the Ten Rounds" of "the Great Prize Fight."[27]

Why did this cheap reenactment of a minor fight sell so well when Lubin's version of a more notorious event had fizzled the previous month? The 1898 Corbett-Sharkey production might have been photographically inferior. Later Lubin catalogs dropped it but kept all other fight titles in stock. Ambitious advertising propelled the newer films into greater circulation as well. Lubin ads in the *Clipper* consistently bettered those of the competition in size and boldness.

With his Sharkey-McCoy reenactment, Lubin hit on a successful variation of an established cinematic and prizefight convention: motion-picture recordings of actors nominally reenacting a lesser-known prizefight of which no recording existed. Earlier boxing pictures had brought genuine

Figure 28. Frames from *Reproduction of the Jeffries and Sharkey Fight* (left) and *Reproduction of the Fitzsimmons-Jeffries Fight* (both Lubin, 1899). (Library of Congress, Motion Picture, Broadcasting and Recorded Sound Division.)

pugilists to pose for the cameras or reproduced a fight already on film (such as *Corbett-Fitzsimmons*), or featured the noted boxers recreating their recent contest (such as *Maher-Choynski*). Lubin's 1899 reproductions built on ring publicity while controlling the on-camera events and the celluloid property. Profits were not as great for reproductions as for originals, but Lubin's strategy allowed his firm to control its own activity rather serve as a for-hire service to the sporting syndicate.

While the success of the Sharkey-McCoy pictures encouraged Lubin to continue fight reproductions, the fortunate circumstances of its next effort led the company to implement a systematic method of production and exploitation of prizefight subjects. When Vitagraph failed to record the Jeffries-Fitzsimmons fight at Coney Island on June 9, 1899, Lubin's scheduled reproduction scooped the market for pictures of the contest. By June 12, a Lubin representative had copyrighted the *Reproduction of the Fitzsimmons-Jeffries Fight,* and the customary *Clipper* advertisements began the next week.

LUBIN'S ROOFTOP RING PRODUCTIONS

Beginning with this important topical film, Lubin improved production standards. The company headquarters moved to a building across from Bradenburgh's Ninth and Arch Street amusement center. Its open-air, rooftop production facility became the location for many Lubin films and all of the subsequent boxing subjects. At least three technicians—James Blair Smith, Arthur D. Hotaling, and production head John J. Frawley—were employed in the cineograph operation, which was now also making comedies and other short subjects. The setup was sparse: a square wooden stage with a frame for hanging canvas backdrops, and a platform for the boxlike camera that stood just above eye level.

The making of the Fitzsimmons Jeffries reenactment can be reconstructed from surviving evidence. Two abbreviated rounds of the film survive. The images reveal a sharper, deeper focus than earlier fight films, confirming the company's claim to superior pictures that were "clear, sharp and distinct in detail."[28] The verisimilitude of the boxing scene is also improved. Replacing the background canvas behind the ring are three rows of bleachers occupied by several dozen young men and boys. The sparring action between the contestants is not unconvincing (save for a staged knockdown), but the acting of the ringside extras upstages the fight itself. Between rounds, two foreground figures stand and wave dollar bills in the air. Playing to the camera, they show money changing hands. Other bettors make their pantomime obvious throughout. One continuous medium-long shot is used. All planes of action—the foreground bettors, boxers in the ring, and the active background spectators—remain in focus, making for a distractingly busy mise-en-scène.

The journalist and referee H. Walter Schlichter later wrote about his experience as a member of the on-camera cast of extras. Like Siegmund Lubin, Schlichter attended the Coney Island prizefight on June 9. He reported that on June 10, Lubin "sent for Billy Leedom, one of Philadelphia's cleverest fighters, and Jack McCormick, a heavyweight." The wiry Leedom was paid to stand in as Fitzsimmons; the burly McCormick, who was in fact a Jeffries sparring partner, represented the new champion. Sports reporter Bert Crowhurst impersonated George Siler as referee. Makeup (greasepaint freckles) was required for Leedom, yet Schlichter judged the film as creating "two almost perfect replicas of the three principals."[29]

Although the choreography of blows never literally reproduced the newspaper accounts of fights (as anecdotes suggest), an off-camera prompter directed the general action of the principals and spectators. The staging of ringside betting remained a favorite device in the Lubin films. As rooftop fights and the passing out of dollar bills became a regular feature of productions at the Arch Street location, larger crowds of extras were employed. Up to two hundred onlookers sometimes jammed the facility.[30]

Other production details are apparent. One spectator in the *Fitzsimmons and Jeffries Fight* reproduction, for example, sports a large shamrock on his lapel, referencing the well-known Irish working-class enthusiasm for prizefighting. Such evidence of preparation reveals that these were more than slapdash productions. As Ramsaye glibly put it: "This was art,—the re-creation of an event—and the 'fight by rounds' column was a scenario, but Lubin did not know it."[31]

Whatever he knew of art, as an entrepreneur Lubin emphasized timely marketing and promotion. Not only did he have his films shot, copyrighted, and ready for exhibition within a week, but he also made them available in multiple forms to accommodate different types of shows. Initial ads for his *Fitzsimmons and Jeffries Fight* offered all eleven rounds. Subsequent sales included six-round highlight films (running fifteen to twenty minutes). Either version could be purchased in rounds abbreviated to one minute of filmed action instead of two (although Queensberry rounds lasted three).[32] Lubin also made free samples available by mail to interested exhibitors. One such "cut-out" of the *Fitzsimmons and Jeffries Fight* (twenty-two frames of a 35 mm celluloid print) was preserved by the exhibitor A. B. Hager, who had used the cineograph in a Los Angeles "store show" in 1899 and 1900.[33] Like other manufacturers, Lubin used telegraph and telephone sales to reach remote and itinerant exhibitors.

Reproduction of the Fitzsimmons and Jeffries Fight was widely exhibited in the summer and fall of 1899. Many theatrical outlets that showed moving pictures were closed during the heat of summer (including Lubin's principal platform, Bradenburgh's Museum), but outdoor amusement centers welcomed the fight pictures. Among the first to feature the championship reenactment was Washington Park on the Delaware, a New Jersey summer resort. After the Lubin films (and "musical carnival") premiered there on June 24, the Philadelphia Police Department sponsored free admission for sixty thousand children.[34] Other prints were projected at parks in Coney Island, Atlantic City, Baltimore, Dayton, Richmond, Montreal, Louisville, and many smaller towns. Like its predecessors, the Fitzsimmons-Jeffries film also served vaudeville (Tony Pastor's in New York), opera houses (Kansas City, New Brunswick), roof gardens (Manhattan, Brooklyn), burlesque shows (the Boston Palace, Philadelphia Lyceum), road troupes (the American-European Vaudeville Company and the Darkest South Company), storefront shows (Vitagraph Hall in Washington, DC), and variety theaters (Buffalo's Court Street Theatre, Cincinnati's People's Theatre, the Denver Theatre, and Norfolk Auditorium).[35]

Audiences accepted the reproduction in lieu of any genuine record. In Atlantic City, conventioneers hearing of the failed Vitagraph films crowded in to see "Professor Lubin's machine." "Whether the pictures were those of the originals or only substitutes requires an expert's eagle eye," the *Philadelphia Inquirer* reported, "for the mill is so clever and so much like the original that the average person would be inclined to think the Fitzsimmons and

Jeffries really were pictured."[36] Screenings were well attended in large cities. Runs lasted several days. A description of a Chicago exhibition indicates how much better *Fitzsimmons-Jeffries* fared than Lubin's Corbett-Fitzsimmons fake.

> Pictures of the Jeffries-Fitzsimmons fight were successfully reproduced by the cinematograph at the Dearborn Theatre yesterday. Considering the adverse circumstances under which they were secured, the pictures are excellent and give a realistic idea of the encounter. There is no time in the progress of the fight when both principals and all their movements cannot be clearly seen.
>
> The area of the pictures [i.e., the ring being photographed] is not large, which is an advantage in many respects. It brings the pugilists into better range and quickens the conception of what happened. A lecturer gives explanations of each round, supplying incidents that cannot be told in a picture.
>
> From the beginning of the tenth round to the close of the contest gets sufficiently exciting. Referee George Siler [i.e., the actor impersonating Siler] appears to have about as much necessity for action as either of the principals. The final scene in the ring, including the knockout, are fortunately clearer than any other part of the pictures. They are shown at the Dearborn continuously from 10 o'clock in the morning to 11 o'clock in the evening. Large crowds witnessed the first productions yesterday.[37]

Such reviews blurred the line between genuine and faked films as readily as the Lubin ads did. The article implies that the presentation may be a recording, but it also suggests that the pictures merely "quicken the conception of what happened" at Coney Island. Such ambiguities reveal that it was not a matter of distinguishing the vile fake from the true document: that evaluative schema was not yet the norm. Viewers of this Chicago cineograph show received the Lubin reproduction as the only available illustration of the event. And if a reenacted version provided clearer, closer views of a fight than the snowy long shots of the veriscope, this could be "an advantage." Because many patrons had never seen any prizefight, much less the real James J. Jeffries, the ability to distinguish the original from the facsimile was moot. (Even A. B. Hager, who exhibited in Jeffries' hometown, failed to make the distinction.)

Boxing insiders, however, criticized the fake. The *Police Gazette*'s expert Sam Austin warned readers off Lubin's work.

> One of the most flagrant cases of a "fake" ever imposed upon a patient, long suffering, innocent and enduring public is the alleged kinetoscope photographs of the Jeffries-Fitzsimmons fight, which are now being

extensively exhibited throughout this country. The unprincipled promoters of the enterprise had the temerity to have a couple of mixed-ale
scrappers, made up with wigs, etc., to represent "Fitz" and Jeffries as
they appeared in the ring at Coney Island on that eventful night, and
go through a lot of fake fighting manœuvres before a reproducing
camera. Nobody who saw the actual fight could be misled or easily
fooled by the "fake" exhibition, but unfortunately there are thousands
of people who did not see the actual fight, and who, for that matter,
never saw either of the fighters, and it is upon the credulity of these
unfortunates that the promoters of the "fake" pictures depend for the
success of their questionable scheme. To satisfy my own curiosity I
attended an exhibit of the pictures . . . [N]ot an incident of the genuine
fight was correctly reproduced. The spectators at the ringside in the
alleged pictures consist of a lot of street gamins, doubtless hired for
the occasion, to make up the assemblage and applaud when called
upon to do so. Not a single face among the spectators is recognizable,
notwithstanding that all around the ringside were men whose faces are
known in every city.

. . . [If] the "fake" exhibitions are as well attended in other cities as
they are in New York, the enterprise, unprincipled as it may be, is at
any rate an extremely profitable one.[38]

For the true believer, not only did the films replace the real ring artists
with inferior stand-ins, but the milieu of the sport was lost. The celebrities,
politicians, sporting men, and business leaders who helped legitimize prizefighting were key elements of the spectacle. Rosters of their names often appeared in sports pages. Austin sought to identify them when he watched
fight pictures. Replacing senators with street urchins took away one of the
sport's few signs of legitimacy. Ring promoters wanted to use motion pictures, but boxing advocates disdained the fake fight film.

Nevertheless, the enterprise proved profitable. Following *Reproduction
of the Fitzsimmons and Jeffries Fight,* Lubin regularized its filming of boxing reenactments. Throughout the 1899–1900 season, the company produced seven versions of lesser fights as well as reproductions of all three
Jeffries title defenses. While none of these enjoyed the exclusivity of
Fitzsimmons-Jeffries, they offered a cheaper alternative to features such as
Biograph's *Jeffries-Sharkey Contest.* When genuine fight pictures proved
photographically inadequate, Lubin reenactments became valuable back-
ups.

The mode of production for the Philadelphia fakes was consistent. Boxer-
actors sparred for the cineograph on the rooftop ring, surrounded by
coached spectators. The resulting 35 mm films were uninterrupted exposures of each round, sold in both full and abbreviated lengths.

CREATIVE COPYRIGHTING

After success with *Fitzsimmons-Jeffries,* Lubin began registering films for U.S. copyright: seventeen different titles in the ensuing year and at least twenty-three in all. The records suggest that Lubin used unconventional, and perhaps deceptive, methods of copyright deposit to give his fight pictures an edge on the commercial competition.

Before 1912, producers obtained legal protection by registering individual frames for copyright as photographs. Motion pictures were often printed on 35 mm strips of paper and deposited at the Library of Congress. A title, application, fifty-cent fee, and a copy (or two) of the work filed with the Register of Copyrights gave the claimant exclusive legal rights to reproduce and sell the work. Some deposited the entire film on paper, whereas others submitted only a few frames or "illustrative sequences." Lubin used strips of four sequential frames from a 35 mm print, like those he placed in advertisements and gave to buyers as samples (see figure 29).[39]

A deposited work supposedly represented a completed motion picture. Yet Lubin secured copyright on titles for which nothing had been filmed. Two surviving copyright booklets reveal how. For *Reproduction of the Jeffries and Sharkey Fight,* shot in early November 1899 just after the real bout, a registration was penciled in on September 9. On November 11, the register stamped "Two Copies Received" on the application. Four frames of a 35 mm strip are stapled to each page, one for each round. The *Jeffries and Corbett* booklet (1900) repeats this practice. The first film strip is labeled "Introduction" and shows a tuxedoed announcer in a ring. Such generic scenes probably were part of the initial registration, with the rounds being added when the film was complete.

Lubin manipulated copyright law to gain greater control of the market for fight pictures. As André Gaudreault demonstrates, "Numerous companies and/or individuals tried from the very start to take advantage of the legal loopholes that existed in a body of law that had never been intended to cover phenomena such as the 'aggregation of photographs' that was the film strip." Lubin's infringements, like those of his competitors, "were a natural extension of aggressive commercial policies" that were the rule in early cinema.[40]

In 1899 Lubin's policy was twofold: he sought to copyright titles in advance of both the fight and the recording of its facsimile, and he copyrighted two titles for each forthcoming product so that the winner's name would appear first regardless of the fight's outcome. For example, on September 8, 1899, four days before the Palmer-McGovern fight, Lubin registered the

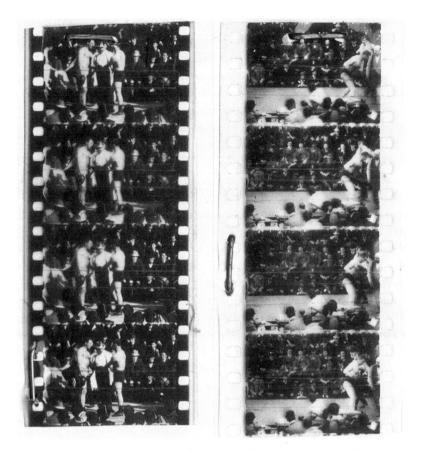

Figure 29. When registering copyright, Lubin deposited booklets with four-frame strips of 35 mm film stapled to each page, one for each round. Samples from *Reproduction of the Jeffries and Sharkey Fight* (1899), left, and *Reproduction of Jeffries and Corbett* (1900). (Library of Congress, Motion Picture Conservation Center.)

titles *Reproduction of the Pedlar Palmer and Terry McGovern Fight* and *Reproduction of the Terry McGovern and Pedlar Palmer Fight*. Although advance ads referred to the *Palmer-McGovern Fight*, after the McGovern's victory the film took on the *McGovern-Palmer* label. Lubin used these methods to deposit eleven boxing films in 1899; in 1900, he copyrighted seven more—the only registrations the Lubin company made that year.[41]

For these productions, however, Lubin sometimes claimed ownership months before they were made. The day following his *Palmer-McGovern* copyright application, copyright was also secured for the Jeffries and

Sharkey titles, although that big battle was two months away. When it became clear that Jeffries' name assured publicity, Lubin expanded this practice. On November 17 he took out applications on four Jeffries titles, even though the Jeffries-Corbett match would not occur until May 1900 and the Ruhlin contest not until December 1900, more than a year later.

Lubin used copyright to prevent others from doing what his company did with rivals' work: duping and selling it for profit without permission. He told buyers of fight pictures that "our copyright will protect you" against pirated screenings.[42] The guarantee meant little, as duping was accepted practice, and the legality of motion picture copyright was not established. Lubin registered his fake fight films through August 1900.

Factors beyond the filmmaker's control curbed his production for the next two years. New York state outlawed prizefighting after August 31, 1900. More serious, however, because they affected all Lubin productions, were lawsuits brought against him by Thomas Edison. In 1901 Lubin shut down operations and moved back to Germany. In March 1902, following the dismissal of Edison's patent-infringement suit, he resumed production in Philadelphia. Lubin revived his boxing recreations, releasing *Reproduction of the Jeffries-Fitzsimmons Fight* in August 1902. The following year he produced *Corbett-McGovern* (April), *Jeffries-Corbett* (an August rematch), *Fitzsimmons-Gardner* (November), and *Dixon-Palmer*.

Conspicuously, Lubin did not copyright these films. When sued for duplicating Edison's copyrighted works, Lubin contended that no motion picture could be granted protection, as U.S. law only specified copyright for single photographs. In consequence, the protection of motion-picture properties was suspended. Amazingly, as Gaudreault points out, Lubin argued that motion-picture claimants should have to pay the half-dollar fee for *every* frame of a film if they were to receive copyrights. The judge agreed that the law failed to protect motion pictures. Until that decision was reversed in 1903, motion pictures could be copied and resold with impunity. The copyright quagmire explains why the business of filming prizefights all but ceased in 1903 and 1904. Neither boxing promoters nor motion-picture companies would invest thousands of dollars in recording a fight if the prints could be freely copied by competitors.[43]

APEX OF THE FAKE FIGHT FILM PHENOMENON

Before the collapse of the fight-picture market, the Lubin reproductions enjoyed a vogue. At a time when cinema found its way into many forms of entertainment, Lubin's boxing presentations proved as versatile and ubiquitous as any type of motion picture. No single reenactment could dominate the market like Biograph's *Jeffries-Sharkey Contest* or Veriscope's *Corbett-Fitzsimmons*. Even an exclusive, such as the *Fitzsimmons-Jeffries* reproduction, commanded less attention than authentic films.[44] However, in most instances recordings were not made, and Lubin's "life motion pictures" proved welcome. By August 1900, with prizefighting on the verge of elimination in New York, the boxing fraternity joined hands with Lubin's Philadelphia operation. Newspapers and sporting journals promoted and praised the cineograph's "honest fakes," allowing Lubin's films to be seen by thousands.

For *Reproduction of the Jeffries and Sharkey Fight*, the company bought huge advertising spreads to rival American Mutoscope and Biograph's. Lubin's imitations could not compete against the full-length original, but they could benefit exhibitors who used moving pictures as side attractions. The ersatz *Jeffries and Sharkey* found audiences through burlesque companies (such as Gus Hill's Masqueraders and Tammany Tigers, or "Howard & Emerson, who took the fight pictures at Coney Island Sport Club"), traveling shows, and circuses.[45] Lubin's fortunes improved when a court enjoined Edison from exhibiting "any copy, real or otherwise," of Jeffries' victory. Despite William Brady's threat "to make an active warfare on all imitations and reproductions,"[46] Lubin pressed on.

At the beginning of 1900, Lubin filmed a trio of reenactments of lesser fights. Reproductions of *Kid McCoy–Peter Maher, Terry McGovern–George Dixon,* and *McGovern–Oscar Gardner* were representations of brief fights (five, eight, and three rounds), making them too short for feature billing but appropriate for filler or entr'acte material. Records of where these films played are sparse, aside from the usual premiere at Bradenburgh's and some touring burlesque shows.[47] Lubin's ability to market *McGovern-Dixon* pictures within a week of the contest gave him a strong advantage over promoters who took three months to release genuine motion pictures. With typical gumption, Lubin tried to invert the meaning of his "fake," suggesting that timeliness was more important to showmen than authenticity: "Our Reproduction of the McGovern-Dixon Fight was ready the day after the fight took place. Don't be a clam and buy pictures of a fight which are made four weeks after the fight took place and called original. Which is the fake, the one SHOWN the day after the fight or the one MADE four weeks after?"[48]

The promoters Tom O'Rourke and Sam Harris labeled Lubin's fakes as the "spurious," "counterfeit" work of an "irresponsible pirate." William Brady promised that "no fake can live a minute" with genuine fight films on the market. But, even with a judge supposedly restraining the exhibition of fake fight films, Lubin's remained the most widely available type of fight picture. By March 1900 the company was advertising all three of its recent reproductions. While its other films were being sold by the foot, fight films and passion plays retained their higher market value as distinct titles.[49]

On May 11, 1900, champion Jeffries defeated a game but aging Jim Corbett in a twenty-three round slugfest at Coney Island. No movie cameras were present. The monopoly on film representations was conceded to Lubin, who had deposited copyright claims on his *Reproduction of the Jeffries and Corbett Fight* the previous November and again in April. He began pushing his full-length film almost exclusively. Along with making the usual claim to have the latest, "greatest set of prize fight films ever made," Lubin reinvented ways of making his mockup sound worthwhile: "When looking at these pictures you imagine yourself seated in the Arena of the Seaside Athletic Club, at Coney Island, N. Y., looking at the real thing." A Corbett comeback might have sparked greater interest than another lumbering Jeffries knockout, but, as it was, the fight attracted only mild interest. As Musser has shown, the business of motion pictures was also beginning to drop off in 1900. The summer months were especially slow for theatrical amusements. By mid-June, Lubin's *Reproduction of the Jeffries and Corbett Fight* was the only motion-picture advertisement in the *Clipper*.[50] Lubin cornered the fight-picture market, but those who patronized his film did so only for lack of anything better.

"HONEST FAKES": *LIFE MOTION PHOTOGRAPHS OF THE FITZSIMMONS AND RUHLIN FIGHT*

As New York's ban on prizefighting approached, Siegmund Lubin embarked on a new strategy. He paid the four top-ranked heavyweight contenders to reenact matches on his Arch Street rooftop. Also in August, cross-promotional events with the *Philadelphia Inquirer* enabled tens of thousands of people to see his fight pictures and other cineograph films. Lubin encouraged press coverage of his operation, gaining positive and wide exposure of his sometimes disparaged practice. The national press and half a dozen Philadelphia dailies chronicled these events. Their reports also indicate that Lubin tried either to record a real fight or, more audaciously, to give the impression he had. As late as December 1900, the press could still misreport that "Professor S. Lubin and a staff of photographers" would travel to Chicago to "take photographs of the [Gans-McGovern] fight for the cinematograph."[51]

When Bob Fitzsimmons knocked out Gus Ruhlin in six rounds on the night of August 10, 1900, the *Police Gazette* noted a "picture machine" in Madison Square Garden for the first time. A week earlier, George Siler reported the event was to be "kinetoscoped" under blazing lights akin to Biograph's setup for the 1899 *Jeffries-Sharkey Contest*. "A photographer of Philadelphia, who has heretofore been declared a fakir by the other fight picture makers, is to take the pictures," noted the skeptical *Brooklyn Eagle*. "He claims to have an extra sensitive photograph film by which he can take excellent pictures of the fight with no other lights than those used ordinarily at Madison Square Garden."[52]

The *Philadelphia Item* mistakenly credited the "enterprising S. Lubin" with actually filming the fight, although it did remark that lighting seemed inadequate for photography. The *New York Journal* suggested that poor illumination defeated a genuine intention to take pictures.[53] But the *Philadelphia Record* suspected a ploy.

> On a temporary stand, about 100 feet from the ring, were two cameras, such as moving pictures are taken with, and a sign on the front of the stand announced that they were the property of S. Lubin, of Philadelphia. Just how moving pictures could be taken from such a distance and by such poor light is a secret never to be divulged. While the outfit was unquestionably only a bluff, it is good betting that Lubin will reproduce the fight in a way to satisfy almost any critic, and that the work will be done in Philadelphia before many days pass by.[54]

Indeed, Lubin was in the Garden with his assistant Jack Frawley to watch the brawl, if not to shoot it. Their camera crew had recorded the pugilists in their training quarters beforehand and contracted them to travel to Philadelphia after their bout, although even this plan was nearly foiled by the severe injuries Ruhlin suffered: "Wonder what Lubin, the moving picture man will do now?" wrote George Siler.[55]

Rather than disguise his method of forgery, Lubin invited press attention. At the company offices, an employee "explained how the fight was to be reproduced": the "picture fight" would take place outdoors, with constructed scenery, rehearsals, and "one hundred men and boys" hired to play the audience. Those at ringside would be "provided with stage money for the purpose of making bets."[56] All these events came to pass on August 13.

The *Police Gazette* described the rooftop production in "Professor Lubin's gallery" as an "honest fake." The "professor" was generously quoted, offering an apologia for his fake (and the fact that even part of the reenactment had to be restaged): "Owing to an accident several of the films were spoiled, which broke the continuity of the action of the two men, and rendered it

Figure 30.   Bob Fitzsimmons and Gus Ruhlin reenact their own August 10 New York bout for Lubin on his Philadelphia rooftop, August 13, 1900. Photo published in local newspapers and *Police Gazette*, September 8, 1900.

necessary for these two men to go through that part of the fight again. The exhibition was in every way satisfactory, and the films are perfect. They are, in fact, the best I have ever taken, and will show the entire fight from the first clash of the gong until Ruhlin was carried out of the ring insensible."

Lubin had to pay for the association with celebrity. He retained only a quarter of the picture receipts: the boxers each got a quarter, and the remainder was divided among the managers and promoter.[57] Lubin was surrendering the profit margin on his only money maker in order to enhance his brand. The local press obliged with copious illustrations on August 14. The *Record* ran a photo of "S. Lubin operating Film Printer on which he prints daily about 35,000 feet of film." Another paper published stills ("Fitzsimmons and Ruhlin in their 'Fake' Fight") taken during the making of the reproduction. Yet another printed a frame enlargement from the cineograph film itself.[58]

The *Police Gazette* picked up the *Record*'s account and added less flattering material. The tabloid condemned the "unprincipled promoter," emphasizing his reenactment's shortcomings. "Sometimes," wrote the reporter who watched the filming, "it was hard to keep a straight face, for the farce was most ludicrous."

> While far from being an exact reproduction of the first wicked encounter the exhibition was a very interesting one, and should look all right in the pictures. S. Lubin, the enterprising individual who engineered the show, says no one will be able to distinguish any difference between the real fight, carried by memory only, and the photographs of the imitation.
>
> The ring was pitched on the roof and the setting was made to look as much as possible like the interior of Madison Square Garden the night of the battle. The crowd in attendance was coatless and hatless, while almost everybody carried a palm fan, just as did the patrons of the real fight. Barring Jim Corbett, the seconds were the same as officiated the original mill, and Charley White, who as the real referee, was also on hand. . . .
>
> An effort was made to reproduce the rounds as they actually occurred and there was where the men made a bad mistake. They of course failed to do the right thing at the right time and the advice and coaching, which was liberally bestowed from every side, only served to make matters worse. . . .
>
> The spectators had not been properly coached in the important duties they were called upon to enact and did not understand just what they were to do to help the fight look lifelike, in the matter of cheering and getting into the ring at the close. The sun persisted in appearing and disappearing in a most tantalizing way toward the end, and it took a lot of shouting back and forth to find just what the sun was going to do next. The last round had to be stopped and started all over again when the film broke, but that was the only mechanical mishap of the day. . . .
>
> An interesting scene was witnessed in Mr. Lubin's office after the mimic battle on the roof was over. There sat Ruhlin, with Fitzsimmons standing over him painting his discolored eyes so that they would not be noticeable on the street.[59]

The motion picture enterprise's tight relationship with the ring establishment was even more evident at the end of the day. After the shoot, the boxers and their entourages went (with reporters) to the company's screening room, where Lubin projected the footage taken at their training quarters. The men jokingly critiqued their performances in the scenes of swimming, sparring, running, and exercising, all of which would be combined with the six-round bout in release prints.

For a boxing insider, the fake fight film held little credibility as an exhibition of fistic skill but was of interest when true ring stars participated. The *Gazette*'s report counters other descriptions of Lubin productions. Rather than telling of blow-by-blow choreography, this is a portrait of playful, controlled chaos. Despite its characterization, the *Gazette* published a pair of Lubin photographs the following week.

The Fitzsimmons-Ruhlin reproduction was also a departure for Lubin distribution and promotion, booked exclusively through the vaudeville agent William Morris. An opening three-week run at Hammerstein's Victoria Roof Garden in Manhattan was the only new ground Morris broke. Otherwise, outlets for the film did not change significantly: burlesque, music halls, and traveling shows (such as the Ferari Midway Exposition Company's "electric theatre").[60]

The film of Fitz restaging his knockout found a much broader audience the following year. When Bob and Rose Fitzsimmons toured with their stage vehicle *The Honest Blacksmith* from 1900 to 1902, theatergoers saw the Lubin footage projected during the play's climax.

"THE INQUIRER'S CINEOGRAPH"

The publicity for *Life Motion Photographs of the Fitzsimmons and Ruhlin Fight* led to Lubin's most successful foray: cineograph exhibitions for thousands of Philadelphians awaiting the results of the last major New York prizefights.

Two weeks after beating Ruhlin, the resilient Fitzsimmons knocked out Tom Sharkey in the second round of their battle of August 24, 1900, at Coney Island. No cameras were installed for this contest, and the combatants did not perform a reenactment for Lubin. However, as with other major events of the period, the results of the Fitzsimmons-Sharkey contest were presented instantaneously to audiences across the nation who gathered in front of newspaper offices to hear them. In Philadelphia, the *Inquirer* invited the public to its headquarters. The "announcement by megaphone" of fight returns became a complete public performance.

> Previous to and during the progress of the battle
>> The Inquirer will furnish
>> Music and Cineograph
> There will be a full military band and moving pictures
>> under the direction of Professor Lubin.[61]

Figure 31. "The Inquirer's Cineograph" projects Lubin films to
a crowd of ten thousand gathered for news of the Fitzsimmons-
Sharkey bout. *Philadelphia Inquirer,* August 25, 1900.

Despite rain, the spectacle was a huge success. A throng turned out
and "watched the great moving picture exhibition." The next morning's
paper featured a front-page illustration of ten thousand people witnessing "the Inquirer's Cineograph" projecting motion pictures across Market
Street onto a tall building. "The style of presentation," the publisher
claimed, "established a new order of things in newspaper bulletin service"
(figure 31).[62]

NEWSPAPER FIGHT BULLETIN SERVICE

The "order of things" to that point had not included motion pictures, although
large crowds and visual presentation were common for election returns,
prizefight announcements, and other news bulletins.[63] The Hearst syndicate made elaborate plans for its Jeffries-Sharkey returns in November

1899. Having seen crowds of twenty-five thousand turn up to learn the fate of the Jeffries-Fitzsimmons contest on June 9, the *Examiner* invested in a complex of telegraph, telephone, and stereopticon technology to display its "flash" bulletins throughout downtown San Francisco. As descriptions were wired in, bulletins were transcribed onto slides (using typewriters and "transparent gelatine or film") and rushed to stereopticons on four different rooftops.[64] Crowds of thirty to forty thousand viewed the texts on canvas screens hung on building fronts. An electric sign also flashed headlines atop the *Examiner* headquarters. In addition, operators telephoned the bulletins to stores, hotels, military posts, and political offices. The *Examiner* repeated this process of patchwork, instantaneous mass communication on election night a few days later.[65] Such public gatherings to hear and see breaking news continued until radio broadcasting displaced them in the 1920s.

Visual enhancement of these announcements remained a novelty. Nevertheless, Lubin's introduction of motion pictures to this carnivalesque public event offers another example of nontheatrical venues for early cinema. It also reiterates the degree to which prizefighting and cinema shared public space and sought mutual legitimation. Both benefited from the newspaper's celebratory treatment of the occasion:

THE CINEOGRAPH

A splendid band was engaged. So were two solo cornetists. And last, but not least, Lubin and his famous cineograph were contracted for.

Think of that! And think of the expense it all involved! . . . [A]n invitation was extended, through the columns of the paper, to all sport-loving Philadelphia to be on hand in front of The Inquirer building at 7:45 o'clock last evening. Accompanying the invitation was the announcement that there would be a continuous performance of music, moving pictures and instantaneous bulletins from the ring side from that hour until the fight was over.

. . . [T]he crowd began to collect. Those who composed it came from all directions and from that time on until after 8 o'clock, when the late comers arrived, the processions Inquirerward were seemingly endless.

"Where are you going to-night?" was the query heard in every section of the city over and over again.

"Down to the Inquirer office to hear the music, see the pictures and get the returns of the fight," came the answer.

[Despite rain] the band concert began promptly on time. So did the cineograph pictures. From that moment until the last returns from the fight were in there was always "something doing" to interest the crowd.

The moving picture exhibition, by the way was one of the longest and certainly the most varied, ever given in Philadelphia.

From three great reels were passed through the cineograph and pictured 5000 feet of life-like and real photographic reproductions of all kinds of scenes and events—nearly a mile, all told.

The reproduction included the Elks parade at Atlantic City, "Scenes on the Brooklyn Bridge," the Chinese funeral held in Philadelphia last May, "Going to a Fire," "Sapho," "Trip to the Moon," "The Darkies' Kiss," "The Irate Model," "A Visit to a Spiritualist," "The Inquisitive Clerk," "Fun in a Photograph Gallery" and many others, including all the principal rounds of the Jeffries-Corbett fight, from the first round to that in which the knock-out blow was administered.

THE CROWD DELIGHTED

Was the great crowd pleased? If applause and cheers and yells of delight indicate anything, it certainly was.

"See Jeffries go for dat mug Corbett," yelled a youngster perched on a point of vantage. "Look at dat upper-cut. Say, it seems almost like bein' right at de fight."

And it certainly did, so distinctly could every move of the contestants and the others in and around the ring be seen.

Besides the moving pictures scores of other pictures were shown by means of a stereopticon. These included, among others, portraits of Mayor Ashbridge, Director English and other city officials, as well as of Fitzsimmons and Sharkey, all of which were greeted with applause.

For all its puffery, the *Inquirer* correctly described Lubin's exhibition as one of the longest motion-picture displays given to that date. Although the emphasis was on variety, the culminating feature was a fight picture: Lubin's reproduction of the most recent heavyweight title bout. The company's ability to pull off such a lengthy and well-received show was a boon to its reputation (particularly as the actual fight was over in five minutes). Even though many of the films were duplicates of competitors' productions, Lubin was promoted from pirate to "Professor."

The public exposure of Lubin's *Jeffries and Corbett* film served as another instance of the motion picture's ability to (temporarily) break down gender and class boundaries within public sphere. The veriscope pictures had given some theatergoing women the opportunity to glimpse images of prizefighters in action. The street showing of Lubin's fight pictures presented another such space. Attention to the moving image was less concerted under these exhibition conditions, as crowd noise and brass bands created a distance not found in the darkened veriscope hall. Yet the opportunity remained.

The *Inquirer* description suggests that the audience was primarily young, male, and working-class, but it also indicates that city dwellers of all sorts came. The *San Francisco Examiner* depictions of similar occasions show mostly male bystanders, but they include a typically foregrounded, lone female figure. Also prominent in both papers' illustrations are streetcars bringing the huge crowds downtown, a reminder that mass transportation was helping reshape the nature of public events. As the "Athletic Woman" columnist wrote from Philadelphia, "The trolley girl is a distinct product of the modern rapid transit." No longer confined to the domestic sphere, the new woman could be "out every night," increasingly integrated into the public.[66] As with the amusement park, the *Inquirer*'s cineograph show offered a mixed-media presentation for a mixed audience, including the women and children otherwise excluded from boxing.

Curiously, no Philadelphia press mentioned that Lubin produced *Reproduction of the Fitzsimmons and Sharkey Fight*, reverting to his use of hired hands to reenact the two-round bout of August 24. Four days later, that film and *Reproduction of the Corbett and McCoy Fight* were both issued copyright registrations. The latter drew renewed press coverage, as the actual participants sparred for Lubin cameras.

On August 30, 1900, the evening of the Jim Corbett–Kid McCoy fight in New York, the *Inquirer* again engaged the cineograph to illustrate its bulletin service, with the 1899 *Reproduction of the Fitzsimmons-Jeffries Fight* providing the main attraction. Its producer was now "the well-known Prof. S. Lubin."[67] Crowds estimated at twenty to thirty thousand packed downtown. A military band played as "the operators in charge of Lubin's wonderful cineograph put their moving pictures in motion." The projection continued for more than two hours before the fight returns were announced to the crowd. The remarkable quantity and diversity of films was unprecedented.

> Through the cineograph were passed 12,000 feet of film containing moving pictures of almost everything under the sun. Parades, dances, fires, trains, comic scenes that convulsed the throng with laughter, runaways, acrobatic performances, everything. The whole eleven rounds of the famous fight in which Jeffries won the championship of the world were given with a vividness that worked the crowd up into the same pitch of enthusiasm those who composed it would in all probability have manifested at the ringside. No such exhibition of moving pictures was ever given before in this country or any other, and to have witnessed it by payment of an admission fee would have probably cost at least $1 per seat.[68]

The newspaper lauded the local filmmaker's "genius." The tribute to Lubin, "the king of the moving picture machine makers and photographers," stressed his fight-picture accomplishments, using exaggeration and misinformation:

> When it comes to prize fight pictures Lubin is doubly the king. Every notable contest in the fistic arena since the Carson City go between Corbett and Fitzsimmons, which he did not take and the pictures of which proved such lamentable failures, his photographers have transferred to yards and yards of films for reproduction for the benefit of the public in his wonderful cineograph. Last night's reproduction by him on the big screen hung across Market street from The Inquirer Building of the Fitzsimmons-Jeffries bout is a sample of what Lubin does. Every motion made by the principals, their seconds and the referee, as well as by those in the audience sitting near enough the ring to be caught by the camera, was pictured upon the screen with a life-likeness that was startling and which aroused the big crowd to the highest pitch of enthusiasm.
>
> In the five years since Lubin entered the moving picture arena he has placed all other moving picture manufacturers in the background. . . . At Lubin's big establishment on South Eighth street, the size and extent of which is a revelation to anyone visiting it for the first time, a trained force of photographers is always on duty, ready to be sent anywhere. . . .
>
> At the big fights the arrangements are not complete unless Lubin is on hand with his picture taking machine. [69]

Lubin cameras, of course, had never filmed a real prize ring. But the company's recruitment of star boxers and its role as illustrator of boxing news lent credence to the misperception that "reproductions" might be recordings. Professor Lubin's months of creative advertising claims were now being reproduced by a major newspaper.

PRIZEFIGHTING'S NADIR: FAKING THE CORBETT-MCCOY FIGHT

The near legitimacy of Lubin fake fight films was upheld briefly when both Corbett and McCoy reenacted their bout in what a headline called "Professor Lubin's Sky Parlor seance." No footage survives, but photographs taken during the production do. The series of images published in Philadelphia newspapers reveal an overflow crowd and the addition of a backdrop representing Madison Square Garden. The *New York Journal* ran five of its own photos as well. "While New York is the greatest city in the country in which to produce fake fights, the fakirs have to come to Philadelphia to get the best reproduction of their contests," jibed the *Record.*[70]

Because Corbett versus McCoy had been the last big battle allowed in New York under the Horton Law, the boxing establishment was glad to have motion-picture reproduction aid its threatened existence. That celebrities like Gentleman Jim and the Kid would hie to Lubin's rooftop indicates how much a part of the American prizefight syndicate Lubin and his company had become.

The *Police Gazette* again sent a reporter to Arch Street.

It seems the correct thing for the participants in a big fight to quietly slip over to Philadelphia a day or two after and go through the motions of continuing the battle before one of Photographer Lubin's continuous picture machines. It wouldn't be Jim Corbett and "Kid" McCoy if, with their inborn instinct for gain, they didn't sight the possibility of gathering a little change for themselves by posing before Mr. Lubin's apparatus. So over they went on September 1 [actually the 4th], and performed, and as the results were satisfactory they will doubtless benefit largely in the shape of royalties, etc., from public exhibitions of the "go."

Unlike the recent Fitzsimmons-Ruhlin reproduction there was in the present instance an entire absence of the secondary personages connected with the fight. Jim Daly, the former heavyweight fighter, represented Charley White as referee; Jack Frawley [head cinematographer] acted as master of ceremonies and timekeeper, and used, in the absence of a gong to announce the beginning and ending of the round, an empty oil can and a hammer.

There was considerable delay over a settlement of the terms of the contract. Corbett and McCoy held out for a larger share of the profits than Professor Lubin felt disposed to give them. After nearly two hours of haggling, a compromise was effected. . . .

Jack Frawley struck the empty oil can with the hammer and the fight was on, but before it had gone two minutes Corbett asked that the rounds be cut short . . . While waiting for the gong to sound in the second round Corbett . . . told the prompter not to forget to remind him of the two wild swings he made in the middle of that round.

From a spectator's point of view the whole proceedings were a farce, but the financial returns to the two men are likely to be very large, if the receipts from the Fitzsimmons-Ruhlin reproduction are to be taken as a criterion.[71]

But the *Life Motion Pictures of the Corbett-McCoy Fight* failed to match the success of *Fitzsimmons-Ruhlin*. Lubin advertisements retreated from their usual hype, and few exhibitions appeared. Occasionally famous names were used in generic endorsements (" 'Greatest Moving Pictures I

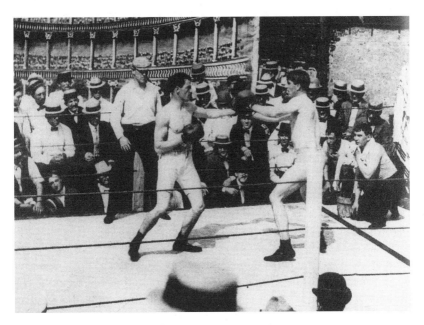

Figure 32.   The real Kid McCoy (left) and Jim Corbett reenact their August 30 Madison Square Garden fight for Lubin on September 4, 1900.

have ever seen.'—Bob Fitzsimmons"). But no mention of fight pictures was made again until *Corbett and McCoy* appeared inconspicuously in a December *Clipper* notice.[72]

"THE HIPPODROMIC EVIL"

Lubin's publicity breakthrough of 1900 coincided with the nadir of prize-fighting's public reputation. With Corbett's unconvincing knockout of McCoy, cries of "Fake!" reached an all-time high among journalists and fans. The *Police Gazette* wrote for months about the "putrid effluvium" generated by the scandal.[73] The fallen idol Corbett still carried the taint of his alleged dive against Tom Sharkey in 1898. The Kid merely added to his reputation as a great boxer who could not always be counted on to perform like "the real McCoy."[74] The Corbett-McCoy fight became so vilified that Lubin's film—a seeming coup de théâtre—turned into a near coup de grâce for the art of the fake.

Boxing had always been marred by its association with gamblers and fixers, but by the turn of the century this connection had brought it to a point of crisis. The word *hippodrome* entered sports lingo to refer to fraudulent, prearranged contests. The Corbett-McCoy affair solidified professional boxing's infamy in New York. Joe Gans's filmed dive before Terry McGovern in December 1900 led to a ban on boxing in Chicago. Philadelphia passed a similar ordinance. By 1901, even the *Police Gazette* lamented the ubiquity of "the hippodromic evil." "Faking as a fine art" was "killing public interest" in the sport.[75]

Motion pictures complicated charges of fraud. When a bout was recorded, suspicions arose that the contest was being altered, if not choreographed, to make for pictures of exploitable length.[76] Filmmakers earned the reputation of being in cahoots with ring promoters. Jack London's novel *The Abysmal Brute* (1911) illustrates this view. His protagonist is a thinly veiled characterization of Jim Jeffries, a natural boxer corrupted by the "ring world syndicate." *The Abysmal Brute* refers often to collusion between boxing and motion pictures. The hero's father warns him to "stay clean . . . no secret arrangements with the movin' pitcher men for guaranteed distance." His shady manager, however, insists the next fight is "not to be shorter than twelve rounds—this for the moving pictures." Before reforming, London's brute agrees to a faked performance: "To the audience it was indubitably a knockout, and the moving picture machines would perpetuate the lie."[77]

Faked fight films, despite their benign roots, added to the patina of deception surrounding prizefights in 1900. When rivals labeled Lubin's work "fake," his films suffered not only from comparison to genuine recordings but also from association with boxing's most illegitimate practices.

LUBIN'S COMEBACK

No fight reproductions and only one prizefight were shot during 1901 and the first half of 1902. The Lubin company produced other genres. When Siegmund Lubin returned from Germany in March 1902, all U.S. production had slowed because of his pyrrhic court victory, which temporarily left motion pictures without copyright protection. The substantial profits he had earned had been lost during his time away.[78] Nevertheless, his firm returned to fight reproduction with the next heavyweight championship, a rematch in which Jim Jeffries again knocked out Fitzsimmons.

Yet this Lubin reenactment, like the sport itself, lacked vitality and cultural currency. The 1901–2 catalog of Lubin films boasted "unsolicited testimonials" from leading boxers, but the *Jeffries-Fitzsimmons Reproduction Prize Fight Films* did little business.[79] Moreover, with boxing's headquarters having relocated to San Francisco, the Philadelphia company no longer had access to its stars and dealmakers.

The following year Lubin's crew shot the last of their heavyweight imitations, *Reproduction of the Jeffries and Corbett Fight* (1903).[80] The actual bout was a tired rematch with predictable results. The film had similar qualities. However fine the cinematography, Lubin fakes could scarcely be differentiated from one another: one-shot recordings of unrecognizable stand-in boxers going through nondescript sparring in the same rooftop ring. Lubin shot three other fight reproductions in 1903, but their subjects offered even less publicity value. The *Dixon-Palmer Fight* (perhaps a dupe of a British film) showed a featherweight contest fought in England. *Reproduction of the Fitzsimmons-Gardner Fight* offered a reenactment of the forty-one-year-old Fitz moving down in class to win a light heavyweight title. Finally, the Lubin catalog pushed *Reproduction of the [Young] Corbett-McGovern Fight (San Francisco, March 31, 1903)*. "We have endeavored to make these fight films as accurate as possible and have even introduced into the pictures the dispute which arose between the fighters and their seconds prior to the fight."[81] Interest in the outcome was dimmed when "Young Corbett II" kayoed the fading ex-champion McGovern for a second time. Bradenburgh's Museum hosted the films' debut, but other venues were scarce.

Further diminishing Lubin's presence, American Mutoscope & Biograph marketed competing fight reproductions in 1903. In shooting its own *Reproduction of McGovern-Corbett Fight* and *Reproduction of Jeffries - Corbett Fight*, Biograph must have felt it could better Lubin at his own game, as both were filmed weeks after the real bouts and the Philadelphia reenactments had occurred.

Biograph offered better-enacted, studio-controlled, condensed depictions that focused on the action in the ring. Its Jeffries-Corbett reproduction shows fighters to better advantage. Shot by Billy Bitzer in the company's new Manhattan studio and lit by overhead Cooper-Hewitt lights, the film reveals only a minimal ringside audience of tuxedoed patrons.[82] The darkened background consists of a painted backdrop of male spectators' faces. Extra, "realistic" touches, such as policemen entering the ring to change Jeffries' gloves, were added but are more restrained than Lubin's wide-open, anarchic pantomimes.

The earlier *Reproduction of McGovern-Corbett Fight* (figure 33) has identical qualities. The *Biograph Bulletin* emphasized that the figures were "shown sharp and clean-cut as a cameo," thanks to the "electric light" photography that had been used in their "great picture of the Jeffries-Sharkey

Figure 33. Left: Biograph's *Reproduction of Corbett-McGovern Fight* (1903). Terry McGovern's corner literally throws in the sponge during the reenactment with "Young Corbett II." Right: *Dixon–Chester Leon Contest* (1906). George Dixon is shown in his only surviving motion-picture appearance. (Library of Congress, Motion Picture, Broadcasting and Recorded Sound Division.)

Contest" in 1899.[83] Although Biograph bouts were half the length of Lubin's (723 feet compared with 1,500 feet for this eleven-round bout), their controlled action made them attractive. The New York company also recruited better talent. Its Jeffries-Corbett reenactors were stand-ins, but the McGovern film boasted the actual participants. Biograph's final boxing venture, the *Dixon-Leon Contest,* also cast the genuine fighters. In February 1906, Bitzer recorded the ring veteran George Dixon (who was retiring) and the journeyman Casper Leon in a straightforward three-round boxing exhibition. Unlike other sparring films, *Dixon-Leon* shows two boxers going at it in earnest. The production, then, was something of an oddity, showing perhaps the only above-board fight between two actual prizefighters performing solely at the behest of film producers. Nevertheless, the mise-en-scène replicates earlier studio reenactments and uses the same set that appears in *Mr. Butt-in,* Bitzer's narrative film shot on February 1 and 2.[84]

Biograph's fight pictures were not in direct competition with Lubin's. These easily produced, one-shot shorts were not intended for feature exploitation. Rather, the fight films, with their on-screen cigar-smoking, sporting-gentlemen spectators, were intended to complement Biograph's extensive catalog of stag, "smoking concert" films. These underground novelties, inspired by burlesque subjects, were produced by several companies (including Edison, Pathé, and Biograph) through at least 1908. Viewed in mutoscope peep shows and specially arranged stag screenings, boxing subjects appeared alongside risqué striptease scenes, much as they did in live burlesque.[85]

PHASING OUT FAKE FIGHT FILMS

In 1904 neither prizefights nor reenactments were filmed in the United States. Boxing's popularity was waning, and motion picture production had shifted to fictional narratives. However, when fight pictures made a come-back between 1905 and 1908, Lubin's ring reproductions did not keep up with changing production practices. But by 1904 the company was success-fully making its own transition to narrative film.

As I show in the next chapter, Miles Bros. of San Francisco dominated the market for prizefight recordings during the early nickelodeon period. With experienced camera operators, an early rental distribution system, and proximity to California and Nevada boxing sites, the Miles operation made complete, authentic films of prizefights widely available. Beginning in 1907, European fight pictures also got extensive distribution in the United States.3

Lubin's last forays into ring reproductions suffered in this new environ-ment. Consistent with its duping practices, Lubin tried to pass off a print of the first Miles recording, *Nelson-Britt Prize Fight,* as one of its own reen-actments. Suspiciously, when Miles Bros. released its $100,000 film in Sep-tember 1905, Lubin shifted his titles from "Reproduction of" to "Imper-sonation." Whereas the former designation suggested authenticity in a fake version, the latter sounded as if the subject truly was an imitation of an original. Yet the print of *Impersonation of Britt-Nelson Fight* deposited in the Library of Congress under Lubin's name is not a recreation but a pho-tographic duplicate of the Miles copyrighted documentary. Lubin also shot a staged version of its own.[86] Where the two versions came into competi-tion, the fake was badly beaten. At the New Orleans Greenwall Theatre, for example, "The Original Britt-Nelson Fight Pictures" attracted record crowds. The proprietor's disclaimer—"$500 will be paid to anyone who can prove that these are not the original pictures taken at Colma, California, September 9"—was aimed at the fake, which showed at the same theater in November 1905.[87]

Further evidence of the decline of the Lubin product came from the same New Orleans theater the following year. Having to compete with the documentarists, the company tried filming reenactments of fights that had not been recorded: *Impersonation of the Fitzsimmons-O'Brien Fight* (No-vember–December 1905) and *Nelson-McGovern Fight* (March 1906). How-ever, when the former played with a burlesque show at the Greenwall in February 1906, it was so poorly received that the manager had to substitute other films before the run ended. With its exclusive reproductions faring so badly, the Lubin company's final attempt to compete head to head presented little threat to the Miles brothers. Lubin's *Reproduction of the Nelson-Gans Fight* was sold by Biograph as well, with the promise that "This is the fight the country is talking about."[88] While it was true that this forty-two-round interracial grudge match had renewed public interest in prizefighting, the illustrated newspaper of cinema now had reliable, authentic and complete motion pictures of such events.

The Lubin Manufacturing Company, as it was now called, continued to expand, joining the other leading American firms in making narrative films its cornerstone. In 1907 it also joined the ranks of indoor studio producers. When Lubin put out one last fake fight film, *Reproduction of Burns-Palmer Fight, London (England), February 10, 1908*, it was ridiculed. *Variety*'s review of the film's appearance as "an extra attraction with the 'Vanity Fair' Company" took note of its poor quality. Lubin's fakery was scorned as anathema and anachronism.

> The picture [has] bogus contestants. The arena and ring are poorly contrived, and at a first glance the film shows upon its face that it is a "fake" pure and simple. About a dozen tiers of benches hold a gathering of observers who have been very poorly rehearsed in their duties, and their enthusiasm over the "fake" is vastly greater than that of the audience which witnesses the picture. There are knock downs galore, many times when no blow is shown to have been delivered, and the final knockout is a ridiculous piece of fakery. . . . If the Buffalo convention [at which distributors formed the Film Service Association] shall have accomplished no more than to prevent reproductions of valuable films it will have achieved a great benefit to the moving picture industry. Several years ago it was a custom in Philadelphia to reproduce any film which seemed to have elements of popularity, and at one time merely mentioning the name of the Quaker City was enough to make film manufacturers outside of that town "throw a fit."[89]

By year's end, Lubin had closed ranks with his rivals to form the Motion Picture Patents Company. Obliged not to copy his colleagues' properties, as well as to concentrate on meeting the cartel's demand for one-reel narratives, Lubin abandoned the genre that had become his trademark. Other MPPC members did likewise.

Ironically, on the only other occasion when filmed boxing reenactments came on the market, Lubin, as an MPPC member, was the one whose film property was threatened. In 1910, America turned its attention to the MPPC-owned film of the controversial Jack Johnson–Jim Jeffries heavyweight championship fight. At least three fly-by-night companies attempted to sell filmed re-creations. The nature of these "impersonations" and "reproductions" was clear to potential distributors and exhibitors. The producers' hopes for a share of the fight-film profits were largely based on a widespread banning of the real fight pictures. The Johnson-Jeffries reenactments were not comparable to the ambiguously advertised Lubin reproductions.

The leading chronicler of prizefighting in this era, Nat Fleischer, wrote in 1946: "In those days boxing publicity was loaded with hooey. As you look over the sports pages of long ago, you wonder why so much piffle was printed and whether the sports editors really thought their public was swallowing all the malarkey they dished out."[90] The genre of fake fight films must be seen in this context. Ring promotion and motion-picture exploitation were infected with ballyhoo. At their intersection came the idiosyncratic phenomenon of the faked fight picture. The surviving fragments of these archaic cinematic attractions hold little meaning to latter-day viewers. As movies, they are opaque and alien.

If we rehistoricize the faked prizefight film as a hybrid of early cinema, the role of "reproductions" becomes clearer. Reenactments of topical events were tolerated, at times welcomed, because there was no expectation of actuality footage. Borrowing from the traditions of boxing, burlesque, circus, carnival, and yellow journalism—each with its "fakirs"—Lubin capitalized on this dubious ethos. When possible, the company sold its films as recordings of actual prizefights. Since genuine motion pictures of popular ring extravaganzas were often not taken, or were botched, these "life-like" approximations were sought by show people and audiences. As *Moving Picture World* said of Siegmund Lubin in 1916, "his 'reproductions' of famous prize fights were clean-up material for the picture promoters" of the 1890s.[91] As reliable location cinematography cut into the market for fakes, Lubin compensated, recruiting star pugilists and offering cheaper, nonexclusive fight pictures. When a flood of authentic boxing films marginalized reenactments, Lubin and others abandoned such productions and embraced the industrial and aesthetic standards of a new era.

5 Fight Pictures in the Nickelodeon Era

Miles Bros. of New York &
San Francisco, 1905–1912

The fortunes of the prize ring are apparently interwoven with those of the moving picture. Without the moving picture your modern prize fight would be shorn of most of its financial glamor and possibilities; without the prize fight the moving picture would not appeal to so many people as it apparently does.

"Pictures and Pugilism," *Moving Picture World*,
December 18, 1909

After the lull in production in 1904, fight pictures began a comeback with the lucrative *Nelson-Britt Prize Fight,* shot in San Francisco on September 9, 1905, by three cinematographers from the local Miles Bros. company. The Miles operation led a return to the exploitation of fight films over the next seven years. For the first three, it was the only company to shoot bouts in the United States. Others followed suit. Production increased each year in both America and Europe, peaking in 1910 with a flurry surrounding the interracial heavyweight battle between Jim Jeffries and Jack Johnson. More than fifty fight pictures were made between 1905 and 1915: at least two dozen in the United States, nearly as many in Britain, and a half dozen more in France. An unknown number of other bouts were recorded for nontheatrical or clandestine screenings. Some survive in private hands, with one noted collector claiming to own recordings of fifty other prizefights from before 1915.[1] Whatever the quantity, a federal ban on their interstate transport caused American fight-picture production to all but cease by 1914.

The genre thus underwent remarkable transformations between 1905 and 1915—from dormant to hot property and back again in a single decade. This was also a period during which cinema was transformed from a small-scale commercial operation open to many enterprising producers to a large-scale, studio-based oligopoly.[2] Motion pictures became a massively popular and influential part of everyday life, with millions of people attending the thousands of movie shows that proliferated after 1905. Throughout this transition, producers, exhibitors, and, for the first time, distributors, looked to fight films for use as features. Major companies supplemented their regular line, and independents sought to exploit single films. The Miles brothers, consummate middlemen, positioned their operation between these two ends of the spectrum. Their business fortunes paralleled those of the fight picture: Miles Bros., Inc., quickly rose to and then faded from prominence.

Simultaneously with the expansion of the motion picture industry, American progressivism implemented an age of reform, critiquing and regulating the practices of cinema and other social institutions. Debates increased about the class, race, gender, and age of audiences for movies in general and fight films in particular. (Boxing's racial tensions dominated this discourse; they are considered in the next chapters.) With the ring in disrepute, the film industry tempered its promotion of pugilism with a professed goal of social uplift, negotiating ways to profit from fight pictures while acceding to restrictions.

THE MILES BROTHERS AND THE RETURN OF THE FIGHT FILM, 1905–1908

In the period 1905 to 1908, the American film industry organized to enable growth. Exhibitors formed trade associations to coordinate their interests. The major manufacturers formed the Motion Picture Patents Company (MPPC) in 1908, agreeing to share technologies and curb competitors. In 1910, the Patents Company consolidated distributorships into the monopolistic General Film Co. All parties communicated through the new trade journals. *Views and Film Index* (begun in April 1906), *Moving Picture World* (March 1907), *Moving Picture News* (May 1908), the British *Bioscope* (October 1908), and the *Nickelodeon* (January 1909) joined *Variety* (December 1905). The key to capitalizing on the efforts of producers and theaters was the establishment of a distribution system. Offering exhibitors an alternative to buying prints, regional businesses bought reels in quantity and rented them for short runs. More than one hundred film "exchanges" set up offices in the United States, making the boom in nickelodeons possible. Miles Bros. soon advertised itself as "the pioneers and originators of film rental service."[3]

Although the Miles company has not been sufficiently studied, historians and contemporaries alike credit it as one of the first successful motion-picture rental businesses. However, its production efforts were limited, focusing mainly on the prize ring. Miles Bros. copyrighted only thirteen original films, all between 1905 and 1907. A dozen were actualities, eight of which were boxing subjects. After success with the *Nelson-Britt Prize Fight* (1905), Miles cameras shot at least seven other prizefights, all in California, Nevada, or New Mexico: *Gans-Nelson Contest* (1906), *O'Brien-Burns Contest* (1906), *Gans-Herman Fight* (1907), *Squires vs. Burns* (1907), a Gans-Nelson rematch (1908), *Ketchel-Papke Fight* (1909), and Jack Johnson's defeat of Jim Flynn (1912). Using three or four cameras at each event, the brothers employed other technicians, including former Biograph cinematographer George Dobson.[4]

Who were the brothers Miles? There were four, all in the family business. The Miles twins, Herbert L. and Harry J., were pioneer filmmakers and exhibitors before launching into the exchange and fight-picture businesses. Photographers by profession, they left Ohio in 1897 with a movie camera of their own design. They traveled to the Klondike goldfields, making and showing motion pictures. In Nome and the Alaskan mining towns they catered to a male, working-class culture that welcomed prizefighting. On their return trek in 1901, the Mileses operated a storefront movie show in Seattle. Later they set up a commercial photography studio in San Francisco, where they also continued shooting motion pictures, some on contract for Edison. Their younger brothers Earle and Joseph joined the business, running a theater and soon an exchange.

In early 1903, Harry Miles, the company president, went to New York. There he sold some thirty of his Alaska and Northwest scenic films to American Mutoscope and Biograph (including *Panorama of "Miles Canyon," Dog Baiting and Fighting in Valdez, Winter Sport on Snake River, Nome*, and *Willamette Falls*). Harry also purchased a batch of secondhand actuality reels and established a distribution office directly across the street. Returning to San Francisco, he recorded topical footage for Biograph, including President Theodore Roosevelt's visit in May 1903. By December, Miles Bros. began renting prints to exhibitors on a weekly basis.[5]

Others hit on the rental idea as well, but the Miles exchanges had the greatest reach, supplying provincial theaters from coast to coast. Three of the brothers also operated one of Manhattan's early nickelodeons (from November 1905 until June 1908) while Earle managed the California operations. Poised to move into the ranks of the major producers, Miles Bros. built a studio and lab in San Francisco in 1906. But fires ignited by the earthquake that rocked the city on April 18 destroyed their facilities. Their own photographs best document the total desolation (see figure 34).

Despite the devastation, Miles Bros. continued as an ambitious film service from its Eastern office, and 1907 was a breakthrough year. When *Moving*

Figure 34.   Members of the Miles family and employees pose in front of
the ruins of their business after the 1906 San Francisco earthquake and fire.
(The Bancroft Library, University of California, Berkeley.)

Picture World began publication in March, Miles was a big advertiser, causing editors to deny reports "that this publication is owned or controlled by Miles Bros., of New York."[6] The journal did, however, hail Miles as "the first who recognized the importance of and catered to the continuous motion picture theaters," later noting that "Herbert Miles controlled a string of 'store shows'" in Eastern cities.[7] He spent that spring in Europe, setting up London and Paris offices and making import deals with eighteen European film manufacturers. In August, a six-story Miles Building opened in Manhattan, billed as the "largest plant in the world devoted exclusively to the moving picture industry."[8] The brand was enjoying such success that, for example, the showman Louis B. Mayer could enter the field in fall 1907 by launching his Orpheum Theater as "the home of refined entertainment devoted to Miles Brothers moving pictures and illustrated songs."[9] In November, Miles Brothers, Inc., was incorporated in New York with $1,000,000 in capital and boasting five million feet of celluloid in its distribution library. Herbert became the founding treasurer of the Moving Picture Exhibitors' Association.[10]

On New Year's Day 1908, the family business suffered another sudden tragedy. Harry J. Miles fell to his death during an epileptic seizure. The front

Figure 35.   A Miles still photographer recorded the Miles Bros. ringside camera platform (ca. 1906–9). The sign reads: "The Moving Picture People, New York and San Francisco." (The Bancroft Library, University of California, Berkeley.)

page of the *New York Times* reported that the forty-year-old bachelor was living with his newlywed brother and wife when he fell from a window of their seventh-floor apartment. The surviving brothers had a staff of employees, but the death of their chief partner, president, inventor, "mechanician," and cinematographer dealt a blow to the corporation.[11]

In May 1910, the Patents Company forced Miles Bros.—and nearly every other American exchange—out of the mainstream distribution business. This strong-arm economic and legal maneuver was a key part of the leading producer-distributors' attempt to monopolize the picture business. MPPC's General Film Company canceled the supply of reels it sent to Miles offices in New York, San Francisco, Boston, and Baltimore, forcing them into bankruptcy. Just weeks before, in "Herbert Miles—A Picture Pioneer," *Moving Picture World* had portrayed the firm as an important one, noting that "Miles nearly boxed the compass of the motion picture field by becoming film manufacturers, but they did not."[12]

The reference to Miles's "boxing" was a pun. From 1905 to 1912, the brothers were known as the specialists in prizefight cinematography. From November 15, 1901, when the Edison Manufacturing Company recorded the Jeffries-Ruhlin pictures, until September 9, 1908, when Selig Polyscope filmed the third Nelson-Gans fight, the Miles brothers were the only camera crew filming prizefights in the United States. During this period, boxing remained a constant presence in cinema, thanks to the recycling of older films, European imports, and Lubin reenactments. But after its banishment from New York in 1900, popular interest in prizefighting had waned. The Miles cameras helped revive it.

THE BATTLING NELSON–JIMMY BRITT FIGHT PICTURES

Although every member of the picture business knew the value of plum fight films, Harry and Herbert Miles's pursuit of them was circumstantial. With offices in both San Francisco and New York (making it the first bicoastal movie company), their company was an ideal agent for boxing promotion as the sport migrated westward. Aside from Edison, which had filmed inside Mechanics' Pavilion in 1901, no companies had been willing to make the train ride to the West Coast to film boxing on the slim chance that both the bout and photography would turn out well. As Miles Bros. was starting to boom in 1905, fight promoters rebounded with the first match-up to capture public interest since the retirement of Jim Jeffries: a lightweight championship bout between the San Franciscan Jimmy Britt and the Danish-born American Oscar "Battling" Nelson.

The Miles firm was developing its production interests when sports promoter James W. Coffroth opened a large stadium in nearby Colma. His open-air ring and "Sunshine Arena" accommodated cinematography. Having made a career of location photography, the brothers struck a deal with Coffroth, paying an astounding $135,000 for the film rights for the battle between Britt and Nelson.[13]

In his punning "Miles of Moving Picture Ribbon," W. W. Naughton wrote of the elaborate preparation by Coffroth and the Miles brothers to insure an exploitable recording of the fight. The Miles crew was armed with "twelve and a half miles of [film] ribbon. . . . I have heard that even if the contest is of moderate length it will take three operators, working shifts of eight hours each, five continuous twenty-four-hour days to develop the films. Coffroth and the picture men are thinking up schemes for encouraging the fighters to get through with their parts of the proceedings as quickly as possible. The cost of snapping the fighters in motion will be about $100 a round, or $33 a minute." Naughton noted that a fight longer than twenty rounds would create a prohibitively high cost in negatives and be too long for theatrical display. "Coffroth and his colleagues are to be pardoned," he said, "for stimulating Britt and Nelson to rapid action," even if the stimulus was a cash bonus to the pugilist who scored an optimally timed knockout.[14]

Photographs and motion pictures of the event demonstrate that Coffroth staged an impressive spectacle and that Miles Bros.' cinematography was successful. An impressive panoramic still taken by a Miles photographer, published in the *San Francisco Examiner*, conveys the import of the moment. The camera platform in the arena is shown off in the moving-picture panorama that preceded footage of the fight itself. The boxing was recorded in unedited fashion, with only slight reframing pans. But the panorama, a common genre of early cinema, was taken from the center of the ring, panning through three hundred degrees to show the fenced-in arena. Midway through the pan the camera stand is visible, bearing a promotional sign for "Miles Bros., the Moving Picture People."[15]

Another preliminary in the film is the ritual introduction of celebrities, including Jim Jeffries, by perennial ring emcee Billy Jordan. Like his Eastern counterpart Joe Humphries, Jordan sometimes worked as a lecturer for fight-picture screenings. His filmed introductions are pitched to the camera, ignoring fans on the other sides of the ring. Next, a photographer enters the ring with a tripod and still camera, documenting the ritual posing of the two boxers in "fighting attitudes."

The footage of Battling Nelson knocking out Jimmy Britt in the eighteenth round survives intact. Cinematically unremarkable, it consists of single long shots from one angle, unedited except for the jump cuts visible when the camera magazines were reloaded. However, the *Nelson-Britt Prize Fight* provides clearer pictures than earlier films. The Miles brothers avoided the mishaps experienced by other ringside camera operators (although the knockout nearly took place out of camera range, as Nelson pushed Britt into a corner).[16]

The Nelson-Britt pictures also reveal a distinctive Miles Bros. production technique. As in later works, the filmmakers hung lettered cards from the ring ropes. At the beginning of each round, we see a man sitting in a back corner replacing the cue card with a different one. The letters have no sequence or pattern. A different cryptic series was used for each production. This practice served two functions. First, the cards indirectly identified the films as Miles property. Second, the scrambled sets of letters functioned as cues for editors assembling the separate camera negatives. The letters told a cutter which pieces of film corresponded to particular rounds.[17] Presumably this odd practice was also meant to frustrate pirates who might steal or duplicate reels.

The *Nelson-Britt Prize Fight* captured a sensational athletic performance that received enormous publicity, and prizefighting rebounded into public interest. A crowd of fifteen thousand men paying $48,000 for tickets cheered the hard-hitting contest. The *Examiner* predicted a huge profit margin for the motion pictures and chronicled their status:

> Pictures of the lightweights have turned out to be thorough successes.
>
> At midnight last night [September 11] the Miles brothers, who handled the apparatus at the ringside, and who have been in their dark rooms with their miles of precious film ever since, were able to see with their own eyes and to make the announcement that . . . the good people of other cities and towns and hamlets who . . . will now be able to pay a dime to get in and sit down to see just everything. . . .
>
> The film, carefully guarded, was carried to the Miles Brothers' establishment on Turk Street immediately after the battle. Experts in the art of photography have been busy ever since. . . . But now the crisis has passed. The film has been toned and fixed.

With uncanny irony, the *Examiner* predicted that the Nelson-Britt fight pictures held such profit potential that "the only way J. Edward Britt, James W. Coffroth and the Miles brothers can lose now is by catastrophe of fire, earthquake or some other equally improbable variety."[18] Seven months later, of course, they met exactly that improbable fate.

The *Nelson-Britt Prize Fight* went to market quickly, appearing in New York and San Francisco before the end of the month. A press screening was organized on September 23, when the pictures "were thrown upon the white wall in Miles brothers' developry" for W. W. Naughton, Coffroth, Britt, and a few others. News items attributed varied reactions to the local hero Britt when he saw the film. One said he thought the films proved him the victim of a lucky punch. Another reported that Britt thought they showed he made a fool of himself. Still another alleged: "The first time Jimmy Britt saw the moving-picture reproduction of his losing battle against the irreducible Dane he fainted." Such talk encouraged curiosity in seeing the replay of a fight. As Naughton suggested, "It will be interesting to learn what story the films will tell to thousands and thousands of wise sports who were not at the ringside."[19]

The story the films told varied depending on where and how they were seen, and by whom. For the socialist Jack London, who witnessed the fight, the battle represented brutal class warfare between Nelson, who "looked like a proletarian that had known lean and hungry years," and Britt, who "looked the well-fed and prosperous bourgeoise [*sic*]." Feeding the reformist push to ban boxing, London described the fight as a demonstration of "the abysmal brute" beating organized intelligence. Watching such an exhibition, he wrote without condemnation, "we are temporarily insane. Reason is gone. The brute has charge of us."[20]

Such rhetoric was repeated when progressives later argued for fight-picture censorship, but in 1905 fans of the Nelson-Britt pictures made the opposite argument. They emphasized that motion pictures made watching a prizefight "cleaner" than experiencing the blood and sweat in person. Some encouraged women and families to see the film.

The recruitment of a female clientele started as a means of garnering publicity and ameliorating opposition. Britt was groomed to be the next Gentleman Jim. A week before the contest, the actress May Irwin enhanced this image with a publicity stunt. A group of women were admitted to Britt's seaside training camp. Armed with cameras, they flocked to snap "souvenir films of the champion" in his swimsuit. This gender-role reversal—women using the camera for the voyeuristic pleasure of seeing a man's exposed body—continued in an interview. Irwin thrived on comic crossings of gender lines. Her San Francisco stage appearance featured a sparring scene in which she knocked out her male costar. Playing on this image, she expounded on feminine respectability for the drama critic Ashton Stevens: "And speaking of respectability, there's just one thing I'd rather do than play Camille [with Jim Corbett] again. I'd rather go to Colma and see that Britt-Nelson fight. Of course my boys will be there. I suppose I'd leave a couple of orphans at the first sight of gore—but just the same I'd like to see the fight. Oh, you lucky men!"[21] May Irwin was hardly a model of respectable middle-class femininity, but her comments helped alter the gender lines in fight attendance.

Additional San Francisco reporting on the Miles films encouraged women to watch the goreless motion-picture reproductions of Britt's knockout. However, the films did not rely on the legitimating trappings of an opera house or academy of music to accommodate female patrons. Instead these "Most Marvelous Moving Pictures" were screened inside Mechanics' Pavilion itself, the headquarters of California prizefighting. The matinee and evening shows were touted as "An Exhibition That Your Family May See." After a successful Sunday premiere, seating accommodations were expanded in the pavilion and continued to be filled. Reviews noted that "the crowd sitting in the darkness gazed at the [knockout] scene in silence,"

and "remarks heard as the tide of the battle ebbed and flowed were" a subdued version of those made during a live fight.[22]

Little of the stigma previously attached to women appearing in a proletarian, male-dominated space was evident. The *Examiner* advocated that respectable women and mothers should enjoy the "Fight Fotos." The Nelson-
Britt film was "like the theatre." Above all it was "fun"—as when the
gallery laughed at the announcer, Billy Jordan, appearing sans his booming
voice; and it was "dramatic"—as when melodramatic boos greeted the images of the betting commissioner, Harry Corbett, and Nelson's manager,
Billy Nolan (who were in the midst of a bribery scandal). The report concluded:

> Taking your mother to the pictures of the Nelson-Britt battle is no
> more a crime than would be the taking of your mother to [actor]
> Wilton Lackaye in [Frank Norris's] "The Pit" or in any other play
> through which he has given quickness to the pulse.
>
> The camera has toned away anything repulsively real in what hap-
> pened to Jimmy several days back. At the same time you are getting all
> that occurred—with the red removed.[23]

Cinema, in reproducing the segregated milieu of the prize ring, again
enabled the breaking of social taboos. By abstracting the real, motion pictures provided the "crack in the curtain" that gave women an entree to
a world previously deemed unsuitable for them. The vested interests of
the sporting and theatrical community encouraged this function of the
movies.

The run of fight pictures again was on. *Nelson-Britt Prize Fight* reached
a national audience more quickly than its predecessors because of the Miles
Bros. exchange network. Before the end of September, the film was already
being booked for its October run in New York. There, *Police Gazette* columnist Sam C. Austin endorsed them: "There is a wonderful fascination about
the pictures of the Battling Nelson-Jimmy Britt fight which I cannot explain. Night after night I have sat in front of the big white curtain watching with interest the recurring episodes which transpired during the memorable battle. There is something which impresses the beholder after it is all
over." [24] By November, Miles prints had reached sites as far-flung as Colorado and Louisiana, playing with burlesque and variety shows. At the
Greenwall Theatre in New Orleans, the film attracted record crowds.[25]

The financial success of the *Nelson-Britt Prize Fight* was great enough
(well over $100,000) to make Jimmy Britt a fiscal loser for selling his share
to Coffroth for $5,000. The profits cannot be gauged accurately, however, as
financial disputes kept the parties in court.[26]

THE GANS-NELSON CONTEST AT GOLDFIELD, NEVADA

After the San Francisco earthquake, it took half a year for the ring enterprise to revive. As the city rebuilt, boxers and their photographers found other headquarters. By Labor Day 1906, new entrepreneurs were mounting boxing's next major production. The first-time promoter George Lewis "Tex" Rickard staged a lightweight championship match between the challenger Battling Nelson and the titleholder, Joe Gans. Rickard became the leading promoter of the sport, bringing its million-dollar profits to New York in the 1920s. The highly anticipated match came off in the mining boomtown of Goldfield, Nevada, when Rickard and a local citizens' council put up a $30,000 purse. Gans retained his title when Nelson struck a foul blow after a marathon of forty-two rounds. Gans-Nelson became a high-profile grudge match, leading to two rematches in 1908. All three fights were filmed and successfully marketed.

A rookie at the fight game, Rickard hired the experienced Miles Bros. team to record the bout. The *Gazette* confirmed Miles's close association with boxing, noting that "the contract has been signed for the moving pictures with Miles Brothers, of San Francisco, the same firm that made the panorama of the Britt-Nelson fight." The Mileses received a cash payment of $2,500, with profits divided equally among Nelson, Gans, and the sponsor. Rickard knew that filming the event was paramount. When a large canvas was suggested to protect fighters from the desert sun, he vetoed it, because it "would interfere with the moving pictures."[27]

Rickard enticed five thousand spectators to make the train trip to Goldfield. Theodore Roosevelt Jr. and the stage star Nat Goodwin brought publicity, appearing alongside John L. Sullivan—whose posing "majestically before the picture machine" elicited a shout of "Quit stallin' for the movin' pictures" from the savvy gallery.[28] Rickard also enlisted a female clientele, announcing, "We are going to make it possible for women—good women— to see the fight."[29] "Out of the usual order," the *Gazette* reported, some "two hundred women of seeming refinement" witnessed the event.[30]

The unusually long bout again signaled to filmmakers the risks inherent in boxing's unpredictability. Miles edited the film to manageable lengths for exhibitors, but the duration of the contest meant that "the 42nd round was taken after six o'clock, and [was] naturally not as distinct as the preceding rounds." The duel thrilled those at ringside but nearly rendered it impossible to record the ending because of the fading light. No doubt in reference to their skill in shooting under these circumstances, the Miles brothers branded their production company Sunset Films, adding a setting-sun logo to their storefront and prints.

Initial reports to the contrary, however, the sunlight lasted long enough. When a "coterie of local [New York] newspaper and sporting men saw the first exhibition" of the *Gans-Nelson Contest,* the replay of the controversial foul blow was the focus of interest. While "a few defects" were noted in the print, this Miles sequel was deemed "much clearer than the Britt-Nelson pictures." The camera distance, much greater than for the Colma fight, left the fighters small within the frame (see figure 37). "The punch is so short and the action so rapid that it is a very difficult thing to see," the *Gazette* reported. "In fact, very few of those present [at the press screening] saw the punch the first time the round was run off. The round was re-run a second time at a slower speed and the foul punch was very evident."[31]

The Nelson camp offered a counterinterpretation. Doctored illustrations, purporting to be "taken from the film and reproduced" for newspapers, showed Nelson landing a clean blow and the referee, George Siler, out of position to see it. Once the Miles pictures were widely seen, however, such misrepresentations were dismissed as typical prizefight yawp. The film debuted successfully at the New York Theater on October 8.[32]

Fight pictures continued to play to diverse audiences in multiple settings. The *Gans-Nelson Contest* found greater success among the working-class, male constituency of burlesque shows than with the mixed audiences of nickelodeons. By December 1906, the Empire Theatrical Circuit reported that picture profits of $10,000 were owed to "the Goldfield Picture Company." Tex Rickard and Billy Nolan disputed the division of the money. Nolan was arrested for embezzlement, but the parties reconciled. Gans was given exclusive film rights in North America; Nelson was allotted two prints to exploit in Europe. Rickard and Nolan had fifteen prints on the Empire circuit.

Empire was one of two theatrical circuits that controlled burlesque. Based in the West, it featured "hot" stag shows for white, working-class men (and shared a building with Miles Bros. before the earthquake); Columbia, the chain of houses in the East, offered "clean" burlesque. In its first two months, the *Gans-Nelson Contest* netted tens of thousands of dollars on the Empire circuit, demonstrating that fight pictures were an important part of burlesque's "boys' night out" entertainment.[33]

Fight pictures also made their way into the burgeoning all-movie shows. When mixed into the nickelodeon's variety programming, prizefight films played to expanded audiences. The *Gans-Nelson Contest* ran in movie houses for a year, alongside short comedies, dramas, and actualities. In July 1907, *Moving Picture World* commented on audience reactions to the film in a neighborhood nickelodeon. "Women and Prize Fights" conveyed the writer's sexist frustration at listening to women talk to one another during

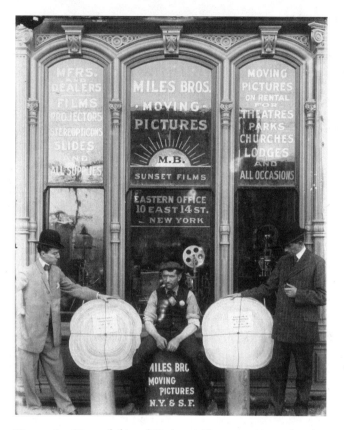

Figure 36.   Harry (left) and Herbert Miles preparing to ship the
biggest paper-print rolls ever deposited for copyright at the Library of Congress, the forty-two-round *Gans-Nelson Contest,
Goldfield, Nevada, September 3, 1906.* (The Bancroft Library,
University of California, Berkeley.)

the screening about a sport of which they professed ignorance.[34] Regardless
of its trivial slant, however, the item confirms that boxing films in the nickelodeon period still had a long shelf life and circulated among both fans and
casual spectators. Even without a heavyweight star, prizefighting was re-
gaining wide exposure through motion pictures.

SUBSEQUENT MILES BROS. FIGHT PICTURES

With another moneymaker under their belt, the Miles brothers maintained
their hold on American boxing footage for another two years. In March 1907,

Figure 37. Frames from the original paper print of the *Gans-Nelson Contest*, scanned one hundred years later. (Library of Congress, Motion Picture, Broadcasting and Recorded Sound Division.)

the first titles the company advertised in *Moving Picture World* were their still-popular *Gans-Nelson* and the more recent *O'Brien-Burns Fight*.[35]

Miles cameras, abetted by Cooper-Hewitt lights, filmed the latter inside a Los Angeles arena in November 1906. "Pictures of Burns-O'Brien Fight Are Great," proclaimed a headline in the *Gazette*. But the match itself was deemed "anything but an interesting boxing exhibition." The new heavyweight titleholder, Tommy Burns, fought "Philadelphia" Jack O'Brien for twenty repetitious rounds before police stepped in (to keep to California's legal limit), and the referee, Jim Jeffries, declared a draw. Miles Bros. promoted the "famous *Burns-O'Brien Contest*" in trade ads, but their terms indicate its diminished value. Prints of the seven-reel film were sold for $1,000 or rented for $35 a day. The stalemated contest made for disappointing sales.[36]

Herbert and Harry Miles's attraction to prizefighting persisted, however. Their crew soon traveled back to Nevada, where the lightweight champion, Joe Gans, fought Chicago's Kid Herman on New Year's Day 1907. Again they successfully illuminated an indoor arena for motion-picture cameras. The mining town of Tonopah, imitating Goldfield, hosted the fight to the finish, awarding $20,000 to Gans for his eighth-round knockout of Herman. Less than three weeks later, Miles's *Gans-Herman Fight* screened in New York. Sime Silverman, the Broadway oracle and founder of *Variety* magazine, reviewed their work approvingly:

> "Miles Bros." stamped upon the opening announcement of the moving pictures of the Gans-Herman fight at Tonopah, Nevada, on last New Year's Day guaranteed the genuineness of the pictures, which speak for themselves. A few preliminaries showed local celebrities of the mining district, including a seven-foot sheriff, all described by Joe Humphreys, the professional announcer. . . . The series is somewhat lengthy, partly occasioned by two changes of reels, but there is no marked delay in the eight rounds between the colored and white fighter. Excepting a slight photographic disturbance in the early part, the pictures are clear and the movements of the men easily followed. In the eighth the "knockout" occurs . . . and when notified in advance by announcer Humphreys of what was coming no one missed it. The after scenes, with Herman insensible, the crowd surging in the ring and the sheriff ordering the building cleared ended the exhibition. The atmosphere of the prize ring being absent, with the women present unaware of the nature or seriousness of the blows, as shown in pictures only, there is no reason why the "Gans-Herman Fight" series should not be a feature act on the bill.[37]

In April 1907, Miles Bros. found they had competition when George Kleine imported the first of many British boxing pictures into the United States. Produced by Urban-Eclipse, the short (half-reel) film showing "Gunner" James Moir defeating "Tiger" Smith for the English heavyweight title attracted minor attention. Later British productions and Kleine Optical Company fight projects proved more successful.

Yet Miles Bros./Sunset Films maintained its unique claim on American prizefights when Tommy Burns again defended his crown. Despite its grandiose title, *International Contest for the Heavyweight Championship: Squires vs. Burns, Ocean View, Cal., July 4, 1907* failed to deliver a ring performance suitable for movie exploitation, as Burns knocked out the

Australian challenger in the first round. Having shot actuality footage surrounding the event, however, the producers assembled a full thousand-foot reel documenting the circumstances of the fight. Herbert Miles recorded Squires in training and Jim Jeffries, now a referee, on his California ranch.[38] When twenty thousand spectators packed Coffroth's Arena for the Independence Day spectacular, Miles filmed surrounding scenes. Two "panorama" films were copyrighted separately. One motion picture (and matching still) were taken from center ring, and a second motion and still pair from the "moving picture stand." Stuck with only a few seconds of fisticuffs, the company puffed up its product as a spectacle-filled topical film. What a *Moving Picture World* ad described as "the shortest, fiercest fight in the history of the prize ring" was a "big, quick money-maker" showing "peculiar" training scenes, "great crowds and 'bunco games' outside the Colma arena," and "celebrities of the ring." The Fourth of July fight also appealed to American viewers' jingoism. Flags were waved to the camera at the end of the film, "showing," ads said, "the champion of Australia at the feet of the victorious American." Burns, a Canadian, played along. Like many boxers of the time, he wore a belt of stars and stripes and unfurled it at the conclusion of the bout.[39]

Although the Miles brothers retained their San Francisco office and were available to film bouts at Coffroth's Arena, they concentrated on New York operations and the manufacture of distribution prints by the hundreds.[40] In February 1908, when representatives of many of the leading exchanges met in Buffalo to form the Film Service Association, Miles Bros. joined and curtailed original production.[41]

With the champion Burns on a European tour for the 1907–8 season, no U.S. producers had access to prizefighting's main events. Some Burns matches in England were filmed and imported for American exhibition. The Urban company filmed the Burns-Moir fight (December 2, 1907), and Hammerstein's Theatre screened selected rounds in Manhattan three weeks later. *Variety* puffed it as "the best of the many [fight pictures] which have been thrown upon the sheet in the past few years."[42] But without press coverage or spectacular athletic displays, *Burns-Moir* and the *Burns-Palmer Fight* (1908) lacked impact.

In America, the boxing story that elicited commentary was the interracial grudge match between Gans and Nelson. Their 1908 rematch repeated boxing's rituals. A large crowd of men gathered on the Fourth of July at James Coffroth's arena, attended by railroad, telegraph, and newspaper services. The Miles camera crew redeployed. A five-reel film of Nelson's seventeen-round victory helped create demand for a rubber match.

The third Gans-Nelson affair skipped the usual year-long publicity efforts and was staged on Labor Day 1908. Returning to Colma, Nelson again beat his older opponent, who was counted out by Jim Jeffries in the twenty-first round. This final set of Nelson-Gans fight pictures scored a major financial success in the United States and Britain.[43] However, this time it was not Miles Bros. that recorded the battle. Chicago's Selig Polyscope provided cinematography for the "Gans-Nelson Film Company." Distribution rights to the four-reel feature were awarded to the Chicago Film Exchange, which reportedly "cleared over $100,000 in rentals."[44] The Chicago companies reflected Nelson's influence, as the "Durable Dane" was loyal to his adopted hometown.

Miles's penultimate foray into fight pictures came with two Stanley Ketchel bouts filmed in Colma in 1909. On July 5 they photographed the twenty-round *Stanley Ketchel–Billy Papke Fight*. Kalem, a Patents Company member, offered the film through its service, although ads credited the production work to the "Eagle Film Co. (Miles Bros.)."[45] By October, when Kalem recorded Jack Johnson knocking out Ketchel, the parenthetical Miles Bros. attribution was gone, although the cinematographer of record was "E. C. Miles." Earle Miles still ran the California office, while the other brothers worked in Manhattan.

In less than a year the Miles Bros. enterprise—large and far-flung in 1907—had faded from the national scene. MPPC's cancellation of the Miles Bros. license agreement in 1910 led the company into bankruptcy. Herbert Miles took on less visible duties. The Film Service Association elected him secretary in 1910. A year later he served in the same post for the Motion Picture Distribution and Sales Company, an alliance of independents.[46] But Miles Bros. remained a second-tier entity, "confining its operations largely to commercial work." By 1912, when Miles cameras anonymously recorded Jack Johnson's title defense for the promoter Jack Curley, the company had been relegated to the role of functionary industrial filmmaker.[47] It retained an invisible but significant afterlife in a series of distribution, export and stock-footage partnerships.[48]

AFTER MILES BROS.: THE ROLE OF FIGHT PICTURES IN THE INDUSTRY

In December 1908, three significant events combined to mark another shift in the status of prizefight films. On December 18, the American film industry entered a new phase of development with the formation of the Motion Picture Patents Company as a trade cartel. On December 24, the mayor of New

York shut down all moving-picture shows in one of the strongest signals of concern about the detrimental influence of motion pictures. Prizefight films were one of the longest-standing sins listed by critics of cinema. And on December 26, Jack Johnson defeated Tommy Burns to win the world heavyweight championship. Although the sporting community recognized Johnson as the most gifted boxer of the day, the press became obsessed with the social consequences of his ascendancy. As white dismay about a proud black champion spread, boxing received more publicity than ever before. In addition to the troubling discourse about race, these events raised two issues about fight films: their role in shifting industrial strategies and their impact on debates about movies and movie houses.

The persistence of fight pictures amid the MPPC's reshaping of motion-picture production and distribution was a major exception to the rule about how the trade worked. Because some of these films attracted a disproportionate share of publicity and profit, leading companies invested in them strategically. The ascendancy of fiction films defined the era. Nonfiction subjects, dominant in the earliest years, made up a far smaller percentage of production during the nickelodeon period. In the heyday of the prizefight film, it fell to a mix of subsidiary companies, independent entrepreneurs, and one-off organizations to record and market topical footage in ad hoc fashion.

Several special nonfiction productions affected the motion-picture market in the early 1910s, generally feature-length presentations with travelogue appeal: *Paul J. Rainey's African Hunt* (1912), pictures of King George V's coronation (1912), footage from Antarctic expeditions (1909–13), and other scenic compilations.[49] Most were presented in upscale theater settings with admissions costing a dollar rather than a nickel or dime. Amid these higher-brow features, prizefight films lasting an hour or more appeared regularly. The genre persisted in nickelodeons, larger theaters, special show-business venues, and nontheatrical settings.

THE VARIETY OF TRADE STRATEGIES

Few generalizations can be made about who produced these fight pictures or how they were distributed: a mishmash of methods were employed. A sampling of cases illustrates the shifting strategies used by industry leaders and small operators from 1909 to 1914:

> In 1909, William Brady returned to the fight film enterprise, obtaining U.S. distribution rights to the *Burns-Johnson Champion Contest* (shot in

Australia by Gaumont, France's second biggest film producer). He sub-contracted distribution rights for individual states to regional distributors.

Great Northern, the American subsidiary of Denmark's influential Nordisk Company, released its half-reel *Boxing Match by Hallberg of Denmark and Young Joe Gaines "Baltimore Black"* (1909). This was an unheralded attempt to film an ersatz Joe Gans and a stand-in for his Danish-born rival, Battling Nelson. (Joseph Miles helped found Great Northern.)[50]

Also in 1909, when Battling Nelson failed to find a company interested in his match against the unknown Dick Hyland, the titleholder hired an anonymous crew to record his fight. "I know that if I knock Hyland out the films will not be worth developing," he said. "But if Hyland should knock me out those pictures would be worth a small fortune." The recording of Nelson's victory received limited screening.[51]

An unaffiliated dealer in fight pictures, John "Doc" Krone of Chicago, brokered a variety of fights, distributing the *Nelson-Gans Fight* in the United States (and personally exhibiting it in England); buying and re-selling states' rights to eighteen prints of *Burns-Johnson Fight;* import-ing ten sets of the British *Summers-Britt Fight* (1909) and renting them for cheap daily and weekly rates; distributing the interracial *Langford-Ketchel Fight* (1910) to capitalize on the upcoming Johnson-Jeffries showdown; and advance-booking films of a Nelson-McFarland fight that never materialized. Krone's success was great enough to allow him to resist Edison's litigation—and win in 1912.[52]

Promoter Sid Hester incorporated the Great Western Film Company of San Francisco in 1910 to exploit films of the Nelson-Wolgast fight (in which Nelson was finally dethroned in a forty-round marathon) and the Langford-Flynn fight. The firm placed trade ads offering wares to all cus-tomers, billing *Nelson-Wolgast* as "a complete story of the making of a new champion, with full lecture description" and topical slides. *Moving Picture World* reported that both films were "on the road under competent managers with paper [i.e., posters and handbills] to announce the films" (see figure 38). Patents Company attorneys sued Great Western for unli-censed use of its camera, while MPPC executives simultaneously hired Hester to help negotiate film rights to the Johnson-Jeffries extravaganza.[53]

In June 1910, Sid Hester and his partner reincorporated as the Clements-Hester Company to import the British *Welsh and Daniels Fight.* Trimmed to a single reel, it was picked up by the anti-MPPC group's

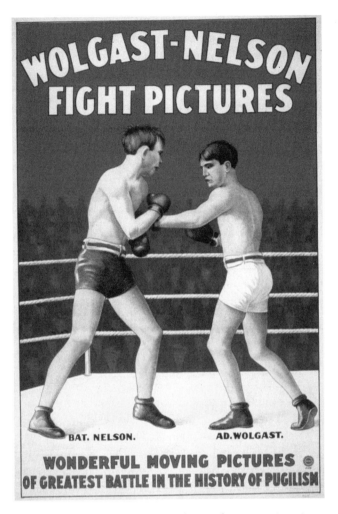

Figure 38.   Poster for *Wolgast-Nelson Fight Pictures* (1910).
The color original is six feet wide and nearly nine feet high.
(Library of Congress, Prints and Photographs Division.)

noisiest dissident, Carl Laemmle, whose Laemmle Film Service exchange purchased rights for six Midwestern states. Other established independents also distributed fights, as when Solax rented British Gaumont's Welsh-Driscoll pictures (1911) to American exhibitors.[54]

Some exploiters entered as unknowns and never achieved prominence. F. S. Eager purchased the U.S. rights to *Sam Langford vs. Sam McVea* (France, 1911). The rare film featuring two African American boxers received little play in America, and Eager's name vanished from the trade. Similar obscurity greeted the *Johnny Kilbane–Abe Attell Fight* (1912). The three-reeler was screened at Hammerstein's Victoria Theater, but neither its producer, the Los Angeles Projection Company, nor its distributor, Columbia Amusement Enterprises, ever resurfaced. Other filmed bouts, such as *Willie Ritchie–Joe Rivers* (1913), circulated out of the public eye, shown only at private clubs.[55]

Vitagraph released a three-reel "feature," *McFarland-Wells Fight* (1912). Unlike earlier features, it rotated into the regular MPPC release schedule.[56]

Often the distinctions between dominant and independent, affiliated and unaffiliated, belied the ways in which business was conducted. Members of the MPPC could break from its policies. Independent entrepreneurs and prizefight managers could aid the Patents Company as readily as oppose it. More typical were cooperative ventures for films, such as the *Nelson-Moran Fight* (1910) and the *Wolgast-Moran Fight* (1911), for which exceptional business documentation exists.

FIGHT-FILM OPERATIONS AND ARTIFACTS

From 1905 to 1910, Battling Nelson appeared in seven prizefight films, taking an active interest in their commercial circulation. When Congress drafted a bill against fight pictures, the House Commerce Committee (chaired by Nelson's congressman) invited his testimony. "I have a number of men on the pay roll exhibiting pictures of boxing contests in different countries," he offered at the May 1910 hearing. In defending the legitimacy of his profession, Nelson described commercial fight picture operations. "Between me and my partners, we must have invested $150,000," he estimated, "because it is the taking of the negatives and the positives that costs." With "at least 25 outfits" exhibiting "the pictures of the Nelson-Wolgast contest," Nelson said, expenses ran to $18,500. Those costs included not only laboratory fees but also salaries for "your booking agent and your advance man and your operator [projectionist] and your lecturer and your manager of the thing."[57]

After the success of the Nelson-Wolgast affair, British lightweight champion Owen Moran came to San Francisco to fight both men. He knocked out Nelson in November 1910, filmed by a crew from Selig Polyscope (an MPPC member). A surviving 1911 financial statement details the arrangements, distribution methods, and fiscal results of this moderately successful fight picture.

TABLE 1. Statement of Moran-Nelson Fight Pictures
up to and including May 20th, 1911.

Receipts		Disbursements	
Film #1	$1016.67	Advertising	$122.60
Film #2	1031.94	Carey Litho. Co.	798.33
Film #3	781.40	Selig Poly. Co.	4881.04
Film #4	497.23	Gen'l Expense	632.02
Film #5	782.32	Show Expenses	1156.27
Film #6	2094.00	Salaries	527.00
Film #7	1247.60	Booking Fees	407.45
Film #8	2009.31	Traveling Exp.	106.00
			$8630.71
Film #9	1114.53	J. W. Coffroth, Dividend	625.00
State Rights, Wash.	1000.00	Geo. A. Kleine, " " "	625.00
State Rights, Calif.	1415.53	Battling Nelson, " " "	625.00
		Chas. J. Harvey, " " "	625.00
	$12,990.07	Total	$11130.71

Recapitulation

Total receipts	$12,990.07
Total disbursements	*$11,130.71*
Net profit	$ 1,759.36

From the George Kleine Collection, Manuscripts Division, Library of Congress.

Several points can be deduced from this record. Many parties had to be cut into the deal, several taking substantial payments off the top. The promoter and the star athlete received the same large percentage of profits. Next, the distributor George Kleine got his own cut for handling procedural details: striking prints, keeping the books, and so on. Kleine also subcontracted a field representative, Moran's manager, Charles J. Harvey. For his share, Harvey traveled North America and Europe conducting trade screenings and subdividing territorial rights. State-rights holders had to line up bookings and promote the pictures locally. Finally, Selig received a substantial disbursement, nearly $5,000, for filming the bout.

The *Moran-Nelson* financial statement itemizes the activities of distribution, exhibition, and promotion. The enterprise spent money on the usual overhead (such as salaries, travel, and booking fees) and direct advertising, and considerably more on the lithograph printing of posters, handbills, and the like. The "show expenses" confirm that Harvey and other agents did their own exhibiting. As agent for the *Johnson-Ketchel Fight* (1909), Harvey "demonstrated" the pictures at a trade show in a London hotel. Claiming to have been one "of about twenty" invited to Edison's production of the Corbett-Courtney pictures in 1894, Harvey gave a recitation of the history of prizefight films during his spiel to potential buyers.[58]

Partners in the *Moran-Nelson Fight Pictures* made money, but net profits were a modest $1,759.36 during the first six months (see table 1). *Moran-Nelson* was neither a hit nor a flop, understandable for a nontitle fight in which the home crowd's favorite lost. Among Moran fans in Britain, however, the pictures were still in circulation two years later.[59]

For the *Wolgast-Moran Fight* (July 4, 1911) similar distribution methods were used, but with better results. The three-reel film of Wolgast's successful title defense was distributed across the United States and England. While there was "almost nothing doing with the Moran Nelson Pictures" in the summer of 1911, Harvey reported, he was having "better luck in selling State Rights with *[Wolgast-Moran]* than any other pictures I have handled." Chicago exhibitions were retained for the partners' own exploitation, with William Selig taking an active interest.[60]

STATES' RIGHTS DISTRIBUTION AND FEATURE-LENGTH FILMS

Two characteristics defined the commercial presence of fight pictures: longer running times and states' rights distribution. Both carried over from pre-nickelodeon successes. Both remained industry standbys after fight pictures. The *Corbett-Fitzsimmons Fight* had established in 1897 that a single motion picture could offer a theatrical "evening's entertainment." More than a dozen fight features preceded the 1910 Johnson-Jeffries pictures, and dozens more followed.[61] Most were marketed by regional agents.

Territorial distribution worked well for enterprises that lacked relationships with exchanges or theaters. As Michael Quinn has shown, states' rights distributors of this era required little startup capital, "could make significant profits with a single film," and could "devote a great deal of energy to selling and marketing" individual features. Ring promoters like Stuart, Hester, and Coffroth could quickly sell rights for individual films to showmen. Large fees could be pocketed before any screenings took place. It was up to the rights buyer (or its licensee) to sell tickets.[62] A states' rights setup could serve other purposes, too. MPPC members, for example, distanced themselves from prizefighting by subcontracting Jack Johnson films to regional entities.

A *Moving Picture World* report illustrates how "small-time" the arrangement of fight picture showings could be for a state rights holder:

> A great deal has been said regarding the lack of enterprise on the part of licensed [MPPC] exchanges in connection with "special" or "topical" subjects, and the Johnson-Ketchel fight films seemed for a time destined to be "passed up" by many of the exchanges who fail to keep their finger on the pulse of the people. The wise ones, however, who ventured have no cause for regret, as for instance, the Lake Shore Film and Supply Company of Cleveland, Ohio. They contracted for one copy of 3,600 feet and now find it necessary to use three copies as exclusive owners of the Ohio rights.

The item relates that "Manager Sam Bullock, of the Johnson-Ketchel fight department" encountered heavy bidding for his Ohio prints, even among small-town show people. Competing managers of two one-hundred-seat theaters in a "tank town" of 1,200 both requested bookings. One claimed to have earlier cleaned up "on that Ganz-Nelson" fight film when he charged up to twenty-five cents. The other asked for advance time to "bill heavy outside" the town: "Send me tew three sheets, six half sheets, six one sheets 'n' five hundert dodgers. By heck, I'll bill it like a cirkus." The lecturer who accompanied the *Johnson-Ketchel Fight* said it "played to the entire population of Tanktown and several villages besides."[63]

Hastening the transition to feature-length productions was the success of multireel dramas using territorial distribution. Italian spectacles such as *The Fall of Troy, The Crusaders,* and *Quo Vadis?* were marketed in this way across North America from 1911 to 1914. The strategy also favored the showmanship practiced by American theatrical and circus promoters who often handled fight pictures. *Moving Picture World* wrongly credited Pliny P. Craft, a circus advance man, with the state-rights concept. Craft said the success of exploiting states' rights to the *Johnson-Jeffries Fight* inspired his exploitation of the features *Buffalo Bill's Wild West and Pawnee Bill's Far East* (1910) and *Dante's Inferno* (1911).[64]

Regardless of distribution method, features were rapidly adopted—despite their association with prizefights. "There is a demand for special feature films on the part of the public that should be developed," said a *Film Index* writer in 1909. "It is not necessary that the 'feature' should be a 'fight film.'"[65] In 1911, *Moving Picture World* crusaded for "great feature films now being released" because they usually were the "better class of films." "The filming of some great opera or a popular literary or dramatic or historical subject requires more than a reel. . . . Quality being equal, quantity counts in every inch of film." An exception in 1911, the multiple reel was majority practice by the end of 1913.[66]

As fight exhibitors had known since 1897, a feature-length film was a property that could be ballyhooed. The show-business authority Epes Winthrop Sargent correctly argued that increased profits would follow the conversion to features. "The multiple reel presents many valuable features," he told exhibitors, "not the least of which is the many forms of special advertising to be had." Even déclassé boxing pictures, Sargent suggested, could elevate the status of the movie house when promoted as features. Feature presentation meant higher ticket prices; higher prices mitigated the reputation of "cheapness," soliciting a "better class" of audience:

> While the nickelodeon has attracted thousands of patrons, other thousands have shunned the pictures because they regard them as something cheap and therefore unworthy of notice. Heretofore most of the special displays at advanced prices have been reels made of prize fights. . . .
>   Once attracted by the special subject, the convert is apt to become a "fan."[67]

REFORM RHETORIC AND THE SOCIAL STIGMA OF NICKELODEONS

The language used by the movie trade and its critics expressed anxieties about class. The Progressive Era debate about moving pictures was led by middle-class and genteel reformers who sought to "uplift," to remake the popular culture that catered to working-class and masculine tastes. Class and gender distinctions were linked. A female audience was presumed to lend bourgeois respectability. Fight pictures contributed to the image of cinema as a vulgar, proletarian domain. They came under intensifying attack as progressivism scrutinized screen content. Producers and exhibitors tried to bring the profitable fight picture into the fold. As they cleaned up pictures and nickelodeons, they also sought to tone down the controversy surrounding cinematic prizefights.

The closing of New York's five-cent movie houses on Christmas Eve 1908 marked a watershed in the debate about motion pictures. Its effect led to the creation of a public advisory board headed by the reformer John Collier. At a hearing called by Mayor George McClellan on December 23, some civic and religious leaders condemned the moving-picture business for showing "low," "indecent," and "immoral" subjects. They were deemed reprehensible because children frequented these shows. However, as Tom Gunning points out, few descriptions of objectionable movie content were reported. "Films of prizefights alarmed some witnesses," he notes, while others offered vague allusions to depictions of crime, vice, or "lovemaking." Indeed, the *New York Times* reported only that "testimony had been given as to pictures showing prize fights"—no doubt elicited by news of Jack Johnson's shot at the heavyweight title, to be filmed three days later.[68]

Motion-picture interests obtained an injunction against the closures. As Gunning points out, however, the confrontation was "entangled in big city politics."[69] Tammany Hall, with its allies in the sporting and theatrical community, feuded with McClellan, a rival Democrat, who next ordered police to enforce new restrictions on theaters using blue laws. The list of performances forbidden on Sundays included "wrestling, boxing (with or without gloves), sparring contests," and "any moving pictures giving a play." Only shows with lecturers presenting films "of an instructive or educational character" were permitted.[70] This exception was intended to allow religious and travelogue presentations. Ironically, fight pictures were the other genre that regularly employed screenside "lecturers" to provide commentary.

A more important result of the New York crackdown was the industry's decision to regulate screen content. Having won their battle to stay open, exhibitors joined manufacturers in promising to eliminate pictures deemed inappropriate. The People's Institute, a public-education wing of the Cooper Union, created the National Board of Censorship, with MPPC approval. Beginning in March 1909, the board previewed prints submitted by manufacturers. Its one hundred volunteers came from an array of reform groups: the Purity League, the Association for Improving Conditions of the Poor, the Federation of Child Study, the YMCA, the YWCA, the Federation of Women's Clubs, the SPCA, the WCTU, and churches.[71] These white, middle-class men and women of New York approved, disapproved, or prescribed revisions for most film content over the next several years.

Theaters complied with the campaign. The first head of the Exhibitor's League allied with the progressive cause, declaring in 1912: "We moving picture exhibitors are educating the industrial classes. . . . [Movie] houses are emptying the saloons, clearing the street corners, gathering together family parties, and preaching greater sermons than the pulpits of our land."[72] Historical literature on the nickelodeon period consistently demonstrates the importance of early movie houses as working-class gathering places. Contemporaneous representations also depicted the nickel show as the haunt of the urban proletariat. John Sloan, to take a noted example, painted pictures of movie houses as part of the Ashcan School's project of rendering the everyday life of ordinary city dwellers. His diaries of 1906 through 1913 are peppered with references to slumming in New York and Philadelphia nickelodeons. "A visit to a moving picture show," he wrote, was "a plebeian treat." Without condemnation, Sloan portrayed movie theaters as part of the Ashcan world. His rendition of a Greenwich Village nickelodeon, *Carmine Theater* (1912), in fact, is the only painting from the school that literally depicts an ashcan.[73]

Despite being rendered as an institution of the unwashed masses, picture theaters were never entirely so, and they quickly shed that reputation.[74] Ironically, the houses that showcased fight pictures were often the higher-class venues. Oscar and Willie Hammerstein's Olympia and Victoria theaters, William Morris' American Music Hall, and the Broadway Theatre were likely places to find fight pictures in Manhattan. In Philadelphia, the commodious Forest Theater hosted the *Johnson-Jeffries Fight* (at $1.50 for admission), replacing the "people's" dime museums and burlesque houses that had presented fight facsimiles.[75] In smaller cities and towns, opera houses presented fight films before used, abbreviated prints filtered down to cheaper shows.

The film industry used this fact to assuage fears about attracting low-brow ruffians. Vitagraph's J. Stuart Blackton represented the manufacturers at the McClellan hearing, vowing to curtail questionable films. As supervisor of the *Johnson-Jeffries Fight* in 1910, he took the initiative to frame the film's reception. "The pictures will go to the best class of houses and rents will be so heavy that the seats will probably sell for 1 to 2 dollars," he reported. This would "freeze out the cheap crowd that might make trouble."[76]

The picture world had to distance itself from the seaminess of the ring while defending operators who capitalized on fight pictures. Many wanted to be rid of prizefighting. One exhibitor railed against the genre in January 1910: "Show better films, such as 'The Passion Play' and other good religious stuff; get the church-going class of people coming to your theaters, and you will not only have the patronage of the church-going class, but you will get along then without their enmity and opposition. . . . The moving picture exhibitor can boost his business if he will show the right kind of stuff. I would much rather have the good-will of the right-thinking class of people than the cheap praise of some barroom tough, whose gratification is to see prize-fights, blood-and-thunder films and other rot."[77] A year later, *Moving Picture News* repeated the case against fight pictures and for class-based betterment: "Everywhere, the world over, protests have come from individuals, from churches, from organizations that tend to uplift humanity;

protests loud and long, and yet the cinematograph industry does not seem to heed the voices of the better class of the communities in which they live. It is giving the industry a black eye every time a fight comes up."[78] When Congress passed a prizefight picture ban, the *News* again applauded on behalf of "every decent exhibitor. . . . This news will be exceedingly gratifying to all who are trying to uplift the industry to a proper plane . . . that such brutal exhibitions as prize fights are now a thing of the past."[79]

Newspapers offered comparable opinions. An editorial cartoon in the *Chicago Tribune*—"Some Fight Pictures That Would Be Desirable"— suggested that "desirable" patrons were not fight fans. The *Tribune* represented the spectators of good pictures as well-attired, white, Republican families cheering their would-be screen heroes: " 'Kid' Consumer"; President Taft golfing; a white member of the "traveling public" punching the black Pullman porter "tipping nuisance"; opponents of child labor; jailers of reckless motorists [i.e., Jack Johnson]; and the ultimate bourgeois champion, "Plain Everyday Decency."

A second cartoon depicted the flip side. "If the Fight Pictures Are Barred in Chicago" implied that the constituency for the *Jeffries-Johnson Fight* was working-class men—street toughs, motormen, liverymen, and farmers— who would attend "clandestine presentations" of "the secret 'film show.' "[80] *Moving Picture World* urged filmmakers to ignore this shadow audience.

> It will be the fate of the fight pictures, if disbarred from the public theaters, they will be shown in other places, in cellars, in out-of-town barns, and perhaps some enterprising men will hire barges and show the fight pictures way out on the ocean, or on our lakes and rivers. The pictures will be shown, and perhaps to larger audiences than if allowed in our regular theaters.
>
> . . . Go to work, forget the fight pictures, . . . try to produce something better; get the patronage of the public, of the exhibitor and of the renter by giving them high-class work.[81]

In many areas, picture people were forced to "forget the fight pictures" because the *Johnson-Jeffries* reels were banned. In response, clandestine projects did crop up. In August, Chicago police arrested the manager of the grand Congress Hotel for showing the Johnson-Jeffries film at a smoker for three hundred men. In December, Tennessee and Arkansas police quashed an attempted screening by a group of men on a Mississippi River barge. No doubt most secret shows went undocumented.[82]

Any screening had to be handled with care, restriction, and disclaimers. When fight pictures were allowed in commercial theaters, measures to control and protect the audience were announced clearly. Women and children would be shielded. "The exhibition of fight pictures," the *Nickelodeon* argued in 1911, would not affect "the attendance of the regular moving picture theaters, because the latter mainly cater to women and children."[83] Managers would contain the number of young or female movie fans happening onto a fight picture. Distributors would deal only with "stag houses": "Any women who attend the production will know beforehand what they are to see." This policy reversed the strategy of early boxing films, which co-opted female spectators. Sellers of the Johnson-Burns pictures in 1909 were among the last to advertise with slogans like "Popular fight pictures attract women," and "Women in Droves See Them."[84]

The film trade also met critics who feared the effects of prizefight films on children—children like twelve-year-old Jimmy Flaherty, a streetwise nickelodeon habitué living on Chicago's Halsted Street. When Jane Addams opened the Hull House Five-Cent Theater at her famed settlement house, *Moving Picture World* asked Jimmy to pass judgment on "the uplift nickel theater show." His response to the wholesome program of fairy tales and travelogues was precocious: "It's pretty, all right . . . but it's too slow to make a go of it on dis street." And his final remark was a progressive's nightmare: "I don't say it's right, but people likes to see fights, 'n' fellows getting hurt."[85]

The largest grassroots group of the Progressive Era, the United Society for Christian Endeavor, campaigned against the *Johnson-Jeffries Fight*. "Harm," the Endeavorers contended, "will be done by allowing children and women to view the production [of brutal fights] by moving pictures." Their "Save the Children!" slogan became the caption for a *New York Tribune* editorial cartoon. The drawing depicted boys and girls at a screening of the infamous prizefight, with the hands of "Public Opinion" and "Christian Endeavor" attempting to block the sight. *Moving Picture World* countered by saying that this illustration "depicting Uncle Sam [*sic*] as shielding children from the baneful influence of fight pictures [demonstrated] the cartoonist's ignorance. He like thousands of other people supposed the pictures were to be spread broadcast among the nickelodeons." But, the *World* argued, "children would not see the pictures at all" because of the high ticket prices. Furthermore, many theaters "strictly barred" anyone under eighteen years of age.[86]

In the ideology of progressivism, children, women, and the "lower classes" required looking after by a responsible elite. As John Collier of the censorship board explained to social workers, the cinema "affects the classes of people who are most impressionable. . . . [T]he motion picture theater audience is made up almost entirely of wage earners and children, many of them from our immigrant population."[87] The masses would not seek out what was best. Stuart Blackton defended censorship, describing how one exchange manager told him there was always a demand for "sensational subjects. . . . His actual words were: " 'They (the public) want red meat and they want it raw.' The fact that the public is now being served cooked viands instead of 'raw' is due to the perspicacity, decency and intelligence of the licensed manufacturers and the restraining influence of the Board of Censors."[88]

The board, however, did not stop, condemn, or even review prizefight films. A 1911 *New York Times* profile of the organization noted that two recent prizefights were "not screened by the National Board of Censorship" because they were "special releases." Such specials, the *Times* reported, "circulate in theatres, as well as ordinary moving picture shows," and were "not particularly objectionable."[89]

The board did not take an official position on fight pictures, but it had internal discussions. In 1910 Collier reported: "There has been much debate among our members about allowing pictures of prize-fights to be reproduced. The final decision was, in effect, tolerant of such films where there was nothing extremely brutal shown and where the persons who took part in them were of a better grade."[90]

The reference to "a better grade," taken in context, was a euphemistic reference to race as well as class. Mixed-race fight pictures were deemed among the lowest grades of screen entertainment. Vachel Lindsay made idiosyncratic reference to the issue in his book *The Art of the Moving Picture* (1915). Seeking to elevate the reputation of movies, Lindsay maintained that to bring in higher-class patrons, it was necessary to remove films that were "actually insulting." "I was trying to convert a talented and noble friend to the films. The first time we went there was a prize-fight between a black and a white man, not advertised, used for a filler. I said it was queer, and would not happen again."[91] Although the National Board of Censorship and the film industry continued to allow pictures of Jack Johnson, racist censorship of them became the law of the land.

As *Moving Picture World* said in 1909, the fortunes of the prize ring were indeed "interwoven with those of the moving pictures" during the nickelodeon era. Fight pictures were never the center of the industry, but from 1905 to 1915 they played an important role. From 1905 to 1908, Miles Bros. held an informal monopoly on the genre. With the success of the Nelson-Britt film in 1905, the Miles brothers resuscitated a dead genre. Their Gans-Nelson and Tommy Burns pictures kept their name visible into 1909, when the company was pushed into obscurity.

The second phase in the genre's history, 1909–15, coincided with the institutionalization of an efficient system for making, renting, and exhibiting film programs, in which fight pictures persisted as an important alternative. When anxiety over fight recordings culminated in a federal ban, it was not a financial blow to leaders of the motion-picture business, who had banked primarily on the more reliable commodity of story films.

The main cause of the animus against prizefighting and its films during these years was interracial controversy. The reign of the audacious African American boxer and movie star Jack Johnson sparked an unprecedented round of debate and action about fight pictures.

6 Jack Johnson Films

Black Exhibition and White
Suppression, 1908–1910

[Whether the public will ever see the Johnson-Jeffries fight pictures] depends upon the opinions of shocked "schoolmarms," elated negro coalheavers, princes of the Church, impassioned sporting gentlemen, conscientious Southern governors, tolerant Northern mayors, filmmakers on the scent of a fortune, newspapers ravenous with the summer news famine and other voices of the people, each of which is yelling in a different key. . . . Every human motive that has made for war and discord from the times of Jacob until today is tangled up in the skein of influences that will determine whether the pictures are shown.

> J.B., JR. "Will You Ever See Those Fight Pictures? That Depends,"
> *New York Tribune,* July 10, 1910

Until recently, historians of early cinema neglected African American film culture. Considerations of movies and race typically began with the racist landmark *The Birth of a Nation* (1915). Most of the recent studies of African American cinema take the productions of Oscar Micheaux as their starting point. Less has been written about its production, exhibition, and reception before 1915—Jacqueline Najuma Stewart's *Migrating to the Movies: Cinema and Black Urban Modernity* (2005) being the stellar corrective.[1]

Fight pictures featuring the controversial heavyweight champion Jack Johnson serve as an entree into the social history of early black filmgoing. His screen presence made him, in essence, the first black movie star. In considering how black, white, and interracial audiences saw the Johnson pictures, we must outline the practices of exhibitors. For Johnson and other black fighters wanting access to the ring, as well as for African American filmgoers seeking pictures of their fights, the color line was a pernicious barrier. Jack Johnson broke boxing's color line but not that of the movie theater. Yet, although the continuing segregation of theatrical space was a constant reminder of coercion, the cinematic image of Johnson projected large on the screen challenged the basis of that segregation.

The reception of the Johnson films predictably divided along racial lines: black communities generally treated screenings as an opportunity for empowerment, while prevailing white opinion held Johnson to be such a threat that traffic in prizefight films was banned by law. In 1915 the Supreme Court twice affirmed film censorship. In *Weber v. Freed* the justices upheld the federal statute that kept Johnson's last fight films from the public eye. In *Mutual v. Ohio* they decided in favor of state censorship boards, but this failed to prevent *The Birth of a Nation*'s bedeviling depiction of white supremacy from being widely seen.

Fight pictures played a major role in Jack Johnson's ascendancy. Issues of race shaped the production, exhibition, and reception of the three feature films showing his first three title fights—against Tommy Burns (1908), Stanley Ketchel (1909), and Jim Jeffries (1910).

BLACK BOXERS ON SCREEN BEFORE JOHNSON

The racial makeup of prizefights was always an issue, although interracial contests were not of primary concern until Johnson won the title in 1908. For many proponents, the sport was a mechanism for sustaining the strength and dominion of the white race. W. W. Naughton opened his 1902 history of fistic champions with an explicit epigraph: "If once we efface the joys of the chase from the land and outroot the stud / Goodbye to the Anglo-Saxon race! Farewell to the Norman blood."[2]

The exclusion of black fighters was a structuring absence before and during the time of the earliest motion-picture bouts. In the United States, widespread black participation at the top levels of the profession was barred. Peter Jackson (1861–1901), a ring professional from the West Indies, challenged John L. Sullivan but saw the star pugilist draw the color line against him.

Jackson's notoriety fed the earliest of fight-film legends. His famous sixty-one round draw against Jim Corbett in 1891 led to talk of an on-camera rematch when the Latham brothers signed Corbett to spar before the Edison camera. But the new champ maintained Sullivan's color line. That fact, however, was displaced by a joke of white wish-fulfillment in which an unnamed black boxer fled the Black Maria, terrified by both Corbett and the camera. Gordon Hendricks's *The Edison Motion Picture Myth* (1961) exposes how Edison biographers perpetuated this "spurious tradition" about Corbett's opponent, embellishing the anecdote with racist stereotyping.[3] A version authored by Edison employees reported "one curious incident" in which "Corbett was asked to box a few rounds in front of the camera, with a 'dark un' to be selected locally. This was agreed to, and a celebrated bruiser was brought over from Newark. When this 'sparring partner' came to face Corbett in the imitation ring he was so paralyzed with terror he could hardly move. . . . The 'boys' at the laboratory still laugh consumedly when they tell about it."[4] A 1931 biography repeated the story of "a Negro fighter . . . paralyzed with terror" who "began to tremble" and ran away while the white ring men laughed.[5] Matthew Josephson's ostensibly more scholarly *Edison* (1959) added that the "third-class pugilist" was frightened by "the lugubrious stage setting."[6]

This account of how camera-ready matches were made is telling in its denial of the color line and its use of derogatory stereotypes. The latter was of course common practice among movie makers. Early film catalogs contained "coon" subjects, the cinematic equivalents of minstrelsy's coon song. This distortion was also prevalent in discourse about the supposed nature of black prizefighters, characterized by the white press as fearful of a true fight. Jack Johnson's "yellow streak" was mentioned frequently—until his deft dispatching of Jim Jeffries.

At the time of Johnson's reign, one camera captured a disturbing contradiction of the stereotype which held that black men were timorous in combat and frightened by technology. In 1909, sailors on the U.S.S. *Vermont* staged a "boxing carnival" in which they induced two "colored mess attendants" to duke it out. Perhaps expecting timid boxers to clown through a scripted knockout, the sailors instead saw David W. Williams beat Harrison H. Foster to death. Rear Admiral Seaton Schroeder came forward to explain: "It was not a prizefight or a boxing bout, but an exhibition for a moving picture machine." No subsequent word surfaced about the fate of the film made aboard the battleship.[7]

When black pugilists appeared on camera, their casting, too, could be motivated by stereotype. The first African American heavyweight to be filmed played a comic foil to the white contender Gus Ruhlin in Edison's *Ruhlin Boxing with "Denver" Ed. Martin* (1901). The catalog description reads: "Here we present Ruhlin in a lively bout with the dusky well known 'Denver' Ed. Martin. The bout is very lively from start to finish and is ended up with a little piece of comedy by Ruhlin presenting Martin with a live chicken, which he receives in a joyful manner."[8]

Much as Peter Jackson was literally consigned to play Tom in *Uncle Tom's Cabin* on his theatrical tours, Martin was pigeonholed into this marginalized role. When Martin made a ringside challenge to Tom Sharkey, the *Police Gazette* recorded one of Sharkey's "characteristic speeches" to the crowd: "Gentlemen . . . I have never barred nobody outside of a nigger. I will not fight no nigger. I did not get my reputation fighting niggers and I will not fight a nigger. Outside of niggers I will fight any man living."[9]

The insistence of the language iterates how deep antiblack feelings ran. The color line remained especially applicable to the heavyweight title, the ultimate symbol of achievement and dominance. In 1901, the *Police Gazette* identified Martin as someone who could be the next champion if given a shot. "No, we won't fight a negro for the championship," the Jeffries camp responded. The reason, said the *Gazette*, was because America would then "have to bow to a negro champion."[10]

EXCEPTIONS FOR LIGHTER FIGHTERS: GEORGE DIXON AND JOE GANS

A few exceptional boxers of African descent, notably George Dixon and Joe Gans, held subheavyweight titles at the turn of the century. Both received praise for their ring skills, although neither was ascribed the celebrity conferred on white champions. Gans and Dixon were slight, light-skinned black men whom the press characterized as mild-mannered and unassuming, well-liked because they did not upset the status quo. In August 1910, while the country was in an uproar over banning Johnson's fight films, Gans died of tuberculosis. The *Washington Post* memorialized him, patronizingly and in contrast to Johnson, as "a negro of humble origin . . . a model of consideration and politeness. He never sought the limelight, kept among his own race, and was the personification of cheerfulness."[11] For Gans, Dixon, and other nonwhite athletes, the ability to advance in a white-controlled social hierarchy was contingent on their ability to appear nonthreatening—even though their profession demanded that they physically dominate their opponents.[12]

Dixon held the bantam- and featherweight crowns throughout the 1890s before losing to Terry McGovern in January 1900. This defining loss was the only one of his many fights to be filmed. His previous appearance in motion pictures epitomized his subservient status. In 1899, he sparred with Sam Bolen, another black journeyman, while Biograph made camera tests for the *Jeffries-Sharkey Contest*. Dixon's only other film performance came just before his retirement in 1906, a sparring match against a white journeyman at the Biograph studios.

The staging of an interracial bout was in line with a growing focus on black-versus-white combats in 1906, the year that Joe Gans developed a rivalry with Battling Nelson. Three of the four feature films showcasing Gans produced between 1906 and 1908 included Nelson. The breaking of the color line resulted from Gans's prowess and a campaign by a few sportswriters for fair play.

Although the *Police Gazette* by no means abandoned racist judgments, its boxing experts often argued for the elimination of the color line. They even ridiculed boxers who enforced it: "Ordinary fighters don't make much of a hit when they draw the color line. The fighting game is not a calling that permits such finely drawn social distinctions. The public does not care [about a boxer's color] . . . as long as he's a good, game fighter and willing to fight any deserving aspirant."[13] By 1906, the *Gazette* said, the "classy lot of dark-skinned" pugilists was dwindling because "the white boxer and the managers of the clubs" excluded them.[14] The argument for breaking the color line was hardly a plea for justice. The tabloid thrived on the sensationalism of interracial conflicts of many sorts, especially lynchings.

Early in his career, Gans was identified as a superlative ring general. But in title contests against Frank Erne and Terry McGovern in 1900, Gans's handlers instructed him "to take a dive." The Selig Polyscope pictures of the infamous McGovern versus Gans fight failed to prove he had "laid down" in the second round, but most regarded the performance as a fake. Gans later admitted the fact but fought for legitimate recognition. In 1902, he knocked out Erne with a single punch to take the title, which he held for six years. In a rare inversion of racial nicknames, Gans partisans dubbed him "the Old Master."[15] In a racist reversion, the champion had to repeatedly challenge the challenger Nelson, the holder of the so-called "white championship." When Tex Rickard made the Gans-Nelson match in 1906, it was pitched as a contest between the best of the whites and the black titleholder.

News that Gans had retained his title was greeted by spirited celebration and violent rebuttal. In New York, the *Times* reported that "many race fights followed" the verdict at "saloon returns." Police barely prevented the hanging of a black Gans supporter by drunken whites. Near Nelson's home, at a "saloon bulletin service," a lynch mob of white men attacked "South Chicago Negroes" cheering Gans.[16]

Screenings of the *Gans-Nelson Contest, Goldfield, Nevada, Sept. 3, 1906* were numerous, though not conspicuous. The boom in moving-picture shows was mounting in 1906–7, but this feature-length presentation ran mostly at burlesque and variety houses. Abbreviated editions later appeared in nickelodeons.[17] Little public debate greeted the pictures themselves. Sporting spectators went to assess the boxing itself. As W. W. Naughton wrote, "Thousands went to see the shadowgraphs of Battling Nelson and Joe Gans at Goldfield over and over again with the object of enabling themselves to form an opinion as to the genuineness . . . of the foul claimed by Gans."[18] Despite that "objectivity," *Gans-Nelson* exhibitions were also specified as images of interracial competition. Biograph catalogs selling

Lubin's reenactment hyped: "This is the greatest fight of the age between a white man and a colored man. . . . This is the fight the country is talking about."

Scant evidence is available of the response to the Gans films in black communities. Few newspapers serving African American readers consistently covered entertainment, theater, film, or sports. Even Gans's hometown *Baltimore Afro-American Ledger* rarely mentioned the local champ. When Jack Johnson won his crown, the paper commented: "We confess that we were not very strongly drawn towards Mr. Joseph Gans, the former lightweight champion, and for many reasons that need not be explained" (presumably his fixing work for gamblers).[19] The *New York Age,* quoting Gans, implied that his potential fandom was undercut because the moving pictures of his victory were being "manipulated unfairly." Gans himself toured on the Empire burlesque circuit, where Nelson's manager, William Nolan, distributed the Gans-Nelson pictures. After attending a *Gans-Nelson Contest* screening in St. Louis, Gans told audiences that, under Nolan's direction, the pictures were made "to show him up in as bad a light as possible."

> [A]ll the rounds that are in Nelson's favor are run off slowly, while those in which he had the better of the argument are run out so swiftly that the spectators cannot get a fair idea of the progress of the battle.
>
> The fouls that Nelson committed, especially the one that ended the fight, Gans says, are thrown on the screen so quickly that it is very hard to get the true story that the pictures should show.[20]

Black audiences for Gans films were also limited by the scarcity of venues for African Americans under Jim Crow laws. Movie houses (or theaters mixing film and stage acts) for black patrons increased in number just after the run of Gans's motion pictures, but few were open in 1906.

Nevertheless, films of Joe Gans helped make loyal fans where conditions permitted. Baltimore's Avenue Theater ("the Only Colored Amusea in the South") revived the *Gans-Nelson* recording of the local hero's glory as a way of celebrating the 1907 Thanksgiving holiday. The black theater manager, Henry H. Lee, offered the "life Moving Pictures of the World's Greatest Champion Joe Gans and Battling Nelson in the Great and Historic Fight at Goldfield" as a "Refined Amusement for Refined People."[21] In New Orleans, the Goldfield film was also presented as an attraction with predominantly African American appeal. Feature presentations of the *Gans-Nelson Contest* were screened as "colored fight pictures" at the Elysium Theatre. Rarely were white-run theatrical spaces so accommodating.[22]

Gans's reign was appreciated primarily by boxing aficionados. The Miles Bros. film of his knockout of an unheralded Kid Herman in 1907 received limited distribution. No other Gans title defenses were filmed until a re-match with Battling Nelson on July 4, 1908. Nelson won this second meeting, so a lucrative rubber match was set up. Selig Polyscope filmed both boxers in training scenes and shot the September 9 bout at Coffroth's Arena in Colma, California. With Gans suffering from tuberculosis, Nelson again won.

Films of Battling Nelson knocking out the black champ grossed more than $100,000. The mainly white audience and promoters clearly were eager to anoint a white athlete. Nelson embraced the epithet "Coon Hunter" in the race-baiting memoir he issued on dethroning Gans. He denied his defeat at Goldfield. "I feel proud of stating *'No Colored Man Ever Conquered Me.'* . . . I was this same negro's master by licking, trouncing, beating and battering him into a mass of 'black jung.'"[23]

The atavistic image of the white master beating a black man registered with many white audiences. As if to underscore the idea of white supremacy, this third set of Nelson-Gans fight pictures was sometimes shown with stage productions of the ubiquitous *Uncle Tom's Cabin*.[24] Pictures of the belligerent Nelson beating and knocking out Gans resonated with the sight of a vicious white owner whipping Tom to death. Neither Battling Nelson nor Simon Legree was necessarily heroic or admirable, but both functioned in popular culture as reminders of white domination. Nelson's own theatrical tour included a "moving picture show of the late fight with Gans." Replays of Nelson's victories increased over the coming year.[25] The *Nelson-Gans* pictures lost their topicality, but their importance as documents of racial competition increased after 1908, when Jack Johnson's image came to American screens.

JACK JOHNSON'S ASCENDANCY

When Johnson defeated Tommy Burns on December 26, 1908, he assumed the world championship of boxing. A film crew from British Gaumont recorded the event from a camera platform amid a massive crowd. The *Burns-Johnson Championship Contest* was distributed internationally. In America, William Brady, John Krone, and others purchased states' rights to the films. The appearance of the *Burns-Johnson* pictures reinvigorated debate about the sport and its propagation through cinema. By the time prints reached American screens in March 1909, a rancorous debate over the politics of race was under way. This controversy governed the film's reception.

Arthur John Johnson began his prizefighting career in 1897 in his hometown of Galveston, Texas.[26] He traveled to Chicago, San Francisco, and Los Angeles, boxing frequently and always winning. In 1902, he knocked out the reigning champion's sparring partner, and brother, Jack Jeffries. As he ascended the challengers' ladder, managers enforced the color line. Consigned to fight mostly other black men, Johnson outboxed Denver Ed Martin, Sam McVey (three times), and others throughout 1903 and 1904, assuming the unofficial title of "Negro champion." In 1904, Jeffries declared that "no logical opponents" were left to take on. "Jack Johnson is a fair fighter, but he is black, and for that reason I will never fight him," Jeffries said. "If I were not champion I would as soon meet a negro as any other man, but the title will never go to a negro if I can help it."[27] The "logic" of white supremacy dictated Jeffries' retirement. He handed his title over to the undistinguished Marvin Hart in 1905.

When Tommy Burns, a middleweight, defeated Hart in 1906, the heavyweight title lost luster. Yet Johnson had a new protagonist to trail, one who needed to earn legitimacy. Burns maintained: "I will defend my title as heavyweight champion of the world against all comers, none barred. By this I mean white, black, Mexican, Indian, or any other nationality without regard to color, size or nativity."[28] Two years later he fulfilled that pledge.

With the established manager Sam Fitzpatrick, who was white, Johnson gained increasing notice. After lining up many fights against black pugilists (including seven against Joe Jeannette), in 1907 Fitzpatrick got the forty-four-year-old Bob Fitzsimmons to box his client. Johnson won easily. In 1908, Johnson shadowed Burns on his European tour. At Plymouth, England, he made his first appearance before motion-picture cameras, knocking out a British fighter, Ben Taylor. The Johnson-Taylor fight pictures were viewed only in local boxing circles. Following Burns to Australia, Johnson found a promoter able to entice Burns into the ring with him. Hugh D. ("Huge Deal") McIntosh was a high-stakes entrepreneur. He had been a boxer himself, then a newspaper owner, theatrical producer, and a member of Australia's parliament. McIntosh promised the titleholder $30,000 and the challenger $5,000, regardless of the outcome.[29]

A stadium seating twenty thousand was built outside Sydney and filled to capacity on Boxing Day 1908. Johnson won, battering Burns throughout. In the fourteenth round, police stopped the Gaumont cameras and stepped into the ring to prevent further humiliation for Burns.[30] McIntosh, who also refereed, later said the pictures "did not half tell how badly he was punished." Johnson's best punches "were delivered while Burns was backed toward the camera and Tommy's head and shoulders completely hid them from the picture machine."[31]

Among those in press row was Jack London. The *New York Herald* syndicated his column widely to white and black papers. As a subscriber to both boxing's primitive ethos and the myth of Caucasian supremacy, London put into stark words a prevalent white reaction. All reporters agreed that Johnson had played with Burns, openly taunting him, punching at will. The new champion laughed and smiled throughout the contest, talking to reporters and spectators as he demonstrated his mastery.

Johnson was depicted as an "Ethiopian," a "colossus," toying "with a small and futile white man." London even suggested he was in control of the image he would project on movie screens: "He cuffed and smiled and cuffed, and in the clinches whirled his opponent around so as to be able to assume beatific and angelic facial expressions for the cinematograph machines." In the most widely quoted words of London's career, the writer concluded with a racial call to arms: "But one thing remains. Jeffries must emerge from his alfalfa farm and remove that smile from Johnson's face. Jeff, it's up to you." Some editions added: "The White Man must be rescued."[32]

White American opinion echoed London's cry. The mentality that dictated Jeffries' retirement demanded his return. Burns was not a true champion, rationalized spokesmen such as John L. Sullivan. Johnson would have to take on the undefeated Jeffries. Raconteur Jim Corbett aggravated the racial anxiety, declaring that "the white man has succumbed to a type which in the past was conceded to be his inferior in physical and mental prowess."[33] Others suggested Burns's defeat was the beginning of the end for white supremacy. "A Negro is the champion pugilist," opined the *Detroit Free Press.*

> [The] dark-colored peoples of the earth are threatening to ply the mischief generally with the civilization of the white man.
>
> Is the Caucasian played out? Are the races we have been calling inferior about to demand to us that we must draw the color line in everything if we are to avoid being whipped individually and collectively?

In the satirical *Puck,* the popular writer Walt Mason responded to Johnson's victory with the doggerel "The Black Peril." His short poem began "How shall the white men save their faces, since Johnsing [*sic*] . . . smothered Tommy Burns?" and concluded with a lament for "the sport Caucasian." No white men remained to challenge Johnson: "The great John L. delivers lectures / And Corbett elevates the stage; / Jeff only fights in moving pictures." Such discourse came, too, from the White House's bully pulpit. President

Theodore Roosevelt endorsed boxing and the "strenuous life," advocating the "ability to fight well and breed well" as a way to prevent "race suicide." Rather than repudiate fisticuffs, TR responded to the result by inviting the white champion Battling Nelson to the White House in January 1909 to discuss who could beat Johnson.[34]

Conversely, most of black America hailed Johnson's victory as a milepost of achievement. "No event in forty years has given more genuine satisfaction to the colored people of this country than has the signal victory of Jack Johnson," the *Richmond Planet* editorialized. The African American newspaper saw political implications in Johnson's title. During the recent Brownsville affair, President Roosevelt had unjustly smeared blacks as undisciplined fighting men; Johnson's honed performance would "rehabilitate the race in the good opinion of the people of the world."[35] The crowning of an African American champion had come at a moment as bleak as any in postslavery America, making him an immediate hero in black America.

REACTIONS TO THE BURNS-JOHNSON FIGHT PICTURES

The reception of the Burns-Johnson films varied according to the conditions of their exhibition. Visceral racist responses were muted, compared to those that greeted later Johnson films. First there was a delay in delivering the prints to American screens from Australia (via Europe). Then, with interest in boxing having fallen to new lows from 1904 to 1908, public and media attention took time to build. Yet the arrival of motion pictures showing a new, charismatic, and controversial heavyweight champion revived the sport.

Gaumont's *World's Heavyweight Championship Pictures between Tommy Burns and Jack Johnson* played on screens in Sydney only three days after the bout, but it was not until February that Hugh McIntosh arrived in England with his film. The promoter and referee of the fight also acted as lecturer at the debut of his ninety-minute fight picture in the National Sporting Club's theater in Covent Garden. He sold British rights to Gaumont, which arranged bookings for twenty prints. McIntosh narrated the film at London music halls before arriving in America the following month.[36]

American bookings of *Burns-Johnson* began immediately after the fight. John Krone's Chicago Film Exchange distributed eighteen sets of pictures. William Brady sold one-year states' rights to independent exhibitors, frankly advertising the films as a workhorse commodity. "The pictures can be used for an entire afternoon or evening's entertainment in first-class houses, and, later, can be reduced to a show of forty minutes duration for vaudeville theatres and cheap moving picture theatres."[37]

The American premiere did not occur until March 21, in Chicago, where Johnson made his home. McIntosh narrated the motion pictures during a two-week engagement at the Chicago Auditorium, a spacious variety venue. The *Chicago Tribune* did not comment on the racial composition of the audience. However, in describing the show as "good pictures of a poor fight," it implied a white reception of the film.[38]

McIntosh next took his film to New York, where opposition arose. A rival impresario, Felix Isman, sought an injunction prohibiting the show, saying that "to produce the pictures would be to lower the dignity of the playhouse."[39] Isman's objection was surely rationalized by the breaking of the color line, as other boxing films had played in New York theaters for a decade. Few locales had legal grounds for prohibiting fight pictures. Iowa was a notable exception, passing a ban immediately after Johnson's win. "No one can show the Johnson-Burns fight in moving pictures in this state without danger of arrest and punishment," one paper reminded the film trade.[40]

Although, as the *New York Times* put it, the *Johnson-Burns Fight* showed "the white man outclassed," its Broadway Theatre debut was produced for a white audience. Spectators were not there to cheer a figure they disparaged. Some boxing fans no doubt wanted to appraise the ring performances, particularly that of the indomitable fighter they had never before seen. Burns had played up the police stoppage of the fight that prevented him from continuing. The "pictures show everything," he said, and indeed they did. "To the majority of those who witnessed the exhibition," said the *Times*, "the pictures were a disappointment on account of the miserable showing made throughout by Burns."[41]

For dispirited white spectators, the screening was an opportunity to rally for Jeffries' return. McIntosh fostered a Jeffries-Johnson grudge match by concluding the Chicago premiere with an offer of a $50,000 purse. The "white hope" himself was appearing on stage at the American Music Hall during the *Burns-Johnson Fight*'s New York run. Jeffries' former manager, William Brady, spoke at the Broadway Theatre premiere, further encouraging an anti-Johnson atmosphere. McIntosh's narration appropriated Jack London's call to remove the smile from Johnson's face. At one McIntosh screening, "it was announced from behind the canvas that some in the [Australian] crowd yelled to knock the grin off Johnson's face. Then Johnson did grin and he could be seen replying to the request."[42] McIntosh reinforced this interpretation, later saying: "It was the first time that Johnson had ever boxed before a moving picture machine and he was overanxious to face the camera. As a result he was continually backing Burns around so that his own face, with its smile of confidence, would be shown in the pictures. All who saw the pictures . . . will recall that the big negro's smile was always in evidence."[43] White audiences were thus urged to see Johnson as a stereotypically grinning "coon," a degrading caricature that they could use to rationalize an act of retribution from "Jeff."

Spectators no doubt had varied and subtler responses to the *Burns-Johnson Fight*, but when public outcry induced Jeffries to make a vaudeville tour in 1909, audiences were nearly univocal in calling for his return to the ring. That the *Burns-Johnson* pictures were presented in order to urge audiences to call for a Jeffries-Johnson battle was confirmed when McIntosh's footage began to be exhibited widely with scenes from the 1899 *Jeffries-Sharkey Contest*—the moment of Jeffries' greatest glory—appended.[44]

Needless to say, African American reception of the pictures took a different tone. Anticipation of the film's arrival was great. The *Indianapolis Freeman,* a widely circulated African American weekly, kept tabs on Johnson's public activities and on the Burns-Johnson films. Immediately after the Sydney fight, the paper informed readers that the pictures would "arrive in the United States in two months." The "English opera house" premiere was reported, with details about the fight, training scenes, and preliminary footage of Johnson's white wife and other celebrities.[45] Images of the dapper new champion appeared frequently in the press and portrayed him as a symbol of "race pride." Johnson's personal appearances, on stage and at train stations, attracted crowds of black (and some white) fans. Songs lionized the achievement of the "black gladiator."[46] However, African American audiences lacked timely access to the *Burns-Johnson Fight.* McIntosh's film deal was unusual, giving him sole possession of the prints, which he insisted on personally unveiling in London, Chicago, and New York. A faster release would have yielded bigger profits.

One showing of *Burns-Johnson* occurred in Chicago on the day of Johnson's first title defense in 1909—and was intentionally wrongly billed. According to the *Freeman* columnist "Juli Jones Jr.," a bunco artist used the black community's anticipation of new Johnson films to scam moviegoers in Chicago's black district.

> One game knight of slot houses put one over on Dehomey to show us how many suckers we have at large. . . . This bright young man rented a closed theater and put out a sign,

"FIRST MOVING PICTURES OF THE JOHNSON-KETCHELL FIGHT."

The funny part of it is that he opened his show at 5 o'clock on Saturday afternoon. The men did not go into the ring until 5:30. He used the Burns and Johnson fight pictures. Nobody woke up until the wise gent had loaded up. He said that he would return next Saturday with the Jeffries and Johnson pictures. Suckers have no class, color, or creed.[47]

That a print of the Burns bout was in ready circulation suggests there were legitimate screenings earlier. However, the 1908 film had less presence than the enormously popular *World Championship, Jack Johnson vs. Stanley Ketchell [sic]* (1909). The sequel received wide distribution through the Motion Picture Patents Company as well as African American theatrical circuits. The proliferation of the champion's cinematic image widened the racial bifurcation over his celebrity.

JOHNSON FILMS IN THE CONTEXT OF BLACK MOVIE EXHIBITION

For African American audiences of the Jack Johnson pictures, two theatrical experiences predominated: white-run venues with segregated seating, and "race theaters" catering to black patrons. The latter were just beginning to emerge. The social experience of being in these spaces was as meaningful as the programming.

The "Negro press" regularly reported on the indignities of being forced into the "cramped cage" of Jim Crow sections. Segregated balcony seating was entrenched in theater culture. From the 1870s whites rationalized it as "nigger heaven," a racist joke suggesting that blacks enjoyed being restricted to the most distant seats. The architecture of entrances, aisles, and stairways directed groups to their assigned places. Staggered showtimes, ushers, and posted instructions also helped sort audiences by race. During the strange career of Jim Crow, nickelodeons and theaters without balconies devised ad hoc means to cordon off black audiences: railings, canvas dividing walls, and even chicken wire.[48]

Commentators differed on how to address the inequality. The *Freeman* columnist Sylvester Russell argued that "given the state of race problems," blacks should not force the issue. Accepting gallery seats was "much better than to be sometimes humiliated, refused, or forced to sit in undesirable quarters." Yet some civic leaders promoted efforts to integrate theaters. In June 1910, a civil rights attorney won a "color-line suit" against Chicago's Colonial

Theater. "Negroes should sue every time they are refused in theaters," said the *Defender*. "Buy your seat anywhere in Chicago theaters and sit there."[49]

Theaters and nickelodeons for African American audiences increased in number from 1908 to 1915. By 1909, the *Freeman* counted "112 Negro theatres owned and operated by Negroes." Many more were white-run. A discernible boom developed during Johnson's reign. Baltimore had six picture theaters in 1909. Sylvester Russell noted in 1910 that "the moving picture theater craze has developed a wonderful stampede among the Negro." Chicago's growing African American district, "the Stroll," was a marketplace for films, with a dozen or more theaters. Most exclusively black and black-owned "show shops" were in the South.[50]

These theaters were seen as preferable for creating "race pride." "There are better five-cent theatres conducted by colored Americans than any controlled by the whites," the *Washington Bee* commented matter-of-factly in 1910. An entrepreneur in Florida said he was opening his theater "to meet prejudice with blunt internal resistance."[51] Whether screening melodramas, westerns, or fight pictures, black houses offered an opportunity for solidarity.

However, even autonomous theaters could not guarantee shelter from the violence of everyday life. In 1911, a thousand white men stormed the opening of a Fort Worth "picture show for Negroes exclusively." The mob beat and stoned moviegoers for "this show of independence," shooting one dead. In Jackson, Mississippi, similar terrorism met the opening of the No Name Theater in 1914. A white mob drove out the black audience and demolished the "moving picture apparatus."[52]

The coercion that kept African American public spaces separate and unequal was ever palpable, even in no-name nickelodeons. The display of Johnson pictures was a reply to such violence, a practice of "blunt internal resistance." Black theaters continued to open, and Johnson films made the circuit.

Where such places were fewer and more constricted, theaters were all the more crucial as rallying points for cultural activity. As Mary Carbine demonstrates in her history of black theaters in Chicago's commercial district, such institutions could describe themselves as the very "Home of the Race." Yet, as Jacqueline Stewart points out, these venues were controversial within their own community because "early Black film culture was also heavily influenced by elements of vice." The first movies to come to Chicago's "Black Belt" neighborhood were shown in a converted saloon run by a gambling kingpin—who developed a fight-picture interest with Jack Johnson himself.[53]

JOHNSON AND THE PEKIN

The most important black-owned venue in early cinema history, Chicago's Pekin Theatre, played a role in disseminating Johnson fight pictures among African American audiences. Its proprietor, Robert T. Motts, incorporated daily film shows into his popular variety house as early as 1905. Considered the "first race theater," "the original and only colored legitimate house" inspired namesakes in Cincinnati, Lexington, Louisville, Memphis, Norfolk, and Savannah. By 1909, thirty-three showplaces bore the name—more than a quarter of the total. When a Motts protégé opened a Cincinnati "moving picture house," the *Freeman* cast it as "'Pekin' fever," noting that the "Pekin Amusement Company" was building a chain.[54] This fever also aided the birth of African American filmmaking. When Peter P. Jones, William Foster, and Hunter C. Haynes began producing films for black audiences in 1913, each used cast members from the Pekin stock company.[55]

In the five years preceding the first African American film production, the films of Jack Johnson were important programming for the Pekin circuit. Robert Motts took a lead in promoting them. He purchased prints of the moving pictures showing Johnson knocking out Stanley Ketchel. The champion himself probably brokered the deal. Johnson demanded personal copies of the fight pictures from the Chicago-based distributor George Kleine.[56] He was personally acquainted with Motts, who organized black Chicago's public reception of its hometown hero. The *Freeman* reported the circulation of the *Johnson-Ketchel Fight* by William H. Smith, who was to manage a new Pekin in Washington, DC, but was "now on the road with fight-moving pictures, owned by Mr. Motts."[57]

The Chicago Pekin revived the Johnson-Ketchel pictures on the eve of the 1910 contest with Jeffries, screening reels between variety acts and announcements of the fight returns. Again the Pekin was "the center of activity," and its cinematic presentation of Johnson's victories energized celebration. On July 4, Johnson's mother and sisters were guests of honor at Motts's theater and led the jubilation when news of victory was wired from Reno. On July 8, the champion appeared before an integrated audience at the Pekin and attended a banquet that Motts hosted for the "black elite."[58]

After the death of Motts in July 1911, white owners bought the Pekin. Friction between Johnson and the management was evident. An independent film producer, C. R. Lundgren, tried to exploit the footage he shot at the funeral of Johnson's wife, Etta Duryea. Her suicide on September 11, 1912, compounded the scandal of their interracial marriage. When the Pekin advertised the film with "flaring signs" on its marquee, Johnson obtained a court order to stop the exhibition.[59]

THE JOHNSON-KETCHEL FIGHT AND THE BUILDUP
FOR JEFFRIES

The film of Jack Johnson's first title defense—against the "Michigan Assassin," Stanley Ketchel, on October 16, 1909—captivated Johnson detractors and fans alike. It also fed demand for a Johnson-Jeffries showdown.

Held at the accustomed site of Coffroth's Arena in California, the event was recorded by cinematographers from Kalem, a major production company. Journalists and fans questioned the legitimacy of Johnson's bout with the overmatched middleweight Ketchel. To guarantee lucrative film receipts, it was rumored, Johnson had agreed not to put Ketchel away for several rounds. Extant prints confirm the original reviewers' perceptions that the champion merely toyed with the challenger for most of the bout.

In the twelfth round, however, a dramatic and unexpected exchange offered a stunning climax. Ketchel swung a roundhouse at Johnson's head. Retreating, the champion fell to the mat—perhaps knocked down, perhaps having slipped. The crowd of white men rose to cheer the underdog. A deliberate Johnson lunged across the ring, smashing Ketchel squarely in the mouth and immediately rendering him unconscious. Johnson leaned casually on the ropes, hand on hip, as the referee counted out his victim (figure 39). Sime Silverman of *Variety* labeled it "a sensational finish to one of the best fight pictures shown."[60]

The Burns-Johnson fight had panicked many whites who saw a white man's possession of the boxing crown as a confirmation of racial superiority—and took it for granted. The filming of Burns's defeat in Australia had at least been stopped by police. The Ketchel pictures, however, depicted a fearsome, indomitable athlete. The legend of Johnson's image grew as replays of his knockout artistry circulated. One interpretation insists that the film shows Johnson scraping Ketchel's front teeth off of his leather glove as the overreaching Assassin lies sprawled on the canvas.[61] The movies and photos of Johnson standing over an unconscious white hope confronted viewers with an unprecedented image of black power. The same pictures offered an antidote to the pervasive negative stereotypes of blacks in popular culture.

The Motion Picture Patents Company distributed the *Johnson-Ketchel Fight,* having George Kleine sell territorial rights to exchanges licensed by

Figure 39. Jack Johnson stands over the unconscious Stanley Ketchel, October 16, 1909, in this retouched press photo. (Todd-McLean Collection, University of Texas at Austin.)

the MPPC (see table 2).[62] Receipts reached into the hundreds of thousands of dollars. The film's prominence raises the question of why a ruling group would permit and promote an on-screen negation of its own ideology.

Several circumstances tempered white reaction to the film. First, many did not take the dubious prizefight as a marker of racial achievement. Devotees, even if they held racist views, could evaluate pugilistic performances apart from supposed racial characteristics. When Joe Humphreys narrated the pictures for fight fans at Hammerstein's Victoria theater, for example, he held forth on pugilistic and financial details rather than race. Furthermore, racial prejudice was not all-consuming. Some whites became Johnson fans. The socialist artist John Sloan, who patronized nickelodeons and Negro League baseball games, appreciated Johnson's performance on film. In his diary Sloan wrote that he and a friend "went up to Hammerstein's Victoria and saw the cinematograph pictures of the recent fight between Ketchel and the negro Jack Johnson. The big black spider gobbled up the small white fly—aggressive fly—wonderful to have this event repeated. Some day the government will wake up to the necessity of establishing a library of Biograph films as history."[63]

TABLE 2. Report of Johnson-Ketchel Partnership Account at close of the books July 30th, 1910

[does not include revenue or expenses for October-December 1909]

General Ledger Accounts

Territorial Rights	$15,029.50 ($35,029.50, less $20,000 to J. Coffroth)
Films [prints]	$20,032.30 (paid to Kalem)
Lithos [posters]	$3,014.04
Slides	$97.11
Titles [for film prints]	$36.76
Photographs	$372
Second-hand films	$1,650
Lectures	$22
[other operating expenses: machine, reels, electro., salary, freight, telephone/ telegraph, travel]	
Profits	$13,698.80

Distributor (location)	Territory	Rights	(film sales)
Amalgamated Film Exchange (Portland, Or.)	Washington-Oregon	$1,625	($750)
American Film Service (Chicago)	Chicago	$1,125	($451.80)
A. P. Negele (?)	(?)	$[?]	($28.80)
Charles A. Calehuff (Philadelphia)	Pennsylvania	$3,000	($1,873.16)
Clune Film Exchange (Los Angeles)	California	$825	($375)
Kleine Optical Co. (Chicago)	Baltimore	$1,000	($762.45)
Kleine Optical Co. (Chicago)	Boston	$1,157	($1,160.11)
Kleine Optical Co. (Chicago)	Chicago	$2,386	($1487.99)
Kleine Optical Co. (Chicago)	Denver	$231	($376.20)
Kleine Optical Co. (Chicago)	New York	$255	($1,401.20)
Lake Shore Film & Supply Co. (Cleveland)	Ohio	$2,500	($1,292.45)
Lyric Amusement Co. (Tacoma)	Alaska	$525	($375)
National Vaudette Film Co. (Detroit)	Michigan	$865	($792)
Nichols Brothers (Grand Rapids, Mich.)	Wisconsin	$1,500	($38.45)
Frank Zepp (?)	North & South Carolina	$[?]	($86.90)
Progressive Moving Pic. Co. (Ogden, Utah)	Utah, Idaho, Wyo., Nevada	$1,500	($375)

TABLE 2. *(continued)*

Distributor (location)	Territory	Rights	(film sales)
Ray Cummings (?)	Minnesota, N. & S. Dakota	$850	($1,062.45)
S. Nye Bass Film Exchange (New Orleans)	Louisiana, Mississippi	$750	($250)
S. Tisher, Star Theatre (Denver)	Montana	$1,125	($375)
S. W. Johnson (Denver)	New Mexico, Arizona	$825	($375)
Yale Film Exchange (Kansas City)	Neb., Tex., Ok., Ark, Kan., Mo.	$6,500	($3,386.20)
+ W. O. Edmunds (Winnipeg, Canada)	Vancouver & Winnipeg	$[?]	(?)
Total cash collected for Territorial Rights		$30,029.50	
Total cash collected in Film Sales			($17,425.06)

Total cash receipts [U.S.]	$53,107.36		
Grand total cash receipts	$63,150.32		
Total profits	$37,471.81		
Dividends paid to George Kleine		$17,666.67	
Dividends paid to A. J. Gilligham		$17,666.67	

Summary of report in George Kleine Collection, Manuscript Division, Library of Congress

Conversely, some white spectators came to see Johnson on display precisely because they envisioned him as a monster. As the films bolstered his reputation as a gladiator, newspapers supplied gossip, anecdotes, and fabricated quotations that made his image larger and more terrible. In the ring, the champion laughed at white opponents, whom he humiliated and dispatched. Outside the ring, Johnson developed a reputation as a profligate spender, drinker, womanizer, and all-around disturber of the peace. He kept company with white prostitutes and married three white women. He was frequently arrested for speeding in his automobiles, and later on more serious charges. For a time his status kept him from jail. But, as Johnson biographers agree, he knowingly fulfilled the role of "bad nigger."[64] A braggadocio and a dandy, he gleefully rebelled against conventional standards of behavior. Many white filmgoers no doubt came as curiosity seekers wanting a glimpse of the controversial, larger-than-life figure.

Consider the *Johnson-Ketchel Fight*'s screening in Louisville. The Buckingham Theater, a deluxe burlesque house, featured the pictures along with its leg show. The Buckingham was part of the Empire burlesque circuit, which "exclusively controlled" the films "for a limited time." Ads for the local premiere appeared in the *Courier-Journal* next to an editorial cartoon showing a razor-wielding black "swell" towering above City Hall, staring at the reader. A white Republican mayor and ineffectual police are depicted as tools of blacks, who are shown gambling, drinking on Sunday, and cavorting with and attacking white women. The political monster projected by the *Courier-Journal* replicated the image of Jack Johnson often conjured by the white press: a predatory miscegenist granted too much power and license. The same issue of the paper reported that Jim Jeffries had at last agreed to fight Johnson.[65]

The return of Jeffries presented a third reason the Johnson-Ketchel pictures played to a large white audience. Spectators knew Johnson had won, but the film previewed the pending bout with Jeffries. Ketchel's supposed knockdown of the champion gave a glimmer of hope that the "Ethiopian colossus" could be vanquished. W. W. Naughton asserted that the scene of the scrappy Ketchel sending Johnson to the mat would be the focal point of the pictures. The knockdown "is registered in the pictures for what it is worth, and will possibly add to their value as a show asset." Naughton predicted that "hordes of people will visit and revisit the Ketchel-Johnson pictures in order to determine whether Johnson sprawled in earnest when Ketchel nabbed him on the mastoid."[66]

In reviewing the premiere of the films at Hammerstein's Victoria, despite Johnson's in-person appearance, the *New York Sun* reiterated the predominant white perspective. "According to the pictures," Johnson's knockout blow was delivered "with so much power that the crowd in the theater was quickly convinced that the only man who has a chance with the negro is Jeffries."[67] Even the staid *New York Times*, on the release of the Ketchel pictures, expressed a racist impulse to see Johnson destroyed: We "wait in open anxiety the news that [Jeffries] has licked the—well, since it must be in print, let us say the negro, even though it is not the first word that comes to the tongue's tip."[68]

The Negro press demonstrated oppositional readings—even though African American reporters reviewed the *Johnson-Ketchel Fight* at presentations presided over by white narrators. Ohio distributor Sam Bullock, for example, lectured at his own bookings. Between white engagements, he scheduled shows for black audiences. He altered his spiel to patronize an audience he looked down on and to diminish Johnson's achievement. Bullock injected humor, *Moving Picture World* commented, "especially when the colored folks are in evidence, as, for instance, when 'filling in' a date at a small show recently in a settlement where the sons of Ham predominate."[69]

Despite such white gatekeeping, African American reviewers typically read the pictures in triumphal fashion. The *Freeman* reported on a Chicago screening. The reviewer described the dispatching of Ketchel with evident delight: "Johnson was right there with a wallop that made the white boy forget all about it." To white racists like Jack London, the champion's ability triggered hopes of salvation by Jeffries; from an African American perspective, Johnson's prowess was worth celebrating in its own right. "According to the pictures," the *Freeman* simply said, "it was a great fight."[70]

However, the *Johnson-Ketchel Fight* had black critics as well. A folksy columnist, "Uncle Rad Kees," said boxing's relationship with motion pictures made Johnson's performance suspect. The fight, he reported, had "many shady appearances."

> If this Johnson-Ketchel fight wasn't a pre-arranged affair, there was some awful clever catering to the moving picture machine. Just imagine Johnson, the cleverest man in the ring today, allowing a little fellow like Ketchel to drop him with a wild swing back of the ear . . .
> After the supposed blow Johnson went down on his hands and toes, rolled over backward on one hand, and facing the moving picture machine all the time; then, seeing that Ketchel was waiting for his cue, he jumped up and rushed at Ketchel like a wild man. . . . The referee stood squarely over Ketchel, counting him out, and all three were in full view of the moving picture machine.[71]

One could have cried "Fake!" said "your old Uncle," but what was the use? Fans were willing to be taken in by "pugilistic pirates." And, as he put it, the whole point of the on-camera performance with Ketchel was to give birth to match between Johnson and Jeffries. "The child was born" with the champion's conspicuous cinematic display.

FRAMING THE JOHNSON-JEFFRIES BATTLE AS PROOF OF RACIAL SUPERIORITY

As soon as the *Johnson-Ketchel* pictures were released, the champion inked a deal to engage Jeffries, now back from retirement. Negotiations were publicized throughout November and December 1909. The boxing fraternity's top promoters met at a hotel in Hoboken, New Jersey, on December 1 and submitted bids. Disposition of the motion-picture rights was a key part of

Figure 40.   Jim Jeffries under the lights, February 1910, while training and touring for his reluctant comeback. (Library of Congress, Prints and Photographs Division.)

the concession. Tex Rickard, who had made his fortune exploiting the interracial Gans-Nelson grudge match, offered the highest bid: $101,000 in prize money and two-thirds of the film receipts to the boxers.[72]

Following tradition, this battle of the century was scheduled for the Fourth of July, placing it at the center of the national stage. In the year preceding it, the meaning of the Johnson-Jeffries showdown was publicly debated. Some played down the contest, saying a boxing match could prove nothing about race. The "battle of brutes," wrote one African Methodist Episcopal minister, would be "an insignificant incident in the great fight the Negro race" had before it.[73]

As buildup intensified, the Johnson-Jeffries match became a symbol of conflicting ideologies about race. Jeffries said he came out of retirement "for the sole purpose of proving that a white man is better than a negro." For whites who took racial superiority as a governing assumption, a Jeffries victory became paramount. As Jeffrey T. Sammons puts it, for many whites, defeating Johnson would be "a lesson akin to a public lynching for blacks who did not know their place."[74]

While celebrities of color were commonly made to stand as representatives of their race, Jeffries became a racial symbol in a way few other white people had done. His predecessors Sullivan and Corbett, stronger advocates of the color line, were seen as individuals. The less charismatic Jeff epitomized whiteness. "Jeffries is the embodiment of all that is powerful and brutish in the white man," Corbett's newspaper column said.[75] Ignoring his advancing age (thirty-five) and extra weight (one hundred pounds!), the white press represented Jeffries as an idealized figure who countered the negative traits attributed to his black opponent. The "White Hope" was sober, the "Black Menace" a drinker. Jeffries was stolid; Johnson was flashy. Jeffries was humble, not a braggart; given to discipline, not dissipation; courageous, not "yellow." Under the Jeffries byline, *Physical Culture* magazine published essays in 1909 reminiscent of Roosevelt's "race suicide" warnings. Jeff advocated boxing as mental and moral training for a weakening nation.[76]

Although Jack London and others portrayed Jeffries as a noble brute, much white hope was pinned on the belief that his innate intelligence would overcome "primitive" instinct in the ring. In 1910, "scientific racism" held that the match was a "contest of brains" as well as brawn. *Current Literature* argued that science dictated Johnson would lose, because "the superiority of the brain of the white man to that of the black . . . is undisputed by all authorities." "The white man, being intellectually superior—as he must be," exercised self-control in the ring, while "the black man's psychology" made him perform "emotionally." The heavyweight crown, as Sammons puts it, was deemed the "true test of skill, courage, intelligence, and manhood."[77]

The black press and public, for their part, made Jack Johnson a signifier of race pride. Booker T. Washington met with him in August 1909. As July 4 approached, this racial solidarity increased. "Thousands of Negroes have nailed your name to their masthead," the *Afro-American Ledger* told Johnson. "Nobody has so much to win or lose as you and the race you represent." In his history of African American athletes, Arthur Ashe concurs with scholars that the Johnson-Jeffries fight represented for blacks not just a signal moment in sports, but the most important event since Emancipation.[78]

As the hype grew to unprecedented proportions, moralist groups lobbied to prevent the match. Protestant ministers petitioned President Howard Taft to intervene, but the White House remained silent. According to gossip, Taft had arranged to receive telegraph reports on the bout, and his son was "betting all his money on the pride of the white race."[79] A coalition of business and church people printed one million postcards saying: "Stop the fight. This is the 20th century." They were addressed to California's governor, who then banished the fight from San Francisco.[80] As with Corbett-Fitzsimmons in 1897, libertine and libertarian Nevada rescued the fight. Tex

Rickard returned to the state where he had made his first boxing fortune, building his stadium in Reno.

The fight gave professional boxing its greatest exposure. Reno became, Rex Beach wrote, "the center of the universe." Three hundred reporters sent out millions of words—including special contributors like Beach, London, Alfred Henry Lewis, John L. Sullivan (whose reports were ghostwritten by the *New York Times*), James J. Corbett, and, for *Variety,* Al Jolson. They painted the event as nothing less than what Al-Tony Gilmore has called "a staging ground for racial supremacy." The Independence Day edition of the *Chicago Tribune* suggested that the "absorbing question of whether a white man or a negro shall be supreme in the world of fisticuffs" in this case meant supreme "in the world at large."[81]

PREPARING TO FILM THE RENO FIGHT

Motion picture coverage of the Johnson-Jeffries contest was far more extensive than for any other. With fifteen years of fight pictures now past, all were cognizant of the role that film played. Journalists closely chronicled the "picture men."

When contracts were signed, *Moving Picture World* made "Pictures and Pugilism" the title of a lead editorial. Filming in Reno was a commercial opportunity. "So we hope Jeffries and Johnson will make a good fight of it and that it will be a good picture and that everybody all around will make money."[82] The *World's* "Man about Town" stated the industry's self-interest.

> The main point at issue is the success of the moving pictures—before and after taking. . . . The object is to place one more winner to the credit of the moving pictures. . . .
>
> These [boxing] people have really gone picture mad, and those who follow up such affairs as spectators or speculators have been stirred to a decidedly suspicious state of mind. An immense amount of money has been made by the owners of the Johnson-Ketchel fight pictures, and the pictures to be taken of the coming fight are looked upon as a gold mine. Think for a moment of the stupendous amount of faith put in them. The purse to be fought for is fixed at $101,000! The receipts from the pictures of the affair are figured at no less than $160,000![83]

That estimate climbed as the day of reckoning approached. *Harper's Weekly* calculated "the moving picture films will be worth at least $1,000,000." As early as May 1909, the Chicago film broker John Krone claimed to "hold an option for producing motion pictures of this fight should it ever materialize." In August, Hugh McIntosh posted advertisements for such films, promising the return of Jeffries would trigger "a great revival of interest in boxing."[84]

The past handlers of fight pictures, the *New York Times* reported, were "up against a big combine." If shut out, the MPPC (often called the Trust) could "bar the pictures" from wide distribution. Eventually a team of Trust and independent representatives managed the films. The original motion picture clause was stricken from the contract. All interested parties formed the J. & J. Co. to handle this special film property outside the regular MPPC distribution system.[85]

To strengthen its hand, the MPPC worked with fight promoter Sid Hester. He and William T. Rock, the president of Vitagraph, negotiated with Tex Rickard and the two camps until the eve of the fight. Both boxers sold their shares of the picture profits. Hester paid Johnson $50,000. The savvy champ said he was glad to take the lump sum rather than be cheated by middlemen distributors.[86] Rickard, forced to pay the cost of moving his arena to Nevada, sold his share to MPPC for $33,000. Jeffries held out for twice that.[87]

Before the main event, independent companies shot footage of the star athletes training. Films with recycled boxing footage as well as new scenes cashed in on the market for Johnson-Jeffries material. Several short films of Johnson in training circulated in Europe and North America; others, such as *Jeffries on His Ranch* (Yankee Film Co.), featured the challenger. The one-off Chicago Fight Picture Company compiled footage from *Burns-Johnson*, the 1899 *Jeffries-Sharkey Fight*, and knockout rounds from other reels, releasing it as *The Making of Two Champions* (1909–10).[88]

Cameras converged on Reno as the battle drew near, documenting training camps and the wide-open town. Photographers and journalists represented the fighters in ways consistent with their stereotypes. Jeffries was quiet and businesslike but made shows of racial solidarity by posing for pictures shaking hands with Sullivan and Corbett. Johnson was more extroverted, treating visitors to flashy sparring displays. Reports depicted him as loose and hammy, thumping his bass viol and, in some footage, "playing cards, chewing gum."[89]

RECORDING THE RENO FIGHT

For the big fight itself, J. & J./MPPC took no chances. Special lenses were made. J. Stuart Blackton supervised twelve camera operators from Vitagraph, Essanay, and Selig. Their equipment was a prominent part of the spectacle. The ring announcer, Billy Jordan, introduced celebrities to the crowd, including "Rock, the moving picture man."[90] Rex Beach wrote: "Across the ring we were faced by the muzzles of a masked battery of moving picture cameras, piled one above the other, while behind each an operator stood with his head muffed in black like a hangman's cap."[91] Shots of this "squadron of cameramen" appeared in the release version of the *Johnson-Jeffries Fight*. According to Alfred Henry Lewis, before the bout "the moving picture men held the platform for an hour, getting photographic action out of the audience. They were voted a pest, and loudly applauded when they at last withdrew."[92] The cinematography of the bout retained the static long shots of earlier fight pictures. At least one camera was dedicated to following Jeffries' movements, framing him as protagonist and privileging white spectatorship.[93]

The film industry desired a Jeffries victory for financial and race reasons. As the *Moving Picture World* bluntly put it, the purpose of the Reno fight was "to wrest the championship from the colored race, and incidentally provide crowded houses for the moving picture men." Another assessment held:

> It is no exaggeration to say that the entire world will await a pictorial representation of the fight. . . . With good light and a battle of, say, thirty well-fought rounds, and the unmistakable victory of Jeffries, these pictures should prove in the current locution, a "gold mine." This is the wish that is father of the thoughts of hundreds of millions of white people throughout the world.
>   . . . if Johnson wins? It is commonly believed that the pictures would then be of comparatively little value, especially among the white section of the community.[94]

But Johnson did win. Camera angles and editing strategies could do nothing to alter the reality of Johnson's dominating performance. Under a sunny sky, before a crowd of twenty thousand, the champion's treatment of the slow-footed Boilermaker resembled his victories over Burns and Ketchel. Johnson mocked his rival as he hit him. He aimed his remarks at the ringside observers Sullivan and Corbett (who race-baited Johnson during the bout) as much as Jeffries.[95] Although the bout was scheduled for up to forty-five rounds (the last fight sanctioned to do so), in the fifteenth Johnson finished off the bloodied and dazed Jeffries. Three times he knocked him down and into the ropes. The referee, Rickard, stopped the contest and declared Johnson the victor, a decision no one challenged. The nearly all-white crowd conveyed disappointment, exiting in funereal silence but without incident.[96]

Immediately, the J. & J. Company sent its thirty thousand feet of exposed celluloid by express courier to the Vitagraph lab in Brooklyn. One report

Figure 41. A doctored photograph of the penultimate round of the
Johnson-Jeffries fight, Reno, Nevada, July 4, 1910. (Library of Congress,
Prints and Photograph Division.)

noted wryly that four smiling Pullman porters happily "bore the trunk con-
taining the precious pictures" as it came off the train on July 8. Two other
sets of camera negatives were sent to the Selig office in Chicago, processed,
then relayed to New York, where a complete negative was quickly assembled and previews printed. On July 10, "a score of men, representatives of
the various of concerns and individuals interested in the J. & J. Co.," assembled at the MPPC offices to examine the product. The pictures were
photographically good and ready for release.[97]

REACTIONARY SUPPRESSION OF THE JOHNSON-JEFFRIES
FIGHT FILM

The first reactions to the news of the fight were violent. A wave of assaults,
some fatal, broke out when results came from Reno. Most were interracial
attacks by vengeful white mobs. Compounding the tense atmosphere was
the social license bordering on anarchy that customarily came with Independence Day. As Roy Rosenzweig has shown, working-class celebrations
of the Fourth in the early twentieth century involved drinking, vandalism,
gun play, unregulated fireworks, and other mayhem. In 1910, reformers

were conducting a "Safe and Sane Fourth" campaign that eventually replaced the unruliness with parades and municipal fireworks displays. As the *Moving Picture World* put it, fans of both boxers "were in a most inflammable condition" on the Fourth.[98]

Attacks on black celebrants overwhelmed police. "Rioting broke out like prickly heat all over the country," the *New York Tribune* reported, "between whites sore and angry that Jeffries had lost the big fight at Reno and negroes jubilant that Johnson had won."[99] At least eighteen African American men were killed and many of both races injured. Most confrontations took place in unsegregated settings, but theater incidents were reported, too. At Atlanta's Grand Opera House a "race clash" followed when "a mixed audience heard the fight bulletins read."[100]

Local and state authorities across the United States banned exhibitions of the fight pictures immediately. As Al-Tony Gilmore and Lee Grieveson document, all the Southern states banned screenings, as did cities elsewhere. Some barred only the Reno film, others all interracial fights, and still others all boxing pictures. "Within twenty-four hours," said the *San Francisco Examiner*, attempts to prohibit screenings had "assumed the proportions of a national crusade."[101] Newspapers headlined the fate of the Johnson-Jeffries pictures throughout the summer. Many endorsed their suppression. Moralist objections to fight pictures intertwined with racist desires to censure this image of black power. Moral suasion failed to keep all previous fight pictures from the screen, but the injection of race prevented many exhibitions of the *Johnson-Jeffries Fight*.[102]

The interdenominational United Society for Christian Endeavor led the crusade. Founded to promote Protestant youth education, by 1910 it and its four million members supported moral reform efforts against "gambling, trash print, king alcohol, and other threats to Christian character."[103] On July 5, the group announced its campaign for prohibition of the film. Letters implored officials to prevent the "evil and demoralizing influences" of the fight pictures from "tainting and brutalizing" "the minds of the young." A year later, the Society opened its national convention before President Taft by again "condemn[ing] the Jeffries-Johnson prizefight pictures."[104]

Other voices—Protestant, Catholic, and secular—also condemned the pictures. The WCTU led a coalition with the same aims. James Cardinal Gibbons, the archbishop of Baltimore, wrote that "it would be wrong to show these horrible pictures." His statement used classic reform rhetoric against the movies: "If the pictures of this contest were permitted, I am sure hundreds of children would see them, and what would be the result? Their morals would not only be contaminated, but they would have the wrong ideal of a true hero. After seeing the pictures a boy would naturally infer that the real American hero was a man bespattered with blood and with a swollen eye given him by another in a fistic encounter."[105] Theodore Roosevelt commented that "it would be an admirable thing if some method could be devised to stop the exhibition of the moving pictures taken" in Reno.[106]

Newspapers caricatured fight-picture interests as crude exploiters. A July 7 cartoon on the *Examiner* front page depicted a cigar-chomping sport carrying the films and a camera around the United States. In cities and the South, he meets rejection. The same hand drew a boorish promoter of the "Jeffries-Johnson Moving Pictures" washed out on a sea of opposition, barred from ports around the globe (figure 42). Indeed, bans on the fight pictures were appearing abroad. In England, Winston Churchill, then the home secretary, supported the restrictions enacted by local councils.[107]

There was a gap between the "Save the children!" rhetoric and the "racialist" rationale articulated by some advocates of censorship. The *Jackson Clarion-Ledger* cartoon "Educational?" used the language of moral uplift while picturing interracial contact as a concern, with two boys studying a movie poster for the fight pictures. In Washington, DC, hundreds of interracial clashes broke out on July 4. Fearing more violence, police prohibited exhibition of the *Johnson-Jeffries Fight*. Other mayors, councils, police, and legislators cited similar concerns when initiating censorship measures. The pictures had to be suppressed, many whites argued overtly, to prevent black empowerment. *Moving Picture World's* statement that "there is an under-current in this matter that is working upon the simplicity and prejudices of certain people" could scarcely have been more understated.[108]

Southern politicians and Northern progressives both categorized children and nonwhites as in need of white adult protectors. As Jane Addams told the newly formed NAACP, the "great race problem in America" was perceived to be caused by "a colony of colored people who have not been brought under social control." Addams herself favored a ban on the Reno fight pictures. Likewise, one white California reformer stated that "a superior people" needed to school the "childlike race."[109]

White Christian campaigners advocated likewise. Sermons argued for quelling the prizefight and films because, as one minister put it on July 4, "if the negro wins, the perfectly natural increase of self-assertion by multitudes of negroes will make life miserable." Aims for a "Christian century" were grounded in the defense of what historian Robert T. Handy describes as "Christian imperialism." Lyman Abbott, who, as editor of the *Outlook*, supported Roosevelt's condemnation of the fight films, revealed the connection

Figure 42. Cartoon commenting on fight-film bans, *San Francisco Examiner*, July 9, 1910.

between race and religion that led Christian progressives to fear the John-son pictures. "It is the function of the Anglo-Saxon race," Abbott wrote, "to confer these gifts of civilization, through law, commerce, and education, on the uncivilized."[110] For some groups, controlling the presumed riotous na-ture of black people by removing inflammatory images was consistent with their view of religion and reform. For others with more overtly white su-premacist opinions, moralist rhetoric served as subterfuge.

ADVOCACY FOR THE JOHNSON-JEFFRIES FIGHT PICTURES

Most African American opinion leaders—and many whites—saw the issue differently. They labeled the ban as hypocritical and race-based. Even those who favored suppressing the films (because the sport was barbaric or be-cause they feared white backlash) recognized that anti-Negro sentiment fu-eled the campaign. The conservative *St. Paul Appeal* confirmed the judg-ment of many black editors.

> The best thing, to our mind, that has come out of the fight is the sudden awakening of the public to the demoralizing effects of the numerous moving picture shows that infest the country and it may bring them under a more strict censorship, to which we say, amen! . . . Yet we are firmly of the opinion that the apparently country-wide objection to the exhibition of the Johnson-Jeffries fight pictures comes more from race prejudice than from a moral standpoint. Who believes for one minute, that had Jeffries been the victor at Reno, there would have been any ob-jection to showing the pictures of him bringing back "the white man's hope?"[111]

Others pointed to a second double standard. As the *Freeman* put it, "Chris-tian organizations" were protesting more fiercely against the *Johnson-Jeffries Fight* than against other immoral films. Most black ministers "view[ed] the opposition as hypocrisy." Prejudiced suppression of the films, the editorial concluded, caused the festering of "race feeling" as much as "the exhibition of the pictures" did.[112]

Two images drive home the intense feeling about the hypocrisy of the anti-fight-picture movement. The *Defender* condemned the criminalization of the films. "The Strong Arm of the American Law" showed Sheriff Uncle Sam ar-resting a "fight picture promoter" while letting lynchers escape. A similar representation in the *Richmond Planet* was captioned "Hypocrisy That Shames the Devil" (figure 43). The "moral wave" against *Jeffries-Johnson* was depicted as an angry white man standing on a "sham platform." He in-vokes "the unwritten law" to condemn the "immoral, unchristian, brutal"

Figure 43. "Hypocrisy That Shames the Devil," *Richmond Planet,* August 6, 1910.

"prize-fight business," while behind his back black men are lynched, hanged, and burned.[113]

Some critics went further, encouraging exhibition of the films. Rationales ranged from simple fairness to the need for black empowerment. One white minister's dissent from the "prejudiced discussion regarding the exhibition of the Jeffries-Johnson prize fight pictures" was reprinted in the black press.

> If the white had won, the white man would have exalted, the negro would have borne defeat, and the pictures would have been shown. The disgrace is to the white man whose mean intolerance belies his boasted superiority.
>
> Isn't it possible that a higher service might be rendered to humanity if the pictures should be shown and every white man who cannot see a

telling blow delivered by the negro without an outburst of race hatred should be treated by the law as an unsafe citizen?[114]

The African Methodist Episcopal Church endorsed the pictures because they would "increase the spirit of independence in the Negro race" and "make the colored man politically more independent."[115] Screening Johnson's victory for African American audiences would have a beneficial political and psychological effect.

A more pragmatic rationalization allowed the *Johnson-Jeffries Fight* to be screened in some areas. The *Washington Bee* explained why reactionary censorship was foolish.

> Because Jack Johnson defeated Jim Jeffries certain officials in certain towns have been appealed to not to allow the pictures of the fight to be placed on exhibition in the moving picture shows. What folly!
>
> . . . There are separate moving picture theatres among the whites and blacks in this country, and certainly the whites, if they fight, will fight among themselves, and the blacks will do likewise. How can there be a clash between the races under these circumstances?
>
> "What fools these mortals be." Let the pictures be shown, and if the whites get mad with themselves and fight themselves, they are to blame. The blacks on the other hand will shout among themselves only.[116]

The debate among the moralists was largely moot. African American filmgoing was regulated by strict codes of segregation. Many towns had no movie venue for black audiences at all.

CIRCUMSCRIBING THE *JOHNSON-JEFFRIES FIGHT*

Despite censures, many places allowed showings of the J. & J. fight pictures, including New York, Philadelphia, Detroit, St. Louis, Kansas City, Buffalo, Denver, Hoboken, Pittsburgh, and smaller towns. They even played in Peoria. To allay criticism, picture people controlled access to their *Jeffries-Johnson World's Championship Boxing Contest* (as it was officially titled) by gender, age, and class, as well as race. Investors in the film tried to take what profits they could without appearing to be scofflaws.

In the case of fight pictures, the National Board of Censorship failed to safeguard against public outrage. The board did not review topical "specials." The day after the fight, the head censor, John Collier, explained his rationale for not tackling the *Johnson-Jeffries Fight*:

> The public demand for this picture is likely to be such that it would probably be of little use for us to try to interfere. . . .

Of course, we have no absolute authority in the matter, and probably if we attempted to suppress such a film we would come into conflict with persons who ordinarily help us very much in our work of trying to see that the usual pictures shown are of a moral character. While the members of the board would naturally be opposed to such pictures, we will not, therefore, be called upon to pass an opinion on them.[117]

Nevertheless, some Board of Censorship allies stood against the film. A former board member, H. V. Andrews, for example, placed a letter in the *New York Times* in favor of barring the film. The group's general secretary responded. While "the board is now censoring over 90 per cent. of all moving picture shows," Walter Storey explained, the "corporation controlling the fight pictures is a syndicate, recently organized for this sole purpose, with whom the board has no agreement. These pictures are therefore not submitted to the board for its decision."[118]

The MPPC had not anticipated the strength of the anti-prizefight opposition. Until the eve of the fight, they had been confident that the Johnson-Jeffries pictures would be in great demand. On July 2, the Patents Company issued a bulletin to exhibitors and exchanges warning that access to the coveted fight film would be denied to any theater in which "unlicensed motion pictures were shown." Violators were threatened with "immediate cancellation."[119]

However, Johnson's victory and the censorship crusade put the film-makers in retreat. "There was never a time," the *Moving Picture World* observed, "when the general interests of the moving picture business were more at stake than during the period immediately following the Johnson-Jeffries fight."[120] Backers of the film balanced exploitation with the rhetoric of social welfare.

The trade press offered split opinions. The *Moving Picture News* came out vigorously against *Johnson-Jeffries*. If Jeffries "had not been hounded by the picture men, no fight would have taken place," they argued. "We hope every exhibitor throughout the country will refuse to pollute his house with such films." The *Moving Picture World* blamed the censorship campaign on "men who failed to secure the coveted privilege of taking the fight pictures [and] are now doing their best to prohibit their exhibition."[121] Non-MPPC producers and exhibitors generally refrained from broad condemnation. They led fight picture profiteering, before, during, and after 1910.

Early on, some film interests rebutted bans, arguing constitutional rights and noble principles. *The Nickelodeon* suggested that film advertisers boycott newspapers as a means of retaliation. The press had hyped the Reno fight and published a multitude of photos, but now hypocritically condemned the movies for exploiting it. A *Puck* cartoon, "Can You Beat This for What Is Known as Gall?" made the same point. Producers discussed opposing fight-film prohibitions in court. As the *Johnson-Jeffries* negatives were being rushed to New York, the picture men raced to the Patents Company offices to confer. A Méliès executive speculated about making this a "test case." Vitagraph's Albert Smith told the *New York Tribune* his company was "not alarmed by the movement against the exhibition of the pictures." If the agitation became widespread, they would "take legal action." William Rock concurred. "We do not mean to yield to the opponents of the exhibition without a fight."[122]

They quickly abandoned this strategy, however. Two publicity fronts were started instead. The producer J. Stuart Blackton addressed the New York press. In Chicago, George Kleine, William Selig, and Essanay's George Spoor lobbied for the right to exhibit the pictures. At first the Chicago triumvirate went along with the compliant mood of the Patents Company, issuing a press release: "No efforts will be made to show the pictures in any city or town where adverse legislation has been taken. It will not be necessary to get out injunctions, for this combine does not intend to buck the law in any city or state. We do not think these pictures are any different from those which have been displayed of the Johnson-Burns and Johnson-Ketchel fights, but if we find that popular sentiment is against them we will lay them on the shelf and not show them at all."[123] A few days later, Kleine and Blackton suggested the National Board of Censorship might be called on after all. With bans and boycotts multiplying, Kleine proposed a two-week cooling-off period before deciding whether to market the film.[124]

Chicago producers went directly to the chief of police, who had the authority to censor moving pictures. On July 11, a private screening was given in a back room of the Selig offices, with two police representatives and several theater managers in attendance. The police chief, Leroy T. Steward, was inclined to permit screening of the fight film. "There is a question in my mind as to whether there would have been any objection made to the showing of the fight pictures if the white man had won. I think there would not." His assistant agreed, saying during the screening: "I don't see anything about these pictures to incite a riot or ruin any one's morals." Spoor was especially glad to hear the report. He had paid the J. & J. Company $60,000 for the right to exploit the film in Illinois.

As protest intensified, however, Steward banned all prizefight pictures from Chicago (including a "farce reproduction"). This decision severely reduced potential profits because the city—the home of Jack Johnson, Battling Nelson, George Siler, and other prominent boxing proponents—was an important venue for fights and films. Spoor took legal action, petitioning for the right to market the timely films immediately. The city rationalized its ban as consistent with the 1907 ordinance forbidding "obscene and immoral kinetoscopes and cinematographs." Spoor countered that permits had always been issued to fight pictures before: Chicago had licensed *Summers-Britt, Burns-Johnson, Johnson-Ketchel, Jeffries-Sharkey,* and films of all three Nelson-Gans matches. The court rejected his plea.[125]

Another Chicagoan, Harold E. Leopold, the owner of a South Side amusement park, sued when police stopped his exhibition of the *Johnson-Ketchel Fight* in late July. Although these pictures had been widely shown, when exhibitors revived them as stand-ins for the Jeffries fight, police extended their crackdown, confiscating prints at both public and private screenings of *Johnson-Ketchel* and *Johnson-Jeffries.*[126]

Yet the fracas in Chicago was an exception to the general conduct of the film trade. Most picture people followed Vitagraph's example, softening the threat of the *Johnson-Jeffries Fight* by assuring it would be handled carefully.

Children were held up as those most in need of protection from screen violence. The mayor of San Francisco banned the pictures on these grounds, arguing that otherwise, "every little boy and girl who had a nickel could gain access to and witness the exhibition." The trade dismissed this argument, pointing out that this fight would not be "spread broadcast among the nickelodeons." *Moving Picture World* rebutted the Christian Endeavor's press campaign, saying "the children whom the daily press so sensationally defend, or pretends to, will not see the pictures at all."[127]

Promoters also vowed to protect women from the spectacle. The Hearst press defended its anti-fight-film stance by arguing that "moving pictures are seen by many millions, mostly women and children who patronize the moving picture shows."[128] The weight of opinion against the *Johnson-Jeffries Fight* caused promoters to assay a "stag" policy. At a press conference, Blackton pledged that "children will be absolutely barred from witnessing the films" and "strictly 'stag' affairs" would ensure that "any women who attend the production will know beforehand just what they are to see. . . . We have taken pains to see that they are not used generally. Oscar Hammerstein offered us a large sum for their use at the Victoria, but we refused, because we did not want them displayed before mixed audiences in the vaudeville houses. The shows will be stag. They will last a couple of hours, and the admission fee will be from $1 to $2." Others repeated Blackton's argument for gender segregation. One correspondent to the *Moving Picture World* wrote that the *Johnson-Jeffries* pictures should not be feared because "they will not be exhibited promiscuously in family theatres."[129]

If the word *promiscuous* suggested sexual transgression, it bespoke a subtle but important level of discourse about screen images of Jack Johnson. Fear of miscegenation motivated containment. The champion was becoming reviled for his conduct with white women. Johnson's violation of this taboo, which surpassed that of any prior national figure, provoked more antipathy than anything he did in the ring. Retribution for this behavior did not peak until 1912, but signs of white fear of Johnson's sexual persona were apparent in discussions of the *Johnson-Jeffries Fight*. The pictures were "demoralizing," reasoned the *Examiner*, not just because they revealed to white "boys and girls" that "their own race was beaten into physical disability by a gigantic negro," but because this might be shown on screens "before white women."[130] As Susan Courtney so convincingly argues in her brilliant *Hollywood Fantasies of Miscegenation* (2004), the Johnson pictures animated, in an aggressive way, a core concern of American culture. Popular films habitually addressed issues of black-white sexual relationships, but few so directly as those showing Jack Johnson.[131]

Reports about the previews also suggested the sexual dynamic of female spectatorship. The first audience for the films consisted of Johnson and his white wife, Etta Duryea, who visited the Vitagraph plant on July 13. While Johnson informally narrated parts of the film, his wife laughed.[132] Soon after, reporters joined the Vitagraph stock company of actors at a second preview. Johnson's sexual menace was hinted at. "The girls clapped their hands for the white hero," said the *New York Times*. "Although he showed his golden smile to them frequently from the screen, the black champion found no favor. Femininity was agreed that he was 'just too horrid for anything.'"[133] The matinee girl's glimpse of Gentleman Jim had been tolerated in 1897, but when a black athlete returned the gaze, the implications brought censure.

Race, gender, age, and class were bound together in the attempts to control the audience for the big fight film. But white fear of racial commingling was at times a sufficient justification for censorship. Again this fear was manifest in cartoon representations. The July 7 *Chicago Tribune* cartoon, "Some Fight Pictures That Would Be Desirable," implied that an all-white audience cheering a white attack on black Pullman porters would be acceptable. The *Examiner* mimicked this idea in "Some Fight Pictures That We Would Permit," condoning white applause for an assault on "Oriental immigration." White opponents of the pictures could not imagine anything other than segregated black and white spheres.

But to the self-interested film trade, exhibiting the *Johnson-Jeffries Fight* had racially charged implications. In August 1910, a cartoon appeared in the *Moving Picture World* depicting a racially desegregated theater audience.

With the ambiguous caption "There's a Reason," the drawing spoke volumes about the racial dynamics of fight film exhibition.[134] The fictional full house reveals disgruntled, sour-looking, middle-aged white men forced to share orchestra seating with black men and women. The gallery remains all-black. The African American patrons are drawn in racist stereotypy, although their smiles and elegant attire are the supposed result of newfound pride and wealth following Johnson's victory. "There's a Reason" was an advertising slogan for Post brand cereals.[135] Post used the vague, suggestive phrase to imply the unspecified benefits of its product. The drawing suggested there was a reason many whites wanted to suppress the film. Encouraging black attendance would allow movement from the controlled environment of the "dark gallery" to integrated facilities. Yet there was also a reason for the trade to allow this one-time privilege: they could profit from black viewers' buying tickets that many whites did not want.

The racially integrated house filled with wealthy African American patrons was a willful misrepresentation. Some whites feared anything approaching such a scenario, but theater owners and picture promoters ensured that strict controls were put on audiences and theater space. While some houses sold tickets to both races, even these maintained white dominion. Efforts to circumscribe the audience for the *Johnson-Jeffries Fight* were largely successful.

ALTERNATIVES TO THE RENO FIGHT PICTURES

Competing productions interfered with the marketing of the genuine films. Independent producers revived the fake fight-film practice. Other forms of visual reproduction and parody also cluttered the market.

At least two faked versions of the Johnson-Jeffries fight were filmed, and multiple editions circulated. Competitors in Chicago and New York hired reputable boxers to imitate the rounds before stadium crowds. With "several of the independent interests in Chicago," the Chicago Sports Picture Company shot a "reproduction." Wrestler Charles Cutler acted the part of Jeffries; Cleve Hawkins played Johnson. They rehearsed for several days and performed in front of bleachers full of excited fans. A two-reel cut was made and advertised as "No Fake." "Johnson-Jeffries Fight Pictures Stopped!!" screamed the ad. "We do not claim to have the original films, but we offer a reproduction of the big fight." The company also marketed Johnson training pictures and claimed "entire exclusive control" of the first and third *Nelson-Gans* fight pictures.[136]

A similar reproduction in New York received greater attention when its producers attempted to pass it off as the real thing. The Empire Film Company hired the well-known Joe Jeannette (who had boxed Johnson ten times) and the white Jim Stewart to "illustrate" the rounds as descriptions were read on July 4. Empire staged the event at the American League Park, attracting a sporting crowd. The company told buyers it had "invaded the ringside" to record the actual contest.

Empire's chief victim was William Morris. Having shown independent fight pictures earlier in the year, Morris was barred by the Patents Company from renting the Johnson-Jeffries pictures. He booked the Empire film to play his American Music Hall sight unseen. On July 9, his advertisements for "a superb set of moving pictures of the Jeffries-Johnson Fight," to be narrated by James J. Corbett, attracted a packed house. After a two-hour delay, projection began. Morris and his restless audience recognized the "'phony' pictures" immediately. "Amid jeers and cries of 'Fake!'" Morris stopped the screening. Fearing more bad publicity for its genuine films, Vitagraph hosted another press meeting, at which. Blackton warned he would take legal action to protect the "patent" on the film. The Empire pictures had been "doctored," he said, and the Chicago one "faked up."

In its report on the episode, *Variety* concluded: "There threatens to be a flood of 'fake' Johnson-Jeffries pictures on the market long before the Rock-Hester originals see the light of day." And in small towns, the writer observed, "the 'outlaw' houses are advertising films of the battle at Reno. Coney Island is fairly ablaze with announcements."[137]

Ads for poor substitutes appeared throughout 1910. The Toledo Film Exchange, for example, offered a two-reel *Johnson-Jeffries Fight* "impersonation which can be shown in any city." A third reel of Johnson in training accompanied the fake. Footage of the Nelson-Wolgast fight could also be rented.[138]

Slide manufacturers intervened in the marketing of "pictures" of the battle of the century. As with cinematic imitations, stereopticon presentations met with mixed reactions. Some sellers glossed over the distinction between still and moving pictures. Louis J. Berger promoted his "Jeffries-Johnson fight pictures" in full-page trade ads. Without mentioning that his product consisted of *New York Herald* news photos, he pitched them as an affordable alternative that was not one of the "numerous 'fakes' and 'doctored' imitators." A Chicago company even sold "Jeffries-Johnson fight pictures" in flip-book form, calling it a "kinetoscope" showing "actual men in moving pictures."[139]

Some audiences rebelled against these deceptions. The Savoy Theater in Manhattan drew a crowd anxious to see the first Johnson-Jeffries footage.

When they discovered that the "ringside pictures" were only snapshots, the spectators, who had paid double admission, rushed the box office, smashing signs and breaking glass. The Savoy continued to offer its lantern slide show but appended a notice to its marquee: "These are not motion pictures."

Some audiences were more accepting. Louisville's Riverview Park promoted "Johnson-Jeffries fight pictures" among its summer amusements. No one deemed it a deception when these proved to be lantern slides. Even this tame display, however, was permitted only because it was outside city limits and "because colored persons" were not admitted at the park.[140]

Lantern slides were not monopolized as motion pictures were. Theater proprietors could find them in varying levels of price and quality. V. L. Duhem, a San Francisco photographer, offered up to one hundred color slides of the Reno bout. In the fall of 1910, Duhem embarked on a more nefarious picture deal. With a nickelodeon manager, he stole prints of the genuine film from a local theater. When the manager was "arrested with four sets of the J. & J. fight films in his possession," Duhem confessed his plan to "manufacture hundreds of copies of the fight pictures and sell them in cities in Germany, France, and England."[141]

In addition to reenactments, bootlegs, and slide series, other ancillary genres emerged to meet the demand for fight pictures. Reissues of older fights, new films of minor bouts, actuality footage of Johnson, race-fight parodies, and wrestling pictures peppered the market. The American Cinephone Company even made a talking picture of the champion delivering his vaudeville monologue.[142] These offerings filled the gap between the hubbub about the *Johnson-Jeffries Fight* and the relative rarity of actual screenings.

The only attraction within professional boxing that fulfilled demand for prizefight material was the publicity drummed up for the black boxer Sam Langford. Although he had lost a fight to Johnson in 1906, the Canadian-born middleweight challenged the champ loudly and often. Twice Langford was filmed boxing Johnson's white opponents. On St. Patrick's Day 1910, Langford knocked out Jim Flynn. MPPC brought suit against its partner, Sid Hester, for photographing the Langford-Flynn fight without a license, hurting the film's market performance. A month later John Krone released the *Langford-Ketchel Fight*, but the no-decision contest generated little interest. After July 4, Langford continued to spoil for a fight with Johnson. He traveled with his films and gained some recognition. Hammerstein's Victoria booked him for a sparring exhibition and a fight film on their "Victoriascope."[143] Langford, tagged as the "Boston Tar Baby," remained pigeon-holed as a racial sideshow. He had to emigrate to Paris to receive acclaim and further movie coverage.

SCREENINGS OF *JEFFRIES-JOHNSON WORLD'S* *CHAMPIONSHIP BOXING CONTEST*

Despite all obstacles, the *Johnson-Jeffries Fight* did appear on many screens. The controversy contributed to its box-office receipts. No riots occurred, as exhibitors practiced established forms of class and race controls on audiences.

The proposed two-week cooling-off period was cut in half as "hundreds of offers from theaters and houses of amusement" came in, and it soon became clear that New York would not bar the film. J. & J. representatives sold the *Johnson-Jeffries Fight* on a straight territorial-rights basis. State and municipal bans cut into their anticipated million-dollar profits, as did the refusal of B. F. Keith and the Independent Managers' Association to book the film. But if the $60,000 Illinois contract, the $150,000 Canadian rights deal, and the $12,000 bid from one Manhattan theater were any indication, the J. & J. Company profited handsomely. When George Smith, the manager of Vitagraph, exhibited the film at London's National Sporting Club in September, he claimed the firm had already made back its investment. Promoters put the total profits at $300,000.[144]

Territorial distributors had less consistent box-office results, as local reactions to the film varied. In suburban Cincinnati, when several theaters on the outskirts of town presented the pictures that had been banned in the city, only a few hundred customers turned up.[145] But the much-hyped recording usually drew substantial crowds.

To bolster the film's debut, Blackton announced that all New York engagements would be booked by the vaudeville magnate Percy G. Williams. Williams engaged two Broadway houses, as well as the Bronx and Colonial theaters in the Bronx, the Gotham and the Orpheum in Brooklyn, and the Alhambra in Harlem as the first showplaces.[146] Counting on the champion's popularity among African American audiences, Williams selected the Alhambra for the premiere.

Methods for controlling audiences on the basis of race were enforced with rigor, holding down black participation even at this heightened moment of "race pride." Raised admission prices did not prevent a full house at the Harlem Alhambra on July 16, where announcer Joe Humphries explained the footage. With pundits having predicted race riots at screenings, the *New York Times* emphasized there was "no sign of race feeling" when the pictures were shown. However, it also described an environment of racial intimidation. At the premiere, the manager (who was white) gave free seating to companies of firemen from New York and Boston, and local police patrolled the theater. Given this show of force, the *Times* ought to have been less surprised

Figure 44. The men of the Comet Theatre, a downtown New York nickelodeon, display posters for *Jeffries-Johnson Fight Pictures* as part of their exhibition of "high class motion pictures." (Daniel Blum Collection, Wisconsin Center for Film and Theater Research.)

that there were "fewer negroes in the audience than had been expected, and these took seats only in the upper parts of the theatre." A review of a Manhattan screening two days later also downplayed the race issue.

For New York's black audiences, alternative viewing opportunities came in August. Olympic Field in the heart of Harlem held outdoor screenings nightly, and a park in Brooklyn presented the film simultaneously. Both advertised to black patrons and received endorsements from the *New York Age* and African American celebrities.[147]

African Americans elsewhere remained interested in seeing Johnson's victory, but antagonistic white attitudes limited their access. In West Virginia, for example, a "Negro teacher" let his students out of school early to see the fight pictures. "The white people" of the town, reported the *Defender*, were "threatening to tar and feather Professor Page." Other exhibitors took extra steps to segregate audiences into separate screenings.[148]

In the end, public debate about the fight picture became more important to black advancement than the film itself was. African American communities celebrated Johnson's monumental victory in public congregations—at theaters, news offices, bars, churches, parks, and street corners—and read about it in newspapers. Johnson's triumph was proof of black achievement. Lack of access to motion-picture replays was secondary. In the estimation of an *Afro-American Ledger* writer, suppression of the film merely made white reactionaries look childish, as it in no way denied Johnson's accomplishment. For the *Defender* reviewer Mildred Miller, the fact that the fight pictures were banned in Chicago, while hateful race melo-dramas (such as William Brady's stage production of "The Nigger") were not, indicated the injustice of local law. "Why not let the Johnson-Jeffries pictures be shown?" she asked. "These show equality in every particular."[149]

Black spectators formed only a small percentage of the *Johnson-Jeffries Fight* audience. Many of the film's largest crowds were exclusively white. Their motivations and reactions were less clearly articulated. Many no doubt attended for the same reasons they saw the Burns-Johnson and Johnson-Ketchel pictures, attracted by the publicity and controversy. Others were boxing devotees. One black columnist even rationalized "there are thousands of white men who bet on Johnson and won, and they are the ones who would like to see the fight pictures and who feel good every time the affair is mentioned."[150]

In areas where black populations were small, the pictures played well. The British *Bioscope* reviewer commented that the pictures were "not brutal, not disgusting," but rather "slow," especially their two reels of preliminary footage. Further, in places without the threat of a black constituency seeking empowerment, white sports fans or thrill seekers could watch Jeffries' Waterloo with more detachment. *Johnson-Jeffries* was a hit in Paris, Dublin, and other parts of Europe (although it had to be "revised" by police in Germany). To cite one instance of similar success in the United States, Madison, Wisconsin, allowed exhibition of the Reno film. It played at the town's main movie venue, the Fuller Opera House, and was revived for a run in 1911. (Yet even in Madison the appearance of Jack Johnson on screen elicited a letter to the editor warning that "every coon in town will turn out.")[151]

Its notoriety gave the *Johnson-Jeffries Fight* appeal beyond that of most boxing movies. Audiences from high and low spheres of influence sought it out, contraband or not. Clandestine shows were held in private hotel suites and on Mississippi River barges. Philadelphia's large Forrest Theater had public screenings as well as private ones for city officials. The Rochester Armory showed pictures of the championship bout to all-male National Guard companies stationed there. The film even held some cultural cachet: having seen it was considered a mark of sophistication. The philanthropist Joseph

E. Widener and his wife screened the film at their Newport summer home. A hundred dinner guests watched a 35 mm projection of the *Johnson-Jeffries Fight* in the millionaire's drawing room while listening to "McLellan's colored singers."[152] Even the sight of a powerful black fighter thrashing the white hope could be reconfigured for the pleasure of some white viewers.

As the film circulated, the scenes of Johnson's formidable performance offered a stiff rebuttal to Jack London's racist call to arms. While making the theatrical rounds in 1910, the champion even posed for ironic photos (with his white wife and entourage) outside a theater marquee advertising "Jack Johnson" alongside a poster for London's *Call of the Wild*. However, Johnson's public appearances and press representations helped diminish the threat that many whites initially saw in the Johnson-Jeffries films. As Roberts describes in his biography, Johnson's tours of burlesque and vaudeville houses presented him to white audiences in a form closer to the accepted, nonthreatening stage and screen stereotype of a "smiling, happy-go-lucky black." Soon his monologues and songs were cut back, literally taking away his voice. He became a freak-show display, a mere posing body on stage.

Other events of 1910 and 1911 diminished the impact of the *Johnson-Jeffries Fight*. A devotee of fast cars, Johnson challenged the champion driver Barney Oldfield to a series of automobile races in October 1910. Cameras filmed Oldfield's victories at Coney Island in front of five thousand spectators. The production was a minor event compared to the fight in Reno, but it caused the *Defender* to remark sarcastically that "white people will be able and willing to find consolation in the Johnson-Oldfield auto-pictures." The film industry itself also searched for an antidote to the Jeffries pictures. *Moving Picture World* reviewed the pictures of a fight between two English heavyweights, Welsh and Driscoll, in March 1911. The journal said it was "looking for [the British] to put the colored fighter out of business."[153]

In the end it was an American, Jess Willard, who finally put Johnson out of business, but not for another four years. The years 1912 to 1915 marked the steady decline of Jack Johnson as a public figure. With a federal statute banning distribution of prizefight pictures, this period also saw the virtual end of the film genre that propagated Johnson's image.

7 Jack Johnson's Decline

The Prizefight Film Ban, 1911–1915

The first confiscation of prize-fight moving-picture films, the
interstate shipment or importation of which is forbidden by a
Federal law passed June 30, was made today in the seizure of 2400
feet of films picturing the Jeffries-Johnson and Gans-Herman fights.
The films were found in the baggage of O. D. Harter, a theatrical
promoter. . . . Harter said he had exhibited the pictures in the Orient
and had not learned of the passage of the law.
  "Seize Prize-Fight Films," *Los Angeles Times*, September 19, 1912

Jack Johnson's three title fights between 1908 and 1910 made him an international celebrity. The three resulting fight pictures added to his fame and
wealth. With the *Johnson-Jeffries Fight*, the visibility and influence of the
genre peaked. Yet the reaction to the film led to the demise of prizefight
films in the United States. During the five years that followed, the films and
Johnson himself met with censure and, finally, banishment.

THE BEGINNING OF JOHNSON'S DECLINE

The victory over Jim Jeffries and its repetition on movie screens marked a
high point in Jack Johnson's career, bolstering his pugilistic reputation and
his status in the African American community. Although most black audiences were prevented from celebrating screenings of the *Johnson-Jeffries
Fight*, they lionized the champion. Black leaders, however, had been careful
to separate pride in Johnson's accomplishment from an endorsement of
Johnson himself. After 1910, support for Johnson faded. Subsequent fight
pictures were received quite differently as the fighter became increasingly
vilified.

As early as March 1910, the *Afro-American Ledger* qualified its appraisal
of Johnson, saying that "the race which in a large measure is proud of him
is not altogether pleased at the pace he is going."[1] Reports of his fast living
and run-ins with the law were thought to adversely affect the environment
in which all African Americans lived. Johnson brushed off scrapes with the
law and flaunted the money with which he paid fines. In March 1911 he

239

Figure 45. Frames from *Jack Johnson: Der Meister Boxer der Welt,* a Dutch version of Kineto's *How the Champion of the World Trains: Jack Johnson in Defence and Attack* (1911). A show of strength and a comic comeuppance. (Nederlands Filmmuseum.)

served jail time for reckless driving. Police harassed him more frequently. While a White Hope boxing tournament was organized to find a man who could unseat him, Johnson returned to Europe.

In London he initially played to cheering audiences on stage. Kineto, Ltd., brought Johnson into a studio and shot an amusing short film replicating part of his stage act. The surviving Dutch distribution print, *Jack Johnson: Der Meister Boxer der Welt* (1911) shows the champ posing and flexing his muscles for the camera (see figure 45). After some bare-fisted shadow boxing, Johnson demonstrates his strength, laughing as he tosses about his white managers. In August, promoters announced a contest against the British titlist "Bombadier" Billy Wells. The topical film specialist Barker took out full-page trade ads proclaiming its forthcoming pictures of Johnson against Wells "the biggest thing ever handled in the cinematograph world" and "the best advertised picture in the history of cinematography." A local official opposed to the fight complained that "without the cinematograph it would never be heard of." The Archbishop of Canterbury and reformers campaigned against the interracial bout, causing Winston Churchill, the home secretary, to rule the fight illegal. The match-up was abandoned.[2]

In France, Johnson and his wife again found a reception more hospitable than that in America. African and African American boxers enjoyed a vogue in Paris during the belle epoque. Shut out from opportunities to box for the title, Sam Langford, Joe Jeannette, Jim Johnson, and Sam McVey emigrated to Paris as early as February 1909, when a Jeanette-McVey match piqued interest in boxing there. In April 1911, Hugh McIntosh promoted a bout between Langford and McVey. Set in the Paris Hippodrome (then also a movie palace), the fight was filmed and the pictures successfully distributed. As for

Figure 46. Frame from *Bill as a Boxer* (Lux, 1910). This French comedy illustrates the prominence of black fighters during the Johnson era. Bill (or Patouillard, played by Paul Bertho, center) encounters a champion boxer named Sam Tapford, played by a white actor in dreadful blackface. The curious mise-en-scène intermixes cinema and boxing posters. Two noted black fighters are referenced. The pair of three-sheet posters shows Joe Jeannette, who fought ten bouts in Paris in 1909. "Sam Tapford" is a play on Sam Langford. Both men were popular athletes in France who squared off fourteen times between 1905 and 1917. (Library of Congress, Motion Picture, Broadcasting and Recorded Sound Division.)

Johnson, he gave stage exhibitions with the French boxing idol Georges Carpentier. But the boisterous champion continued to have confrontations with the authorities. He returned to the United States in 1912 to train for another title defense.[3]

THE JOHNSON-FLYNN PICTURES

Although his popularity was diminishing, talk of a Johnson fight picture still created excitement. As the *Freeman* noted when a large African American movie theater opened in January 1912, anxious patrons at the grand opening "acted as if Jack Johnson and Jim Jeffries were on the inside."[4] But the challenger, Jim Flynn, failed to attract the same level of interest. Johnson had defeated Flynn on his way up. The ersatz Irish brawler (born Andrew Chariglione) had been knocked out on St. Patrick's Day, 1910, by Sam Langford. The Langford-Flynn pictures hardly enhanced his image as a white hope. Yet he was the only contender to land a financial backer.

Neophyte promoter Jack Curley put up $30,000 to entice Johnson back into the ring. In January, Johnson signed an agreement that guaranteed him a third of the film receipts and "the lion's share of the 'training camp pictures.' "[5] New Mexico, having just been granted statehood, had no anti-prizefight law. Boosters in the declining boom town of Las Vegas, New Mexico, agreed to host the championship. Local investors put up $100,000, hoping to attract the national press corps. They envisioned "motion picture cameramen taking city scenes to be displayed after the boxing bout in moving picture theaters in every town and city in the United States."[6]

Their investment soured, however. Johnson remained news, but papers devoted little attention to his upcoming Fourth of July battle. An independent Chicago outfit, incorporated as the Johnson-Flynn Feature Film Company, produced a two-reel film in March. *Jack Johnson and Jim Flynn Up-to-date* (1912) showed the pugilists in training but did little to spark interest.

The commercial value of Johnson fight pictures had plummeted. No major companies bid for the chance to shoot the fight in Las Vegas. They did, however, continue to market white fight films. Vitagraph released the *Mc-Farland-Wells Fight*. On July 4 the lightweight championship upstaged Johnson's victory. *Ad Wolgast vs. Joe Rivers*, shot in Vernon, California, captured dramatic footage of the boxers knocking each other out simultaneously. The lightweight contest attracted more fans and grossed more money than the heavyweight duel. Its film also received wider and more timely distribution and more favorable reviews.[7]

The motion picture copyrighted as *Jack Johnson vs. Jim Flynn Contest for Heavyweight Championship of the World* listed Jack Curley as the producer, although he hired Miles Brothers to shoot it. The quality of the original 35 mm film is difficult to judge based on the extant 16 mm version, in which the boxers' heads are partially cropped. This flaw is particularly noticeable because the overmatched Flynn tried to head-butt Johnson repeatedly. Otherwise, the pictures revealed the expected and familiar scenes of Johnson toying with his opponent and engaging ringside spectators in repartee. Police stopped his bloodying of Flynn in the ninth round.

The Johnson-Flynn pictures had only a small audience. Advertisements for the film were scarce, although it was shown in Albuquerque, San Francisco,

Figure 47.   Frame from *Johnson-Flynn Fight* (July 4, 1912), taken from a 16 mm reduction print of the Miles Bros. 35 mm original. (Library of Congress, Motion Picture, Broadcasting and Recorded Sound Division.)

and New York. The only interest in them, said the *Police Gazette*, was among aficionados who wanted to see whether the champion's skills had diminished. They had not, but his reputation had. Johnson's reliance on picture profits to sustain his extravagant lifestyle helped tarnish his professional image. "Joe Jeannette Dubs Johnson a 'Moving Picture Fighter' " ran a headline to Jim Corbett's column just before the Flynn fiasco. The now-familiar charge against boxers stuck to Johnson. The *Gazette* confirmed the observation: "Just why Jack wanted to hold instead of fight is a question that is hard to explain, except on the ground that the negro was desirous of making those moving pictures worth while from a financial standpoint."[8]

THE FEDERAL BAN ON FIGHT PICTURES

The *Jack Johnson vs. Jim Flynn Contest* failed commercially, in part because Congress outlawed the traffic in prizefight pictures. After the bout, a statute barring the interstate transport of fight films went into effect on July 31, 1912. As debate about the action made clear, the main intention of the framers of the law was to quash the cinematic glorification of Jack Johnson. Anti-prizefight reformers were pleased as well. For several years, commercial distribution of such films ceased in the United States, making fight picture production unprofitable. Clandestine and private screenings continued in America, while the recording of bouts continued in England. The federal ban stayed on the books until 1940, although officials gradually began to ignore the law after Johnson's reign.

The "act to prohibit the importation and the interstate transportation of films or other pictorial representations of prize fights" was the culmination of attempts to restrict the prizefight business. Congress first debated attempts to outlaw fight films in 1897. With the rise of a black heavyweight champion in 1908, state legislatures had issued restrictions. And even before the reactionary municipal ordinances against the *Johnson-Jeffries Fight*, the U.S. Congress had reconsidered fight film legislation.

In May 1910, Rep. Walter I. Smith (R-Iowa), whose state had been the first to enact a boxing film ban, introduced a bill "to prohibit the exhibition of moving pictures of prizefights" and telegraphed fight descriptions. Some religious groups lobbied for it, but most agitated to stop the Johnson-Jeffries bout itself. With Jeffries given a chance to win, the white, male Congress demonstrated no desire to pass the Smith bill. At Commerce Committee hearings on May 17, the Speaker of the House set a decidedly pro-boxing tone. Speaker Joseph Cannon, an Illinois representative, called on his fellow Illinoisan Battling Nelson to testify. "Uncle Joe" sparred with the "white world's champion" for Capitol Hill reporters. In the committee hearing, Rep. Thetus Sims (who led the charge against Johnson films) even asked Nelson for an exhibition of his skills. No action was taken. In 1911, Smith alone testified when his bill failed to get beyond a committee hearing.[9]

The next Congress took up more carefully drafted legislation, this time more obviously motivated by race issues. As another big "race fight" approached in 1912, the subject came to the floor of Congress. Although the proposed act did not single out films on the basis of racial difference, its sponsors did. Unreconstructed Southern Democrats steered the bill.

Representatives Sims (Tennessee) and Seaborn A. Roddenbery (Georgia) managed the House vote, while Furnifold M. Simmons (North Carolina) and Augustus Bacon (Georgia) led Senate action. No opposition to censorship per se was raised, although there was confusion as to whether the law ought to target production, distribution, exhibition, or viewership. In the final draft, the Sims Act was modeled after existing federal controls on "obscene" publications and birth control and abortion literature. Rather than try to stop production or punish recipients, Congress used its constitutional power to regulate commerce and forbade interstate transport of fight films. Most non-Southern members agreed that the spread of brutalizing prize-fight scenes ought to be stopped for religious, moral, and ethical reasons, but they prevented swift passage of the bill.

The Southern delegation pushed for immediate action, pleading the dangers of racial conflict. On June 10, Sen. Bacon said there were "some impending performances" he hoped to prevent. As late as July 1, Rep. Sims brought the issue to the House floor, describing it as a bill to stop "interstate commerce of moving-picture films of prize fights, especially the one be-tween a negro and a white man, to be held in New Mexico on the 4th of July." Some House members took exception to the virulent racism ex-pressed and delayed a vote until after the fight.

When Sims laid his bill before the House again following Johnson's lat-est show of force, the excessive rhetoric of his ally nearly sidetracked the de-bate again. Rep. Roddenbery linked his aversion to fight pictures with his racist aversion to interracial affairs: "It is well known that one of the chief inducements and incentives to these prize fights now is the sale of the films under contracts. . . . [T]he recent prize fight which was had in New Mexico presented, perhaps, the grossest instance of base fraud and bogus effort at a fair fight between a Caucasian brute and an African biped beast that has ever taken place. It was repulsive. This bill is designed to prevent the display to morbid-minded adults and susceptible youth all over the country of repre-sentations of such a disgusting exhibition." Ohio representative William Sharp interrupted Roddenbery's tirade to ask if it was "more indefensible for a white man and black man to engage in a prize fight than for two white men to engage in such a conflict?" Roddenbery responded: "No man de-scended from the old Saxon race can look upon that kind of a contest with-out abhorrence and disgust."[10]

It was not the last time Roddenbery invoked the "principles of a pure Saxon government" to defame Jack Johnson in Congress. Later that year, when Johnson married a second white wife, Roddenberry pressed for a con-stitutional amendment against miscegenation. Nothing, he said, was as de-grading, "villainous," or "atrocious" as the laws "which allow the marriage of the negro, Jack Johnson, to a woman of Caucasian strain." Roddenbery warned that granting license to "black-skinned, thick-lipped, bull-necked, brutal-hearted African" men like Johnson would lead to another civil war. Meanwhile, some exhibitors and authorities were seeking to bar new films documenting Johnson's interracial wedding.[11]

When Northern representatives challenged Roddenbery's venomous grandstanding, Sims intervened. He cut off his ally and reminded the

House that there was a consensus in favor of stopping immoral prizefight films. The bill passed and was signed into law on July 31, 1912.[12] So obvious were the white fears of black power that animated the legislative process that even a boxing insider like William Brady mistakenly thought the act specifically "prohibit[ed] even a motion-picture reproduction of any such a mixed-color contest."[13] In fact, the statute criminalized only interstate transport of the pictures. However, with distribution legal only in the state where a bout was recorded, no significant profits could be realized. Fight film production ceased in the United States.

EUROPEAN FIGHT FILMS

Prominent bouts were still being shot and distributed by British and French companies. Although Britain quashed the Johnson-Wells fight, the nation still welcomed pictures of its native sons winning pugilistic glory. The camera-ready National Sporting Club turned out many British fight films. In 1911, *Bioscope* and *The Sportsman* noted that " 'contests on canvas' are, thanks to the advance in the art of photography, the rule nowadays, rather than the exception, and everything of note is quickly placed before the public." The British trade argued that this widespread distribution was, in part, due to its "open market" for boxing films, in contrast to the American practice of treating them as "exclusives."[14] More than twenty prizefights were recorded in Britain during the Johnson era, making the genre, as Rachel Low notes, "of especial importance."[15]

In France, the popularity of fight pictures was tied to the rise of Georges Carpentier. While a teenager, he was promoted by the showman François Descamps, who turned him from a champion of *savate* kick-boxing *(la boxe française)* into his country's first master of *la boxe anglaise*. By the age of nineteen he had won the welter-, middle-, light-heavy-, and heavyweight championships of Europe. A series of successful film recordings bolstered his career. In March 1912, pictures of his two-round defeat of Jim Sullivan in Monte Carlo ran for several weeks at the American Biograph in Paris and elsewhere. In June, the box office for the *Carpentier-Willie Lewis Fight* caused *Bioscope* to remark on the "phenomenal success in topical films." *Georges Carpentier v. Frank Klaus* followed within the month. A year later, motion pictures of the *Bombadier Wells–Carpentier Fight* showed the young sensation knocking out the English heavyweight. But Carpentier was no "moving picture fighter." His appearances drew broad and select audiences, especially in Paris, but his quick knockouts made for short films. One film renter rationalized this difficulty to exhibitors by contending that fight pictures "are the finest moneymakers out, when not too long. A long fight film becomes monotonous."[16]

Carpentier films were good box office. He drew noticeably more women to boxing displays than any of his predecessors had. The handsome athlete was billed as the "Orchid Man" for the elegance he was perceived to bring to the world of working-class pugs. Although Carpentier pictures could not be imported into the United States after the passage of the 1912 Sims Act, they expanded European interest in boxing, as did the emigration of African American boxers. Thus it was in Paris—only days after Carpentier was filmed beating Ed "Gunboat" Smith to take on the dubious title of "white heavyweight champion of the world"—that Jack Johnson fought his last successful title defense in June 1914.

JOHNSON IN EXILE: *THE JOHNSON-MORAN FIGHT*

In 1912, cameras had captured a gleeful champion dominating Jim Flynn. In 1914, motion pictures revealed a lackluster Johnson dragging around the little-known white hope Frank Moran for twenty uneventful rounds. Between those events, Johnson's career changed dramatically. Public perceptions of him altered. For many white Americans, Johnson had become a public enemy. For many African Americans, too, his heroism diminished; for some he became persona non grata.

Johnson's activities are unusually well documented during this period. The thousands of records generated by federal officials building a criminal case against Johnson reveal the troubled public and private life of a figure who was sometimes justly accused but often unjustly persecuted.

After his 1912 victory in New Mexico, Johnson motored back to Chicago, where he opened a South Side night club, the Café de Champion. Activities at the club exacerbated his reputation for lowlife carousing. Worst of all, in September his wife Etta committed suicide. A month later he was arrested for the abduction of Lucille Cameron, one of two white prostitutes who were his regular companions. The federal Bureau of Investigation had already been gathering evidence against Johnson for smuggling jewels. Now the government pressed trumped-up charges of violating the White-Slave Traffic Act (the Mann Act) of 1910, which made it illegal to transport women across state lines for immoral purposes. Johnson was quickly indicted, jailed, and bailed. Once released, he inflamed an already intense race hatred by marrying Cameron.

There was some sympathy for Johnson in the black community. The *Richmond Planet* initially suggested "the whole thing [was] a 'frame-up' against him because of his color." But soon the paper joined others in acknowledging the need for African Americans to distance themselves from the man whom white America took as a representative of his race. Black leaders rebuked him. In Harlem, Rev. Adam Clayton Powell asked that the race not be indicted for Johnson's sins. Booker T. Washington issued a formal statement condemning the boxer's behavior.[17]

The *Afro-American Ledger* began 1913 by editorializing: "We hope Mr. Jack Johnson will form a resolution to keep out of the lime light" and stop doing "irreparable injury" to his race.[18] Johnson stayed out of the ring, but not out of the limelight. In May he was convicted of the white slavery charges and sentenced to a year in prison. But he skipped bail, crossed the Canadian border, and sailed to Europe. His music-hall performances in Paris, Brussels, London, and other cities drew mixed responses. To meet expenses, he fought exhibitions against outclassed boxers and wrestlers. That December, in the bohemian Montmartre, he made a dubious effort in a ten-round draw with Jim Johnson, an unranked sparring partner. That the underfinanced Johnson-Johnson affair yielded no motion-picture coverage indicates the degree of Jack's decline (as well as the fact that this was not a white-hope fight).

After a year of ignominy, Johnson, still holding the title of champion, found a promoter willing to offer him prize money and motion-picture receipts. Manager Dan McKetrick set up a title defense against Frank Moran. Arc lights and a camera platform were installed in the Velodrome d'Hiver for the June 27 bout. Georges Carpentier acted as referee, helping to attract a crowd of seven thousand that included aristocrats and celebrities. Surviving portions of the film reveal Johnson in his usual playful form, able to hold off attacks. Early on, according to a London report, the "cinematograph people" feared a short-lived contest. But Johnson let the fight go the distance before being declared the winner. As the pair sparred coyly for the entire twenty rounds, the crowd turned ugly, shouting that the competition was a disingenuous fake.

The *Johnson-Moran Fight* had little distribution. Johnson was vilified for his poor showing. The de rigueur charges of playing to the camera were leveled by both black and white commentators. The pictures were condemned as low-class screen fodder. As the *Richmond Planet* and *New York Sun* put it: "The suspicion is unavoidable that a desire to make a longer exhibition for the motion pictures had much to do with his failure to end the contest early. . . . But the pictures of the black loafing for twenty rounds against a competitor plainly not in his class can scarcely be worth watching. Even the familiar Western 'dramas' of the movies are preferable to this."[19] The world champion had become such a pariah that films of his victories had become all but worthless. No profits were made on the Paris bout. The Great War in Europe, which began a month later, pushed Johnson even further out of the public eye.

THE JOHNSON-WILLARD FIGHT PICTURES

A motion picture which would hold keen appeal for the white mass audience was footage of Jack Johnson being knocked out by any white underdog. Conventional wisdom held that should he lose, the Sims Act would be reversed or ignored. When such a film—the *Willard-Johnson Boxing Match*—came into being on April 5, 1915, however, the ban was still enforced. On more than one occasion, agents seized prints of the film showing Jess Willard flooring Johnson in the twenty-sixth round. Despite popular sentiment, undoing the statute was not high enough on the legislative agenda for Congress to accomplish it (the Senate was about to act on the matter when it adjourned).[20] Attempts were made to subvert the law, and the film's owners challenged it all the way to the Supreme Court. The *Willard-Johnson Boxing Match* stayed in the national spotlight as part of a contentious public discourse about race, motion pictures, and censorship. Debates about the meaning of the Johnson films became entangled in the stormy discussion of *The Birth of a Nation* and other racially inflammatory films of 1915.

Johnson's last title defense had to be held in a place remote from regulated civic life, yet accessible to the sporting class who would pay to see it. For several months, promoter Jack Curley tried to secure a bout in Juarez, but factions in the ongoing Mexican civil war threatened to interfere. With Johnson a fugitive from United States authorities, the gamblers' playground of Havana served the purpose. The champion arrived in Cuba after travels in Europe, Argentina, and elsewhere. His brushes with the law had continued. He was favored to win, but at thirty-eight he was slowing and out of shape. The awkward and little-known Jess Willard was ten years younger, half a foot taller, and solid.

"For twenty rounds Johnson punched and pounded Willard at will," the Associated Press reported, "but his blows grew perceptibly less powerful as the fight progressed, until at last he seemed unwilling or unable to go on." In the twenty-fifth round, Willard landed a wild windmill "heart punch" into

Johnson's chest. Before the next round began, the champion reportedly signaled the end, asking his wife to leave the arena. When another blow sent
Johnson to the mat in the next round, he did not rise until the referee's count
was done. Spectators poured into the ring to celebrate Willard's victory.[21]

The ring establishment recognized the chance for a changing of the
guard. Curley had to outbid Jim Coffroth for the contract, promising the
champion $30,000 and half of the movie profits. He realized the huge po-
tential in exploiting pictures of Johnson going down for the count. In contrast to his Las Vegas promotion three years before, Curley's Havana efforts
brought in three influential partners and elevated the motion-picture coverage. Films of the fight would be profitable outside the United States and—
the promoters hoped—allowed into America if Johnson lost.[22]

Harry H. Frazee, like William Brady, played a major role in sporting and
theatrical circles. He was an advance man for theatrical troupes and then a
Broadway producer. He managed Jim Jeffries for a time and, after his success with the Johnson-Willard match, bought the Boston Red Sox baseball
team in 1916. His partner, L. Lawrence Weber (figure 48), a "colorful showman, sports promoter" according to *Variety*, had a hand in founding Metro
Pictures just a month before the fight. Well connected in Broadway, variety,
and burlesque, Weber managed distribution plans for *Willard-Johnson
Boxing Match* and handled the court appeals when U.S. customs agents
seized his film. The experienced movie director and actor Fred Mace supervised the film production. Mace was well known in the new Hollywood
community. He worked for Keystone, where he was credited with inventing the comedy gag of the pie in the face. Mace also had a penchant for boxing subjects, creating a comic boxer persona for himself called One-Round
O'Brien. Just a month before the Havana shoot, he directed and starred in
What Happened to Jones for William A. Brady and World Film, a comedy
with a prizefight sequence.[23]

The quartet of Curley, Frazee, Weber, and Mace shared promotional re-
sponsibilities. Film work commenced in late March, when Mace took four
cameramen to Cuba to shoot preliminary footage of training camps and the
Oriental Park Racetrack, the site of the bout. The organizers admitted they
were taking a risk by holding the fight outdoors. Rain would mean no moving pictures, but the bigger arena yielded a larger crowd. Admission receipts
of $100,000 were collected on a sunny afternoon.

The fact that promoters had chosen a Hollywood professional instead of
an old-guard or industrial cinematographer showed in the finished product.
In place of the static long shots that made up previous fight films, Mace's
Willard-Johnson Boxing Match employed a variety of camera distances and

Figure 48.   L. Lawrence Weber, the producer and distributor of
the *Willard-Johnson Fight. New York Clipper,* March 13, 1897.

angles. In surviving editions of the film, medium and close-up shots alternate with master shots of the ring, even during the rounds. Camera operators with tripods are seen setting up shots in and beside the ring. Also apparent are setups designed to follow Willard during the fight, although the boxers are covered equally in the posed prefight scenes.

The close-ups of Willard in action are consistent with the promoters' view that they were there to frame a film of his victory. "The moving picture men say there is no question but they will show the films all over the world if Willard wins, owing to the popular demand," said the *New York Times.* Film-industry commentators predicted success. "It is not expected," wrote *Variety,* "that the authorities will hold the same antipathy against the exhibition of a white champion on the sheet as it did against the black one."[24] Black newspapers expressed similar, albeit more cynical, opinions. Lester Walton said he "would not be surprised to see the mayors of the various cities change their minds about the exhibition of the moving pictures showing a colored and a white man fighting." The *St. Louis Herald* predicted: "Had Johnson won a ban would've been placed on the fight pictures, but now—we expect to see some law passed compelling the exhibition of the fight. Of this we are assured: there will be no nationwide clamor against showing the pictures . . . and the moving picture owners will make their millions."[25] Indeed, there was no clamor against *Willard-Johnson*— because the film was almost totally suppressed in the United States, confiscated by customs officials at several ports of entry.

Events surrounding the *Willard-Johnson Boxing Match* recapitulated the problematic history of fight-picture production, distribution, exhibition, and reception. But the crackdown also closed a chapter in that history. The fate of the Havana film insured that post-Johnson prizefights would not be part of the mainstream movie industry.

Three factors marginalized the Willard-Johnson fight pictures. In addition to the federal ban on their import, racial controversy and cutthroat competition played roles. The last began even before Mace and Weber's pictures left Cuba. A pirate outfit filmed the bout and rushed its inferior footage to market. According to the *New York Times*, "The fight management, seeing the possibility of moving picture machines equipped with telescopic lenses operating from the hills, had guards stationed at all vantage points." Nevertheless, an unidentified party filmed parts of the bout from a hillside near the racetrack. A few days later these bootleg pictures were showing in Havana movie houses. "All showed fragmentary films, evidently taken by a pirate a long way away." Jack Johnson himself "raced to theatres warning them not to show the films." Cuban courts disregarded his pleas: the producers of these fugitive prints even obtained the Cuban copyright to the *Willard-Johnson Fight*. The clandestinely made recording was "shown nightly around Cuba," while "the real pictures" could not be "shown in Cuba without consent of the piraters."[26]

In the United States, other film interests tried to cash in on demand for pictures of the new champion. Universal Pictures had a one-reel melodrama, *The Heart Punch*, "thrown on the market" immediately after the fight, showing Willard in its advertisements and claiming he played "the leading part." In fact, the movie merely inserted training footage of Willard, shot months earlier Slides of the Havana bout played at Hammerstein's Victoria.[27] Weber's court brief claimed that "many spurious pictures have been and will be advertised and the public may be induced to believe that such spurious pictures represent the authentic moving pictures of the Willard-Johnson contest. An attempt is now being made to place before the public a

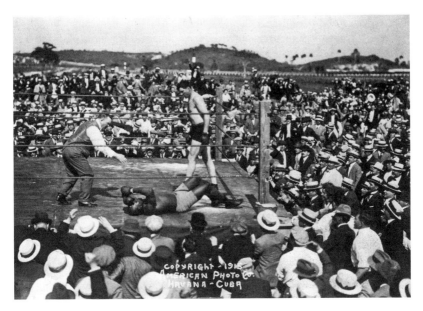

Figure 49. News photo of Jess Willard's knockout of Jack Johnson, Havana, April 5, 1915. (Library of Congress, Prints and Photographs Division.)

picture representing the said Willard-Johnson contest, which was posed by two parties who are not the aforesaid Willard and Johnson, or either of them."[28] The brief even claimed that fakers planned to record a different reenactment in each state. Weber further complained to the courts that any slide presentations were "spurious" because they were deliberately misrepresented as moving pictures.

The white press made ideological and racial capital out of Johnson's defeat. Willard had "restored pugilistic supremacy to the white race," said the *New York Times* front page.[29] Lacking cinematic replays of the events in Havana, the press seized on the final image of the giant Willard striding away from the vanquished Johnson, prostrate on the canvas. As Al-Tony Gilmore points out, the image became a "standard wall decoration" in white sports bars for many years, a signifier of white supremacy and retribution (see figure 49).

Black newspapers and Johnson himself offered a different interpretation. The ex-champ claimed he had thrown the fight for money, citing the picture as evidence. The photograph showed him holding his gloves over his eyes as the referee counted ten. This proved, he suggested, that he had consciously shielded his eyes from the sun while deliberately staying down for the count. The *Richmond Planet* printed the famous photo and offered Johnson's interpretation to black readers. It also eulogized the fallen champion.

> It will be observed that he is holding his hand over his head. . . . His pose had been perfect for the purposes of the moving picture men, who regarded this part of the affair as the climax to the earning of a great fortune by showing the motion pictures all over the world. It would be an appeal to the white man's vanity. That pose of Jack Johnson won for him $32,000 in cash and rights in the moving pictures valued at a quarter of a million dollars. There are few white men who would not have laid down for that amount just as Jack Johnson did. Study the picture again, and then imagine that you see more than a quarter of a million in the dim distance.
>
> Jack Johnson was supreme in the pugilistic field, supreme in getting money as result of that supremacy and supreme in angering both the white and the colored race in this country. . . . We shall never gaze upon his like again. Farewell, Jack Johnson![30]

Although Johnson's sworn "confession" is regarded as a fabrication, the tale persisted. The boxing authority Fred Dartnell implied that his viewing of the *Willard-Johnson Boxing Match* in 1915 lent credence to the story. Watching the film in a London picture house with Johnson himself present, Dartnell claimed that as the knockout scene was replayed and "the film unrolled its dark secret," he saw Johnson "wreathed in smiles."[31]

Such views were rare. The Johnson defeat was seen as the end of an era for black fighters. Willard announced a return of the color line. "There will never be a black heavyweight champion, or a colored champion in any division for that matter, at least as long as the present generation endures," boasted the *Detroit News*. "The Ethiopian has been eliminated." Most of the Negro press bid a quiet adieu to the problematic celebrity.[32] In April 1915, and for years after, black opinion focused on film censorship of another kind: the campaign to suppress *The Birth of a Nation*. Discourse about the Johnson fight pictures greatly diminished amid the avalanche of commentary on the epic film that libeled the entire race.

JOHNSON FIGHT PICTURES VERSUS *THE BIRTH OF A NATION*

Much has been written about the impact of D. W. Griffith's *The Birth of a Nation* and its main sources, Thomas Dixon's novel and play *The Clansman* (1905). Situating these works in the context of Jack Johnson's reign offers another view of their reception. Another race play of the period, Edward Sheldon's exploitative title *The Nigger,* also contributed to the debate about race, representation, and censorship. In the spring of 1915, the Fox Film version of *The Nigger,* Griffith's *The Birth of a Nation,* and the *Willard-Johnson Fight* were all generating headlines and provoking civic and state actions. The black press campaigned against the double standard that allowed venomous race melodramas on the screen but censored pictures of Johnson.

It is more than coincidental that these texts glorifying white supremacy and the suppression of black resistance appeared during the time of Johnson's sporting dominance. Gerald Early begs the question: "Who did D. W. Griffith have in mind when his 1915 epic, *The Birth of a Nation* . . . depicted scenes of black men asking white women to marry them, a stark contrast to Dixon's novels, where rape is the thing that pricks the conscience of the white man? Johnson's mad gestures cried out for equally mad responses."[33] Griffith and his audiences would have linked Johnson's image to other representations of miscegenation.

The press connected the rise of Jack Johnson with the race melodramas of Dixon and Griffith. Following Johnson's title victory, the *Afro-American Ledger* published a satirical piece (reprinted from a white newspaper) by "Jim Nasium" that belittled race baiters. The color line "invented" by Sullivan was simply "subterfuge behind which a white man can hide to keep some husky colored gentleman from knocking his block off and wiping up the canvas with his remains," the columnist said. "Next to Mr. John L. Sullivan, probably the Rev. Thomas Dixon, Jr., author of The Clansman, is the greatest living exponent of the color line. Mr. Sullivan would never fight a Negro, and Rev. Dixon won't fight anyone else."[34] The pugilist and the playwright were cast as ideological spokesmen for principles of racial governance.

In this context, Jack Johnson films became, for many African Americans—even those excluded from seeing them—a counter to the new wave of vicious anti-Negro dramas. Condemnation of *The Clansman* predated Johnson's fame. This criticism was often low-key, as in the call by one black publication in 1907 for "colored people everywhere [to] cease giving plays like 'The Clansman' unmerited publicity" by generating "so much loud talk." With suppression of the *Johnson-Jeffries Fight* in 1910 came pleas for equitable policing of Dixon's work.[35]

Then came *The Nigger,* a story of the South's race problem as depicted by a white, Harvard-educated Chicago playwright. In Sheldon's melodrama, a Southern governor is a paragon of white virtue (though he fails to stop a lynching) until he discovers that he is a "quadroon." This trace of

Negro blood he deems sufficient to turn him into a lowly brute. Believing only pure-blooded whites are entitled to power and privilege, he resigns his office, gives up his plantation, and renounces his white fiancée. Repertory productions toured successfully throughout 1910, when America's interracial conflict was at a fever pitch. William Brady's production of the play led the *Defender* to complain that if *The Nigger*—calculated to incite race hatred—could go on, why not the Johnson-Jeffries pictures? When Fox Film Corp. produced a feature-length version of the play and released it concurrently with *The Birth of a Nation,* further ire was directed at the story. Protest diminished when Fox changed the release title, but the film was still the target of censorship.[36]

Far more attention, however, focused on Griffith's momentous photoplay. News of Johnson's defeat shared front pages with reports on the efforts of the NAACP and others to have *The Birth of a Nation* barred.[37] Black publications linked the two stories for months. The *Amsterdam News* inquired:

> Now that 'Jack' Johnson has been detached . . . what?
> Will [colored people's] influence be felt with that of those who demand a halt to the prejudice creating, history distorting lies of *Birth of a Nation?*
> Will the white race celebrate its "victory" with the birth of a new era of justice and freedom, or by the continued run of *Birth of a Nation* and the prejudice and wrongs which the picture so prominently represents?[38]

As the campaign to keep the film from playing in Chicago peaked in May and June, the *Defender* followed suit: "Why were they so anxious to keep the Jeffries-Johnson fight off the screens? We, then, demand The Dirt of a Nation canned." Black leaders in Baltimore reminded the police board it "had refused to allow the presentation of the Johnson-Jeffries fight pictures on the alleged ground that they arouse race antagonism," and therefore should ban *Birth of a Nation* for the same reason.[39]

The national effort of a biracial coalition to prevent exhibitions of Griffith's feature met with mixed results. Some areas kept the film out, but most allowed it, with various editorial changes. The notoriety of the pro-Klan spectacle grew.

Ironically, white officials' newfound tolerance for racially divisive films led to a local revival of screenings for the *Johnson-Jeffries Fight.* As a counter to the white supremacist fiction, Chicago's Black Belt neighborhood welcomed the factual recording of Johnson beating the white hope, a picture it had been denied in 1910. In September 1915, the *Defender* "unearthed a scheme whereby the pictures of the late Johnson-Jeffries fight will be

Figure 50.   Ad for revival of the *Johnson-Jeffries Fight* (1910), *Chicago Defender*, January 21, 1922.

shown" in a tent set up near the Stroll. For the *Defender*, screening the pictures was important as a rebuttal not to Willard's supporters but to Griffith's. "How great is the difference between this picture and The Birth of a Nation?" they asked censors. "In the former, we view the camp life of trained athletes, and subsequently their wonderful skill. In the latter, terrible pictures of white men raping colored girls and women and burning of colored men at the stake."

In 1921, when Chicago police permitted the Jack Dempsey–Georges Carpentier fight pictures to be screened, they were forced to grant a permit for the same theater to show the Johnson-Jeffries pictures. As Juli Jones Jr. noted, the latter had been "cut and doctored so much" they looked "ordinary" next to the new Dempsey film. The worn print also revealed that the *Johnson-Jeffries Fight* had been watched often during the years it was contraband. The *Tribune* movie columnist Mae Tinee also criticized the print quality but found the viewing "more exciting" than *Dempsey-Carpentier*. She did not describe the audience, except to quip that the air in the crowded Star theater was "democratic with odors." After playing the Loop, the pictures came to Black Belt theaters in January 1922. Ads in the *Defender* included a recent photo of Jack Johnson (figure 50). They also boasted "a new process of enlargement" that allowed viewers to see the action "far closer than ever before in any fight film."[40] Apparently, interest remained high enough for someone to invest in reprinting the entire film with tighter framing.

Judging which images and narratives were capable of engendering race hatred remained problematic, as was evident in disagreements within the black community. Following the suppression of *Johnson-Jeffries*, but not the Dixon and Sheldon dramas, the *Defender* pressed for equality in the censorship of racial representations. In 1914, with movie houses multiplying along the Stroll, the paper began a close monitoring of screen content. When a Stroll theater showed a comedy that depicted a game called "Hit the Nigger" (a common carnival attraction in which ticket buyers hurled baseballs at a black man's head), the press accused both the Chicago Board of Censors and the community for failing "to suppress moving pictures that breed race hatred."

The *Defender's* exposure of the fact that African Americans were excluded from the Chicago board led to the appointment of the Rev. A. J. Carey. As censor, Carey was praised for "revolutionizing pictures portraying his race" and for "cutting race pictures okayed by the National Board." Ironically, his first action was to censor *One Large Evening*, a comedy that ridiculed black clergy, even though its director, Hunter C. Haynes, was one of the first African American filmmakers. Carey's ban was praised because the film "represent[ed] the race at its worst." The *New York Age* argued: "The duty of the film manufacturer should be to emancipate the white American from his peculiar ideas and incorrect notions of the colored American, not enslave him in additional ignorance which is hurtful to both races."[41]

The collision between bans on fight pictures and *The Birth of a Nation* heightened awareness of black screen images. The confrontation also points to the existence of a substantial African American film culture that predated Griffith's far-reaching racist imagery. Films of Jack Johnson, especially when exhibited by the Pekin and other black theaters, constituted an early and powerful cinema for black audiences. These were followed by motion pictures made by, with, and for African Americans. In addition to Haynes and his Afro-American Film Company in New York, two Chicago producers, William Foster and Peter P. Jones, were active between 1913 and 1915. Each produced black-cast two-reel comedies that dealt in stock characters. Each also made nonfiction films (usually of black business, religious, and fraternal groups in parades), as Jones put it, to "awaken the conscience of men and women to do the right thing."[42] In September 1915, Jones offered his own response to *The Birth of a Nation*. He recorded five reels documenting events at the recent Illinois National Half Century Exposition and Lincoln Jubilee, a commemoration of Emancipation. It was sold nationally on a territorial-rights basis.[43]

These films are not known to have survived. Only sketchy details exist with which to surmise what they were like. Press accounts cannot give a complete accounting of the reception they received, especially the work of Foster, who was writing his own reviews as "Juli Jones Jr." Yet the mere existence of such productions—as with the establishment of black theaters, resistance to coercive seating policies, and the lifting of a voice in the politics of controlling film content—helped create a black film culture that offered its audiences more than "the dirt of a nation."

ENFORCING THE FEDERAL BAN ON
FIGHT-PICTURE TRANSPORT

Both the Willard-Johnson pictures and *The Birth of a Nation* were subject to government censorship. Only the Johnson films were confiscated and destroyed by federal authorities. However, even this measure was not totally successful.

Initially the federal statute looked as if it would be repealed. The motion-picture trade hoped for this, as did the many who wanted to view the ousting of the black champion. One Southern newspaper, according to the *Defender*, "suggested a special session of Congress to repeal the fight film law." Despite such desires, the Treasury Department decided not to allow the Havana films to be imported. The *New York Times* accepted the feds' action as "irritating" but "all right."[44]

Meanwhile, the owners of the Willard-Johnson pictures followed a three-pronged strategy for exploiting their hot property: overseas distribution, clandestine exhibition in the United States, and legal challenges to the statute. Johnson himself was largely responsible for taking the *Willard-Johnson Boxing Match* abroad. Unable to enter the United States, he told a skeptical press he "expected to ally himself with moving picture concerns in Europe, and that he probably would lecture before and during the exhibition of the pictures of the fight." In his autobiography, Johnson said he "was to take the films of the fight and exhibit them in South America and Europe." After some legal entanglements, and an attempt by Curley and Mace to keep the pictures out of Johnson's hands, the ex-champ claimed that he intercepted the film at the London office of American Express. He then had the Barker company make prints. He also sold the rights to a South American company and "the Australian right to the pictures to Rufe Nailor," an old-school sporting and theatrical impresario who controlled racetracks, legitimate theaters, and movie houses in Australia and South Africa. The Willard films also screened in Canada and other non-U.S. markets.[45]

The film's box-office potential in the United States was too great for promoters simply to surrender. They made persistent attempts to get the *Willard-Johnson Fight* shown in America. Only a couple of their successes are recorded. At least some prints crossed the border, however, and these no doubt had an extensive, undocumented life in backroom and after-hours screenings. The first documented American showing of the film occurred two weeks after the bout. On April 19, "hundreds stood in line" at the Monroe Theater in Detroit to see twelve rounds and preliminary scenes of the Havana event. Local police "let it go" for one performance.[46] The only other documented screening took place a year later in New York City. On April 11, 1916, at the offices of the Duplex Motion Picture Corp., members of the boxing establishment saw several rounds projected. However, authorities stopped a plan to exhibit this print in New York. No other public screenings of the *Willard-Johnson Boxing Match* were held in America for many years.[47]

During the year between these two exhibitions, L. Lawrence Weber and other interested parties made great efforts to get courts to allow their film into the country. No less than three federal cases resulted from the wily promoters' colorful attempts to circumvent the law.

Few violations of the anti-fight-picture statute were reported during its first three years. A minor incident involving the *Johnson-Flynn Fight* occurred in 1912, when a distributor was arrested and fined $100 for attempting to transport a print across state lines. The action discouraged the trade, however. "It will seldom be worth while to take pictures," *Motography* noted, "when their scope is limited to the state in which the bout occurs." The only other known attempt to import a prizefight film was an obscure case involving the *Ritchie-Welsh Fight* (1914). British distributors argued that their product should be permitted because it had been filmed under the "select auspices" of the National Sporting Club. Although this film preceded the Willard-Johnson pictures, authorities used the latter as a test case for the new law.[48]

Attempts to bring the footage of Willard's victory into the country resulted in three decisions upholding the Sims Act: *Weber v. Freed* (1915), *Kalisthenic Exhibition Co. v. Emmons* (1915), and *Pantomimic Corp. v. Malone* (1916). Unlike the Mutual Film Corporation, which appealed to the Supreme Court on grounds that motion pictures should have First Amendment protection, these complainants sought technical or disingenuous evasions of the law.

The first to reach adjudication involved the Kalisthenic Exhibition Company. In July 1915, Willis Emmons, the U.S. customs agent in Portland, Maine, confiscated negatives of the *Willard-Johnson Fight*. The carriers of the negatives, working for Harry Frazee, had taken them from Cuba to Montreal. Whether they were really trying to smuggle in the contraband or deliberately setting up a legal challenge is unclear. Kalisthenic argued that the law did not apply, first, because the company intended to use the film for "private exhibitions" in clubs, associations, and the like, and, second, because it was importing photographic negatives "which could not be used for purposes of exhibition." In August a court found the company in violation of the federal act, a decision upheld on appeal in January 1916.[49]

More attention came to Lawrence Weber's two challenges, the first because it was taken to the Supreme Court, and the second because of the publicity surrounding this last attempt to bring the movies into the United States. *Weber v. Freed* was initiated three weeks after the bout. Throughout April 1915, the film company received signals that its prints would not be allowed past port authorities. Customs officials, treasury agents, and the secretary of the National Board of Censorship affirmed that the Willard-Johnson films would be confiscated. Anticipating smugglers, federal authorities alerted inspectors.[50] At Newark, Deputy Collector Frederick S. Freed confiscated a set of the Havana films; Weber challenged the ban on constitutional grounds.

Weber prepared for a major confrontation, hiring former U.S. senator Charles Towne to argue the matter. The Justice Department, recognizing that the case could set a legal precedent, expedited the challenge and prepared a strong defense. By April 30 arguments were heard in New Jersey district court. *Moving Picture World* reported on courtroom events. "There is no doubt about the volume and the sincerity of the effort to get the Willard-Johnson fight films past the frowning watchfulness of Uncle Sam" without resorting to smuggling, they asserted. "Film men and sporting stars," including Curley and Mace, attended the New Jersey hearing.

Judge Thomas Haight found Weber's arguments unconvincing. Throughout the hearing he voiced doubts about the tenets of the challenge: that Congress had overstepped its power to regulate commerce; that films were not "articles" of commerce; that the exhibition of moving pictures did not constitute "traffic, sale, or commerce"; that, as Weber was both owner and distributor, his exhibition of the film was not commerce, because "no man can trade with himself." Haight even cited punishment for Jack Johnson's violation of the Mann Act as an example of how Congress had constitutionally regulated "interstate traffic."[51]

Weber appealed to the high court. In arguments heard on December 1, 1915, Weber's bill of complaint expanded. But the new brief sounded like press-agent hype. Towne lauded Weber's credentials as a long-time expert in "furnishing amusement and entertainment to the public." He emphasized the great cost and effort expended in making these "perfect, exact and clear reproductions" that "represent[ed] the highest type of the moving picture art." He even asked the court to consider the commercial demand that existed "due to the great enthusiasm of people in the United Sates caused by the said Jess Willard having wrested the titled of Champion heavyweight of the world from the said Jack Johnson." Up to $2,000,000 in net profits stood to be made. Needless to say, this argument contradicted the contention that prizefight films were not "commerce."[52]

This legal strategy repeated the missteps Mutual Film Corp. had made in trying to persuade the court to declare state censorship boards unconstitutional. Earlier in the year, the justices had considered Mutual's appeal to free speech and press but determined that its true motive was commercial. That "the exhibition of moving pictures is a business, pure and simple, originated and conducted for profit" was a point made more clear by *Weber v. Freed* than by *Mutual v. Ohio*. With that precedent, the court declined to hear the state's rebuttal to Weber. Chief Justice Edward Douglas White issued a unanimous opinion, rejecting Weber's "fictitious assumption."[53]

A RUSE AT ROUSES POINT?

The mainstream movie industry did not react with alarm to *Weber v. Freed*. Its feature film factories in California and international distributorships were expanding rapidly. The censorship practices upheld by *Mutual v. Ohio* did not slow takings at the box office. But as an independent showman, Lawrence Weber continued to push for a way to exploit his prints of the *Willard-Johnson Fight*.

On the first anniversary of the Havana fight, Weber's colleagues staged a publicity stunt on the U.S.-Canada border, leading to a third court case, *Pantomimic Corp. v. Malone*. Pantomimic was another misleading company name created when Weber copyrighted his prizefight film on May 4, 1915. How he was able to obtain official imprimatur on a motion picture that it was illegal to bring into the United States is another question. Presumably two frame excerpts from each of the twenty-six rounds were deposited, as the copyright catalog lists "52 prints."

With an invited customs official and reporters in attendance, a half dozen Pantomimic representatives pitched a tent at Rouses Point, New York, on the Canadian border. They carried with them reels of 35 mm celluloid: a print of the footage Fred Mace had shot in Havana (which had been stored at the Toronto offices of Universal) and an equal amount of raw stock. Newspapers reported that a projection of the *Willard-Johnson Boxing Match* was set up on the Canadian side, while inches away on the American side a specially built camera and printer captured a "secondary negative" of the motion pictures. According to the reports, R. W. Ulmer made the tedious but ingenious reproduction in public from Sunday, April 4, 1916, through

Thursday. After Ulmer had duplicated all seven reels, Duplex labs made a positive print, which was screened at the Duplex office on April 11. The promoters hoped this creative evasion of the law would allow them to show the fight pictures all over New York state. However, customs officials again seized the film, forcing Pantomimic to argue its case in court.[54]

The company contended that it had not violated the law because only rays of light had crossed the border. The new film negative thus produced in New York was literally made in America. But the district and appeals courts found the clever attempt "within the mischief of the act." Seizure of Pantomimic's negatives and prints was upheld. Commercial exhibitions of the *Willard-Johnson Boxing Match* had to take place outside the United States.[55]

The film's promoters derived the desired publicity from this episode even if they were not allowed to capitalize on it. However, there is some question as to whether their public show at Rouses Point was genuine. Richard Koszarski has speculated that perhaps the "entire media event, with reporters and lawmen in tow, was a fraud." He argues that, given "the chemical and mechanical properties of film equipment and film stock" in 1916, synchronization, duplication, and print quality would have been at best problematic. The project may have been "an elaborate ruse" to garner publicity. Had the court judged the importation legal, Pantomimic could then have smuggled its first-generation prints into New York and exhibited those.[56]

Yet reporters who witnessed the event accepted that Ulmer's "newly developed synchronizing device" had indeed duplicated the film by this "new and unusual method." The judges who heard the detailed evidence of the case from customs agents and U.S. attorneys never doubted the "two plants connected together" actually worked. The circuit judges' written opinion even offered a technical description of the camera, lens, film, synchronizing chain, and reels. But spurious renditions of the event have been written into legend. Terry Ramsaye's 1926 version of the incident admits that "the facts began to get hazy" immediately after the Rouses Point transfer. His account of "Jack Johnson's film knockout" further obscures the matter by claiming that anonymous "master manipulators" from Washington power circles offered to facilitate the Pantomimic scheme, for a fee. "A plan was evolved by which the picture was to be very freely handled in the normal and usual manner with the projection-importation method used as a mere publicity blind, an alibi to be used in explaining things to the Department of Justice."[57]

In the end, it does not matter whether the *Johnson-Willard Boxing Match* was actually duplicated in this peculiar manner. The Rouses Point anecdotes encapsulate the role, reputation, and uses of prizefight films during this period. From 1908 to 1915, motion pictures of Jack Johnson provoked extraordinary social reaction and drew moviegoers. The escapades of Weber, Curley, Mace, Frazee, and the rest in Cuba and Canada illustrate how well policed Johnson's image had become and the lengths to which exploiters of fight pictures would go to cash in on it.

The case of the Jack Johnson fight films demonstrates the dynamic social history of black film culture that predated *The Birth of a Nation*. The pictures constituted an early black cinema and arguably made Johnson not only the first African American screen star but one of the earliest moviemade celebrities.

It would be a fallacy to read the Jack Johnson films purely as signifiers of black empowerment, although they have been put to that use. Johnson became a symbol of the Black Power era: his autobiography was reprinted in 1969 and his life story turned into a Broadway play (1967) and a movie, *The Great White Hope* (1970). Jim Jacobs's Academy Award–nominated documentary *Jack Johnson* (1970) reanimated period photographs and footage with an edgy, angry score by Miles Davis. Muhammad Ali had 16 mm film prints of the Johnson-Burns and Johnson-Ketchel fights projected on the walls of his dressing room before taking on a latter-day white hope in 1970. In the 1980s, the next-generation champion Mike Tyson spent hours watching videotapes of Johnson and other early boxers, courtesy of his manager Jim Jacobs, owner of the world's most comprehensive fight film collection.[58] In 1993, footage of Johnson was also a key part of NBC television's adaptation of Arthur Ashe's *Hard Road to Glory*. The program cast Johnson as part of the American civil rights struggle, as did HBO's documentary *The Journey of the African American Athlete* (1996). Finally, Ken Burns used the images in his PBS production *Unforgivable Blackness* (2005, with a less angry score by Wynton Marsalis), retelling John Arthur Johnson's narrative in respectful, centenary tones. When the Librarian of Congress named *Jeffries-Johnson World's Championship Boxing Contest* to the 2005 National Film Registry of historically and culturally significant works, the film became canonical.

As their initial reception showed, however, there was no single interpretation, black or white, of the Jack Johnson fight pictures. In the end, Johnson's opponents succeeded in reframing his image. When he reappeared on the screen in 1919, it was on their terms. Motion pictures were made of the "white slaver" giving boxing exhibitions in Leavenworth prison, where he served a year after surrendering to federal authorities for his Mann Act conviction. He later appeared in some black-cast feature films in the 1920s, but there he was relegated to the nonthreatening role of a clown. When Fox Movietone newsreels recorded him in 1929, he did not speak but simply mugged and mimed while conducting a jazz orchestra.[59] Audiences no doubt remembered the power of his fight-picture exhibitions, but the retribution against those pictures was such that no black fighters would repeat his success until Joe Louis won the heavyweight title in 1937.

8 Bootlegging

The Clandestine Traffic in Fight Pictures,
1916–1940

> Fight film suppression keeps a person dizzy.
> The pictures can't be seen for love or money.
> One judges Mr. Dempsey's friends are busy—
> Or can it be the friends of Mr. Tunney?
> L.H.R., "These Days," *New York Times,*
> October 16, 1927

Following the legal suppression of prizefight films in 1915, ring promoters continued to record big matches, but fight pictures were never again integrated into the mainstream American film industry. Hollywood loved boxing and star boxers, but the major producer-distributors left the handling of bouts to others. The sport itself continued to grow, even with limited movie replays. The emergence of live radio broadcasts of bouts in the 1920s (and the televising of them in the 1940s and 50s) significantly displaced the fight film. However, theatrical screenings did not disappear. Instead the topical prints arrived in theaters without organized promotion or marketing and through clandestine distribution methods. Fight pictures also had significant nontheatrical exhibitions in clubs, casinos, rented halls, and private venues. Even amid the prohibition of interstate commerce in any film "of any prize fight or encounter of pugilists," Tex Rickard and Fred Quimby's film of the 1921 contest between Jack Dempsey and Georges Carpentier earned six-figure profits. By the end of the decade, film bootleggers had overwhelmed attempts to suppress prizefight films. Hundreds of people were involved in the making, copying, pirating, selling, distributing, and exhibiting of dozens of films, short and long. After movies of the 1927 rematch between the champion, Gene Tunney, and the ex-champ Dempsey flooded the market, the American press and public deemed the prohibition of fight-picture transport a failure on par with the contemporary federal prohibition of the "transportation of intoxicating liquors." Yet it took another full decade to legalize what became, throughout the 1930s, a routine form of film production. When Congress decriminalized prizefight recordings in 1940, independent producer-distributors, itinerant exhibitors, and some Hollywood units revalued and "repurposed" old fight pictures, both from early cinema and from this later bootleg era.

Certainly American movie culture of the 1920s was dominated by Hollywood. Fight films returned from their banished state, however, surfacing in surprising places by colorful means. With its own stars and fans, the sport found ways to distribute its movies independently. Using creative, often illicit tactics, a cohort of high-rolling promoters successfully conspired to distribute its popular merchandise worldwide. Bootleggers—which is to say transporters of contraband films and dupers of pirated prints—eventually forced the repeal of fight-picture prohibition.

THE RISE OF JACK DEMPSEY AS SCREEN CELEBRITY

With Jack Johnson dispatched and exiled, a white majority returned support to boxing as a spectator sport. Movie lights and cameras continued to be standard paraphernalia at nearly every publicized title bout and at many lesser fights, even though it was a crime to carry prints or negatives across a state line. Distribution overseas and within state borders remained an option. More to the point, the organizers of professional boxing, a group with considerable behind-the-scenes influence, constantly challenged the 1912 statute. New York promoters were still attempting to circumvent the law when Jess Willard made his only successful title defense. The Madison Square Garden bout of March 25, 1916, marked the return of professional boxing to New York, which had again legalized the sport.

Motion pictures of Willard's sluggish, no-decision bout with Frank Moran failed to generate much response. With Tex Rickard's promotion, the contest earned a record $152,000 in attendance receipts and attracted nearly fourteen thousand spectators. But Willard was already known as a performer without charisma. When his bout with Moran proved uneventful, there was little call for an encore. Film reviewers who saw the *Willard-Moran Fight* within New York's borders spoke approvingly of its documentary qualities. Training scenes and footage of a preliminary bout (Levinsky-Savage) preceded the main event, as did close-ups of celebrities at ringside. A telephoto lens also permitted closer framing of the ring action, with medium shots cut into the standard extreme long shots. Green-tinted Cooper-Hewitt lights, although disconcerting to spectators in the Garden, provided clear images for movie viewers. However, the hype of the Champion Sports Exhibition Company's only trade advertisement for the film was a laughable misrepresentation: "The Motion Picture Sensation of All

Time! . . . The Greatest Display of Physical and Mental Development . . .
The Most Talked About, Successful and Fascinating Encounter in the History of the World's Sports." In 1916, when legal challenges to the fight picture ban failed for promoters of the Willard-Johnson pictures, exhibition of
the Willard-Moran film died as well.[1]

The Willard-Moran contest was deemed such a fiasco that the New York
legislature again changed state laws on boxing. Prizefighting was returned
to criminal status in 1917. Only a 1920 bill sponsored by state senator
Jimmy Walker (later mayor of New York City) gave the sport permanent
protection.[2]

The boxing world remained subdued commercially until Rickard
mounted a Fourth of July spectacle between Willard and Jack Dempsey in
1919. Willard stayed out of the ring for more than three years, attracting
only a freak-show following when he joined a traveling circus. His appearance in an obscure movie melodrama, *The Challenge of Chance* (1919), did
not enhance his reputation; nor did his lack of participation in wartime
morale-boosting efforts.[3]

The lull in boxing hype resulted from the national focus on the war in
Europe, particularly after U.S. forces joined the combat in 1917. However,
while the war effort distracted from the business of prizefighting, it did
more to legitimize and institutionalize boxing than any efforts by partisans
of the professional sport. Boxing was chosen as the means for "changing the
ordinary lay minded individual into a fighting machine" during the First
World War. In October 1917, the war department's Commission on Training Camp Activities announced that motion pictures would be the key to
teaching "confidence, aggressiveness," and the athletic skills to make men
"better bayonet fighters." It had already completed one training film showing Kid McCoy, Jim Corbett, and other ring stars. The army even made its
own recordings of some routine civilian prizefights for recreational camp
screenings. Some commercial opportunists exploited the moment. Sports
promoters, for example, put together *Champions of the Athletic World*
(1917), a two-reel compilation film that began with clips from the *Johnson-
Jeffries Fight* and climaxed with a "patriotic thriller"—footage of six thousand military officers in pugilistic training.[4]

Eventually, millions of servicemen trained in boxing. Military tourna-
ments produced champions, including Gene Tunney (the "Fighting Marine"), who won the heavyweight title from Jack Dempsey in 1926. After
World War I, veterans brought a recreational version of the sport into more
schools, gyms, and other institutions. Collegiate boxing became sanctioned.
Moralist attacks abated.

Although fight-picture distribution remained illegal, the U.S. government itself, along with commercial newsreel services, produced dozens of nonfiction films showing American troops being made "fit to fight" via boxing. The awkward champ Willard stayed out of the limelight, but the popular middleweight champion Mike Gibbons became, as Jeffrey T. Sammons recounts, "the premier physical fitness specialist of World War I." Gibbons appeared in training and recruiting films. Other military productions showed boxing as a regular part of soldier and sailor life.[5] After Dempsey won the heavyweight title from Willard in 1919, twenty-five thousand members of the American Expeditionary Force in Europe petitioned to see the film. But even this one-reeler bound for nontheatrical screenings was quashed.[6]

Even though fight pictures could not be transported, they continued to be produced as the sport grew to unprecedented levels of profitability and popularity. Several companies bid for the rights to the Dempsey-Willard contest, including Pathé's international newsreel service. Tex Rickard awarded the contract to a freelance operator, Frank G. Hall's Independent Sales Corporation.[7] The film showed a brutal and bizarre spectacle. Dempsey earned his "mauler" reputation, sending his giant opponent to the mat seven times in the opening round and breaking Willard's jaw and ribs. The bout ended after three merciless rounds. Rickard attracted twenty thousand ticket buyers to Toledo, Ohio, including a growing number of the rich and famous, but motion pictures of the event had to be screened in private or abroad. The Ohio board of censors prevented exhibition of the *Dempsey-Willard Fight* in the only state where federal law would have permitted it.[8]

Nevertheless, boxing boomed in the 1920s, a period characterized as a golden age for American sports. Jack Dempsey rose to a level of fame comparable to that of baseball's Babe Ruth. Movies could not easily exploit his prizefights, but they capitalized on his celebrity. Dempsey appeared in serials, shorts, and feature films, married Hollywood actress Estelle Taylor in 1925, and socialized with Hollywood's biggest stars, including boxing fans Charlie Chaplin and Douglas Fairbanks.

Master promoter Rickard continued to bolster pro boxing. After every big contest, he challenged the fight-film statute. Liberated by the Walker law of 1920, Rickard made Madison Square Garden the center of professional boxing, leasing the facility for ten years with the circus magnate John Ringling.[9] After cameras recorded Dempsey's knockout of Bill Brennan there on December 14, 1920, Rickard and the champion's handlers announced a plan "to test [the] law prohibiting the transporting of fight films." The *Dempsey-Brennan* pictures would be exhibited in Milwaukee at a nonprofit show and federal authorities "invited" to arrest the cooperative exhibitors.

When the scheme was traced to Rickard, he denied it, saying that all of the motion-picture negatives would remain in his possession.[10]

However, Rickard and his associates instigated a calculated challenge to the law, leading to a series of fines and ultimately their conviction on conspiracy charges in 1925. Neither the fines nor the conviction, however, much diminished the exploitation of fight pictures.

THE WORLD'S HEAVYWEIGHT CHAMPIONSHIP CONTEST BETWEEN JACK DEMPSEY AND GEORGES CARPENTIER

The signal event in boxing's new era of million-dollar gates was the Jack Dempsey–Georges Carpentier title bout of July 2, 1921. The Rickard publicity machine hyped it for months, pitting the plebeian American champion (and reputed draft dodger) against the socialite French challenger (and war hero). A stadium was built outside Jersey City, where seventy-seven thousand patrons paid more than a million and a half dollars at the gate, easily making up for the unprecedented fees promised to Dempsey and Carpentier: $300,000 and $200,000 respectively, plus movie profits to both.[11] A battery of cameras, including one for slow-motion coverage, were on hand. The film producer Fred Quimby hired the newsreel pioneer George McLeod Baynes of Canada's Associated Screen News for the camerawork. The final edit presented the fifteen-minute bout in an hour-long process documentary, with extensive intertitles, training scenes, aerial shots, and footage of the stadium and crowds. The film also deliberately framed the event as a legitimate undertaking. It opens with a close-up of Tex Rickard and shots of him inspecting his arena with the governor of New Jersey. It ends, curiously, with statistics on how much money was paid at the gate, how much each boxer was paid, and "how much the government received"—reminding audiences that the Uncle Sam who made fight pictures illegal was nonetheless taking a share of prizefight revenues.[12]

However, Dempsey's four-round victory was more notable for its historic coverage by radio. The live blow-by-blow broadcast description of the contest was one of the medium's first mass-audience productions. Radio promoter J. Andrew White coordinated the event for Rickard, Madison Square Garden Corporation, the Radio Corporation of America, and the National Amateur Wireless Association. RCA set up a five-hundred-watt transmitter in New Jersey for the broadcast. Using the call letters WJY, the signal reached an estimated two hundred thousand listeners, relayed by amateur operators and played through loudspeakers in theaters and halls.[13]

Figure 51. Tex Rickard (right) and Fred C. Quimby with newsreel cameras, promoting the Dempsey-Carpentier fight (1921). The photo op was a brazen reminder that they would be recording the fight knowing that the film's distribution would be illegal. (Library of Congress Prints and Photographs Division.)

Boxing became an important part of radio programming. The National Broadcasting Company's radio networks, and many stations, carried increasing numbers of live fights, pro and amateur, throughout the twenties. Although promoters were cautious at first, fearing that free, live broadcasts would hurt paid attendance, both radio and live audiences increased. When Tunney twice beat Dempsey in 1926 and 1927, hundreds of thousands of fans saw the bouts in person, while tens of millions listened on network radio. As the pioneer ring broadcaster Sam Taub wrote in 1929, "The radio makes fans."[14]

Broadcast descriptions did not replace films. Fans still wanted to see replays, especially when controversies (such as the famous "long count" in the second Tunney-Dempsey bout) could be reviewed and analyzed in slow motion. Fred C. Quimby, Inc.'s *The World's Heavyweight Championship Contest between Jack Dempsey and Georges Carpentier* played in New Jersey theaters two days after the fight. (A second, unauthorized recording of the fight also circulated before police intervened. Pathé News cameramen with telephoto lenses poached footage from atop a building overlooking the stadium.)[15]

Before the bout, Rickard's partners had laid plans to challenge the law again, or at least to circumvent it, by transporting prints of the *Dempsey-Carpentier Fight* out of New Jersey. They engaged in a broad and complex conspiracy abetted by political operatives. The first screening of Dempsey's victory was at a private party on July 4, 1921, at the palatial home of the *Washington Post* publisher, Edward B. McLean. Among the many attending were President Warren Harding, Vice President Calvin Coolidge, and Secretary of State Charles Evans Hughes (who had been a Supreme Court justice when *Weber v. Freed* upheld the statute banning fight-picture distribution). Also in attendance was the attorney general, Harry M. Daugherty, who had been at the New Jersey bout and had posed for photos with Dempsey when visiting his training camp.[16] Later, during the 1924 Senate investigation of Daugherty's many alleged misdeeds (which forced his resignation), witnesses testified about the workings of the conspiracy, part of what the press called an "amazing story of 'deals' in whisky, prize-fight films, drugs and big politics."[17]

Rickard, Quimby, and Dempsey's manager Jack Kearns hired a political fixer, memorably named Jap Muma. They mistakenly believed he could get the Justice Department to ignore their venture. Muma was part of the "Ohio Gang" that came to Washington in 1921 with Daugherty and the Harding administration. Employed by a McLean newspaper, he delivered a *Dempsey-Carpentier* print to his boss's Fourth of July party. Quimby, Inc., had prints taken to more than twenty states, each carried by a different person. These anonymous couriers delivered unidentified packages to hired attorneys, who knowingly received the contraband, then either sold prints with state distribution and exhibition rights or left reels for theater managers to screen. If arrested, each distributor pleaded guilty and simply paid a fine. The $1,000 maximum penalty became "tantamount to a license," a mere operating expense for fight-film distributors.[18]

Exhibition of the *Dempsey-Carpentier Fight* thus continued legally. Often a free screening at a veterans' hospital was held first to garner sympathy. Movie theaters then conducted commercial screenings, advertised with large posters and newspapers. In New York, Rickard and Quimby even had their film approved by the Motion Picture Commission, the state's new censorship board. The Dempsey-Carpentier picture was on the Commission's first review docket when it began operation on August 1, 1921. Rickard hired the attorney William Orr, a former secretary to the governor, to lobby the contested film through the censorship and licensing process.[19] Orr also handled publicity and tracked receipts. (He remained in the picture business, in 1925 arranging a White House screening of *The Big Parade* for the newborn company MGM.)[20]

Dempsey's assistant Teddy Hayes trucked the first seven prints of the movie into Manhattan from West Orange, New Jersey, in July. Quimby meanwhile suggested that the films might have been brought into New York by the military, as he had donated a copy to an army welfare group in New Jersey. In September, Madison Square Garden's matchmaker, Frank Flournoy, took films to Connecticut and later to Ohio. He alerted the U.S. attorney that he intended to transport the reels, plead guilty, and pay the fine. In Los Angeles, Denver S. Dickerson did the same, delivering a print from Nevada, where he had been governor during Tex Rickard's Johnson-Jeffries event in 1910.

Chicago politics proved the toughest obstacle. For three months, city officials battled over whether the *Dempsey-Carpentier Fight* would be permitted. Rickard took a rare public stance, telling reporters, "We are going right ahead with our plans to exhibit the pictures." He continued, disingenuously, "They can hardly be called fight pictures. They are views of training quarters, trainers, crowds, the big arena and a boxing match." And he concluded with a class-based argument about picture prohibition: "It is the poor man who is hit by the ban on these pictures just the same as he is hit by the high price of whisky. A rich man can pay $50 for a ringside seat, but the poor man cannot even see the pictures." Chicago's police chief unexpectedly granted a permit to Rickard's film, triggering a city council investigation. Having approved *Dempsey-Carpentier,* he was forced to allow showings of the contraband *Johnson-Jeffries Fight* of 1910, as well as Battling Nelson pictures already in the city.[21]

The Dempsey film was popular overseas as well, but not without its troubles. One of Pathé's cinematographers smuggled the incomplete, pirated footage out of the United States and sold it cheaply to a British distributor. The authorized dealer arrived in London to find the footage already "showing in every theater."[22]

This Rickard-Quimby distribution scheme generated big profits but led to years of scrutiny and, in 1925, a federal trial and conviction. In 1921, Quimby netted over $125,000 (half of which was paid to a "dummy," who passed cash installments to Muma and Orr).[23] He dropped out of the dealings, however, when informed that U.S. attorneys were building a felony conspiracy case and seeking prison sentences. In 1922, the Justice Department's Bureau of Investigation compiled a report on fight-picture trafficking. It documented an active ad hoc network of dealers, especially for films of Dempsey. Eighteen violators had already been fined, with seven more indicted in Los Angeles. Bootleggers of pirated prints included repeat offenders, such as William H. Rudolph, who was arrested seven times in seven cities in the South. By 1924, twenty-five federal cases were pending in as many cities. Rickard, Quimby, and others were charged with 148 violations.

The 1924 Senate investigation of Attorney General Daugherty exposed, among other things, the Dempsey-era fight-film trade. A parade of witnesses, including Rickard, Muma, Orr, and Quimby, described their activities, most alleging that Daugherty had facilitated the 1921 *Dempsey-Carpentier Fight* scheme. The special agent in charge told senators that Muma brought Quimby to meet the Bureau of Investigation's chief, and that the attorney general referred them to his Washington crony Alfred Urion, who lined up sympathetic lawyers to receive the films in various states.[24]

Such fight-picture exploitation remained a feasible, semiclandestine activity, but Hollywood distributors and mainstream exhibitors stayed out of it. Fred Quimby was an exceptional figure in this regard, going on to become a major Hollywood executive. He went from Montana exhibitor to independent producer in 1920 by signing Jack Dempsey to star in the serial *Daredevil Jack*. Quimby also released the one-reel *A Day with Jack Dempsey* (1921), showing the champ's dawn-to-dusk training. He joined Universal (which made the 1924 Dempsey serial *Fight and Win*) and then Pathé as a producer of short subjects. From 1926 to 1956, he held the same position at MGM, where he produced many sports films, with pugilism a favorite topic. Quimby's name, however, eventually became synonymous with the MGM animation unit that brought him eight Academy Awards. His federal conviction was forgotten.[25]

THE TUNNEY-DEMPSEY FIGHTS

Scuffles between fight-picture interests and federal authorities continued throughout the 1920s. Dozens of independent producers and distributors— and hundreds of exhibitors—peddled boxing documentaries despite the threat of fines and jail terms. So many agents, brokers, contractors, and subcontractors were involved in the gray market for fight pictures that prosecutors could not keep pace. Much of the genre's popularity remained linked to the celebrity of Jack Dempsey during his 1919 to 1926 reign and beyond. His 1926 and 1927 title bouts against Gene Tunney were among the greatest media events of the era, leading to a surge in fight-picture exhibition.

Motion pictures of Dempsey's 1923 defenses against Tommy Gibbons and Luis Firpo were shot and exhibited, but not boldly marketed. Aggressive law enforcement initially stemmed their distribution. Federal agents in Los Angeles impounded the Dempsey-Gibbons pictures just as they were being developed at the lab of Horsley Studios. Harry Grossman, who filmed the Fourth of July fight in Shelby, Montana, was found nearby at Dempsey's Hollywood home, but no one was arrested for transporting the goods. In any case, other copies of the film had already been flown to Chicago on July 5.[26]

Just two months later, with the Dempsey-Firpo pictures, authorities again energetically sought to cut off interstate traffic. The ring moguls ensured the profitability of the picture by holding the contest in New York, premiering the film on Broadway forty-eight hours later. Dempsey's manager, however, slowed the film's circulation. Although Dempsey knocked out Firpo in less than four minutes, Jack Kearns insisted that part of the footage be excised from release prints. He did not want the public to see the remarkable moment (now legendary) when the champion was awkwardly bulled from the ring and pushed back into it by men in press row. Eventually the uncut version made its way to screens.

Novel attempts were made to get around the law. One had Dempsey-Firpo films sent to Canada and Mexico, in hopes that prints could be transported into each border state. Another invited a Justice Department agent to a screening in New Jersey, so that the exhibitor could be arrested and then argue in court that "the films were developed and assembled in New Jersey," so they did "not come within the meaning of the inter-State ordinance." Neither prevailed. Some exhibitions were permitted in cities outside New York; elsewhere, films were seized.[27]

The international market for fight pictures remained strong, too. In South America films of the Argentinian Firpo were in high demand. His wealthy patron installed a projection system in his Buenos Aires home, so that Firpo could study films of Dempsey's technique. One American sports writer scoffed "when a prize-fighter can call on the camera to help him win the title, there will be nothing left for Will Hays to do in the capacity as czar of the movies, for then the pictures will cure all human ills."[28]

Although Dempsey's two 1923 defenses garnered comparatively minor interest, when he took on Gene Tunney in September 1926, the boxing establishment heavily promoted his return to the ring. In Philadelphia, the largest sports crowd in history, some 125,000, saw Tunney's ten-round victory. Rickard sold the film contract to an obscure figure, Leon Britton, who paid $25,000 for the right to distribute the *Dempsey-Tunney Fight* in Pennsylvania and abroad. Curiously, only a few screenings occurred before Britton told a skeptical press that his films had been stolen. They might have been; prints could be copiously duped without penalty, as such works were not copyrighted. But given the revelations at Rickard's recent conspiracy trial, Britton's claim sounded like a ruse to distract from the illegal circulation of prints. Quietly, throughout 1926 and 1927, *Dempsey-Tunney* screenings cropped up nationwide.[29] Tunney himself attended a screening in Cleveland, made possible by a man who accepted the penalty (two days in jail) so that he could exploit the film in Ohio. Even with federal policing and confiscation, copies of Dempsey films remained plentiful. In July 1927, one entrepreneur drew audiences by editing together celluloid highlights of the ex-champ's fights against Carpentier, Firpo, and Tunney. Another compiled two reels showing knockout rounds of seven championship tilts, presented with live narration by ring announcer Joe Humphries. Another wildcat outfit copyrighted a compilation film, *The Rise and Fall of Jack Dempsey* (1928).[30]

Even after Dempsey lost the heavyweight crown, his stardom continued to drive investment in motion picture production. On July 21, he knocked out Jack Sharkey before eighty thousand fans at Yankee Stadium. Tex Rickard contracted a new production company, Goodart Pictures, to document the event with slow-motion cameras. The finished edition showed the seven rounds in both regular and slow motion, attracting enthusiastic audiences to theaters throughout New York. In a now-familiar scenario, the authorized dealers had to contend with both bootleg recordings and a federal investigation. International Newsreel shot parts of the bout, then rushed *Vivid Highlights of the Dempsey-Sharkey Million Dollar Battle* to theaters. United States attorneys were more concerned with Goodart's role in an alleged "scheme to send a single film into a State, where local laboratories would produce hundreds of duplicates."[31]

The copies and editions circulating in so many venues overwhelmed the Justice Department. Its agents resorted to seizing film prints and even to arresting entire movie theater staffs in the middle of screenings. Courts often dismissed such charges, however. The final major confrontation between fight-picture interests and federal authorities followed the hyped rematch between Tunney and Dempsey. The spectacle of September 22, 1927, at Chicago's Soldier Field was another Rickard extravaganza, with more than one hundred thousand tickets sold for $2.5 million. Live radio coverage reached tens of millions of listeners.[32]

Goodart Pictures again handled the movie operations. Its president, Henry Sonenshine, subcontracted the filmmaker Joseph Seiden to shoot the main event. The completed movie bore a title card proclaiming: "Tex Rickard presents the Official Motion Pictures of the Heavyweight Boxing Contest between Gene Tunney, Heavyweight Champion of the World, and Jack Dempsey, Contender, for the Heavyweight Championship of the World." Twenty-four hours after Tunney's victory, however, U.S. marshals arrested Sonenshine in Illinois "as he was loading five sets of films and one set of negatives of the fight into an airplane."[33] Prosecutors struggled for two years trying to get an indictment, but within days after the fight, "Tunney-Dempsey II" movies were showing nationwide. In New York City alone, thirty-five theaters were running them. Large posters advertised the films on short notice. Even without an organized promotional strategy, the Goodart films attracted many moviegoers curious to see pictures of the fight about which they had heard and read so much. Complicating matters, Goodart was seeking to restrain rivals from showing bootleg copies—and neither Sonenshine nor U.S. attorneys knew whether those were copies of prints stolen from Goodart or different footage shot by unauthorized cameras.[34]

The machinery of media coverage and the ready availability of moving pictures could not be contained by the outmoded 1912 law. Interest in watching ring stars reached into sectors public and private, the spectacular and the everyday. The Paramount in Times Square ran the *Tunney-Dempsey Fight* as a daily special, as did first-run family theaters. The movie house aboard the SS *Leviathan* showed the film to 1,300 American Legionnaires returning from London. The Montmartre in Brooklyn even booked it with a revival of the 1920 art-house sensation *The Cabinet of Dr. Caligari* (!).

"I saw the fight pictures last night," Will Rogers began his popular column a week after Tunney won. A movie star writing from Hollywood about a first-run 35 mm screening enhanced the fight picture's status. But local laboratories across the nation were also making thousands of nontheatrical prints in film gauges that did not exist when Dempsey first became champion. Kodak's 16 mm and Pathé's 9.5 mm formats brought boxing films into homes, sometimes while they were still news. One Chicago camera store offered 16 mm copies of *Tunney-Dempsey Fight Films* for use in home movie projectors, boasting that prints were being made available less than eighteen hours after the bout.[35] No doubt such reels also wound up at screenings outside the home.

Countering authorities who had raided private showings were events such as one described in the *Washington Post*. In her "Moviegraphs" column, Felicia Pearson told of a show-at-home version of the hot topic of '27: "There was a party in New York the other night. After dinner the lights

Figure 52. The ubiquitous Tunney-Dempsey pictures appeared on a program with the famous German art film. *New York Times*, October 30, 1927.

went out and the Dempsey-Tunney fight pictures were projected by a baby Pathe onto a perpendicular white sheet. . . . and, really, it was great." She continued with giddy pleasure:

> The entire seventh round was shown in slow motion. . . . It was thrilling to see Tunney's jab, to see the birth of a sudden idea in Dempsey, which could be read so plainly that even his back muscles re-solved themselves into a "You're-gonna-get-it-now, Mr. Tunney." To see Tunney spar. To see Dempsey's sudden blow—then another—another. And then Tunney crumpled into a dazed, half-sitting, the pic-tures of which we've all seen. . . . And then the counting begins, and a tremor of excitement went through the party watching the picture projected by the baby Pathe.[36]

The horizons of film reception had been greatly altered since the Matinee Girl of 1897 encountered the Veriscope projections of the *Corbett-Fitzsimmons Fight*. By 1927, fans, families, and the smart set could all view fisticuffs as cinematic spectacle. Women, especially jazz babies like Felicia Pearson (a twenty-two-year-old countess and newspaper heiress), could freely comment on the pleasure of watching the Manassa Mauler's rippling muscles.

"A NEW CLASS OF BOOTLEGGERS" VERSUS THE LAW

With such promiscuous encounters between audiences and fight pictures, the law became a joke. Editorials complained of its "inanity" and the "futile attempt to attack prizefighting" by curbing films. In *Life* magazine, Robert Sherwood protested the "singularly outrageous" prohibition imposed by the government "in its infinite stupidity." The *New York Times* editorialized for a repeal, saying the law created "a new class of bootleggers." Even the circumspect Motion Picture Producers and Distributors Association in Hollywood signaled support for a repeal. "The law is silly in view of the fact that it does not prevent the making and showing of fight films," said the chief counsel to MPPDA head Will Hays. Charles Pettijohn personally found the statute "foolish," he told a reporter, although his office was officially agnostic because "the producers and distributors of the regular pictures have nothing to do with fight films." Still, it was possible, he offered, that if the law were revoked "the motion picture industry might become interested in making such films."[37]

Of course there was a picture industry, active but sub rosa, cranking out such films. It proved so difficult to regulate that traffickers made a mockery of some prosecutions. When questioned, distributors and theater owners caught with prizefight movies told investigators that they did not know where their prints had come from or that they got them from someone they just "bumped into." Preposterous as those stories were, the conspiracy of silence often held. In other cases, the state proved simply out of touch. One exhibitor on trial for showing the Tunney-Dempsey pictures in Texas embarrassed prosecutors by showing the film in court and challenging prosecution witnesses to identify the boxers on the screen. None could.[38]

The tide of opinion and policy against prizefight films soon shifted, however. In 1922, national crusades in favor of movie censorship peaked. At a hearing on a bill to create a federal board of censorship for motion pictures, critics had pointed to the ineffectiveness of the anti-prizefight law. The reformer Wilbur F. Crafts called the situation a scandal, charging that Attorney General Daugherty was complicit in ignoring it.[39] However, Will Hays, a Harding administration official, had become head of the new MPPDA that year and managed to stem calls for federal censorship. Ironically, he had

Figure 53. One of the fight pictures available for home movie projection was the Pathex 9.5 mm film *Boxing Form* (1925). Gene Tunney (left) spars with the old-timer Jim Corbett on a New York rooftop (see n. 36). (Charles Gilbert Collection, Northeast Historic Film.)

succeeded William A. Brady (fight-film promoter par excellence), who, as president of the National Association of the Motion Picture Industry from 1916 to 1921, had unsuccessfully campaigned against censorship. Hays was also linked to Terry Ramsaye's celebratory movie history, *A Million and One Nights* (1926), which made much of prizefighting. Just before its publication, Hays called for "motion-picture companies to search their vaults for ancient films" of "historical interest" and join with the federal government to preserve important footage. A 1926 *New York Times* Sunday magazine piece about the Hays proposal devoted much of its space to the thesis that prizefight films were of "genuine historical importance."[40]

As early as 1926, some members of Congress were trying to reverse the fight-picture prohibition.[41] With radio and newspapers supplying fight coverage to mass audiences and ring celebrities enjoying widespread adulation, the suppression of motion pictures was incongruous. Courts began loosening their interpretation of what constituted a violation of the law.

The turning point came in late 1927, when the Justice Department tried one last serious dragnet. Investigating the broad cinematic circulation of the second Tunney-Dempsey bout, U.S. attorneys in several states impaneled grand juries, which heard testimony from many distributors, bootleggers, and exhibitors of *Tunney-Dempsey II*. But the attempt to quash the popular films was undone by judgments against the prosecutors. One month after the big fight, a federal judge ruled that it was neither illegal to exhibit fight pictures nor to receive them from a person who was not a "common carrier," even if the parties involved intended to profit from what they knew to be contraband. Other judges made identical rulings in the days that followed, forcing U.S. attorneys to return confiscated prints to their owners—who put them back on exhibition.[42] Headlines reduced the news to "Fight films legalized." For several years prosecutions and press coverage were negligible.

FILMING FIGHTS IN THE 1930S

Fight pictures thus populated American movie screens into the sound era. The kingpin George Lewis "Tex" Rickard died in 1929, still under investigation for his latest film deals. Throughout the 1930s, dozens of prizefight films were produced, distributed, and even registered for copyright, most with the cooperation of Rickard's successor Mike Jacobs or the Madison Square Garden Corporation. The company even controlled big matches in other cities, employing a full staff of box-office managers, construction supervisors, security men, and publicists.

Copyrighting these motion pictures helped establish their standing, but it posed a legal paradox. To obtain copyright entailed depositing a print with the United States Copyright Office at the Library of Congress; transporting the said print to Washington was of course a criminal act. Only two of the many fight films shot during the 1920s were copyrighted. An impasse was broken when Gold-Hawk Pictures obtained copyright for *World Heavyweight Championship Boxing Contest between Gene Tunney and Tom Heeney* (1928), a record of the champ's last title defense. In a letter to the Register of Copyrights, the pioneering motion-picture copyright attorney Fulton Brylawski made a compelling argument for recognizing fight pictures. He pointed out that the Library granted his application to copyright the *Dempsey-Carpentier Fight* in 1921. When he received two prints from Fred Quimby for copyright deposit, federal agents had questioned him but taken no action when he explained his purpose. Creators of fight films, Brylawski said, needed to have their works copyrighted to protect them in international markets. Further, copyright would allow them to exploit their properties in the future—when the ban surely would be repealed. As evidence that Gold-Hawk Pictures was not seeking to evade the law, Brylawski's novel claim stated, only a photographic negative was being deposited. There were no projectable prints for sale. (In reality, *Tunney-Heeney* prints were already being screened commercially; officials reported "scores of copies of the negative had been made for local motion picture houses.") Whether or not this successful case directly influenced other producers, dozens of prizefight films were copyrighted throughout the 1930s.[43]

Still nominally illegitimate, fight pictures remained the purview of non-Hollywood companies. Most were subsidiaries of the now huge and incorporated apparatus of professional boxing, taking names such as Sporting Events, Inc., Madison Pictures, Inc., Garden Pictures, and Super-Sports Attractions. The journeymen who did the shooting and editing also worked in other fringe genres for which speed of release and economy of style were characteristic: industrials, newsreels, exploitation pictures, race movies, and Yiddish films. Joseph Seiden, for example, made features as diverse as *My Yiddishe Mama* (1930), *Sex Madness* (1938), and *Paradise in Harlem* (1940) after shooting the second *Tunney-Dempsey Fight*. Jack Rieger, who coproduced *The Yiddish King Lear* (1935) with Seiden, was the most active filmmaker for hire at heavyweight fights in the thirties. He also made Poverty Row features, compilation documentaries, and exploitive "ethnographic" films. Producer and editor Jack Dietz profited from several Joe Louis fight pictures (and bootlegs of a dozen more) between 1936 and 1939, while he also managed the Cotton Club in Harlem and produced B movies. The unrefined production values of the films did not prevent them from being lauded on occasion. Otis Ferguson, for example, wrote in *The New Republic* about the replay of Max Schmeling's upset of the undefeated Joe Louis in 1936. "There is nothing on the screen this week, there is nothing anywhere this week, that for implications and sheer electric excitement can come up to the pictures of the Joe Louis–Max Schmeling fight." Dietz sold the German rights to this $25,000 production for $400,000. So much of his income came from the U.S. gray market, however, that he was imprisoned for tax evasion.[44]

By 1930 some fight pictures were clearly linked to organized crime. Bill Duffy, who coproduced and copyrighted several heavyweight title films with Dietz in the midthirties, was a longtime underworld associate. He was with Al Capone at the Dempsey-Tunney fight in Chicago. In 1931, the *New York Times* noted "rumors that Al Capone's men brought" the film of the Schmeling-Stribling bout into the state. Theater owners complained of "the racket" that ran "an undercover distribution system."[45] Joe Louis wrote that before 1940 "the New York mob had a set-up where they would sell fight films for a flat price in other states." He even identified George Jean "Big Frenchy" De Mange, a rich racketeer who died in 1939, as the one who "bought the rights on all fight films." After 1940, Louis gained a legal interest in his own fight pictures, with RKO helping to produce and distribute. For his two victories over Jersey Joe Walcott in 1947 and 1948, he said, "I was named producer of my own fight pictures."[46]

For more than a decade, the fight-picture statute was seldom enforced. When authorities tried to discover who transported the 1931 *Schmeling-Stribling Fight* from Ohio to New York, they got nothing out of witnesses in court. The "consensus in movie circles," the *New York Times* said derisively, "was that the films" crossed the state lines "all by themselves."[47] Sometimes authorities worked at cross purposes. When the New York Department of Corrections invited a retired Gene Tunney to speak to prisoners in 1932, he brought with him "several reels of fight films, showing all the important moments of the last decade." In 1935, the *Washington Post* described the de facto traffic in fight films after the Yankee Stadium bout between Joe Louis and Max Baer: "Motion pictures, as everyone knows, were made of the four rounds," wrote the movie-industry reporter Nelson B. Bell. "These pictures, as a matter of cold fact that might as well be admitted, will be shown in all corners of the United States before the emulsion on the celluloid is fairly set!" The sports columnist Shirley Povich accurately summed up the situation at the end of the decade.

> State, county and city officials for several years have been winking at the Federal statute. . . . Prosecutors know they could not gain a conviction of an exhibitor for the mere showing of the films. He could always say "I found the films in the lobby and decided to run them."
> Forty-eight hours after big title fights of the past few years, the films have been shown in States from coast to coast.[48]

Povich was summarizing what had been made clear at congressional hearings of May and June 1939. The head of the Southeastern Theater Owners Association told the Senate Interstate Commerce Committee that "every prize-fight film that has been made has been shown" in numerous independent theaters. He described the anonymous trafficking in prints but also testified that the distribution of fight films had become so open that no concealment was necessary. Prints were now routinely "shipped out from central distribution points" alongside the legitimate ones.[49]

After more than a decade of deliberation, Congress unanimously repealed the prohibition on fight-picture commerce in 1940. The bill's author and perennial champion was the New Jersey senator W. Warren Barbour. As the U.S. amateur heavyweight titleholder in 1910–11, Barbour had been touted as a "white hope" of the Jack Johnson era. At the 1939 hearings, he presented Jack Dempsey, who testified that the "nuisance" law had cost him a "couple million dollars pin money" from motion-picture receipts. A state boxing commissioner told senators "the prize fight film in slow motion" had become "the mainstay of college boxing coaches." J. Reed Kilpatrick, president of the Madison Square Garden Corporation, even testified that "television broadcasts of fights" were "coming soon"—if the 1912 statute could be repealed. President Franklin D. Roosevelt signed the bill "divesting prize-fight films of their interstate character" into law on July 1, 1940.[50]

"REPURPOSING" EARLY CINEMA IN THE CLASSICAL ERA

After 1940, the mode of production for recording prizefights did not change significantly. The major studios did not start producing or distributing fight pictures. However, some Hollywood features did make use of the liberated "old" prizefight footage. Twentieth Century–Fox, for example, released *The Great American Broadcast* (1941), a musical and dramatic version of the first radio coverage of boxing. However, the studio reportedly found footage from the 1921 *Dempsey-Carpentier Fight* in "very bad shape" and chose not to use it. (It also happened to be under copyright to Fred Quimby at rival MGM.) Instead, Fox incorporated "sepia-colored" footage of the 1919 Willard-Dempsey contest. The mix of historical actuality and studio scenes brought praise. "Insertion of the clips is one of the best examples of expert production judgment and editing of the past year," said *Variety*. The *New York Times* called it "one of the film's most exciting moments." "By giving both the newsreels and the sequences leading up to the championship struggle a sepia bath, the studio alchemists have managed an exceptionally smooth transition from the photography of the present to that of 1919."[51]

However, *The Great American Broadcast* used not a print of the *Dempsey-Willard Fight* but shots from *The Birth of a Champion* (Fistic Film Co., 1940), a two-reeler that recycled the twenty-year-old footage. It was the work of Henry Sonenshine, whose Goodart outfit had twice filmed

Dempsey in 1927. The veteran actor Clarence Muse, writing from Holly-wood for the *Chicago Defender,* objected to Sonenshine's claim that the film showed "the rise of the most colorful champion of all times." With "Joe Louis and Jack Johnson still around," Muse suggested that *The Birth of a Champion* (not to say *of a Nation*) played to white audiences' nostalgia for a 1920s white hero during the 1940 reign of another black champion.[52]

Even Sonenshine's repurposed images of Dempsey's rise derived from an earlier version of the same footage. In late 1939, an unidentified promoter sold the American press on the idea that "recently unearthed pictures" of Willard fighting Dempsey in 1919 were akin to historical finds rather than exploitation material. Newspapers published frames from the recording said to have been " 'lost' for many years."[53] Clearly the promoter was providing cover for the deployment of fight pictures in advance of Congress's repeal. Treating them as ancient and buried treasures was an apt rhetorical strat-egy, given how obscure early silent cinema seemed to moviegoers.

With the release of *Kings of the Ring* (Stadium Films, 1944), a new au-dience reacted to pre-1912 cinema as primitive. Independent film dealer Martin J. Lewis rounded up prints dating from the Johnson era and ear-lier. "Where they dug up that 1907 film of Burns knocking out Bill Squires is a mystery," said the *Hartford Courant.* Shirley Povich went further, mistakenly saying it "was the first ever filmed in motion pictures," and adding, "Amazingly, the films were not half bad." For most reviewers, the "breath-taking" sight of Johnson kayoing Stanley Ketchel with a single punch in 1909 was the most memorable moment. Lewis's film included a voice-over narration by Nat Fleischer of *The Ring* magazine and Bill Stern of NBC radio, which Povich found "a refreshing contrast to the bootlegged movies of the big fights that barnstormed in Washington a few months ago."[54]

THE KEROSENE CIRCUIT: VESTIGIAL
FIGHT-PICTURE EXHIBITION

From 1940 until the establishment of broadcast television networks, prizefight films remained part of an alternative practice of exhibition and exploitation. Much as they had at the turn of the century, itinerant exhibitors bargained for the territorial rights to fight pictures—or they projected bootleg copies. They traveled town to town with 35 mm prints, booking venues on a freelance basis. As Eric Schaefer has described the practice, exploitation artists (Povich's barn-storming bootleggers) did their own advance work, drummed up audiences,

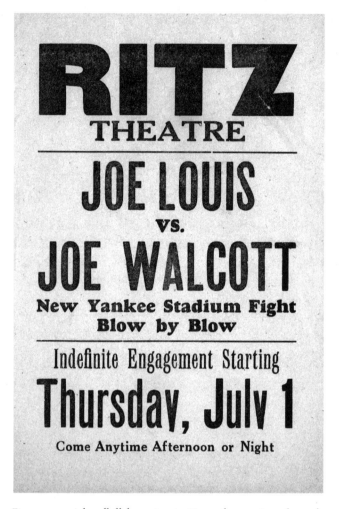

Figure 54.   A handbill from Austin, Texas, for movie replays of
Louis's second victory over Walcott and his last title defense.
The fight had been broadcast live to a small television audience
on June 25, 1948. (From the author's collection.)

and showed their wares until business ebbed. Even before the ban had been
lifted, for example, the promoter Leland Lewis assembled a highlight package
of twenty-one films showing twenty years of ring history. He traveled the
"kerosene circuit" of the Southwest, projecting films to rural and small-town
audiences who had no movie theaters and sometimes no electricity.[55] Others
worked urban venues outside first-run houses. The ring promoter Jack Laken,

for example, toured in 1942 and 1943 with "The Greatest Cavalcade of Fight Pictures Ever Assembled," a compilation showing highlights of bouts from the Dempsey and Louis eras.[56] A handbill promoting the 1948 *Joe Louis–Joe Walcott* pictures (figure 54) is an even later example. It invited spectators to the Ritz Theater, the only racially integrated theater in Austin, Texas. As with Jack Johnson films a generation earlier, Joe Louis pictures became causes for celebration in most African American communities. His films were in demand in all-black movie houses as well as in white-owned theaters. Louis's impact on American culture has been well chronicled, although the role that films played in his career merits further study.[57]

TELEVISION FIGHTS

"Just at a time when movie companies are envisioning profits from fight films, with the Federal law permitting their transportation nearing passage," Shirley Povich wrote in 1939, "television is coming along to knock the bottom out of fight pictures."[58] His obituary for fight films was premature. Theatrical, itinerant, and kerosene-circuit screenings continued well into the fifties. Fans and collectors also purchased 8 mm and 16 mm reduction prints into the 1970s.

As it had been for cinema and radio, boxing was a common subject for television. J. Andrew White, as president of CBS, could say in 1928, "The first and most logical application of television apparatus would be for events such as championship boxing matches."[59] As early as the 1920s and 30s, experimental telecasts showed boxing matches. Successful closed-circuit television displays of championship prizefights were shown in theaters in England in 1938 and became common in the Unites States in the 1940s. NBC telecast its first prizefight on June 1, 1939, and resumed regular boxing coverage as soon as World War II concluded. The network installed TV sets in veterans' hospitals, telecasting fights in order to polish their production skills. NBC's 1946 prime-time schedule contained only a few shows, but among them were the *Gillette Cavalcade of Sports* on Mondays and Fridays and a half hour of "fight film filler" on Thursdays. Its coverage of the Joe Louis–Billy Conn fight that year was the first heavyweight title contest on live television.[60] By 1948, two-hour telecasts of *Boxing from St. Nicholas Arena* (NBC), *Boxing from Westchester* (CBS), and *Boxing from Jamaica Arena* (Dumont) aired weekly. ABC added *Tomorrow's Boxing Champions* in 1949, and Dumont, *Boxing from Sunnyside Gardens, Boxing from Dexter Arena,* and *Madison Square Garden.* Tim Brooks and Earle Marsh recount:

There were periods in the late 1940s and early 1950s when it was common to have as many as five or six network boxing shows on during the same week, not to mention the local shows. . . . Boxing was an institution on early television for several reasons. It was easy to produce, the camera-coverage area was limited to the relatively small space occupied by the ring, and it had tremendous appeal to the first purchasers of television sets in the late 1940s—bars. Even a TV with a ten-inch screen could become a magnet to sports-minded drinkers.[61]

As television audiences grew in the late 1940s and 50s, films taken of boxing bouts were generally intended for later broadcast. Their theatrical life, however, could continue. A big bout like the 1948 Louis-Walcott rematch traveled to movie theaters on film long after its live broadcast. And at a weird, short-lived interface between the two media, there was also Paramount's theater-television system, which debuted with a boxing exhibition. In the absence of any means of projecting a video signal onto a twenty-four-foot movie screen, the process captured a live television signal by recording it on motion-picture film. The film was fed through a developer and then into a projector, allowing spectators to see a 35 mm kinescope some sixty-six seconds later. On June 25, 1948, viewers at the Paramount Theatre on Times Square watched the "instantaneous newsreel" of the television signal showing Louis and Walcott boxing at Yankee Stadium. As new forms of TV appeared throughout the late twentieth century—satellite distribution, subscription channels, pay per view—prizefight spectacles continued to play a prominent role.

Much has been written about the relationship between television and boxing. As Jeffrey Sammons documents, broadcast rights and profits became and remain an integral part of the corporate business of professional fights. Critics have offered a diversity of evaluations about television's effects on the sport, from Leslie Bell's 1952 estimation that "TV is the greatest thing that ever happened to boxing," to A. J. Liebling's judgment that saturation coverage ruined the "sweet science." However, television unquestionably expanded the audience and revenue for professional boxing.[62]

The meaning and significance of the sport, its celebrities, and boxing matches are ever changing, but the issues they raise persist: controversies over gender, race, class, and violence as public spectacle. Each mass medium has affected professional boxing, yet it would be a mistake to overgeneralize about diverse historical moments. The conditions of production and reception derive from the practices of distinct groups at particular times. To understand the significance of fight pictures, a social-history approach is the most revealing.

To dispel any doubt that one must go beyond the screen image to discern the ways in which meanings were created, consider three uses of prizefight films in Europe in the 1920s. In Paris, a year after his fight with Dempsey, Georges Carpentier lost to an obscure pugilist from Senegal, "Battling Siki" (this despite the typical rumor that the fight had been set up for Carpentier "to make a good newsreel film" by knocking out Siki). The 1922 movie played widely in France, but the conditions of its reception led to interpretations quite distinct from those that had greeted its predecessors. The surrealist poet Robert Desnos provocatively suggested that the movie illustrated cinema's powers of eroticism. "It's because, despite everything, it is protected by an objective representation of reality that the cinema escapes the control of its legal guardians," the twenty-two-year-old film critic wrote in *Paris-Journal*. Cinema "transforms external elements to the point of creating a new universe: this is how the slow-motion film of the Siki-Carpentier fight in fact simulates gestures of passion."[63]

A second intriguing episode occurred in Germany soon thereafter. A vogue for boxing among both leftist bohemians and nascent Nazis generated new horizons of reception for fight pictures. Artists and intellectuals followed the sport, including Bertolt Brecht, who wrote about it in the new sports journal *Die Arena*. Brecht found the rapt prizefight audience and the starkly lit boxing ring apt paradigms for the kind of theater he envisioned. His biographer also notes: "Paul Samson-Koerner, the German light-heavyweight champion, became his friend and constant companion. In July 1926 Brecht announced that he was writing Samson-Koerner's biography. And when the film of the Dempsey-Tunney fight of 1926 was shown at a Berlin cinema, the performance was preceded by a poem by Brecht, recited by the well-known actor, Fritz Kortner."[64] Another German film used Dempsey footage in a different context still. The 1925 documentary from the UFA studio, *Wege zu Kraft und Schönheit*, released in the United States two years later as *The Way to Strength and Beauty*, intercut scenes of nude models with shots of Jack Dempsey as well as of the swimmer Johnny Weissmuller and the dancer Leni Riefenstahl—both of whom also went on to movie stardom, propelled by their bodies beautiful and athletic.[65]

Explanations of these incidents need not be unraveled here. Suffice it to say they represent vastly different forms of the genre's exhibition and reception. Shifting the time, place, and audience for such films transformed their historical meaning and the role they played in the culture that engaged them.

If we were to take our cues primarily from the moving image on the screen, there would be little indication that the history of early fight pictures was as complex or important as it was. Most of these films are now lost or exist only as fragments, making traditional film interpretation impossible. Further, the imagery in surviving fight films carries no hint of the vast interest and controversy that surrounded them. The popularity of *A Trip to the Moon*, *The Great Train Robbery*, *The Lonely Villa*, or *Cabiria* can be attributed to aesthetic quality or cinematic novelty, but the static camerawork of the *Johnson-Jeffries Fight* piques little curiosity in itself. Only the extracinematic aspects of the movie's production and reception explain why so much commentary and frenzy surrounded it.

Cultural and social histories create a "usable past." They historicize motion pictures by placing them within their original contexts of reception. But this does not mean that only their original audiences could make sense of them. Latter-day producers and spectators have put those movies to different uses. Celluloid images of Jack Johnson victories, for example, were revived as protest against *The Birth of a Nation* in 1915; as a reminder, in 1922, that Jack Dempsey dodged black challengers; as part of the Black Power movement of the 1960s and 70s, along with the influence of Muhammad Ali; and as precursors of African American struggles for equality and civil rights in the Ken Burns documentary *Unforgivable Blackness: The Rise and Fall of Jack Johnson* (2004).

Even though many of these hundreds of early fight pictures may never be revived and reinterpreted, we can still make this cinematic sporting past usable. By reconstructing the historical conditions of the fight picture, we reveal the ways in which cultural artifacts were constructed, exhibited, interpreted, fought over, celebrated, condemned, suppressed, revived, and repurposed. In short, they offer us a model of how society, culture, media, and power worked at particular points in history. That history becomes usable as an alternative vision, instructive because it is so different from, at times even alien to, contemporary experience. By following the precepts of social history—recovering the lost and suppressed parts of the past, valuing the experiences of everyday life, and focusing on local practices—we can best understand the significance of fight pictures.

Filmography

Footage of actual prizefights is underscored.
Asterisks denote extant films.
AMB = American Mutoscope & Biograph

[*Men Boxing*],* May–June 1891, Edison

Boxing, ca., October 1892, Edison

[*Boxing Match*] *Newark Turnverein*, ca. March 1894, Edison

Boxing [Jack McAuliffe?], ca. May 1894, Edison

Leonard-Cushing Fight,* June 14, 1894, Edison/Kinetoscope Exhibiting Co.

Hornbacker-Murphy Fight,* August 1894, Edison/Raff & Gammon

Corbett and Courtney Before the Kinetograph,* September 7, 1894, Edison/Kinetoscope Exhibiting Co.

[*Moore-Lahey Fight*], November–December 1894, Chinnock

[*McDermott Fight*], January 1895, Chinnock

Billy Edwards Boxing, January–February 1895, Edison/Raff & Gammon; *Billy Edwards and The Unknown 5 Rounds; Billy Edwards and Warwick*

Boxing Match/Boxing Contest, March–June 1895, Birt Acres

Young Griffo–Battling Barnett, May 1895, Eidoloscope

[Unidentified, Atkinson No. 41], 189?–190?

[*Herman Casler and Harry Marvin sparring for the Biograph camera*], June 1895, American Mutoscope Co.

[*Prof. Al. Leonard–Bert Hosley sparring exhibition*], August 5, 1895, American Mutoscope Co.

*Boxeurs,** 1896, Lumière

*Pedlar Palmer v. Donovan, Boxing,** 1896, Lumière; filmed in England

A Prize Fight by Jem Mace and Burke, 1896, Birt Acres

A Boxing Match in Two Rounds by Sgt. Instructor F. Barrett and Sgt. Pope, January 1896, Birt Acres

[*Fitzsimmons-Maher Fight*], February 21, 1896, Kinetoscope Exhibiting Co.; Enoch Rector (failed cinematography)

Boxing Contest between Tommy White and Solly Smith, August 1896, Edison/Raff & Gammon

[*Boxing Match between a Man and a Woman*], 1896, Edison

*Boxing Match,** August 1896, Robert Paul–Birt Acres

Prize Fight by Skelly and Murphy, August 1896, New Orleans

Sparring Contest, Canastota, N.Y., copyright December 18, 1896, American Mutoscope Co.

Boxing Match between Toff Wall and Dido Plum, 1896–97, Robert Paul

Downey-Monaghan Round 1, 1897, American Mutoscope Co.

Downy vs. Monaghan [Prize Fight, Downey vs. Monahan], 1897, American Mutoscope Co.

Maher-Choynski Glove Contest, January 1897, Zinematographe/Harry Davis, Pittsburgh

*Corbett-Fitzsimmons Fight,** March 17, 1897, Veriscope

*Corbett and Fitzsimmons, Films in Counterpart of The Great Fight,** April 1897, Lubin

Prize Fight with "knock out," April 1897, Electroscope

The Great Hall and Mitchell Glove Contest, June–July 1897

*Boxing for Points** [Pvt. Darrin v. Cpl. Healy], September 9, 1897, Edison

Downey-Paterson Fight/The Downey and Patterson Fight, November 27, 1897, International Film Company

A Magnificent Glove Fight, December 1897, Interchangeable Automatic Machine Syndicate

Boxing Match, 1898, Eberhard Schneider

A Boxing Match, 1898, Warwick, U.K.

Corbett and Sharkey Fight, November 1898, Lubin

[*Living Pictures of a Boxing Contest*], 1898, Randall Williams and Chittock, U.K.

Train vs. Donovan, 1898, American Mutoscope Co.

Fight, November 1898, G. A. Smith, U.K.

Country Prize Fight, 1899, E. H. Amet/Magniscope

Re-enactment of Sharkey-McCoy Fight, January 1899, Lubin

[*Test Pictures for the Upcoming Jeffries-Fitzsimmons Fight*], May 1899, Vitagraph

Prize Fight, May 18, 1899/copyright October 14, 1902, AMB

[*Jeffries-Fitzsimmons Fight*], June 9, 1899, Vitagraph

Reproduction of the Jeffries-Fitzsimmons Fight, June–July 1899, Vitagraph

Jeffries-Fitzsimmons Fight, June 1899, Edison

Reproduction of the Fitzsimmons-Jeffries Fight in Eleven Rounds Showing the Knock Out, copyright June 12, 1899, Lubin

Chuck Connors and Chin Ong, August 1899, AMB

Chuck Connors vs. Chin Ong [*windup*], August 1899, AMB

Reproduction of the Pedlar Palmer and Terry McGovern Fight, copyright September 8, 1899, Lubin

Reproduction of the Terry McGovern and Pedlar Palmer Fight, copyright September 8, 1899, Lubin

Reproduction of the Jeffries and Sharkey Fight, copyright September 9, 1899, Lubin

Reproduction of the Sharkey and Jeffries Fight, copyright September 9, 1899, Lubin

Great International Battle Between Pedlar Palmer and Terry McGovern, September 12, 1899, American Sportagraph

[*George Dixon–"Sam" Bolan Fight*], September 1899, AMB

Test, Coney Island Athletic Club, November 1899, AMB

Mysterious Billy Smith–Jim Jeffords, October–November 1899, AMB

The Battle of Jeffries and Sharkey for Championship of the World,*
copyright November 4, 1899, James H. White /Edison; C, Albert E.
Smith, James B. French, Joe Howard

The Jeffries-Sharkey Contest,* copyright November 4, 1899, James H.
White

Jeffries-Sharkey Contest,* copyright November 10, 11, 13, 15, 1899,
AMB

Reproduction of the Corbett and Jeffries Fight, copyright November 17,
1899, Lubin

Reproduction of the Jeffries and Corbett Fight, copyright November 17,
1899 and April 21, 1900, Lubin

Reproduction of the Jeffries and Ruhlin Fight, copyright November
17, 1899, Lubin

Reproduction of the Ruhlin and Jeffries Fight, copyright November
17, 1899, Lubin

*Reproduction of the Peter Maher and Kid McCoy Fight (Maher-
McCoy, Rounds),* copyright November 21, 1899, Lubin

Reproduction of the [Kid] McCoy and [Peter] Maher Fight, copyright
November 21, 1899, Lubin

Great Glove Fight [Frank Lewis and Fred Gausden Gaydon?], ca. 1900,
James Williamson, U.K.

Great Glove Fight, Continuation, ca. 1900, Williamson

Reproduction of the McGovern and Dixon Fight, copyright January 8,
1900, Lubin

McGovern-Dixon Fight, January 9, 1900, Tom O'Rourke and Sam H.
Harris

Reproduction of the Sharkey and Fitzsimmons Fight, copyright March
7, 1900, Lubin

Reproduction of McGovern-Gardner Fight, March 1900, Lubin

Reproduction of the Jeffries-Corbett Fight, May 1900, Lubin

Life Motion Photographs of the Fitzsimmons and Ruhlin Fight, copyright
August 10, 1900, Lubin

Reproduction of the Corbett and McCoy Fight, copyright August 28, 1900, Lubin

Reproduction of the Fitzsimmons and Sharkey Fight, copyright August 28, 1900, Lubin

<u>*McGovern-Gans Fight Pictures,*</u>* December 15, 1900, Selig Polyscope

Ruhlin Boxing with "Denver" Ed. Martin, December 1901, Edison

<u>*Jeffreys [i.e., Jeffries] and Ruhlin Sparring Contest at San Francisco, Cal., November 15, 1901—Five Rounds,*</u>* copyright December 9, 1901, Edison; Kleine Optical

Jeffries-Fitzsimmons Reproduction Prize Fight Films (second fight), July 1902, Lubin

Dixon-Palmer Fight, 1903, Lubin

*Reproduction of Jeffries-Corbett Contest,** 1903, AMB

*Reproduction of Jeffries-Corbett Fight,** 1903, Lubin

Boxing Match on Board the U.S. Cruiser "Raleigh," January 1903, Lubin

Sparring Exhibition on Board the U.S.S. "Alabama," February 1903, Edison

An English Prize-Fight, April 1903, Warwick, U.K.; AMB

Reproduction of Corbett-McGovern Fight San Francisco, March 31, 1903, April 1903, Lubin

Reproduction of Corbett-McGovern Fight (rematch), copyright June 2, 1903, AMB

<u>*Light Heavyweight Championship Contest Between Root and Gardner,*</u>* copyright July 11, 1903, Selig Polyscope

*Reproduction of Jeffries-Corbett Contest,** copyright September 22, 1903, AMB

Reproduction of Fitzsimmons-Gardner Fight, 1903, Lubin

Sparring Match on the "Kearsarge," August 7, 1903; copyright January 3, 1905, AMB

Great Prize Fight; Open-Air Boxing Match [Dido Plum v. Johnny Hughes], pre-1905, U.K.

[Jack Johnson–Joe Jeannette], ca. 1905–8

Nelson-Britt Prize Fight for Lightweight Championship, San Francisco, September 9th, 1905,* copyright September 15, 1905, Miles Bros.

Nelson-Britt Prize Fight, copyright September 27, 1905, Miles Bros.

Impersonation of Britt-Nelson Fight,* copyright September 29, 1905, Lubin

Sparring at the N.Y.A.C.,* copyright November 7, 1905, AMB

Impersonation of the Fitzsimmons-O'Brien Fight, copyright November 8, 1905, Lubin

Dixon–Chester Leon Contest,* copyright March 6, 1906, AMB

Nelson-McGovern Fight, copyright March 23, 1906, Lubin

Impersonation of Gans-Nelson Fight, copyright August 17, 1906, Lubin

Reproduction of Nelson-Gans Fight, copyright August 17, 1906, Lubin

Gans-Nelson Contest, Goldfield, Nevada, September 3, 1906,* copyright October 4, 1906, Miles Bros.

O'Brien-Burns Contest, Los Angeles, Cal., November 26[28]th, 1906, copyright December 17, 1906, Miles Bros.

[Tommy Ryan–Kelly],* 1907

Gans-Herman Fight [World Lightweight Championship of January 1, 1907 Held in Tonopah, Nevada],* 1907, Miles Bros.

Match de boxe anglaise [Pat O'Keefe vs. Charlie Allum]; Boxing Matches in England, April 1907, Pathé

Gunner Moir–Tiger Smith Fight, April 27, 1907, U.S. release, Urban-Eclipse, U.K.; Kleine Optical

Panorama, Crowds at Squires-Burns International Contest, from Center of Ring, Colma, July 4th, 1907, copyright July 11, 1907, Miles Bros.

Panorama, Crowds at Squires-Burns International Contest, from Moving Picture Stand, July 4th, 1907, copyright July 11, 1907, Miles Bros.

International Contest for the Heavyweight Championship, Squires vs. Burns, Ocean View, Cal., July 4th, 1907,* copyright July 18, 1907, Miles Bros.

Moir-Burns Fight, December 2, 1907, Urban, U.K.

Burns-Palmer Fight, February 1908, U.K.

Reproduction of Burns-Palmer Fight, London, February 10, 1908, copyright February 15, 1908, Lubin

Gans-Nelson Fight (second fight, July 4, 1908), copyright April 27, 1908, Miles Bros.

[*Jack Johnson–Ben Taylor*], July 31, 1908, U.K.

Burns-Squires Fight (third fight), August 24, 1908

Nelson-Gans Fight Pictures (third fight), copyright September 9, 1908, Selig Polyscope, for the Gans-Nelson Film Co.

Moran-Attell Fight, September 7, 1908, J. W. Coffroth

World's Heavyweight Championship Pictures between Tommy Burns and Jack Johnson,* December 26, 1908, Gaumont

[*Fitzsimmons-Lang Fight*],* December 27, 1909, Australia

Jim Driscoll versus Seaman Hayes, February 14, 1909, National Sporting Club

The Summers-Britt Fight Pictures, February 22, 1909, Gaumont, U.K.

Boxing Match [by Hallberg of Denmark and Young Joe Gaines "Baltimore Black"], May 1909, Nordisk; Great Northern

Ian Hague-Sam Langford Fight, May 24, 1909, Gaumont

[*Nelson-Hyland Fight*], May 29, 1909

Ketchel-Papke Fight,* July 5, 1909, Eagle Film Co. (Miles Bros.); Kalem

[*Nelson-McFarland Fight*], July 5, 1909, John Kronc promoted film; bout canceled

[*David W. Williams–Harrison H. Foster on the Battleship "Vermont"*], July 30, 1909, U.S. Navy

[*Digger Stanley–Jimmy Walsh Fight*], October 1909, Gaumont, U.K.

*World Championship, Jack Johnson vs. Stanley Ketchell** [i.e., Ketchel], copyright October 24, 1909, J. W. Coffroth/Kalem; Kleine Optical/ MPPC and Gaumont, U.K.

Summers-Welsh Fight, November 8, 1909, Gaumont, U.K.

Middle Weight Boxing, pre-1910, Alfred J. West, U.K.

Kid Sharkey–Young Dority, 1910, Chicago Fight Picture Co.

An English Boxing Bout, January 7, 1910, U.S. release, Pathé

Nelson-Wolgast Fight, February 22, 1910, Great Western Film Co.

*Sam Langford and Jim Flynn Fight,** March 17, 1910, Great Western Film Co.

Langford-Ketchel Fight, April 27, 1910, John Krone

*Welsh and Daniels Fight,** April 25, 1910, U.K.; Clements-Hester Co.; Laemmle Film Service

Welsh v. MacFarland, May 30, 1910, National Sporting Club

*Jeffries-Johnson World's Championship Boxing Contest, Held at Reno, Nevada, July 4, 1910,** also known as the *Johnson-Jeffries Fight,* copyright December 7, 1910, J. & J. Co.; Vitagraph/MPPC

Impersonation of the Johnson-Jeffries Fight, July 1910, Toledo Film Exchange

[Reenactment of] Jeffries-Johnson Fight, July 1910, Empire Film Co.

Reproduction of Johnson-Jeffries, July 1910, Sports Picture Co.

Joe Bowker versus Digger Stanley, October 17, 1910, National Sporting Club

Tom Thomas versus Jim Sullivan, November 1910, National Sporting Club

*[Sam McVey–Battling Jim Johnson],** November 19, 1910

Nelson-Moran Fight, November 26, 1910, Selig/J. W. Coffroth

Stanley-Condon Contest, December 1910, Gaumont, U.K.

[Jim Driscoll–Freddie Welsh], December 20, 1919, Gaumont, U.K.; Solax, U.S. March 1911

Moir-Wells Fight, January 1911, U.K.

Ian Hague v. William Chase, January 30, 1911, National Sporting Club

Jim Driscoll v. Spike Robson, January 30, 1911, National Sporting Club

*[Sam Langford–Bill Lang],** February 21, 1911, U.K.

Sam Langford vs. Sam McVea [i.e., McVey], April 1, 1911, Hugh D. McIntosh

Wolgast-Moran Fight, July 4, 1911, Charles J. Harvey

Kilbane-Attell Fight, February 22, 1912, Los Angeles Projection Co.; Columbia Amusement Enterprises

Jim Sullivan versus Georges Carpentier, March 1912, Warwick, U.K.

McFarland-Wells Fight, May 1912, Vitagraph

Carpentier–Willie Lewis Fight, June 1912

The Great Carpentier v. [Frank] Klaus Fight at Dieppe, Middleweight Championship of the World, June 24, 1912, The Film Service, U.K.

Ad Wolgast vs. Mexican Joe Rivers,* July 4, 1912, Tom McCarey

Jack Johnson vs. Jim Flynn Contest for Heavyweight Championship of the World, Las Vegas, New Mexico, July 4, 1912,* copyright July 18, 1912, Jack Curley/Miles Bros.

[*Willie Ritchie–Joe Rivers*], July 4, 1913

Carpentier-Wells Fight, December 1913

Johnson-Moran Fight,* June 27, 1914, Paris

Ritchie-Welsh Fight, July 7, 1914, London

Joe Bayley vs Johnnie O'Leary Canadian Light Weight Championship Boxing Match, Brig House Arena, Vancouver, July 11, 1914,* Capitol Film Company, Victoria, BC, Canada

Carpentier and Gunboat Smith, July 16, 1914, Topical Budget, U.K.

Jimmy Wilde vs. Joe Symonds,* November 16, 1914, National Sporting Club

Jimmy Wilde vs. Tancy Lee,* January 25, 1915, National Sporting Club

Willard-Johnson Boxing Match,* April 5, 1915; copyright May 4, 1915, Pantomimic Corp. (Fred Mace), for L. Lawrence Weber

[*Willard-Johnson Fight*] (clandestinely filmed version), April 5, 1915

FILMS OF RELATED INTEREST

[*Monkey and another, boxing*], May–June 1891, Edison

The Boxing Cats Prof. Welton's,* ca. July 1894, Edison

[*Alleni's Boxing Monkeys*], August 1894, Edison

Glenroy Brothers, September 13, 1894, Edison/Raff and Gammon

Glenroy Brothers [no. 2], September 22, 1894, Edison/Raff and Gammon

Glenroy Bros., Boxers* aka *Boxing Bout*, October 6, 1894, Edison/Raff and Gammon

Glenroy Bros., Farcical Pugilists in Costume, October 6, 1894, Edison/ Raff and Gammon

Walton and Slavin, October 6, 1894, Edison/Raff and Gammon; four films of a comic routine

Boxing Kangaroo,* May–June 1895, Robert Paul–Birt Acres

Das boxende Känguruh* [Mr. Delaware and his boxing kangaroo], November 1895, Skladanowsky Bioscop

Ringkampf zwischen Greiner und Sandow [wrestling match between a "ringer" and Eugen Sandow], November 1895, Skladanowsky Bioscop

[*Boxing Match between a Man and a Woman*], July 1896, Edison/Raff and Gammon

Bag Punching [by Mike Leonard], October 1896, Edison/Raff and Gammon

First Round, Glove Contest between the Leonards and *Second Round, Glove Contest between the Leonards*, *1897*, American Mutoscope Co.

Comedy Set-to* [Belle Gordon and Billy Curtis], April–May 1898, Edison

Comic Boxing Match, 1899, Warwick, U.K.

The Boxing Horse [vs. "a powerful colored man"], 1899, Lubin

The Automatic Prize Fight, May 1899, AMB

Boxing Dogs, July 1899, AMB

Jeffries and Brother Boxing, November 1899, AMB

Jeffries Boxing with Tommy Ryan, November 1899, AMB

Jeffries Throwing Medicine Ball, June 7, 1899, Vitagraph

Jeffries Skipping Rope, June 7, 1899, Vitagraph

Prize Fight [Glove Fight between John Bull and President Kruger]* and *The Set-To between John Bull and Paul Kruger*, Warwick, copyright March 15, 1900, Anglo-American Exchange; U.K.

Boxing in Barrels,* 1901, Lubin

*Gordon Sisters Boxing,** copyright May 6, 1901, Edison

Jeffries Sparring with His Brother, December 1901, Edison

Jeffreys [i.e. Jeffries] in His Training Quarters, copyright December 2, 1901, Edison

Ruhlin in His Training Quarters, copyright December 2, 1901, Edison

Ruhlin Boxing with "Denver" Ed. Martin, 1901, Edison

The Interrupted Prize Fight, 1902, Warwick, U.K.

French Boxers, November 1902, AMB

Prize Fight in Coon Town, 1903, Selig Polyscope

Barrel Fighters, 1903, Selig Polyscope

Prof. Langtry's Boxing School, 1903, Lubin

*The Last Round Ended in a Free Fight,** copyright January 22, 1903, AMB

English and French Boxers, May 1903, Edison

*A Scrap in Black and White,** copyright July 8, 1903, Edison

*Expert Bag Punching,** copyright July 23, 1903, AMB

Miniature Prize Fighters, 1903, Robert Paul

Boxing Horses, Luna Park, Coney Island, 1904, Edison

*A Couple of Lightweights at Coney Island,** copyright July 28, 1904, AMB

Bokserparodi; Ihles and Antonio, Boxers, 1907, Nordisk; Great Northern

*Dancing Boxing Match, Montgomery and Stone,** copyright May 7, 1907, Winthrop Moving Picture Co.

Jim Jeffries on His California Ranch, copyright June 8, 1907, Miles Bros.

Squires, Australian Champion in His Training Quarters, copyright June 8, 1907, Miles Bros.

Boxing Mania, 1908, Carlo Rossi, Italy; Kleine Optical

The Girls Boxing Match, 1908, AMB

Burns and Johnson Training, 1909, U.K.

How Jack Johnson Trains, 1909

Jack Johnson in Training, 1909, Kineto, Ltd., U.K.

*[Langford-McVey training],** 1909

The Making of Two Champions, 1909, Chicago Fight Picture Co.

Jim Smith, the Champion Boxer, January 1909, Nordisk; Great Northern

Blindfold Boxing, ca. 1900–1910, Alfred J. West, U.K.

There Is a Fight, ca. 1900–1910, Alfred J. West, U.K.

Boxing Contest, ca. 1900–1910, Alfred J. West, U.K.

Boxing on Stools, ca. 1900–1910, Alfred J. West, U.K.

Feather-Weight Boxing, ca. 1900–1910, Alfred J. West, U.K.

Boxing Fever, 1910, Cricks and Martin, U.K.

The Making of a New Champion, 1910

The Man to Beat Jack Johnson, 1910, U.K.

Pimple Meets Jack Johnson, 1910, Davison's, U.K.

Dooley Referees the Big Fight, February 1910, Bison; New York Motion Picture Co.

Jack Johnson Training Pictures, May 1910, Kineto, Ltd., U.K.

Johnson Training for His Fight with Jeffries, May 16, 1910, Chicago Film Picture Co.

How Championships Are Won—and Lost, June 1910, Vitagraph

*Jeffries on His Ranch,** June 15, 1910, Yankee

The Other Johnson, July 6, 1910, Essanay

Mr. Johnson Talks [Jack Johnson's Own Story of the Big Fight], August 1910, American Cinephone Co.

How the Champion of the World Trains, Jack Johnson in Defence and Attack, 1911, Kineto, Ltd., U.K.; *Jack Johnson, Der Meister Boxer der Welt,** 1911, Dutch print

Jack Johnson, Champion du Monde de Boxe Poids Lourds, June–September 1911, France

Jack Johnson Paying a Visit to the Manchester Docks, June–September 1911, U.K.

The Night I Fought Jack Johnson, 1912, Vivaphone, U.K.

Jack Johnson and Jim Flynn Up-to-date, copyright March 20, 1912, Johnson-Flynn Feature Film Co.

One-Round O'Brien, July 4, 1912, Biograph

[*Etta Duryea Johnson's Funeral*], September 1912, C. R. Lundgren

[*Cameron-Johnson Wedding Films*],* December 1912

Pimple Beats Jack Johnson, 1914, Phoenix, U.K.

Wizard-Blackson Fight, A Cartoon Comedy by Fred E. Johnston, May 1915, J. B. Felber, Fort Pitt Film Co.

Notes

Unless noted otherwise, all motion picture catalogs cited are from Charles Musser et al., eds., *Motion Picture Catalogs by American Producers and Distributors, 1894–1908: A Microfilm Edition* (Frederick, MD: University Publications of America, 1985).

The following abbreviated titles are used throughout:

Clipper	*New York Clipper*
Defender	*Chicago Defender*
Examiner	*San Francisco Examiner*
Freeman	*Indianapolis Freeman*
Gazette	*National Police Gazette*
Inquirer	*Philadelphia Inquirer*
MPW	*Moving Picture World*
NYT	*New York Times*
Post	*Washington Post*
TAED	Thomas A. Edison Papers Digital Edition (edison.rutgers.edu)
Trib	*Chicago Tribune*

PRELIMINARIES

1. Jon Elsen, "ESPN Steps into the Ring with Big Fights," *New York Post*, May 13, 1998; Jon Saraceno, "Ex-Tyson Boss Cayton Still Rolls with Punches at 80," *USA Today*, August 21, 1998; Jim Jacobs obituary, *NYT*, March 24, 1988. See also Earl Gustkey, "Old Fight Films," *Los Angeles Times*, March 24, 1982, and "Collectors of Films Back a Champion," *NYT*, November 28, 1986.

2. Tom Gunning, "The Cinema of Attractions: Early Film, Its Spectator and the Avant Garde," *Wide Angle* 8, nos. 3–4 (1986): 64.

3. Terry Ramsaye, *A Million and One Nights* (1926; reprint, New York: Simon and Schuster, 1986), 107, 413.

4. Charles Musser, *The Emergence of Cinema: The American Screen to 1907* (New York: Scribner's, 1990), 193–208.

5. The concept of writing history to create a "usable past" is a well-established one. Warren I. Susman, in *Culture as History: The Transformation of American Society in the Twentieth Century* (New York: Pantheon, 1984), 293, credits the phrase to Van Wyck Brooks in his article "On Creating a Usable Past," *The Dial*, April 11, 1918. Miriam Hansen applies this concept in "Early Silent Cinema: Whose Public Sphere?" *New German Critique* 35 (1985): 147.

6. The best account of these issues is Charlie Keil and Shelley Stamp, eds., *American Cinema's Transitional Era: Audiences, Institutions, Practices* (University of California Press, 2004). See especially the essay by Ben Brewster, "Periodization of Early Cinema," 66–75.

7. Robert C. Allen and Douglas Gomery, *Film History: Theory and Practice* (New York: Knopf, 1985), 153–72.

8. Robert C. Allen, "From Exhibition to Reception: Reflections on the Audience in Film History," *Screen* 31, no. 3 (1990): 349.

9. Elliot J. Gorn and Warren Goldstein, *A Brief History of American Sports* (New York: Hill & Wang, 1993), xii. Reviews of sports history include Benjamin G. Rader, "Modern Sports: In Search of Interpretations," *Journal of Social History* 12 (Winter 1979): 307–21, and Nancy L. Struna, "In 'Glorious Disarray': The Literature of American Sports History," *Research Quarterly* 56, no. 2 (1985): 151–60.

10. John Rickards Betts, *America's Sporting Heritage, 1850–1950* (Reading, MA: Addison-Wesley, 1974), 61–64, 160–69; John R. Betts, "The Technological Revolution and the Rise of Sport, 1850–1900," in Paul J. Zingg, ed., *The Sporting Image: Readings in American Sport History* (Lanham, MD: University Press of America, 1988).

11. Elliott J. Gorn, *The Manly Art: Bare-Knuckle Prize Fighting in America* (Ithaca, NY: Cornell University Press, 1986), 180–82; Melvin Adelman, *A Sporting Time: New York City and the Rise of Modern Athletics, 1820–1870* (Urbana: University of Illinois Press, 1989), 2–6; Steven A. Riess, *Sport in Industrial America, 1850–1920* (Wheeling, IL: Harlan Davidson, 1995); Steven A. Riess, ed., *The American Sporting Experience* (New York: Leisure Press, 1984); Allen Guttmann, *A Whole New Ball Game* (Chapel Hill: University of North Carolina Press, 1988). See also Donald J. Mrozek, *Sport and American Mentality, 1880–1910* (Knoxville: University of Tennessee Press, 1983); Richard D. Mandell, *Sport, A Cultural History* (New York: Columbia University Press, 1984); S. W. Pope, ed., *The New American Sport History* (Urbana: University of Illinois Press, 1997); and Benjamin G. Rader, *American Sports,* 5th ed. (Upper Saddle River, NJ: Prentice Hall, 2004).

12. Steven A. Riess, "Sport and the Redefinition of American Middle-Class Masculinity," *International Journal of the History of Sport* 8, no. 1 (1991): 5–27. (Aaron Baker brought this article to my attention.) See also Clifford Putney, *Muscular Christianity: Manhood and Sports in Protestant America, 1880–1920* (Cambridge, MA: Harvard University Press, 2001).

13. Gorn, *Manly Art*, 19, 28–29, 254. The term *fancy* continued to be used in the twentieth century: see, for example, Jeffrey Farnol, *Famous Prize Fights, or Epics of "the Fancy"* (Boston: Little, Brown, 1928).

14. Timothy J. Gilfoyle, *City of Eros: New York City, Prostitution, and the Commercialization of Sex, 1790–1920* (New York: Norton, 1992), 18–20, 92–115; Howard P. Chudacoff, *The Age of the Bachelor* (Princeton, NJ: Princeton University Press, 1999): 217–50.

15. Gorn, *Manly Art*, 216–47; Michael T. Isenberg, *John L. Sullivan and His America* (Urbana: University of Illinois Press, 1988), 300–323.

16. Ian Morrison, *Boxing: The Records* (London: Guinness, 1986), 88–89.

17. Randy Roberts, *Papa Jack: Jack Johnson and the Era of White Hopes* (New York: Free Press, 1983); Geoffrey C. Ward, *Unforgivable Blackness: The Rise and Fall of Jack Johnson* (New York: Knopf, 2004); Steven A. Riess, "In the Ring and Out: Professional Boxing in New York, 1896–1920," in *Sport in America: New Historical Perspectives*, ed. Donald Spivey (Westport, CT: Greenwood, 1985), 95–128. Other recent books also neglect the role of motion pictures: see, for example, Thomas R. Hietala, *The Fight of the Century: Jack Johnson, Joe Louis, and the Struggle for Racial Equality* (Armonk, NY: M. E. Sharpe, 2002) and Graeme Kent, *The Great White Hopes: The Quest to Defeat Jack Johnson* (Gloucester, U.K.: Sutton, 2005).

18. Tom Gunning, *D. W. Griffith and the Origins of American Narrative Film* (Urbana: University of Illinois Press, 1991), 291.

19. Mary Beth Haralovich, "Film History and Social History," *Wide Angle* 8, no. 2 (1985): 10.

20. E. P. Thompson, *The Making of the English Working Class* (London: Victor Gollancz, 1964), 12, 832. See also I I. J. Perkin, "Social History," in *The Varieties of History*, ed. Fritz Stern (New York: Vintage, [1956], 1972), 434, 455; John Clarke et al., eds., *Working-Class Culture: Studies in History and Theory* (London: Hutchinson, 1979).

21. Peter N. Stearns, "Toward a Wider Vision: Trends in Social History," in *The Past before Us*, ed. Michael Kammen (Ithaca, NY: Cornell University Press, 1980), 210, 213.

22. Stearns, "Toward a Wider Vision," 216. See also Arthur S. Link and Richard L. McCormick, *Progressivism* (Arlington Heights, IL: Harlan Davidson, 1983).

23. Rudyard Kipling, "Mrs. Bathurst," in *Traffics and Discoveries* (New York: Doubleday, Page, 1904).

24. Elliott J. Gorn, "The Wicked World: The National Police Gazette and Gilded Age America," *Media Studies Journal* 6 (1992): 1–15; Gene Smith and Jayne Barry Smith, eds., *The Police Gazette* (New York: Simon and Schuster,

1972); Gilfoyle, *City of Eros*, 133–34. See also Guy Reel, *The National Police Gazette and the Making of the Modern American Man, 1879–1906* (New York: Palgrave Macmillan, 2006).

1. THE SPORTING AND THEATRICAL SYNDICATE

1. "The Kinetograph," *New York Sun*, May 28, 1891, quoted in Charles Musser, *Edison Motion Pictures, 1890–1900: An Annotated Filmography* (Washington, DC: Smithsonian Institution Press, 1997), 78. Other reports also wed Edison's invention to pugilism: according to "The Wonderful Kineto-graph" (*New York Herald,* in *Current Literature,* July 1891, 451), "it can be applied to the ring, and a whole prize fight or sparring exhibition, with the motions, blows, and talk, can be reproduced."

2. The Kinetoscope Company, Bulletin no. 2, January 1895, description of *Billy Edwards and the Unknown, Boxing Bout in 5 Rounds.*

3. "Some of Edison's Latest," *Albany Telegram,* January 7, 1894 (TAED SC94001A).

4. Rebecca Solnit, *River of Shadows: Eadweard Muybridge and the Technological Wild West* (New York: Viking, 2003), 228; *Photographic News,* March 13, 1882; "Athletes Boxing," in Eadweard Muybridge, *Attitudes of Animals in Motion* (1881), plate 111.

5. "The Kinetograph," *Phonogram,* October 1892, 217–18. In 1994, the Edison National Historic Site (NHS) restored a boxing scene taken in 1891. *[Men Boxing]* appears on the Library of Congress website "Inventing Entertainment: The Motion Pictures and Sound Recordings of the Edison Companies" (http://memory.loc.gov; accessed January 13, 1999). Musser reproduces seven frames said to be from *[Men Boxing]* (*Edison Motion Pictures*, 75). However, the action and mise-en-scène they show are not present in the restored version. Therefore, Dickson may have taken a second 1891 motion picture of men boxing. For the 1892 *Phonogram* image and article, see Charles Musser, *The Emergence of Cinema: The American Screen to 1907* (New York: Scribner's, 1990), 74.

6. George Parsons Lathrop, "Edison's Kinetograph," *Harper's Weekly,* June 13, 1891, in *The Movies in Our Midst,* ed. Gerald Mast (Chicago: University of Chicago Press, 1982), 8–12. Lathrop had collaborated with Edison on an unpublished novel.

7. W. K. L. Dickson and Antonia Dickson, "Edison's Invention of the Kineto-Phonograph," *Century Magazine,* June 1894, in Mast, *Movies in Our Midst,* 12–19. Also, W. K. L. Dickson and Antonia Dickson, *History of the Kinetograph, Kinetoscope, and Kineto-phonograph* (1895), facsimile ed. (New York: Museum of Modern Art, 2000).

8. Correspondence between Otway Latham and William E. Gilmore, May 16 and 19, 1894 (TAED D9427): Motion Pictures—Kinetoscope Exhibiting Co.; Charles Musser, *Before the Nickelodeon: Edwin S. Porter and the Edison Manufacturing Company* (Berkeley: University of California Press, 1991), 45–47;

Stephen Herbert and Luke McKernan, eds., *Who's Who of Victorian Cinema: A Worldwide Survey* (London: BFI, 1996), s.v. "Latham." Extensive research on the kinetoscope era, including its boxing films, can be found in Ray Philips, *Edison's Kinetoscope and Its Films: A History to 1896* (Westport, CT: Greenwood, 1997), and Gordon Hendricks, *The Kinetoscope* (1966), in *Origins of American Film* (New York: Arno, 1972).

9. Hendricks, *Kinetoscope*, 75.

10. *New York World*, June 16, 1894.

11. *Brooklyn Standard Union*, August 16, and *Brooklyn Citizen*, August 18, 1894, quoted in Hendricks, *Kinetoscope*, 92–93. The Kinetoscope Exhibition Co. was incorporated in Tilden's home town of New Lebanon, New York, and capitalized at $30,000 ("Newly Incorporated Companies," *NYT*, August 17, 1894).

12. Edison Films, Catalogue no. 94, March 1900, 27; Lubin Company catalog of "Life Motion Pictures," 1907, 102.

13. Musser, *Emergence of Cinema*, 193–337.

14. Hendricks, *Kinetoscope*, 91, reprints items from the *New York Sun*, June 16, 1894, and others. It remains unclear whether Jack McAuliffe performed at the Black Maria. Musser (*Edison Motion Pictures*, 90, 101–2), lists *Boxing* (no. 39) as featuring McAuliffe, shot by May 1894. He indicates that a fragment of the film is extant, but none is reproduced. What do exist are twenty-four frames (captioned "Kinetoscopic Records") from a Black Maria film that appeared in *The Electrical World*, June 16, 1894, 799, and *Literary Digest*, July 21, 1894 (captioned "Kinetoscopic Record of a Boxing Exhibition"). Musser identifies this as *[Boxing Match]* (no. 25), recorded by mid-March 1894. Musser notes that McAuliffe's "appearance before Edison's camera was never shown commercially" (*Edison Motion Pictures*, 90). A lone item in Edison's press clippings fails to clarify whether a McAuliffe scene was actually photographed: "Some time ago an attempt was made to have Jack McAuliffe fight a man of his own choice, but he took his side partner to East Orange, and Mr. Edison and his friends were anything but satisfied with the sparring exhibition to which they were treated" ("Fight for Edison: Clever Boxers Have a Finish Bout for the Wizard," *New York Journal*, June 16, 1894 [TAED DSC94009C]).

15. Edison Films, Catalogue no. 94, 27; Terry Ramsaye, *A Million and One Nights* (1926; reprint, New York: Simon and Schuster, 1986), 109.

16. *New York World* and *New York Sun*, June 16, 1894, and *Newark Evening News*, August 10, 1894, quoted in Hendricks, *Kinetoscope*, 92–97.

17. Edison Films, Catalogue no. 94, 27; Hendricks, *Kinetoscope*, 92–97.

18. *New York Sun*, June 16, 1894.

19. Ramsaye describes the *Leonard-Cushing Fight* as being advertised in the Latham kinetoscope parlor with the aid of signs and a storefront barker (*Million and One Nights*, 109).

20. See Dennis Brailsford, *Bareknuckles: A Social History of Prize-fighting* (Cambridge, U.K.: Lutterworth, 1990); Elliott J. Gorn, *The Manly Art: Bare-Knuckle Prize Fighting in America* (Ithaca, NY: Cornell University Press, 1986); Michael T. Isenberg, *John L. Sullivan and His America* (Urbana: University of

Illinois Press, 1988); and Jeffrey T. Sammons, *Beyond the Ring: The Role of Boxing in American Society* (Urbana: University of Illinois Press, 1988). Less than a year before his death, Sullivan formed the John L. Sullivan Motion Picture Company. "John L. Sullivan in New Role," *Chicago Tribune,* March 25, 1917.

21. *New York World* and *New York Sun,* June 16, 1894; "Fight for Edison" (TAED DSC94009C); G. Wilfred Pearce, "Edison Defended," *Boston Advertiser,* September 18, 1894 (TAED SC94029A).

22. Musser, *Edison Motion Pictures,* 36.

23. These include a photograph of an unidentified bar featuring a row of six kinetoscopes, each labeled "Corbett Fight," in Musser, *Emergence of Cinema,* 85; a photograph of Thomas Tally's phonograph and picture parlor in Los Angeles (ca. 1897–98), in which the only visible sign reads "See the Corbett Fight," in Musser, *Before the Nickelodeon,* 86; an earlier photograph of Tally's in Robert Sklar, *Movie-Made America* (New York: Vintage, 1975), 8; a photograph from the Edison NHS, showing five "prize fight kinetoscopes" with posters and signs in the "Arcade at Tabor Opera House, Denver, set up to show a five-round prize fight" between Corbett and Courtney, in Bob Fisher et al., "A 100-Year Start on Tomorrow: In Celebration of the Invention of Motion Picture Film," reprinted from *American Cinematographer,* n.d., 2a–3a (provided by Tom Streible); and the cover illustration for Dickson and Dickson, *History of the Kinetograph,* which includes W. K. L. Dickson's rendering of *Corbett and Courtney before the Kinetograph.*

24. Hendricks, *Kinetoscope,* 100, 79.

25. Rex Lardner claims that John L. Sullivan turned down Edison's offer (*The Legendary Champions* [New York: American Heritage Press, 1972, 98–99]). Lardner's several errors about *Corbett-Courtney* appear to be derived from William A. Brady, *Showman* (New York: Dutton, 1937). The documentary *The Legendary Champions* (1968; written and directed by Harry Chapin, and nominated for an Academy Award) is more reliable.

26. See Patrick Myler, *Gentleman Jim Corbett* (London: Robson, 1998); Armond Fields, *James J. Corbett* (Jefferson, NC: McFarland, 2001); and Bob Peterson, *Gentleman Bruise: A Life of the Boxer Peter Jackson, 1860–1901* (Sydney: Croydon, 2005).

27. Alan Woods, "James J. Corbett: Theatrical Star," *Journal of Sport History* 3, no. 2 (1976): 162–75. Brady had acted in stage productions of *After Dark.* In 1915, William A. Brady Picture Plays, Inc., produced a film adaptation. See Lawrence Jacob Wilker, "The Theatrical Business Practices of William A. Brady" (Ph.D. diss., University of Illinois, 1973.)

28. Nat Fleischer and Sam Andre, *A Pictorial History of Boxing* (New York: Citadel Press, 1959), 66. Edmund E. Price, a New York prizefighter and dramatist, wrote Sullivan's theatrical vehicles: *Honest Hearts and Willing Hands* (1891–92), *The Man from Boston* (1892–94), and *A True American* (1894–95). Each concluded with a ring battle in which the hero knocked out the villain ("Sorrow over the Death of Price, Boxer-Lawyer," *NYT,* February 1, 1907).

29. Woods, "James J. Corbett," 165–73.

30. Brady, *Showman*, 83.

31. "Snap-Shot Gladiators," *New York Journal*, August 10, 1894 (TAED SC94027A); "The Big Fight and Kinetoscope," *Newark Evening News*, August 10, 1894, in Hendricks, 100–101.

32. *New York Sun*, September 8, 1894.

33. Hendricks refers to the fight as occurring on September 8 (*Kinetoscope*, 79), though he later documents the correct date, September 7. The detail would be insignificant except for the fact that William Brady later wrote: "We were two solid days getting a picture of those six minutes of fighting" (*Showman*, 161). All other evidence indicates, however, that Corbett arrived in West Orange on the morning of the seventh, sparred, and returned to Manhattan that same afternoon for his scheduled performance at the American Theater.

34. "Latest Edison Films for Projecting Machines," F. M. Prescott catalog, June 1897; Edison Films, Catalogue no. 94, 27.

35. Brady, *Showman*, 160.

36. "Knocked Out by Corbett," 3, 8. See also the series of drawings titled *Corbett and Courtney before the Kinetoscope*, "recorded by the *New York World* artist at the scene" (*World*, September 8, 1894, reproduced in Fleischer and Andre, *Pictorial History*, 73). Citations of Corbett-Courtney as an actual contest include W. W. Naughton, *Kings of the Queensberry Realm* (Chicago: Continental, 1902), 101; *Life and Battles of Jack Johnson* (New York: Richard K. Fox, 1912), 81; Bert Randolph Sugar, ed., *The Ring 1981 Record Book and Boxing Encyclopedia* (New York: Atheneum, 1981), 472; and Fleischer and Andre, *Pictorial History*, 73 ("This was a legitimate fight and to a finish").

37. Hendricks, *Kinetoscope*, 101.

38. Tom Gunning, "'Primitive' Cinema—A Frame-Up? Or, The Trick's on Us," *Cinema Journal* 28, no. 2 (1989): 3–4.

39. *Cincinnati Enquirer*, March 25, 1894, in Woods, "James J. Corbett," 170; "The Pugilistic Drama," *NYT*, September 4, 1894.

40. "Pugilist Corbett May Be Indicted," *NYT*, September 9, 1894; Hendricks, *Kinetoscope*, 108–9. "Corbett May Be Indicted," *NYT*, September 12, 1894, specified that the judge charged a grand jury to indict "the principals and spectators," but the "newspaper men" who could testify as witnesses were "not amenable."

41. Musser also attributes *[Boxing Match between a Man and Woman]* to Raff & Gammon, but says that this attribution may have been mistakenly based on an inaccurate advertisement for the *White-Smith* film (*Edison Motion Pictures*, 223).

42. Hendricks, *Kinetoscope*, 114–15. On January 16, 1895, Maguire & Baucus ordered "6 Prize Fighting Kinetoscopes" (the Lathams' expanded model) and "2 sets 'Leonard Cushing' films."

43. Billy Edwards, an aged British lightweight, was by this time a boxing instructor and had just published a book showing pictures of many of the best-known prizefighters of the nineteenth century (*The Portrait Gallery of Pugilists of England, America, Australia*, 1894). See also Marshall Deutelbaum, "A

Collection of Edison Films," in *"Image" on the Art and Evolution of Film* (New York: Dover, 1979), 9–19; Musser, *Edison Motion Pictures*, 172–73.

44. Ramsaye, *Million and One Nights*, 116. "Pugilists' Managers Fight," *NYT*, March 15, 1895; "Fights with His Manager," *NYT*, February 5, 1896.

45. Deac Rossell, "A Chronology of Cinema, 1889–1896," *Film History* 7, no. 2 (1995): 133–34; "Charles E. Chinnock Dead," *NYT*, June 12, 1915.

46. The American Mutoscope Company became American Mutoscope and Biograph in 1899. Paul Spehr, "Filmmaking at the American Mutoscope and Biograph Company, 1900–1906," *Quarterly Journal of the Library of Congress* 37 (1980): 413–21.

47. Ramsaye, *Million and One Nights*, 211; Gordon Hendricks, *Beginnings of the Biograph* (1964), in *Origins of the American Film* (New York: Arno, 1972), 2.

48. Hendricks, *Beginnings of the Biograph*, illustration 4.

49. *Canastota Bee*, August 10, 1895, in Hendricks, *Beginnings of the Biograph*, 20. Canastota, New York, near Syracuse, became home to the International Boxing Hall of Fame in 1989.

50. American Mutoscope and Biograph catalog, 1903. It is unclear whether the Leonard-Hosley round was preserved as one of these four films. A pair of paper-print frames survives from a motion picture titled *Sparring Contest [at] Canastota, N.Y.*, which were copyrighted by the American Mutoscope Company—though not until December 18, 1896. These frames show a makeshift ring. With cornermen and a referee looking on, the younger fighter delivers a knockout blow; in frame 2, the older "victim" is seen carried to his corner. The pair of boxers could be the "professor" and "pupil" referred to in the newspaper article.

Later Biograph boxing subjects in this catalog include *Prize Fight, Downey vs. Monahan* (1897), *Glove Contest between the Leonards* (1897), *Train vs. Donovan* (1898), and *Chuck Connors and Chin Ong* (1899).

51. John Barnes, *The Beginnings of the Cinema in England, 1894–1901* (Exeter: University of Exeter Press, 1997); *Clipper*, April 10, 1897, 101; Sylvester Quinn Breard, "A History of the Motion Pictures in New Orleans, 1896–1908" (master's thesis, Louisiana State University, 1951).

Jem Mace (1831–1910) boxed an exhibition against Dick Burge (rather than "Burke," as the Acres title has it) in London on October 14, 1895. Paul's two-round film featured Charles "Toff" Wall, a British heavyweight, and Dido Plum, a middleweight champion.

52. American Mutoscope and Biograph Picture Catalogue, November 1902, 26.

53. "The Championship Match," *Clipper*, November 4, 1894, 562.

54. "Pantopticon Rivals the Kinetoscope," *NYT*, April 22, 1895; Woodville Latham, Patent No. 707, 934, for improvements in the projecting kinetoscope, granted August 26, 1902; *Motion Picture Patents Co. v. Universal Film Mfg. Co., et al.* 243 U.S. 502 (1917). See also Ramsaye, *Million and One Nights*, 121 ff.; David Samuelson, "Strokes of Genius," *American Cinematographer* 80, no. 3 (March 1999): 166–74. The senior Latham's role in film history was recognized

and romanticized in the *New York Times Sunday Magazine*'s story on the Museum of Modern Art's opening of its film department. Frank S. Nugent wrote: "Woodville Latham . . . screened the first picture (at 153 Broadway) presenting, in four minutes of boxing, Young Griffo vs. Battling Charles Barnett. So, in combat, was an art born. The Latham Pantoptikon rescued the movies from the penny arcades" ("Celluloid Pageant: The March of the 'Art' Is Vividly Portrayed in a New Museum Devoted to the Film," *NYT,* January 19, 1936).

55. Fleischer and Andre, *Pictorial History,* 96.

56. Merritt Crawford, "William Kennedy Laurie Dickson: Movie Pioneer," ca. 1935, quoted in Mast, *Movies in Our Midst,* 27–31.

57. George C. Pratt, "Firsting the Firsts," in Deutelbaum, *"Image,"* 20–22, citing the *New York Sun,* April 22, 1895.

58. Eidoloscope's boxing debut remained in the picture trade's memory, as evidenced in a *Moving Picture World* collection of oral histories: "The first store show in New York was a prize fight picture," on Broadway, according to Arthur Hotaling, a director for Lubin (Epes Winthrop Sargent, "New York City Holds Record for Earliest Exhibiting," *MPW,* July 15, 1916, 371).

59. Pratt quotes the *Rochester Democrat and Chronicle,* January 19, 1896, which itself was citing a Chicago paper, possibly the June 11, 1895, *Chicago Inter-Ocean:* "The entire ring is reproduced. The men are seen to shake hands and begin the preliminary sparring when Griffo lands a stinger. . . . At the call of time the men take their corners to be fanned and rubbed down by their seconds. The referee walks around the ring and going to the ropes orders a spectator to stop blowing smoke into the ring" ("Firsting the Firsts," 21).

60. Crawford, "William Kennedy Laurie Dickson," 29; "Eugene A. Lauste, Inventor, 78, Dies," *NYT,* June 28, 1935.

61. James S. McQuade, "Chicago Reports Many Variations in Picture Shows," *MPW,* July 15, 1916, 414.

62. Pratt, "Firsting the Firsts," 20–22; Rossell, "Chronology of Cinema," 136, 145, passim. The eidoloscope at the Olympia was drawing bigger (and more respectable) crowds than the "living pictures" posed by undraped female models, which had attracted large audiences previously. "The Theatres," *NYT,* May 24, 1896.

63. After leaving the film business, Gray and Otway Latham worked in New York real estate. Gray Latham was married to the author and illustrator Rose Cecil O'Neill (the inventor of the Kewpie Doll) from 1896 until their divorce in 1901. Gray died in 1907 after falling from a Broadway streetcar, Otway in 1910, and their father in 1911. See *Who's Who of Victorian Cinema,* as well *New York Times* items: "Legal Notices: The Eidoloscope Company," October 21, 1898; "Vitascope Company of New Jersey," January 15, 1898; *"George Carr et al. vs. Otway Latham,"* January 10, 1901, passim; "Gray Latham Stricken," March 27, 1907.

64. Ramsaye, *Million and One Nights,* 281.

65. Hendricks, *Kinetoscope,* 141.

66. Gerald Bordman, ed. *The Concise Oxford Companion to American Theatre* (New York: Oxford University Press, 1987), 409.

67. Hendricks, *Kinetoscope*, 142.

68. Robert C. Allen, "Vitascope/Cinématographe: Initial Patterns of American Film Industrial Practice," in *The American Movie Industry: The Business of Motion Pictures*, ed. Gorham Kindem (Carbondale: Southern Illinois University Press, 1982), 3–11; Robert C. Allen, *Vaudeville and Film, 1895–1915: A Study in Media Interaction* (New York: Arno, 1980).

69. Michelle Aubert and Jean-Claude Seguin, *La production cinématographique des frères Lumière* (Paris: Bibliothèque du Film, 1996), 109, 287; J. Rittaud-Hutinet, *Le cinéma des origines* (Seysset, France: Champ Vallon, 1985), 171.

70. Ramsaye, *Million and One Nights*, 241. The term *colors* refers to prints with hand-painted frames.

71. Multi-image poster "Cinématographe perfectionne" (Paris, 1896), reproduced in Gregory J. Edwards, *The International Film Poster* (Salem, NH: Salem House, 1985), 21.

72. Oskar Messter, *Mein Weg mit der Film* (Berlin: M. Hesse, 1936), unnumbered plate.

73. Henry Tyrell, "Some Music-Hall Moralities," *The Illustrated America*, July 11, 1896, 76.

74. Gorn, *Manly Art*, 100–106, 181 ff.; Isenberg, *John L. Sullivan*, 92–102 ff.; John Rickards Betts, *America's Sporting Heritage, 1850–1950* (Reading, MA: Addison-Wesley, 1974), 38–39, 61–62.

75. Albert McCleery and Carl Glick, *Curtains Going Up: Theatre Americana* (New York: Pitman, 1939), 5. The Latham brothers' Virginia-born father had been an officer in the Confederate army, but Gray and Otway were Manhattanites, making at least one appearance in a society column (*NYT*, December 16, 1893). On the father's background, see Woodville Latham, letter to the editor, "Seward's Idea of Lincoln's Ideas," *NYT*, March 21, 1907.

76. Timothy J. Gilfoyle, *City of Eros: New York City, Prostitution, and the Commercialization of Sex, 1790–1920* (New York: Norton, 1992), 224–28; Robert C. Allen, *Horrible Prettiness: Burlesque and American Culture* (Chapel Hill: University of North Carolina Press, 1991), 73–77; Edward Van Every, *The Sins of New York, as "Exposed" by the Police Gazette* (New York: Frederick A. Stokes, 1930); Gorn, *Manly Art*, 183–84; Isenberg, *John L. Sullivan*, 4–5, 96–97; Lloyd Morris, *Not So Long Ago* (New York: Random House, 1949), 33.

77. Steven A. Riess, "In the Ring and Out: Professional Boxing in New York, 1896–1920," in *Sport in America: New Historical Perspectives*, ed. Donald Spivey (Westport, CT: Greenwood, 1985), 95–128; Daniel Czitrom, "Underworlds and Underdogs: Big Tim Sullivan and Metropolitan Politics in New York, 1889–1913," *Journal of American History* 78, no. 2 (September 1991): 536–58.

2. THE CORBETT-FITZSIMMONS FIGHT

1. Paul Rotha, *The Film till Now* (London: Spring Books, 1930, 1967), 69–70.

2. William Brady commissioned Charles T. Vincent to write this star vehicle. Corbett toured in *A Naval Cadet* for three seasons, playing an Annapolis student who boxes, invents a machine gun, and goes to the slums of Paris to catch criminals who have stolen his patent. *NYT*, November 29, 1896; October 12, 1897.

3. "That Championship Match," *Clipper*, November 3, 1894, 562. Fitzsimmons was indicted in January 1895 and acquitted in July. Damond Benningfield, "The Boxing Championship That Wasn't," *American West* 23, no. 1 (1986): 64; *Clipper*, November 24, 1896; W. W. Naughton, *Kings of the Queensberry Realm* (Chicago: Continental, 1902), 117.

4. "Having Hot Times Down at Austin," *Dallas Time Herald*, October 2, 1895; James William Madden, *Charles Allen Culberson* (Austin: Gammel's, 1929), 35–38.

5. Daniel Albert Stuart (1846–1909) had a rivalry with Culberson that began in the 1870s. He headed gambling interests that controlled the boom town of Jefferson. Culberson, as county attorney, attempted to drive Stuart out.

Stuart qualifies as a carpetbagger, one of the Northern mercantile class who sought opportunities in the South during Reconstruction. Vermont-born, he came to Texas in 1872 after involvement with Kentucky horse racing. By 1895, he was said to have dictated who held elective office in Dallas. He moved to Manhattan in 1897. See *Memorial and Biographical History of Dallas County, Texas* (Chicago: Lewis Publishing, 1892), 547; "XXIV Legislature Meets," *Austin Statesman*, October 3, 1895; Frank X. Tolbert, "Stuart Proposed Fight in Balloon," *Dallas Morning News*, September 19, 1962; Robert L. Wagner, "Governor vs. Gambler," *Texas Parade*, November 1963, 22–24; "Gov. Culberson and Dan Stuart," *Dallas Times Herald*, October 8, 1895; "That Grand Jury Down at Austin," October 9.

6. J. C. M., "Hot Springs is the 'Hot' Town," *Dallas Times Herald*, October 10, 1895; William A. Brady, *Showman* (New York: Dutton, 1937), 165–70.

7. H.R. 5566, 54th Congress, 1st sess., February 5, 1896.

8. "Fitzsimmons To Fight Maher," *NYT*, December 17, 1895; Grace Miller White, "When Judge Roy Bean Pulled a Prize Fight," *Frontier Times*, August 1941, 478; Tolbert, "Stuart Proposed Fight."

9. Dick King, "The Fight that Almost Kayoed Boxing," *Frontier Times*, Summer 1959, 56–57; Banks, "Roy Bean," 24–25.

10. "The Big Mill Pulled Off," *Galveston News*, February 22, 1896.

11. Even before the train arrived in Langtry, "it became certain that the kinetoscope could not be operated during the light." *Clipper*, February 29, 1896, 829; "The Day Was Too Dark for the Kinetoscope," *Austin Statesman*, February 22, 1896.

12. Rex Lardner, *The Legendary Champions* (New York: American Heritage Press, 1972), 107; Peter Arnold, *History of Boxing* (Secaucus, NJ: Chartwell, 1985), 39; Fred Dartnell, *"Seconds Out!"* (New York: Brentano's, 1924), 133–34.

13. "The Big Mill Is Pulled Off," *Galveston News*, February 21, 1896.

14. Peter F. Stevens, "'Wyatt Earp's Word Is Good Enough with Me!'" *American West* 25, no. 1 (1986), 44–47; *I Married Wyatt Earp: The Recollections*

of Josephine Sarah Marcus Earp (Tucson: University of Arizona Press, 1976), 150–55; Stuart N. Lake, *Wyatt Earp, Frontier Marshal* (Boston: Houghton Mifflin, 1931), 66–70. Secondary accounts of the Fitzsimmons-Maher bout include Jimmy Banks, "Roy Bean: Boxing Promoter," *Texas Parade*, September 1950, 24–25; Denis McLoughlin, *Wild and Woolly* (Garden City, NY: Doubleday, 1975), 39; Robert H. Davis, *"Ruby Robert": Alias Bob Fitzsimmons* (New York: Doran, 1926).

15. William H. Swanson, "The Inception of the 'Black Top,'" *MPW*, July 15, 1916, 369; Sylvester Quinn Breard, "A History of the Motion Pictures in New Orleans, 1896–1908" (master's thesis, Louisiana State University, 1951); Dan Streible, "A History of the Boxing Film, 1894–1915," *Film History* 3, no. 3 (1989): 237 (broadside of "The Great Corbett Fight" provided by Richard Koszarski); Charles Musser, *The Emergence of Cinema: The American Screen to 1907* (New York: Scribner's, 1990), 169. The Corbett-Courtney films were featured in New Orleans at Vitascope Hall (July 1896), Tally's Los Angeles film parlor (December 1896), and Siegmund Lubin's first cineograph projections in Philadelphia (March 1897).

16. The kinetoscope exhibitor Frank J. Howard, illustrating the pervasiveness of fight pictures and spectators' supposedly naive understanding of cinematography, recollected: "One of the first films was of the Courtney-Corbett Fight. It was just after this that Corbett was knocked out by Fitzsimmons. We advertised 'The Great Corbett Fight.' We did not state which one. One day a man stopping at the door said, 'You had better fix that machine. There's something the matter with it. Corbett knocks out Fitzsimmons instead of Fitzsimmons knocking out Corbett.' He supposed he was seeing the Fitzsimmons fight and that the mechanism of the machine caused the error." William M. Flynn, "New England Figures Theater Value by Millions," *MPW*, July 15, 1916, 408.

17. C. Francis Jenkins, *Animated Pictures* (Washington, DC: H. L. McQueen, 1898), 24, lists 110 " 'scope' and 'graph' machines."

18. The sketch opened on March 21. Ad in *Clipper*, April 3, 1897, 81. Armond Fields and L. Marc Fields, *From the Bowery to Broadway* (New York: Oxford University Press, 1993), 131 (book generously provided by Annie Bright).

19. Terry Ramsaye, *A Million and One Nights* (1926; reprint, New York: Simon and Schuster, 1986, 284–87; Musser, *Emergence of Cinema*, 195; Jan-Christopher Horak, "Introduction to Film Gauges," in *Electronic Encyclopedia of Moving Image Archive Studies* (UCLA, 2000), www.cinema.ucla.edu/tank (accessed August 1, 2005).

20. "Siler Gives His Views," *Examiner*, March 18, 1897; Barratt O'Hara, *From Figg to Johnson* (Chicago: Blossom Book Bourse, 1909), 171.

21. 54th Cong., 2nd sess., *Congressional Record*, 29 (March 1, 1897): H 2587–88; Jeffrey T. Sammons, *Beyond the Ring: The Role of Boxing in American Society* (Urbana: University of Illinois Press, 1988), 24; David Pivar, *The Purity Crusade: Sexual Morality and Social Control, 1868–1900* (Westport, CT: Greenwood, 1973), 234.

22. Musser, *Emergence of Cinema*, 84; Brady, *Showman*, 166. The cagey manager may also have arranged his own exhibitions of *Corbett-Courtney*. Some of the earliest "shows in store rooms were conducted by William A. Brady, who had some early fight pictures" ("The Evolution of Exhibiting," *MPW*, July 15, 1916, 368).

23. "Delaney's Ideas of the Kinetoscope," *Examiner*, April 9, 1897; Brady, *Showman*, 171; Musser, *Emergence of Cinema*, 194–97. Fitzsimmons sold his share of the film profits to Brady for ten thousand dollars.

24. "The Championship Match," *Clipper*, October 4, 1894, 562.

25. *Boston Herald*, March 17, 1897, cited by Musser, *Emergence of Cinema*, 196.

26. "Kinetoscope Works Like a Charm," *Trib*, March 16, 1897; "[Sen. John J.] Ingalls Describes the Fight," *Examiner*, March 18, 1897.

27. T. J. Williams, "One Punch Was Worth a Fortune," *Examiner*, March 18, 1897.

28. Madden was Sullivan's original manager and promoter; he was also a former boxer and a press agent for Buffalo Bill's Wild West Show. He helped supply acts for the Black Maria productions and is visible as an on-screen spectator in the Billy Edwards boxing film shot by W. K. L. Dickson. Gordon Hendricks, *The Kinetoscope* (1966), in *Origins of American Film* (New York: Arno, 1972), 135, and "A Collection of Edison Films," in *"Image" on the Art and Evolution of the Film*, ed. Marshall Deutelbaum (New York: Dover, 1979), 9–10; Michael T. Isenberg, *John L. Sullivan and His America* (Urbana: University of Illinois Press, 1988), 96–102 ff.

29. "Fitzsimmons Is Now the Champion," *Clipper*, March 27, 1897, 64.

30. "Kinetoscope Views Are Good in Spots," *Examiner*, April 18, 1897.

31. "The Fistic Kinetoscope Exhibits," *Clipper*, April 10, 1897, 96; "Kinetoscope Scheme Is a Failure," *Examiner*, April 4.

32. "Predictions," *Examiner*, March 16, 1897; "That Kinetoscope Story," *Examiner*, March 28, 1897.

33. "Another Fight Anticipated," *Examiner*, April 5, 1897; "Donohoe Makes Strong Denial," *Examiner*, April 14, 1897.

34. *Transmission by Mail or Interstate Commerce of Picture or Any Description of Prize Fight*, H.R. 10369, 54th Cong., 2nd sess., February 26, 1897.

35. All quotations from 54th Cong., 2nd sess., *Congressional Record* 29 (March 1, 1897): H 2587–89.

36. "To Stop Pugilism by Kinetoscope," *New York Tribune*, March 25, 1897, added to Sen. Hoar's description of technologies, reporting "a bill which prohibits the reproduction by kinetoscope, kitascope *[sic]*, biograph, or any kindred device of a pugilistic encounter of any sort." The bill was unsuccessfully reintroduced in 1900. "Against Prizefight Pictures," *NYT*, March 10, 1900.

37. "Against Prizefight Pictures," *New York Tribune*, April 16, 1897. Of the forty-two signers, the article named: "Justice [Stephen Johnson] Field of the U.S. Supreme Court, Governors Oferrall of Virginia, Cooke of Connecticut, and Grout of Vermont; Bishops Whitaker, Coleman, and Cheney," and others. The

bill came up for debate on May 12, but the Utah senator Joseph Rawlins objected; no further action was taken. 55th Cong., 1st sess., *Congressional Record* 30 (May 12, 1897): S 1046.

38. *New York Tribune* editorial, March 22, 1897.

39. "Anti-Kinetoscope Fight Bills," *New York Tribune*, March 20, 1897; "To Cut Off Exhibition of Prize Fight Pictures," *NYT*, March 21; "To Prohibit Prize-Fight Pictures," *Examiner*, March 21; "No Kinetoscope for Canada," *Examiner*, April 16; "No Prizefight Pictures," *NYT*, April 18; "To Bar Fight Pictures," *Examiner*, June 5.

40. "Pulpit Views on the Fight," *Examiner*, March 15, 1897; "The 'Veriscope,'" *NYT*, May 26, 1897; Rep. Elijah Morse (R-Massachusetts) and Rep. Aldrich, 54th Cong., 2nd sess., *Congressional Record* 29 (March 1, 1897): H 2586–87.

41. Gregory A. Waller, "Situating Motion Pictures in the Prenickelodeon Period: Lexington, Kentucky, 1897–1906," *Velvet Light Trap* 25 (1990): 12–28; "A Knock-Out for Kinetoscopic Reproductions of the Corbett-Fitzsimmons Fight Planned by Women," *Lexington Herald*, March 24, 1897; *Clipper*, May 8, 1897, 171.

42. "Fitzsimmons Will Fight," *Examiner*, March 27, 1897.

43. *Examiner*, April 4, 1897.

44. "Another Fight Anticipated," *Examiner*, April 5, 1897; Jimmy Swinnerton's cartoon, April 8.

45. "Fitz Hobnobs with Greatness," *Examiner*, May 19, 1897.

46. "Pugilists Give a Mimic Show," *NYT*, March 18, 1897.

47. Ads in *Clipper*, April 3, 1897, 83. Amet might never have filmed his recreation. His ad stated: "Parties purchasing an outfit from us will be informed as soon as the films are ready for the market."

48. Musser, *Emergence of Cinema*, 255–57; Ramsaye, *Million and One Nights*, 299–302, 390–91.

49. *Clipper* ad, April 17, 1897, 115.

50. *Clipper*, April 24, 1897, 134. Thomas Armat failed in his try to have Veriscope exhibitions halted by the courts. *New York Dramatic Mirror*, July 10, 1897, 14.

51. Ad in *Clipper*, May 1, 1897, 146.

52. Ad in *Clipper*, May 15, 1897, 180.

53. Ads in *Clipper*, May 29, 1897, 214, and June 5, 232.

54. Ramsaye, *Million and One Nights*, 288; Musser, *Emergence of Cinema*, 201; Ephraim Katz, *The Film Encyclopedia* (New York: Perigee, 1979).

55. Lubin's 1897 Corbett-Fitzsimmons production is labeled "Unidentified. LACMNH [Los Angeles Museum of Natural History] #9. Early Boxing Film. 38' 190?" The 35 mm print (Library of Congress shelf number FEA 6392) runs thirty-three seconds at 18 feet per second.

56. John Rickards Betts, "Sports Journalism in Nineteenth-Century America," *American Quarterly* 5, no. 1 (Spring 1953): 56.

57. For the Fourth of July crowds, New Orleans exhibitors added *The Great Hall and Mitchell Glove Contest*. Breard, "A History of the Motion Pictures,"

1–35; *New Orleans Times Picayune,* June 26–27 and July 4–5, 1897; Blake McKelvey, "The Theater in Rochester during Its First Nine Decades," *Rochester History,* July 1954, 22.

58. Musser, *Emergence of Cinema,* 169; "Corbett Sues Edison," *New York Tribune,* April 30, 1897. Edison sued Veriscope for patent infringement. *New York Herald Tribune,* February 24, 1898. "The Great Corbett Fight and Knockout" was advertised in the *Bakersfield Californian* as part of a May 29, 1897, presentation of Edison motion pictures. The local press, then and a century later, mistook it for the actual *Corbett-Fitzsimmons Fight.* See Gilbert Gia, "The Fight of the Century in Bako," *The Blackboard,* May 2003, www.theblackboardfreepress.com (accessed June 1, 2005).

59. *Clipper* ad, May 1, 1897, 150. The May 29 edition included an ad from a New York exhibitor: "6 Corbett-Fitzsimmons Counterpart Films for Sale. Used Once," 215. The Nickelodeon in Boston solicited films and noted "Corbett Fitzsimmons counterpart preferred," *Clipper,* June 19, 1897, 264.

60. Musser, *Emergence of Cinema,* 202.

61. Charles H. Tarbox, *Lost Films, 1895–1917* (Los Angeles: Film Classic Exchange, 1983), 28–29; "Arthur Hotaling Recalls the 'Good Old Days,' " *MPW,* July 15, 1916, 380–81; *Post,* June 20, 1897.

62. Musser, *Emergence of Cinema,* 200–208.

63. The $750,000 figure is given by William A. Brady in *Fighting Man* (Indianapolis, IN: Bobbs-Merrill, 1916), 131–48. Musser cites the lower, net profit amount (*Emergence of Cinema,* 200). Prior to the premiere, the first Veriscope press screening had to be postponed because the Academy of Music lacked the direct-current electrical power the projector required ("Self-Defense," *Philadelphia Item,* May 15, 1897).

64. "Fitz Fouled Jim Corbett," *Examiner,* May 13, 1897.

65. W. W. Naughton, "Apropos of that Fitzsimmons Foul," *Examiner,* May 14, 1897. The phrase is used again in "Shadows of Fitz and Corbett," *Examiner,* July 13, 1897.

66. Dion Boucicault, *The Octoroon* (New York: n.p., 1861), 32; David Krause, ed., *The Dolmen Boucicault* (Chester Springs, PA: Dolmen Press, 1965), 25; Townsend Walsh, *The Career of Dion Boucicault* (New York: Dunlap Society, 1915), 64–68. The familiar line might have been suggested by William Brady, who had acted in this scene.

67. Naughton, "Apropos of that Fitzsimmons Foul."

68. "Here's What the Veriscope Discloses," *Examiner,* May 29, 1897. The *Clipper* noted the "assertions made by irresponsible people, which were emphasized by alleged veriscope reproductions in certain sensational newspapers" [i.e., the *New York World*]. "The 'can't tell a lie' veriscope pictures," it was said, "proved" the allegations about Fitzsimmons' foul wrong. "The Championship Fight Reproduced," *Clipper,* May 29, 1897, 214.

69. Musser, *Emergence of Cinema,* 48–49; Gordon Hendricks, *Eadweard Muybridge: The Father of the Motion Picture* (New York: Grossman, 1975).

70. *Examiner,* July 13, 1897.

71. Brady, *Showman*, 179–81; Edward Van Every, *Muldoon* (New York: Frederick A. Stokes, 1929), 231–33. If Brady was describing the Veriscope's opening night, his story is at odds with contemporary reviews. The *New York Tribune*, for example, said that during the sixth round, "the crowd became so much excited that the lecturer who was explaining the incidents had to give it up" ("The Veriscope Shows the Fight," *New York Tribune*, May 23, 1897). The *New York Journal* did not mention Brady but reported that Muldoon caused an uproar by rising midway through the screening to shout, "What the announcer just told you . . . is a mistake" (*Journal* report, reprinted in "Objections from Muldoon," *Philadelphia Item*, May 27, 1897).

The methods of manipulation in cinematography and projection became standard in moving-picture primers. C. Francis Jenkins observed that objects "can be photographed slowly and afterwards reproduced rapidly, thus falsifying the record." He added: "In a fisticuff encounter, when the knockdown is struck the vanquished fighter falls in the most leisurely manner imaginable" (*Animated Pictures*, 77–78). Elsewhere, he made a schematic drawing of the Jenkins-Armat projector that showed a boxing film being projected on a screen. See *"United States v. Motion Picture Patents Co.,"* reprinted in *Film History* 1, no. 3 (1987).

72. For example, the "look of agony" on Corbett's face as he hits the canvas—a description the San Francisco paper (July) ascribed to the New York press (May)—was a phrase repeated in advertisements in Dallas (October) and in a New Orleans review. See reviews in *Examiner*, July 13, 1897; *Dallas Time Herald*, October 21, 1897; *New Orleans Picayune*, March 28, 1898.

73. *Clipper*, April 24, 1897, 134.

74. "Chas. P. Scribner Killed," *NYT*, June 7, 1897; *Clipper*, April 24, 1897, 128; Musser, *Emergence of Cinema*, 199; Carl Louis Gregory, "The Early History of Wide Films," *American Cinematographer*, January 1930, 5. In November 1902, profits from the Corbett-Fitzsimmons pictures were still being contested. *The Veriscope Company v. William A. Brady*, City Court of New York, 39 Misc. 835; 81 NYS 498 (1902).

75. Curt Dalton, *When Dayton Went to the Movies* (1999), www .daytonhistorybooks.citymax.com (accessed June 23, 2005), citing 1897 *Dayton Journal* coverage.

76. "The 'Veriscope,' " *NYT*, May 26, 1897; *Examiner*, July 12, 1897; *Clipper*, May 29, 1897, 214; *New York Tribune*, May 23, 1897; "Success of the Veroscope," *San Francisco Chronicle*, July 13, 1897; *New Orleans Democrat*, March 28, 1898; and Musser, *Emergence of Cinema*, 199. In the midst of its first Chicago run, the *Chicago Tribune* noted: "Complete new films were received from the Veriscope company, taken from the new process of reproduction. . . . They are immensely clearer than the first batch" ("Grand Opera House," June 20, 1897). The July 25 *San Francisco Chronicle* reported likewise: "The lights and projecting machine have been improved during the last weeks" at the San Francisco Orpheum.

77. Police arrested the managers and boxers at the Academy of Music exhibition bout between Mike Leonard and George Dixon. "Dixon and Leonard

Arrested," *NYT*, August 20, 1895; Luc Sante notes that the "old-line Academy" for the rich "jumped class," becoming a vaudeville theater. *Low Life: Lures and Snares of Old New York* (New York: Farrar, Straus, Giroux, 1991), 86.

78. "The Veriscope Exhibited," *New York Dramatic Mirror*, May 29, 1897, 13; "The Championship Fight Reproduced," *Clipper*, May 29, 214; "The Veriscope Shows the Fight," *New York Tribune*, May 23.

79. Musser, *Emergence of Cinema*, 221–23; Charles Musser and Carol Nelson, *High-Class Moving Pictures: Lyman H. Howe and the Forgotten Era of Traveling Exhibition* (Princeton, NJ: Princeton University Press, 1990). Musser applies the term "operational aesthetic" from Neil Harris, *Humbug: The Art of P. T. Barnum* (Boston: Little, Brown, 1973).

80. "Said at the Theaters," *Post*, September 19, 1897.

81. Review in *New Orleans Picayune*, March 28, 1898, cited in Breard, "A History of the Motion Pictures."

82. Musser, *Emergence of Cinema*, 512; Dartnell, *"Seconds Out!"* 133. Henry V. Hopgood observed: "In practice there is no limit to the length of scene capable of reproduction if so minded, one could sit out a three-quarter hour prize-fight at the Aquarium" (*Living Pictures: Their History, Photo-Production and Practical Working* [London: Optician and Photographic Trades Review, 1899], 231). Hopgood also indicates that the London print of the film was adapted for a different projection system: "This apparatus [the "Anglo-Continental Company's 'Kinematograph'"] was used by the Aquarium for the exhibition of the celebrated prize-fight, the negatives of which were secured by 'the Veriscope.' " (166).

83. Waller, "Situating Motion Pictures," 12–28; "Introducing the 'Marvellous Invention' to the Provinces: Film Exhibition in Lexington, Kentucky, 1896–1897," *Film History* 3, no. 3 (1989): 223–34. Waller also cites "A Knock-Out," *Lexington Herald*, March 24, 1897; items in the *Lexington Herald*, September 27, 1897; and *Lexington Leader*, October 1, 1897.

84. *Twenty-third Annual Meeting of the Women's Christian Temperance Union of Rhode Island* (Providence: Providence Press, 1897), 11; Breard, "A History of the Motion Pictures," 48.

85. *Dallas Morning News*, October 10, 23–29, 1897; "Corbett and Fitzsimmons," October 25; *Dallas Times Herald*, October 6, passim.

86. "William S. (Doc) Waddell [*nee* William Shackleford Andres, 1863–1952]," July 23, 1952, in *Variety Obituaries* (New York: Garland, 1988); "Doc Waddell Dies," *NYT*, July 17, 1952. The "bishop of the Big Top" also began "lecturing and exhibiting in opera houses" with Edison pictures in 1896.

87. Musser (*Emergence of Cinema*, 200, 299–301) charts the Searchlight Theater of Tacoma. The Searchlight was using 35 mm projection in 1901, so it is unclear whether it screened Lubin's *Corbett-Fitzsimmons* or a reduction print of the Veriscope recording. A temporary storefront show of *Corbett-Fitzsimmons* was presented during the 1897 Toronto Industrial Exhibition. Gerald Pratley, *Torn Sprockets* (Newark: University of Delaware Press, 1987), 18.

88. Miriam Hansen, "Individual Responses," *Camera Obscura* 20–21 (1989–90): 179. Hansen's other writings on *Corbett-Fitzsimmons* include

"Reinventing the Nickelodeon: Notes on Kluge and Early Cinema," *October* 46 (1988): 178–98; "Adventures of Goldilocks: Spectatorship, Consumerism and Public Life," *Camera Obscura* 22 (1990): 51–72; and *Babel and Babylon: Spectatorship in American Silent Film* (Cambridge, MA: Harvard University Press, 1991).

Overviews of scholarship on female audiences for cinema include "The Spectatrix," special issue, *Camera Obscura* 20–21 (1989–90); Antonia Lant and Ingrid Periz, eds., *Red Velvet Seat: Women's Writings on the First Fifty Years of Cinema* (London: Verso, 2006); Jennifer M. Bean and Diane Negra, eds., *A Feminist Reader in Early Cinema* (Durham, NC: Duke University Press, 2002); Shelley Stamp, *Movie-Struck Girls: Women and Motion Picture Culture after the Nickelodeon* (Princeton, NJ: Princeton University Press, 2000); and Janet Staiger, *Interpreting Films* (Princeton, NJ: Princeton University Press, 1992).

89. Musser, *Emergence of Cinema,* 200; "View the Carson Fight," *Trib,* June 9, 1897; "Women and Men See the Big Fight," *Trib,* June 13, 1897.

90. "The Shadows of the Corbett and Fitzsimmons Fight," *Examiner,* July 18, 1897; "Corbett and Fitzsimmons," *Dallas Morning News,* October 25, 1897; *New Orleans Picayune,* March 28, 30, 1898; *New Orleans Democrat,* March 30, 1898.

91. Tooker promoted *The Black Crook,* the 1866 Broadway spectacle featuring chorus girls in flesh-colored tights, by inventing a "public indignation build-up." He was also a respected member of the political, press, and theatrical establishments in New York. Brady, *Showman,* 131–33; Tooker obituary, *NYT,* July 8, 1896.

92. Waller, "Situating Motion Pictures," 17–18.

93. *Twenty-third Annual Meeting of the WCTU,* 11.

94. "Annie Laurie" (pseudonym of Winifred Black), quoted in Barbara Belford, *Brilliant Byline: A Biographical Anthology of Notable Newspaperwomen in America* (New York: Columbia University Press, 1986), 140. Belford gives no specific date for Black's 1892 *Examiner* story but adds: "It was said she was the first woman to report a prize fight."

95. Nat Fleischer and Sam Andre, *A Pictorial History of Boxing* (New York: Citadel Press, 1959), 62–63; *Gazette,* February 18, 1899, 10. Brady alludes to a woman who smuggled herself into the 1892 Corbett-Sullivan fight in men's clothing (*Showman,* 77). See also "Woman Would See Prize Fight," *New York Herald,* August 23, 1898; "Sporty Young Woman at the Bouts," *Gazette,* May 26, 1900, 8. The movie *Opportunity* (Metro, 1918) recycled the tale as a comedy, in which a young, athletic woman dresses in her brother's clothes in order to attend a prizefight that her father has forbidden her to see.

96. "Two Women Fight with Gloves in Approved Pugilistic Style," *Gazette,* November 17, 1894, 3; *Gazette,* January 19, 1895, 5. Steven A. Riess, "Sport and the Redefinition of American Middle-Class Masculinity," *International Journal of the History of Sport* 8, no. 1 (1991): 16–22.

97. Sen. John J. Ingalls, "The Blow a Fluke," *Examiner,* April 4, 1897; Sammons, *Beyond the Ring,* 54–55; Lardner, *Legendary Champions,* 104.

98. T. J. Williams, "One Punch Was Worth a Fortune," *Examiner,* March 18, 1897; Hansen, *Babel and Babylon,* 10.

99. Timothy J. Gilfoyle, *City of Eros: New York City, Prostitution, and the Commercialization of Sex, 1790–1920* (New York: Norton, 1992).

100. "Corbett and Fitzsimmons," *Examiner,* April 1, 1897.

101. Robert C. Allen, *Horrible Prettiness: Burlesque and American Culture* (Chapel Hill: University of North Carolina Press, 1991), 186; Hansen, "Adventures of Goldilocks," 52; B. F. Keith, "The Vogue of Vaudeville," *National Magazine,* November 1898.

102. Waller cites advance publicity telling "those thousands of ladies and gentlemen who, in a quiet way, take a keen interest in sporting matters" that Veriscope shows were "perfectly proper." Musser cites the *Boston Herald* as describing them as "quite the proper thing" for ladies (*Emergence of Cinema,* 200, 512). See also "Dramatic and Musical," *San Francisco Chronicle,* July 18, 1897.

103. Hansen, "Reinventing the Nickelodeon," 190; Musser, *Emergence of Cinema,* 200.

104. "The Matinee Girl," *New York Dramatic Mirror,* June 12, 1897, 14.

105. Hansen, "Adventures of Goldilocks," 52.

106. "Was It Another Fake Fight?" *Philadelphia Item,* August 31, 1900; Kurt Gänzl, *William B. Gill: From The Goldfields to Broadway* (London: Routledge, 2002), 271–72; "Mrs. Fitzsimmons Tells How She Will Star with the Pugilist in a Fight Play," *New York World,* September 9, 1900.

107. "Robert Fitzsimmons in the 'The Honest Blacksmith,' " *Post,* April 14, 1901; "Ex-champion Fitz in Paint and Powder," *Los Angeles Times,* November 3, 1902; "Fitz Accused by Wife," *Post,* April 17, 1901.

108. "Alice Rix at the Veriscope," *Examiner,* July 18, 1897.

109. *The Bay of San Francisco, The Metropolis of the Pacific Coast and Its Suburb Cities: A History,* vol. 2 (Chicago: Lewis Publishing, 1892), 313, lists William Rix (b. 1863, San Francisco) as a lawyer and son of the San Francisco settler Alfred Rix. *Woman's Who's Who of America* (New York: American Commonwealth, 1914), 691, cites Harriet Hale Rix (b. 1863, San Francisco), a socialist suffragist, as the daughter of Hale and Alice Pierson (Locke) Rix. G. S. Rix, in *Genealogy of the Rix Family* (1906), 95, identifies Hale (1828–1903/4) and Alice Locke Rix as a New Hampshire couple who moved to San Francisco following the gold rush of 1849. Alice Rix bore four daughters between 1855 and 1863.

110. Belford, *Brilliant Byline,* 2–5; Phyllis Leslie Abrahamson, *Sob Sister Journalism* (New York: Greenwood, 1990).

111. Antonia Lant, "Individual Responses," *Camera Obscura* 20–21 (1989–90): 217–19. "Spectatrix" was also the nom de plume of a theater reviewer for the *London Daily News* in the 1890s.

112. Thomas Waugh, "Strength and Stealth: Watching (and Wanting) Turn of the Century Strongmen," *Canadian Journal of Film Studies* 2, no. 1 (1991): 1–20.

113. Gilfoyle, 135–36. Gerald Early writes that boxing's spectacle of "male bodies often locked in embrace" represents only a "latent homosexuality" denied

by most of its audience and participants. In its violence, prizefighting arguably "becomes virulently antihomosexual theater" ("James Baldwin's Neglected Essay: Prizefighting, the White Intellectual, and the Racial Symbols of American Culture," in *Tuxedo Junction* [New York: Ecco Press, 1989], 189).

114. "Women and Prizefights," *MPW*, July 13, 1907, 374.

3. UNDER THE LIGHTS

1. Steven A. Riess, "In the Ring and Out: Professional Boxing in New York, 1896–1920," in *Sport in America*, ed. Donald Spivey (Westport, CT: Greenwood, 1985), 99–106. Riess puts the number of fights held in New York under the Horton law at 3,350. See also Jeffrey T. Sammons, *Beyond the Ring* (Urbana: University of Illinois Press, 1988), 22.

2. John Barnes, *The Rise of the Cinema in Great Britain* and *Pioneers of the British Film* (London: Bishopsgate, 1983); Hauke Lange-Fuchs, *Birt Acres* (Kiel: W. G. Mühlau, 1987); Vanessa Toulmin, *Randall Williams, King of Showmen* (East Sussex, U.K.: Projection Box, 1998); *Clipper*, March 4, 1899, 14.

3. *International Photographic Films*, winter 1897–98, 21.

4. The Selig Polyscope Company *1903 Complete Catalogue* (22, 24) described its *Prize Fight* as one in which "two bad coons" fight, with the knockout victim getting hosed with water to revive him. Biograph wrote of *Chuck Connors vs. Chin Ong:* "A lively set-to with the gloves, between the well-known Bowery character and a new Chinese aspirant for pugilistic honors. The fighting is exciting and very funny . . . the Chinese champion is knocked down three times." Connors was described by the *Police Gazette* as "Mayor of Chinatown, Bowery Boy, ex-knuckle pusher, sport, guide," and author of the book *Bowery Life*. "Chuck's Big Night at Tammany Hall," *Gazette*, February 10, 1906, 6.

5. Sam C. Austin, "Interest in the Big Fight at Fever Heat," *Gazette*, June 17, 1899, 11; Riess, "In the Ring and Out," 101.

6. Sam C. Austin, "Lively Bidding for the Jeffries-Sharkey Fight," *Gazette*, July 29, 1899.

7. Charles Musser, "The American Vitagraph, 1897–1901: Survival and Success in a Competitive Industry," in *Film before Griffith*, ed. John L. Fell (Berkeley: University of California Press, 1983), 22–66; Rex Lardner, *The Legendary Champions* (New York: American Heritage, 1972), 126.

8. Albert E. Smith and Phil A. Koury, *Two Reels and a Crank* (Garden City, NJ: Doubleday, 1952), 13–14; William A. Brady, *Fighting Man* (Indianapolis, IN: Bobbs-Merrill, 1916), 181–82.

9. "Fight Takes Place at Night," *Examiner*, May 23, 1899; "The Films that Failed; Emergency Experiences in Trying to Electrically Illuminate a Prize Fight," *Phonoscope*, May 1899, 14.

10. "Fitzsimmons and Jeffries Will Fight a Square Fight," *Gazette*, June 3, 1899, 11.

11. "Fitzsimmons and Jeffries Will Fight," 11; "Corbett-Sharkey Fiasco," *NYT*, November 24, 1898.

12. W. W. Naughton, "When Once in the Ring the Principals Intend to Punch Diligently without Posing for the Picture Machine," *Examiner,* May 31, 1899.

Boxers posed for cameras on the eve of the fight. Reporters following Jeffries' hour-by-hour regimen wrote that after lunch on June 7, "the Vitascope artists appeared and the next four hours were spent in posing for pictures which are to be exhibited in connection with the fight. The first picture taken represents Jeffries tossing the medicine ball to his brother, Jack, Jim Daly and Tommy Ryan. He knocks all three down with hard throws. . . . Other pictures taken represent Jeffries jumping the rope and being rubbed down" (H.H.D., "Both Big Men Supremely Confident," *Inquirer,* June 8, 1899).

13. "Politics Inspire Devery to Threaten the Finish of the Fight," *Examiner,* June 8, 1899; Brady, *Fighting Man,* 170. The most influential figure in Tammany's control of the boxing underworld was the politician Timothy D. ("Big Tim") Sullivan, "the boss of the Bowery." One of the most powerful men in New York, he owned theaters, ran a gambling operation, and was "the head of a syndicate that controlled and exacted tribute from every prize fight in the city" during this period. Harold C. Syrett, *The Gentleman and the Tiger: The Autobiography of George B. McClellan, Jr.* (Philadelphia: Lippincott, 1956), 252. The police chief, William Devery, was a Tammany crony who had a reputation for not enforcing gambling and prizefight laws. A noted sportsman, in 1903 he and his gambling partners purchased the New York Yankees baseball team. Riess, "In the Ring and Out," 100.

14. Charles Michaelson, "Vitagraph Mars View," *Examiner,* June 10, 1899; Julian Hawthorne, "Crowd at Ringside Viewed by Novelist," *Examiner,* June 10.

15. "Scenes at the Island Ringside," *Examiner,* June 10, 1899; "Jeffries Wins the Boxing Championship of the World," *Philadelphia Ledger,* June 10; Smith and Koury, *Two Reels and a Crank,* 14–15.

16. Austin, "Interest in the Big Fight at Fever Heat," 11.

17. "Jeffries Wins from Fitzsimmons," *NYT,* June 10, 1899.

18. "Topics of the Times," *NYT,* June 25, 1899.

19. Sam C. Austin, " 'Fake' Photographs of the 'Fitz'-Jeffries Fight," *Gazette,* August 5, 1899, 11.

20. Ad in *Clipper,* July 8, 1899, 380.

21. *Clipper,* August 12, 1899, 474, and August 19, 502. These *Clipper* ads do not mention the participation of Jeffries or Fitzsimmons. The tale-spinning John V. Grombach says "the two boxers were brought back at a later date to try to re-create the fight. . . . officially for the movies" (*The Saga of the Sock* [New York: A. S. Barnes, 1949], 58).

Pieces of two different films survive that appear to be reenactments of the Fitzsimmons-Jeffries bout; neither features the original participants. The Library of Congress print (FEB 4779, *Reproduction of the Fitzsimmons-Jeffries Fight,* 1899) is identified as Lubin's, although the catalog misidentifies the boxers as the real Jeffries and Fitzsimmons. A second piece of archival film, Harry Chapin's documentary *The Legendary Champions* (*Turn of the Century Fights,*

1968), purports to be a Jeffries-Fitzsimmons recreation. Further complicating proper identification, Lubin also shot a reenactment of the 1902 Jeffries-Fitzsimmons rematch.

22. "Jeffries on the Casino Roof," *NYT,* June 18, 1899.

23. " 'Bob' Fitzsimmons Acts with Admirable Discretion," *Gazette,* July 8, 1899, 11.

24. "Threatened Trouble over the McGovern-Palmer Match," *Gazette,* August 19, 1899, 11.

25. Charles Musser, *Before the Nickelodeon* (Berkeley: University of California Press, 1991), 139–40.

26. Ad in *Clipper,* September 9, 1899, 571.

27. "M'Govern-Palmer Contest Was Postponed by a Storm," *Gazette,* September 23, 1899, 3; Musser, *Before the Nickelodeon,* 139–40.

28. "McGovern Beats Palmer," *Gazette,* September 30, 1899, 2; Austin, "Palmer's Boxing Talent Was No Match for M'Govern's Fighting Quality," *Gazette,* September 30, 11.

29. Sam C. Austin, "Sharkey and Jeffries to Select a Battleground," *Gazette,* September 16, 1899, 11; G. W. Bitzer, *Billy Bitzer: His Story* (New York: Farrar, Straus, and Giroux, 1973), 4.

30. Sam C. Austin, "Sharkey and Jeffries to Select a Battleground," *Gazette,* September 16, 1899, 11.

31. American Mutoscope and Biograph Catalogue, 1903, film nos. 1308–9.

32. "Clandestinely Took Pictures of the Fight," *Examiner,* November 6, 1899; "Pictures Taken by Stealth," *Gazette,* November 25, 1899, 11; Musser, "American Vitagraph," 50.

33. *Clipper,* November 4, 1899, 752.

34. "Clandestinely Took Pictures of the Fight," 7; "Row over Fight Pictures," *New York World,* November 9, 1899; "Jeffries-Sharkey Pictures," *NYT,* November 10; ad in *Clipper,* November 18, 797.

35. Ad in *Clipper,* December 2, 1899; George C. Pratt, "No Magic, No Mystery," in *"Image" on the Art and Evolution of the Film,* ed. Marshall Deutelbaum (New York: Dover, 1979), 45.

36. "Brady and O'Rourke Win," *Clipper,* December 30, 1899, 924. "Pictures Attached; Suit against Exhibition of Jeffries-Sharkey Fight Pictures," *Hartford Courant,* January 13, 1900.

37. F. M. Prescott, *Catalogue of New Films,* Supplement no. 3, November 20, 1899; *Clipper,* November 18, 1899, 802, 804, and November 25, 828.

38. "Pictures Taken of the Fight Are a Great Success," *Gazette,* December 2, 1899, 7, 10; Sam C. Austin, "Biograph in Trouble," *Gazette,* November 25, 11. Frame enlargements of the film were captioned "Copyright, 1899, by the American Mutoscope and Biograph Company," in *New York World,* November 11 and 14; *New York Journal,* November 11.

39. *Clipper,* October 7, 1899, 651, November 18, 792; "Jeffries Dodged Arrest," *New York World,* November 8; "Biograph Fight Pictures," *NYT,* November 21.

40. Several New York dailies ran stories titled "Round New York in 80 Minutes": *NYT,* October 28; *World,* November 5, 7; and *Herald,* November 5, 26. See also "Jeffries and Sharkey Pose as Roman Gladiators," *Journal,* December 11.

41. George W. Lederer, "New York Theatre," *Clipper,* November 25, 1899, 814; "Spectators Applaud Sharkey," *Gazette,* December 9, 8.

42. Ads in *Clipper,* November 18, 1899, 799, 887. Musser estimates that there were at least six traveling Biograph units (*Emergence of Cinema,* 203).

43. Lillie Devereaux Blake, "Brutality, says Mrs. Blake, in Prize Fight Pictures; She Sees the Sharkey-Jeffries Biograph Exhibition and Couldn't Stand the 'Hideous Brutality,' " *New York World,* November 21, 1899; "Prizefighting Attacked," *NYT,* December 19, 1899.

44. Ads in *Examiner,* February 11, 12, 16, 1900.

45. Sam C. Austin, "Corbett as a Fender to Fight Jeffries," *Gazette,* December 9, 1899, 11.

46. Ad in *Examiner,* February 11, 1900.

47. "Sharkey Loses to Jim Jeffries," *Gazette,* November 18, 1899, 3; "Pictures Taken of the Fight Are a Great Success," *Gazette,* December 2, 7; "Biograph Pictures Success," *Clipper,* November 11, 771.

48. William A. Brady, *Showman* (New York: E. P. Dutton, 1937), 203; Brady, *Fighting Man,* 183; Pratt, "No Magic, No Mystery," 45.

49. Dan Parker, "Some Unwritten Fight History," in *POST Boxing Records, 1934 Boxing Records and Sports Annual,* ed. John J. Romano (New York: POST Sports Records, 1934), 11–12.

50. "Sharkey Looked the Winner," *New York World,* November 21, 1899.

51. "Big Earnings Made by Our Champion Pugilists," *Gazette,* June 8, 1901, 7; Austin, "Biograph in Trouble," 11; "Biograph Pictures Success," 771; "Jeffries and Corbett," *Gazette,* December 9, 1899, 7.

52. Ads in *Clipper,* March 3, 1900, 19, March 17, 66. Secondhand sales of the 35 mm non-Biograph *Jeffries-Sharkey* films were also advertised by a West Virginia exhibitor.

53. "Prize-Fighting Legislation," *Clipper,* March 10, 1899; "Horton Law Repealed," April 7, 134; Riess, "In the Ring and Out," 95–124.

54. Ad for *"Jeff" Skipping the Rope, Throwing the "Medicine Ball,"* and *Fun in the Training Quarters, Clipper,* April 21, 1899, 192; Ad in *Clipper,* April 7, 1900, 138.

55. "Sharkey and Fitzsimmons Probably at Coney Island," *Gazette,* March 24, 1900, 7, italics added.

56. Sammons, *Beyond the Ring,* 24–29; "Gov. Nash Takes Legal Steps," *Gazette,* February 16, 1901, 10.

57. "Jeffries Beat Ruhlin in Five Rounds," *Gazette,* November 30, 1901; Musser, *Before the Nickelodeon,* 157–92.

58. Jack London, "Gladiators of the Machine Age," *Examiner,* November 16, 1901.

59. W. W. Naughton, "Poor Fight from a Spectator's Point of View," *Examiner,* November 16, 1901.

60. "The Pictures of the Fight," *Examiner,* November 16, 1901.

61. Library of Congress, Print No. FLA 5499. Musser cites White as "lacking strong photographic skills" (*Before the Nickelodeon,* 154).

62. James White, testimony, May 4, 1910, quoted in Musser, *Before the Nickelodeon,* 191.

63. Edison Manufacturing Co., *Edison Films,* May 1902, 12–13, and September 1902, 27–29.

64. *New Orleans Democrat,* December 27, 1901, cited in Sylvester Quinn Breard, "A History of the Motion Pictures in New Orleans, 1896–1908" (master's thesis, Louisiana State University, 1951).

65. "Dan Stuart Will Bid," *Gazette,* November 24, 1900, 10; "Champion Boxers Matched," *NYT,* February 16, 1902; "In 8 Rounds Jeffries Whips Fitzsimmons," *NYT,* July 26, 1902.

66. "Horton Law Repealed," *Clipper,* April 7, 1900, 134.

67. W. W. Naughton, *Kings of the Queensberry Realm* (Chicago: Continental, 1902), 308.

68. "Jeffries Whips Corbett," *Gazette,* August 22, 1903, 1.

69. Jim Jacobs claimed that film existed of a Joe Walcott–Joe Gans fight from September 30, 1904 (from "a list of fight films from 1894 thru 1930," compiled by Jacobs, provided by Phil Guarnieri). Jacobs also wrote that he "had the opportunity to show the Jeffries-Monroe . . . fight to Jack Dempsey at his home" in 1960 (Jimmy Jacobs, "I Saw All of These Fights Tuesday Night," *The Ring,* September 1961, 47). There is no corroboration for these claims.

70. Selig Polyscope Company, *1903 Complete Catalogue,* 43.

71. Sam H. Harris (1872–1941) became one of New York theater's most powerful producers, with hits including *The Jazz Singer, Animal Crackers, Of Thee I Sing, Dinner at Eight, You Can't Take It with You,* and *The Man Who Came to Dinner.* Gerald Bordman, *The Concise Oxford Companion to American Theatre* (New York: Oxford University Press, 1987), 206–07.

72. Ad in *Clipper,* February 10, 1900, 1066; "Dixon Meets His Waterloo," *Clipper,* January 20, 986.

73. Ads in *Clipper,* April 7, 1900, 138, and March 31, 104.

74. "Fitzsimmons Won Fight," *NYT,* August 11, 1900.

75. "Fitzsimmons Beat Ruhlin in Six Rounds," *Gazette,* August 28, 1900, 7; "Ruhlin and Fitz To Get Pictures of the Fight in the Ring Again," *Gazette,* September 1, 10; "Fitzsimmons Again Victorious," *Clipper,* September 1, 595; ads in *Clipper,* September 8, 612, 622.

76. Lardner, *Legendary Champions,* 143; Nat Fleischer and Sam Andre, *A Pictorial History of Boxing* (New York: Citadel Press, 1959), 158; Musser, *Emergence of Cinema,* 290–92.

77. "M'Govern Wins a 'Fake' Fight," *Trib,* December 14, 1900; "Prohibit Prize Fighting," December 15; "Aims to Prohibit Prize Fights," December 16. The *McGovern-Gans Fight Pictures* I had presumed to be lost. However, a video copy of the complete Selig film was posted to YouTube.com on August 22, 2006.

This version opens with the title "Forrest Brown presents," a nontheatrical reissue done decades later.

78. "Joe Gans was an Easy Mark for Terry McGovern," *Gazette*, January 5, 1901, 11.

79. Selig Polyscope Company, *1903 Complete Catalogue*, 43.

80. "Referee Siler Freely Criticized," *Gazette*, January 12, 1901, 11.

81. "Gans-McGovern Affair Causes Mayor Harrison to Stop Boxing in Chicago," *Gazette*, January 19, 1901, 11; "Pictures Which Tell That Gans Failed to Try," *Gazette*, February 2, 10; George Siler, "Joe Gans Confesses," February 25, 1906, in *The Greatest Sport Stories from the Chicago Tribune*, ed. Arch Ward (New York: A. S. Barnes, 1953), 73–75. See also *Life, Battles, and Career of Battling Nelson, Lightweight Champion of the World, by Himself* (Hegewisch, IL: n.p., 1912), 220.

82. Ads in *Clipper*, December 29, 1900, 980, 986; Hurtig and Seamon ad, *Trib*, December 27; Musser, *Emergence of Cinema*, 276; Robert C. Allen, *Horrible Prettiness: Burlesque and American Culture* (Chapel Hill: University of North Carolina Press, 1991).

Burlesque was not the only arena that called for segregating audiences in order to promote the quasi-legitimate images of prizefighting. Often such films made their way to the sub rosa world of the carnival. Arthur Hotaling operated itinerant movie shows (which included fight reproductions) in 1896–97. He reported using "the old familiar device of the county fair man—the 'blow off' " to round up curious male audiences. "Word was passed that at half-past eleven in the evening we would run a show for men only and the boobs used to begin to gather shortly after ten." There the late-night fraternity would be shown burlesque-like material. "Arthur Hotaling Recalls the 'Good Old Days,' " *MPW*, July 15, 1916, 380.

4. FAKE FIGHT FILMS

1. Robert Darnton, *The Great Cat Massacre and Other Episodes in French Cultural History* (New York: Basic Books, 1984), 4–5.

2. Neil Harris, *Humbug: The Art of P. T. Barnum* (Boston: Little, Brown, 1973), 61–62; Jane Gaines, "From Elephants to Lux Soap: The Programming and 'Flow' of Early Motion Picture Exploitation," *Velvet Light Trap* 25 (1990): 31.

3. Samuel L. Clemens, "The Only True and Reliable Account of the Great Prize Fight, for $100,000, at Seal Rock Point, on Sunday Last, Between His Excellency Gov. Stanford and Hon. F. F. Low, Gov. Elect of California" (1863), in *The Wit and Humor of America*, vol. 5, ed. Kate Milner Rabb (Indianapolis, IN: Bobbs-Merrill, 1907), 1903–12.

4. Naomi Rosenblum, *A World History of Photography* (New York: Abbeville, 1981), 461.

5. *Benét's Reader's Encyclopedia of American Literature*, ed. George Perkins, Barbara Perkins, and Phillip Leininger (New York: HarperCollins, 1991), 772.

6. "The Great Fight at Carson," *Examiner*, May 25, 1897; "Kinetoscopic Glimpses of the Hawkins-Dixon Glove Contest," July 24, 1897; "Boxers Pose before 'The Examiner's' Camera to Portray the Great Championship Battle," November 4, 1899.

7. *Examiner*, July 8, 1902; August 16, 1903.

8. "After the Fight" and "Straight Left Reaches Jeffries' Chin," *Gazette*, December 2, 1899, 7, 10; "Solar Plexus Punch in the Second Round" and "Ruhlin Struggles to His Feet," *Gazette*, September 8, 1900, 10.

9. Miriam Hansen, *Babel and Babylon: Spectatorship in American Silent Film* (Cambridge, MA: Harvard University Press, 1991), 30–34.

10. "An Invention Disgraced," *New York Dramatic Mirror*, January 26, 1895. John Edward McCullough (1832–85) was committed to a mental institution in 1884 and released shortly before his death. Gerald Bordman, *The Concise Oxford Companion to American Theatre* (New York: Oxford University Press, 1987), 280.

11. "Fight Pictures That Are Fakes," *Examiner*, May 22, 1897.

12. C. H. Claudy, "The Degradation of the Motion-Picture," *Photo-Era*, October 1908, 161–65.

13. Harold Wentworth and Stuart Berg Flexner, eds., *Dictionary of American Slang* (New York: Crowell, 1975), 322; Charles Musser, *The Emergence of Cinema: The American Screen to 1907* (New York: Scribner's, 1990), 201 (citing *Phonoscope*, June 1897, 12).

14. "Arthur Hotaling Recalls the 'Good Old Days,' " *MPW*, July 15, 1916, 381.

15. "Through Lubin's Lens: A Silent Film Sampler," program notes, National Museum of American Jewish History (Philadelphia, 1984); H. Walter Schlichter, "The Name 'Lubin' Revives Memories of Posed Movies of Title Bout," *Inquirer*, November 3, 1940 (copies kindly provided by Joseph Eckhardt). Lubin also advertised the cineograph in *Scientific American*, December 11, 1897, 384.

16. For biographical information about Siegmumd Lubin, see Joseph P. Eckhardt, *The King of the Movies: Film Pioneer Siegmund Lubin* (Madison, NJ: Fairleigh Dickinson University Press, 1997); Linda Woal, " 'When a Dime Could Buy a Dream': Siegmund Lubin and the Birth of Motion Picture Exhibition," *Film History* 6, no. 2 (1994): 152–64; Joseph P. Eckhardt and Linda Kowall, *Peddler of Dreams: Siegmund Lubin and the Creation of the Motion Picture Industry, 1896–1916* (Philadelphia: National Museum of American Jewish History, 1984); Linda Kowall, "Siegmund Lubin: The Forgotten Filmmaker," *Pennsylvania Heritage*, Winter 1986, 18–21; Gene Fernett, *American Film Studios: An Historical Encyclopedia* (Jefferson, NC: McFarland, 1988), 130–36; *Lubin: Clear as a Bell*, video (n.p., 1980).

17. Eckhardt and Kowall, *Peddler of Dreams*, 4.

18. "The Championship Fight Reproduced," *Clipper*, May 29, 1897, 214, and June 5, 1897, 232.

19. A *Clipper* ad of September 4, 1897, 447, brought responses of "Fraud!" from Maguire and Baucus.

20. *Clipper,* May 28, 1898, 222; Kowall, "Siegmund Lubin," 20; Fernett, *American Film Studios,* 133; Terry Ramsaye, *A Million and One Nights* (1926; reprint, New York: Simon and Schuster, 1986), 377.

21. Musser, *Emergence of Cinema,* 224–61.

22. Ads in *Clipper,* December 3, 1898, 671, 686; "Corbett Loses to Sharkey on a Technicality," *Philadelphia Public Ledger,* November 22, 1898.

23. Ad in *Clipper,* December 17, 1898, 718.

24. "New Field For The Fighters," *Trib,* December 4, 1898. The report curiously erred in saying Lubin "declined an offer to photograph the Corbett-Fitzsimmons fight."

25. Ad in *Clipper,* January 28, 1899, 818, and February 4, 836.

26. *Philadelphia Public Ledger,* March 23, 1899; *New Orleans Picayune,* April 7, 23, 1899; *The Graphic* (London), August 5–September 30, 1899.

27. Musser, *Emergence of Cinema,* 284–85.

28. Ad in *Clipper,* August 19, 1899, 502. The print is *Reproduction of the Fitzsimmons-Jeffries Fight in Eleven Rounds Showing the Knock Out* [or *Knockdown*], Library of Congress, AFI/LACMNH Collection, FEB 4779, 190 feet, copyright S. Lubin; 12 June 1899. The catalog erroneously describes the film as "starring the original participants . . . verified by contemporary photos."

29. Schlichter, "The Name 'Lubin,' "; Rex Lardner, *The Legendary Champions* (New York: American Heritage Press, 1972), 126.

30. Eckhardt and Kowall, *Peddler of Dreams,* 2–6; Joseph P. Eckhardt and Linda Kowall, "The Movies' First Mogul," in *Jewish Life in Philadelphia,* ed. Murray Friedman (Philadelphia: Institute for the Study of Human Issues, 1983), 18–21; Fernett, *American Film Studios,* 132.

31. Ramsaye, *Million and One Nights,* 288.

32. The first "complete set of films" consisted of 1,700 feet "showing the knockout" and was priced at $250 (ads in *Clipper,* July 1, 1899, 360). Lubin then offered "the Six Most Important Rounds for $125" (*Clipper,* August 19, 1899, 502), and later a 1,200-foot version ($180) and a 600-foot cut for $90 (*Clipper,* September 9, 1899, 572).

33. "Reproduction of Film Exposed 40 Years Ago," *American Cinematographer* 20, no. 12 (December 1939): 546, misidentifies the film as being a record of the authentic fight, even though the daylight cinematography is supposed to be a recording of an event it describes as having occurred indoors at night. Did A. B. Hager also think he was exhibiting genuine fight pictures forty years earlier?

34. Notice in *Inquirer,* June 29, 1899.

35. *Clipper,* June 24–August 12, 1899. See also Roger William Warren, "History of Motion Picture Exhibition in Denver, 1896–1911" (master's thesis, University of Denver, 1960).

36. "Sea Side Gossip," *Inquirer,* June 25, 1899.

37. "Those 'Fake' Jeffries-Fitzsimmons Pictures Again," *Gazette,* August 19, 1899, 11.

38. Sam C. Austin, " 'Fake' Photographs of the 'Fitz'-Jeffries Fight," *Gazette,* August 5, 1899, 11.

39. Kemp R. Niver, "From Film to Paper to Film," in *Wonderful Inventions,* ed. Iris Newson (Washington, DC: Library of Congress, 1985), 199–209; Erik Barnouw, "Introduction," xv, and "Preface," in Kemp R. Niver, *Early Motion Pictures: The Paper Print Collection in the Library of Congress* (Washington, DC: Library of Congress, 1985), xv, ix–xii. Reproductions of Lubin's 35mm film strips were published, for example, in his *Jeffries and Sharkey* ad (*Clipper,* November 25, 1899, 828).

Patrick G. Loughney documents that in 1896 and early 1897, motion picture copyright registration included the deposit of "duplicate copies of short pieces of positive nitrate film" of four to six frames each ("A Descriptive Analysis of the Library of Congress Paper Print Collection and Related Copyright Materials," PhD diss., George Washington University, 1988, 60). I thank George Willeman for providing access to two Lubin copyright deposit booklets.

40. André Gaudreault, "The Infringement of Copyright Laws and Its Effects (1900–1906)," in *Early Cinema: Space-Frame-Narrative,* ed. Thomas Elsaesser (London: British Film Institute, 1990), 114.

41. Loughney, "A Descriptive Analysis," 168; ads in *Clipper,* September 16, 1899, 596; September 23, 1899, 620. C. Francis Jenkins described copyright practice at the time: motion picture titles were registered along with "short pieces of film," but two full-length copies of each subject were also deposited some time later. "If no copies are filed, the copyright is void and a penalty of $25 incurred" (*Animated Pictures* [Washington, DC: H. L. McQueen, 1898], 93–94).

42. Ad in *Clipper,* September 16, 1899, 596.

43. Gaudreault, "The Infringement of Copyright Laws," 114–22; Musser, *Emergence of Cinema,* 330–31.

44. Gregory A. Waller documents that a presentation of the "International Cineograph film of the eleven-round Jeffries-Fitzsimmons fight was not accorded any special treatment" ("Situating Motion Pictures in the Prenickelodeon Period: Lexington, Kentucky, 1897–1906," *Velvet Light Trap* 25 [1990] 17–18).

45. Ads in *Clipper,* November 25, 1899, 828.

46. "Brady and O'Rourke Win," *Clipper,* December 30, 1899, 924.

47. Gus Hill's Tammany Tigers, for example, carried Lubin's *McGovern-Dixon* pictures. Ads in *Clipper,* February 10, 1900, 1052.

48. Ads in *Clipper,* February 17, 1900, 1092, and February 24, 1113. It is unclear what Lubin meant by "made." The first ad for the genuine films appeared a month after the fight, but there is no evidence that the pictures released in April were anything other than those taken at ringside on January 9.

49. Ads in *Clipper,* February 10, 1900, 1066; March 17, 72; May 26, 304; "Pictures of the Fight Are a Great Success," *Gazette,* December 2, 1899, 7.

50. Ads in *Clipper,* May 26, 1900, 304, and June 16, 363.

51. Selig Polyscope recorded the suspicious bout and released the *McGovern-Gans Fight Pictures;* Lubin did not attempt to film the fight or a reenactment. See "Philadelphia Sports Are Coming," *Trib,* December 11, 1900.

52. "Fitz Beats Ruhlin in Six Rounds," *Gazette,* August 25, 1900, 7; Slick, "Fitzsimmons Beats Ruhlin," *Philadelphia Item,* August 11; George Siler, "Big

Fight to Be Kinetoscoped," *Trib,* August 4; "Fitz-Ruhlin Pictures," *Brooklyn Eagle,* August 5.

53. Slick said that Lubin "and Jack Foley [Frawley], his assistant took moving pictures of the fight. No intense light was shed over the scene as in the Jeffries-Sharkey fight, and if they are a success they will be a credit to Mr. Lubin's improved methods" ("Fitzsimmons Beats Ruhlin," *Philadelphia Item,* August 11, 1900).

Before the original bout, the *New York Journal* reported: "Pictures, if possible, will be taken of the battle. Failing this, arrangements have been made to have Fitz and Ruhlin show their daily training camp life and work before the moving picture machine as soon after the battle as practicable" ("Ruhlin Off to Garden," August 10, 1900). After the reenactment, it mentioned: "An effort was made to take pictures of the fight there, but the light was not strong enough" ("Ruhlin and Fitz Go Over Big Fight," *New York Journal,* August 14, 1900).

54. "Notes Taken at Ringside," *Philadelphia Record,* August 11, 1900.

55. George Siler, "Ruhlin's Lack of Condition," *Trib,* August 12, 1900.

56. "Fitz and Sharkey to Meet Next," *Philadelphia Item,* August 13, 1900.

57. "Fitz and Ruhlin Fight the Fight Over Again," *Inquirer,* August 14, 1900. Lubin's share of the profits was 25 percent, as were shares for Fitzsimmons and for Ruhlin. See Sam Austin, "Jeffries Raises Trouble," *Gazette,* April 21, 1900, 11

58. "Big Fight Reproduced," *Record,* August 14; "Fitzsimmons and Ruhlin in a Bogus Fight before the Camera," *Philadelphia North American,* August 14, 1900; "Fitzsimmons and Ruhlin 'Fight' Six Rounds on the Roof of an Arch Street Building," *Philadelphia Press,* August 14, 1900 (the accompanying image was captioned "The Knock-Out, Enlarged from a cineograph film taken during the reproduction of the fight in this city yesterday"). The *Pittsburg Press* was dismissive, saying pictures of reenactments would always be "counterfeits pure and simple" ("Fake Pictures of the Fight," August 13, 1900). Cropped versions of these photos ("copyrighted by S. Lubin") appeared in the *Gazette* on September 8, 1900, 10.

59. "Ruhlin and Fitz to Get Pictures of the Fight in the Ring Again," *Gazette,* September 1, 1900, 10.

60. Ads in *Clipper,* September 8, 1900, 612, 622, and September 15, 635.

61. Notice in *Inquirer,* August 24, 1900.

62. "Inquirer Gave First News of the Fight to Thousands," *Inquirer,* August 25, 1900.

63. The idea was not totally unknown, however. Philadelphia's Lyceum burlesque house provided "returns by rounds" of the Jeffries-Corbett fight during its run of the *McGovern-Dixon Fight* (which was followed by a "Tobascope" presentation of the *Reproduction of the McCoy-Maher Fight*). *Inquirer,* May 11, 13, 1900.

64. Jenkins says the process "for rapidly producing announcements of current events, as war news, elections, etc. etc., on a lantern canvas, is to write the desired amounts with a typewriter, as needed, on transparent gelatine or film,

and while the ink is still moist to dust it over with a tuft of cotton dipped in finely divided lamp black, soot, or the like" (*Animated Pictures*, 90).

65. "Read 'The Examiner' Bulletins of the Fight," *Examiner*, November 1, 1899, 14; "Immense Crowds Watch for the Results on 'The Examiner' Bulletins," *Examiner*, November 4, 1899, 3.

66. "Athletic Woman," *Inquirer*, June 15, 1899.

67. Notice in *Inquirer*, August 30, 1900.

68. "Inquirer's News of the Fight Away Ahead of All Others," *Inquirer*, August 31, 1900.

69. "Marvelous Work, Lubin Has Placed the World within Reach of the Humblest," *Inquirer*, August 31, 1900.

70. The articles in Philadelphia newspapers publishing photos on September 5, 1900, included "Corbett and M'Coy Fight in Professor Lubin's Sky Parlor," *North American;* "Corbett and McCoy Reproduce their Fight Before the Camera," *Press;* and "Fake Fight Reproduced," *Record.* Also, "Journal Camera Snaps Corbett and M'Coy in the Ring," *New York Journal*, September 5.

John Durant and Edward Rice, *Come Out Fighting* (New York: Essential Books, 1946), 54, reprints a Corbett-McCoy Lubin photo with the incorrect caption "before Edison's motion picture camera." The same image is reprinted in Nat Fleischer and Sam Andre, *A Pictorial History of Boxing* (New York: Citadel Press, 1959), 158.

71. "Big Pictures Taken of the Fight between Corbett and M'Coy," *Gazette*, September 22, 1900, 11.

72. Ads in *Clipper*, October 6, 1900, 720, and December 8, 920.

73. "Was the Corbett-McCoy Fight a Prearranged Fake?" *Gazette*, September 29, 1900, 4; "Jeffries and Sharkey," *Gazette*, December 1, 1900, 10.

74. Although the origin of the phrase "the real McCoy" is disputed, W. W. Naughton applied it to Norman "Kid McCoy" Selby in 1899. Robert Cantwell's *The Real McCoy: The Life and Times of Norman Selby* (Princeton, NJ: Vertex, 1971), also presents erroneous information about *Corbett-McCoy* and fight films. If some thought McCoy was acting for the cameras when he took a dive, then it is apropos that his post-ring career included acting in Hollywood feature films between 1916 and 1930.

75. "Faking as a Fine Art," *Gazette*, June 22, 1901, 7.

76. Sam Austin's comments before the Fitzsimmons-Jeffries bout exemplify this tendency:

In my opinion the kinetoscope picture business is responsible for whatever belief exists that a hippodrome affair is contemplated. The management has made no secret of its intentions to have a photographic reproduction of the fight made for exhibition purposes. The public argues that if the affair is ended quickly, say in a round or two, the pictures will be comparatively valueless for exhibition. It will be remembered that after Corbett was defeated by Fitzsimmons he made a statement . . . that if he had not had an arrangement with

Dan Stuart and the veriscope people to get at least five rounds of the fight in a picture he would have beaten Fitzsimmons in the first two or three rounds. In all his conversations with me Corbett blamed the veriscope affair for his defeat.

"Fitzsimmons and Jeffries Will Fight a Square Fight," *Gazette,* June 10, 1899, 11.

77. Jack London, *The Abysmal Brute* (New York: Century, 1913), 32, 65–66, 116. The story appeared originally as a syndicated newspaper serial in 1911.

78. Musser, *Emergence of Cinema,* 330.

79. *Lubin's Films* [ca. 1901; 1906], 12–13.

80. Library of Congress 35 mm film print FEB 7596, *Corbett Fight Film ("Big Fight"),* appears to be Lubin's *Reproduction of Jeffries and Corbett* (1903). The mise-en-scène, framing, and action match that of *Reproduction of Fitzsimmons-Jeffries* (1899), and the actors resemble Jeffries and Corbett.

81. *Lubin's Films,* June 1904, 25.

82. Library of Congress print FLA 5660, 1903, 640 feet; Musser, *Emergence of Cinema,* 337–38.

83. "Bulletin No. 7," June 1, 1903, in *Biograph Bulletins, 1896–1908,* ed. Kemp R. Niver (Los Angeles: Locare, 1971), 85.

84. Niver, *Early Motion Pictures,* 210. Charles Keil brought this film to my attention.

85. Robert C. Allen, *Horrible Prettiness: Burlesque and American Culture* (Chapel Hill: University of North Carolina Press, 1991), 265. During this period, burlesque consisted of a "variety show with comics, song & dance girls, acrobats, and boxing and wrestling matches." Charles McGraw, *The Encyclopedia Americana: International Edition* (Danbury, CT: Grolier, 1990), 801.

86. The Library of Congress holds three items associated with this fight. *Nelson-Britt Fight for Lightweight Championship, San Francisco, Sept. 9th, 1905,* copyrighted by Miles Bros., September 15, 1905 (registration number H65558), is a panorama photograph of the arena. *Nelson-Britt Prize Fight* (copyright September 27, 1905, H66202 through H66206) is the Miles recording of the entire event, viewable as a 16 mm reference print (LC shelf numbers FLA 5596 through 5599). Lubin received copyright number H66293 on September 29 for his *Impersonation of Britt-Nelson Fight.* However, the reference print (FLA 5934, taken from a paper-print original) that is identified as Lubin's *Impersonation* is an identical copy of the opening portion of the Miles film.

When Lubin premiered his film (apparently not the dupe but the reenactment), it was advertised as "First Presentation Anywhere of the Great Moving Picture Reproduction of the Recent Britt & Nelson Championship Fight at Colma, Cal. Most successful and Realistic Life Motion Pictures ever taken of a championship battle. Pictures taken and exclusively exhibited under the direction of Prof. S. Lubin" (*Inquirer,* September 17, 1905).

87. Sylvester Quinn Breard, "A History of the Motion Pictures in New Orleans, 1896–1908," master's thesis, Louisiana State University, 1951.

88. Biograph catalog, 1906.

89. *Variety,* February 29, 1908, 12.

90. Nat Fleischer, *The Michigan Assassin: The Saga of Stanley Ketchel* (New York: C. J. O'Brien, 1946), 81.

91. Epes Winthrop Sargent, "New York City Holds Record for Earliest Exhibiting," *MPW,* July 15, 1916, 371.

5. FIGHT PICTURES IN THE NICKELODEON ERA

1. The collector Jim Jacobs amassed some seventeen thousand boxing films, but he exaggerated about his impressive collection. Phil Guarnieri, a fight film collector, graciously provided a list of his own holdings, as well as information about Jacobs (personal correspondence, February 29, 1992). Jimmy Jacobs, " 'I Saw All of These Fights Tuesday Night,' " *The Ring,* September 1961, 28–29, 47; Jacobs obituary, *NYT,* March 24, 1988; "Collector's Films of Boxing's Glory Days Still Pack a Punch," *Los Angeles Times,* January 16, 1986.

2. Eileen Bowser, *The Transformation of Cinema, 1907–1915* (New York: Scribner's, 1991); Charlie Keil and Shelley Stamp, eds., *American Cinema's Transitional Era: Audiences, Institutions, Practices* (University of California Press, 2004); Richard Koszarski, *An Evening's Entertainment: The Age of the Silent Feature Picture, 1915–1928* (New York: Scribner's, 1990).

3. *MPW,* October 12, 1907, 516; Janet Staiger, "Combination and Litigation: Structures of U.S. Film Distribution, 1896–1917," *Cinema Journal* 23, no. 1 (1983): 41–72.

4. Patrick G. Loughney, "A Descriptive Analysis of the Library of Congress Paper Print Collection and Related Copyright Material," PhD diss., George Washington University, 1988, 355. Fred J. Balshofer and Arthur C. Miller mention Dobson's working for Miles around 1907–8, "photographing what we today call industrial films . . . [including] sporting events" (*One Reel a Week* [Berkeley: University of California Press, 1967], 11).

5. Herbert LeRoy Miles (1867?–1941) might have been born about a year earlier. Henry "Harry" J. Miles (1867–1908) is "H. J. Miles" in Biograph credits. The *AFI Catalog* and others conflate them as "Herbert J. Miles." The younger brothers were Earle C. and Joseph Ralph Miles. Max Alvarez, personal correspondence, June 5, 2006. Alvarez generously shared his research notes, including his interview with Herbert's son Bill Miles of July 11, 1990.

Terry Ramsaye, *A Million and One Nights* (1926; reprint, New York: Simon and Schuster, 1986), 401–3; Charles Musser, *The Emergence of Cinema: The American Screen to 1907* (New York: Scribner's, 1990), 312, 367; George Kleine, letter to Benjamin Hampton, September 12, 1927, in the George Kleine Collection, Manuscripts Division, Library of Congress (calling "Herbert Miles of the Pacific Coast" one of "two or three early exchange men" predating the nickelodeon); "Miles Brothers, Pioneers," *MPW,* July 10, 1915, 248; T. A. Church, "San Francisco, Cal., Dates Back to the Year 1894," *MPW,* July 15, 1916, 399–400; George M. Cheney, "New Orleans, La., Records Wonderful Development,"

MPW, July 15, 1916, 403. According to Loughney, Miles Bros. "made, on a contract basis, a significant number of the scenic and travel films that were copyrighted under the Edison name. The Edison Company was either uninterested in buying boxing films or was unable to induce the Miles Brothers to sell the rights" ("A Descriptive Analysis," 168). Robert Grau describes the firm as "one of the earliest moving-picture concerns in the country and active factors in every phase of the industry almost from the outset of the evolution" (*The Theatre of Science* [New York: Broadway Publishing, 1914], 17).

6. "$1,000, No. 00," *MPW*, April 27, 1907, 116; Miles Brothers ad in first issue of *MPW*, March 9, 1907, 16.

7. "The Evolution of Exhibiting," *MPW*, July 15, 1916, 368; Musser, *Emergence of Cinema*, 417, 424; Charles Musser, *Before the Nickelodeon* (Berkeley: University of California Press, 1991), 374; Max Alvarez, "The Origins of the Film Exchange," *Film History* 17, no. 4 (2005): 431–65.

8. *MPW*, August 17, 1907, 384.

9. Mayer's Orpheum was in Haverhill, Massachusetts. Eric Foner and John A. Garraty, eds., *The Reader's Companion to American History* (New York: Houghton Mifflin, 1991), s.v. "Mayer, Louis B."

10. "Miles Brothers, Inc. (amusement enterprises)" listed its directors as Harry and Herbert Miles and H. Heaton Van Matre. *NYT*, November 20, 1907. Items in *MPW* include the following: May 4, 1907, 136; November 13, 1907, 298; and November 16, 1907, 604. Miles Brothers commercial photography was still active in California. Oxoniensis, "Winter Motoring in California," *Overland Monthly and Out West Magazine*, March 1907, 3.

11. "Plunged to Death in a Fit," *NYT*, January 2, 1908; *Film Index*, January 11, 1908; *Billboard*, January 25, 1908, 17. Another hindrance was an alleged case of industrial sabotage. Two employees were arrested for grand larceny when a cashier confessed to a scheme involving stealing reels and sending "junk heap" and "repeater" film prints to "subscribers." This was at the behest of an unnamed rival company. "Miles Bros.' Late Employees," *MPW*, November 9, 1907, 577.

12. "Herbert Miles—A Picture Pioneer," *MPW*, March 19, 1910, 416. Herbert Miles testified for the government in *United States v. Motion Picture Patents Co.* (1915). "Brief for the United States," reprinted in *Film History* 1, no. 3 (1987): 241, 248, 260.

13. "Fight in Coffroth's Arena," and "Tex Rickard's Bid for Fight Accepted," *NYT*, December 3, 1909. Because of Miles and Coffroth, fight films became for a time synonymous with their town. In 1911 the *Moving Picture News* mistakenly attributed the genre's origins to "the first fight [film] made in San Francisco fourteen or fifteen years ago." "Those Fight Pictures," *Moving Picture News*, September 30, 1911, 6.

14. W. W. Naughton, "Fifty-Five Thousand for Fighter Who Gains the Day," *Examiner*, September 1, 1905.

15. *Nelson-Britt Prizefight*, Library of Congress, print no. FLA 5596. The wide photo appeared as "made exclusively for the Examiner" and copyrighted by the Miles Brothers, *Examiner*, September 10, 1905, reprinted in Battling

Nelson, *Life, Battles and Career of Battling Nelson, Lightweight Champion of the World* (Hegewisch, IL: n.p., 1912).

16. The action in the corner is only partly visible on the 16 mm reduction print at the Library of Congress, although the outer portion of the 35 mm original may have been cropped. No reviewers complained of missing the dramatic knockout.

17. A card marked "LL" is visible in the right-hand corner of the ring in an image captioned "Snap Shot Photograph of the Finish of the Britt-Nelson Fight," *Examiner*, September 10, 1905. Also, a young man holding a card with the legend "U" appears in a photo taken from the Miles camera platform at the 1906 Gans-Nelson fight, reproduced in Nat Fleischer and Sam Andre, *A Pictorial History of Boxing* (New York: Citadel Press, 1959), 248.

18. "Film Showing Fight Toned and Fixed," *Examiner*, September 12, 1905.

19. W. W. Naughton, "Britt More Than Ever Convinced That He Was Victim of Lucky Punch," *Examiner*, September 24, 1905; E. B. Lenhart, "Jimmy Britt Says He Made an Awful Fool of Himself," September 27, 1905.

20. Jack London, "Brain Beaten by Brute Force," *Examiner*, September 10, 1905.

21. Ashton Stevens, "May Irwin and 'Some Sons,' " *Examiner*, September 3, 1905; "The Ladies Press Button on Jimmy," September 1.

22. *Examiner*, September 25, 1905; "Fight Views Operated Nicely," September 26.

23. E. B. Lenhart, "Fight Fotos Give the Women Some Idea of a Queensbury Contest; Boxing Photos Please the Women," and "Some Questions Answered," *Examiner*, September 25, 1905; "$7000 Corruption Fund Was Raised to Kill Ralston's Anti-Prizefight Bill [in California Senate]," September 14.

24. Sam C. Austin, "Terry and Young Corbett," *Gazette*, November 4, 1905, 10.

25. Shown at Greenwall's Theatre, New Orleans, November 20–26, 1905, with vaudeville. From January 7 to 14, 1906, a "special attraction" of *The Original Britt-Nelson Fight Pictures* accompanied the play *The Devil's Daughter:* "$500 will be paid to anyone who can prove that these are not the original pictures taken at Colma, California, September 9." Sylvester Quinn Breard, "A History of the Motion Pictures in New Orleans, 1896–1908" (master's thesis, Louisiana State University, 1951), 215–16); Roger William Warren, "History of Motion Picture Exhibition in Denver 1896–1911" (master's thesis, University of Denver, 1960).

26. Sam C. Austin, "Britt and Nelson Still Wrangling over Money Matters," *Gazette*, January 27, 1906, 10, reported Nelson was owed $5,666 on the fight pictures. Nelson claimed: "I sold my interest in the fight pictures to the manager of the club for $5000. I never received a cent of this picture money. . . . Later I was presented with one set of films of this fight." Nelson, *Life, Battles and Career*, 175.

27. "Gans is Slight Favorite to Win over Nelson," *Gazette*, September 1, 1906, 10; Nat Goodwin, *Nat Goodwin's Book* (Boston: Badger, 1914), 294.

28. T. P. Magilligan, "Larry Sullivan as an Orator," *Gazette*, September 29, 1906, 10. A similar anecdote indicating the crowd's familiarity with ringside cameras is noted by Musser: according to the *New York World*, a fan shouted at the president's son, "Show yourself and turn your face toward the moving pictures" (*Emergence of Cinema*, 484). However, the referee, George Siler, wrote: "Theodore Roosevelt Jr was not present, all reports to the contrary notwithstanding" ("Goldfield Wants Gans and Britt," *Trib*, September 5, 1906).

29. Charles Samuels, *The Magnificent Rube: The Life and Gaudy Times of Tex Rickard* (New York: McGraw-Hill, 1957), 145. Rickard's wife reported the following exchange with her husband:

WIFE: "You and I know that the best people don't go to prize-fights."

TEX: "Someday fine ladies may be goin' to see prize-fighting."

Mrs. Tex Rickard with Arch Oboler, *Everything Happened to Him* (New York: Frederick A. Stokes, 1936), 208

30. "Gans Is Slight Favorite," *Gazette*, September 1, 1906, 10; "Gans Wins from Nelson on a Foul," September 15, 1906, 3; "Teddy Roosevelt, Jr. Saw Gans-Nelson Fight," *NY World*, September 4, 1906. .

31. "Moving Pictures Will Show Foul Blow Nelson Struck," *Gazette*, October 10, 1906, 10. When the films began their public run in New York, the fight was cut to the first twenty and the final six rounds, making up a feature-length presentation. "New York Sports See Pictures of Goldfield Battle," *Gazette*, October 29, 1906, 10. According to an initial report, "It was announced that the moving-picture films had given out at the end of the 38th round so that the final [blow] will not be shown" ("Gans and Nelson May Fight Again for Championship," *NY Journal*, September 5, 1906).

32. "New York Sports See Pictures of Goldfield Battle," 10; "Will Fight Pictures Answer?" *Post*, October 8, 1906; Nelson reproduces the drawing, captioned "Was It a Foul? The Exact Blow Which Lost Nelson His Fight With Gans" (Nelson, *Life, Battles and Career*, 208).

33. "Nolan and Battling Nelson in the Picture Squabble," *Gazette*, December 15, 1906, 10; "Gans and Nelson Agree," *Post*, November 30, 1906; Robert C. Allen, *Horrible Prettiness: Burlesque and American Culture* (Chapel Hill: University of North Carolina Press, 1991), 191–92.

34. "Women and Prize Fights," *MPW*, July 13, 1907, 374.

35. *MPW*, March 30, 1907, 62.

36. "Pictures of Burns-O'Brien Fight Are Great," *Gazette*, December 19, 1906, 10; *MPW*, May 18, 1907, 176.

37. Sime [Silverman], "Miles Bros.' Film. 'Gans-Herman Fight," *Variety*, January 19, 1907.

38. *Jim Jeffries on His California Ranch* and *Squires, Australian Champion in His Training Quarters* were copyrighted June 8, 1907. The deposit print of *International Contest for the Heavyweight Championship: Squires vs. Burns* (copyright July 18, 1907) contains no footage other than the single-camera shot

of the ring where the introductions, fight, and celebration occur. Two title cards differentiate it from previous films. The first identifies "Miles Bros. New York and San Francisco" as the producers and includes a logo of a setting sun with the initials MB. The second title card, which precedes the boxing, reads "The Shortest and Fiercest Contest on Record."

39. *MPW*, July 13, 1907, 304.

40. Illustrations of the Stanley Ketchel–Jim Thomas contest in Colma on Labor Day 1907 depict the presence of a motion-picture camera. Nat Fleischer, *The Michigan Assassin* (New York: C. J. O'Brien, 1946), 38.

41. *MPW*, August 24, 1907, 400; Musser, *Before the Nickelodeon*, 377; Bowser, *Transformation of Cinema*, 27–28.

42. Sime. "Burns-Moir Fight," *Variety*, December 21, 1907; "The Moir-Burns Fight," *MPW*, October 26, 1907, 686.

43. Sime., "Gans-Nelson Fight," *Variety*, September 26, 1908; "Nelson-Gans Fight at Chicago [sic]," *Bioscope*, November 13, 1908, 4.

44. "More Fight Films," *MPW*, March 13, 1909, 299.

45. Ad in *Billboard*, August 14, 1909, 13.

46. *MPW*, February 12, 1910, 211; *MPW*, May 21, 1910, 841; *Bioscope*, December 7, 1911, 711; "A National Board of Censorship," *MPW*, June 19, 1909, 825–26; Staiger, "Combination and Litigation," 50–56.

47. Church, "San Francisco," 400. Geoffrey C. Ward found documentation (in the *Chicago Examiner*, July 11, 1912) of Miles Bros. shooting the Johnson-Flynn fight, and kindly shared it (personal correspondence, November 6, 2003).

48. Joseph and Herbert's Atlas Film venture was quashed by Edison legal actions in 1911. Herbert created the short-lived Republic Film, which became the International Education Film Company in 1912 (the same year he was arrested for bigamy). In 1913 and 1914, the two brothers operated the Exclusive Supply Company with the producer-director Herbert Blaché and Great Northern's Ingvald Oes. Joseph had better fortune with his Joe Miles Library ("Miles of Stock Shots") and Lloyds Film Exchange through the teens, and then with Lloyds Film Storage Corporation. These became the Progress Film Company, one of the major stock footage companies outside Hollywood in the 1920s and 1930s. Herbert Miles filed another bankruptcy petition for Miles Bros. in 1917. He was a dealer in educational films when another fire struck his holdings in 1922. *MPW*, November 18, 1911; *NYT*: "Arrest Herbert L. Miles," November 30, 1912; "Miles Bros., Inc. in Bankruptcy," June 29, 1917; "Film Blaze," September 19, 1922; Anthony Slide, *Nitrate Won't Wait* (Jefferson, NC: McFarland, 1992), 140; Alvarez, "Origins of the Film Exchange," 448; and Alvarez, personal correspondence, June 5, 2006.

49. Titles include *Buffalo Bill's Wild West and Pawnee Bill's Far East* (1910); *[Ernest Shackleton's South Pole Expedition]* (Gaumont, 1910); *Picturesque Colorado* (1911); two versions of *With Captain Scott, R.N., to the South Pole* (1911, 1912); *Coronation Pictures* (Kinemacolor, 1911); *Carnegie Museum Expedition [to Alaska]* (1912); *Paul J. Rainey's African Hunt* (1912) and *Rainey's African Hunt* (1914); *Mexican Revolution* (1912); Pathé's *Olympic Games at Stockholm* (1912), *Panama Canal Pictures* (Kinemacolor, 1912); *Witney and*

Scott Hunting in the Arctic (1913); *Pendleton Oregon Roundup* (1913); *Jack London's Adventures in the South Sea Islands* (1913); *Frontier Celebration (in Honor of Theodore Roosevelt)* (1913); *How Wild Animals Live* (1913); and *Mexican War Scenes* (1913). A variety of other films were released around 1910 through 1912 with footage of Roosevelt, British royalty, and the Delhi Durbar of India. Daniel G. Streible, "Origins of the Feature Film: 1897–1913" (master's thesis, University of Texas at Austin, 1987).

50. *MPW*, May 1, 1909, 572, 575; June 12, 1909, 811; *New York Dramatic Mirror*, May 8, 1909, 15, 17. Joseph Miles noted in *Motion Picture News*, April 18, 1914, 30.

51. "Battling Nelson Pays for Pictures," *Nickelodeon*, July 6, 1909, 8.

52. *MPW*, January 2, 1909, 90; "More Fight Films," March 13, 299; August 14, 290; *Billboard*, May 8, 1909, 14; *Moving Picture Annual and Yearbook for 1912* (New York: MPW, 1912), 16.

53. *MPW*, March 19, 1910, 411; "Langford and Flynn Pictures," *MPW*, April 30, 688; "Fight Picture Held Back in New York City," *Variety*, July 9, 4; "Clash on Pictures of Wolgast Fight; Hammerstein Advertised Them for His Theatre and Now Loses License of Company," *NYT*, March 23.

The success of *Wolgast-Nelson* was widespread but varied by region. In Chicago, "a local moving picture agent" purchased Nelson's interest in the film for $15,000. With the victory by Adolph Wolgast, a Milwaukee resident, the pictures received positive treatment in Wisconsin. The *Nelson-Wolgast Fight* was the first featured motion picture at the Fuller Opera House in Madison, the state capital's first regular movie venue. W. W. Naughton, "Wolgast to Take Rest; Nelson Gone to Chicago," *Examiner* February 24, 1910, 9; *Wisconsin State Journal*, March 26, 1910, cited in Janet Staiger, "The Fuller Opera House: A Transition from Theater to Cinema" (unpublished MS, 1977).

54. *Bioscope*, May 26, 1910, 34; *MPW*, March 4, 1911, 486.

55. *MPW*, June 24, 1911, 1418; "Kilbane's Easy Victory," *NYT*, March 6, 1912; article describing Columbia Amusement Enterprises, Cleveland, opening its New York headquarters by exploiting the Kilbane Attell prizefight, *Bioscope*, March 28, 1912, 911.

56. *Moving Picture Annual and Yearbook for 1912*, 110; "Wolgast Holds Title," *NYT*, July 5, 1912.

57. *Prohibition of Interstate Transportation of Pictures and Descriptions of Prize Fights: Hearing before the Committee on Interstate and Foreign Commerce*, 61st Cong., 2nd sess., May 17, 1910, 3–9; "Battling Nelson Is Held in Chicago," *NYT*, February 26, 1927. Nelson's interest in his reels later took an obsessive form. In 1927, police arrested him for allegedly stealing a print—from Butte, Montana—of his filmed loss to Ad Wolgast in 1910. He was put under "psychopathic" observation, but cleared.

58. "A Pugilistic Panorama: Johnson Ketchel Moving Pictures," *Bioscope*, December 23, 1909, 58; "Johnson-Ketchel Fight Goes to Gaumont's," *Bioscope*, February 3, 1910, 15. A figure comparable to Harvey was R. S. Edmondson, manager of American Film Releases in England. In 1911, *Bioscope* published a

full-page drawing depicting him as a giant leading boxers by the hand, saying, "He has successfully exploited several famous fight films" (*Bioscope* supplement, September 28, 1911, xxvii).

59. *Bioscope*, July 11, 1912, 13; October 3, 1912, 59.

60. *MPW*, July 29, 1911, 251; Charles Harvey, letter to George Kleine, August 9, 1911, in George Kleine Collection. (Harvey had also just been made the founding secretary of the New York State Athletic [i.e., Boxing] Commission. *NYT*, July 28, 1911.) The Kleine Optical Company retained the New York and New Jersey rights to *Johnson-Ketchel*. "The Fight Pictures in New York," *MPW*, January 8, 1910, 54.

61. The list included Biograph's *Jeffries-Sharkey Contest* (1899, 6 reels); Lubin's reproductions of *Jeffries-Sharkey* (1899, 4 reels) and *Corbett-Jeffries* (1899, 4 reels); *Root and Gardner* (1903, 3 reels); *Nelson-Britt* (1905, 5 reels), *Gans-Nelson* [I] (1906, 5 reels), *O'Brien-Burns* (1906, 8 reels), *Gans-Herman* (1907, 3 reels), *Gans-Nelson* [II] (1908, 5 reels); *Nelson-Gans* [III] (1908, 4 reels); *Burns-Johnson* (1909, 5 reels); *Johnson-Ketchel Fight* (1909, 4 reels); and *Nelson-Wolgast Fight* (1910, 4 reels).

62. Michael Quinn, "Distribution, the Transient Audience, and the Transition to the Feature Film," *Cinema Journal* 40, no. 2 (2001): 49. State-rights distribution also abetted fly-by-night schemers, companies said to be part of "a 'bunco' game" and fleecing " 'hayseeds.'" ("The Feature Film," *Moving Picture News*, June 22, 1912, 1, and June 29, 6).

63. "Funny Facts about the Johnson-Ketchel Fight Films," *MPW*, January 8, 1910, 54.

64. Hugh Hoffman, "The Father of the Feature," *MPW* July 11, 1914, 272–73; Bowser, *Transformation of Cinema*, 192–93; Epes Winthrop Sargent, "The Special Release," *MPW*, February 24, 1912, 666. On the transition to feature films and the role of states' rights, see Quinn, "Distribution," 35–56.

65. *Film Index* item reprinted in *Bioscope*, December 30, 1909, 25

66. Editorials in *MPW*, July 29, 1911, 184; August 19, 1911, 436; September 6, 1913, 1043. See also Bowser, *Transformation of Cinema*, 121, 191–216; Janet Staiger, "Blueprints for Feature Films," in *The American Film Industry*, ed. Tino Balio (Madison: University of Wisconsin Press, 1985), 185–89; William Uricchio and Roberta E. Pearson, *Reframing Culture: The Case of the Vitagraph Quality Films* (Princeton, NJ: Princeton University Press, 1993).

67. Sargent, 666; "The Special Release and the Small Exhibitor," *MPW*, September 30, 1911, 965. Sargent (also known as Chicot or Chic.) was a cofounder of *Variety* and the author of *The Technique of the Photoplay* (1912) and *Picture Theatre Advertising* (1915).

68. Tom Gunning, *D. W. Griffith and the Origins of American Narrative Film* (Urbana: University of Illinois Press, 1991), 152; "Says Picture Shows Corrupt Children," *NYT*, December 24, 1908.

69. Gunning, *D. W. Griffith*, 151. George Brinton McClellan Jr., son of the Union Army general who ran as the Democratic challenger to Abraham Lincoln's reelection, counted among his political enemies "Big Tim" Sullivan of Tammany

Hall. Sullivan aligned with the exhibitors because he was a stakeholder in theaters. Harold C. Syrett, *The Gentleman and the Tiger: The Autobiography of George B. McClellan, Jr.* (Philadelphia: Lippincott, 1956), 252.

70. "Police Act as Critics," *NY Tribune*, December 27, 1908.

71. Garth Jowett, *Film: The Democratic Art* (Boston: Little, Brown, 1976), 126; "The Standards of the National Board of Censorship," (1909), in National Board of Review of Motion Pictures Records, New York Public Library; Charles V. Tevis, "Censoring the Five-Cent Drama," *World Today*, October 1910, in *The Movies in Our Midst*, ed. Gerald Mast (University of Chicago Press, 1982), 69.

72. Our Roving Commissioner, "The Motion Picture Exhibitors' League of America," *Moving Picture News*, June 22, 1912, 8, and June 29, 6.

73. *John Sloan's New York Scene*, ed. Bruce St. John (New York: Harper & Row, 1965); Guy Pène Du Bois, *John Sloan* (New York: Whitney Museum of American Art, 1931), 117.

74. Ben Singer, "Manhattan Nickelodeons: New Data on Audiences and Exhibitors," *Cinema Journal* 34, no. 3 (1995): 5–35; Roy Rosenzweig, *Eight Hours for What We Will: Workers and Leisure in an Industrial City, 1870–1920* (New York: Cambridge University Press, 1983), 191–221; Judith Mayne, "Immigrants and Spectators," *Wide Angle* 5, no. 2 (1982): 32–41; Kathy Peiss, *Cheap Amusement: Working Women and Leisure in Turn-of-the-Century New York* (Philadelphia: Temple University Press, 1986); Miriam Hansen, *Babel and Babylon: Spectatorship in American Silent Film* (Cambridge, MA: Harvard University Press, 1991); David Nasaw, *Going Out: The Rise and Fall of Public Amusements* (New York: Basic Books, 1993). Excellent review essays are Robert Sklar, "Oh, Althusser! Historiography and the Rise of Cinema Studies," *Radical History Review* 41 (1988): 10–35, and Janet Staiger, "Class, Ethnicity, and Gender: Explaining the Development of Early American Film," *Iris* 11 (1990): 13–25.

75. "Among the Theaters," *Nickelodeon*, August 1, 1910, 80.

76. "At 'Stag' Houses Only," *NY Tribune*, July 11, 1910; J.B., Jr., "Will You Ever See Those Fight Pictures? That Depends," *NY Tribune*, July 10.

77. L.B., letter to the editor *MPW*, January 8, 1910, 53–54.

78. "Those Fight Pictures," 6.

79. "Fight Films," *Moving Picture News*, June 22, 1912, 8.

80. *Trib*, July 7, 1910.

81. J.M.B., "On the Big Fight," *MPW*, July 16, 1910, 194.

82. "Fight Pictures on the Mississippi," *Nickelodeon*, January 7, 1911, 12. The existence of this "smoker circuit" was well known. John Collier wrote: "A few obscene films are always being secretly passed around for private exhibition before festive gatherings of men" ("Censorship; and the National Board," *The Survey*, October 2, 1915, 9).

83. "Among the Theaters," 80. Similar arguments were reported from British sources. "Our London Correspondent" said to American exhibitors: "Truth to tell, fight films are not great drawing cards here. Many showmen will not feature them, realizing that many members of their audiences do not like them." *Moving Picture News*, October 28, 1911, 27.

84. *Billboard*, August 14, 1909, 13; "At 'Stag' Houses Only," 3.

85. *MPW*, July 6, 1907; J. A. Lindstrom, "'Almost Worse than the Restrictive Measures': Chicago Reformers and the Nickelodeons," *Cinema Journal* 39, no. 1 (1999): 90–112.

86. "'Man About Town' on the Jeffries-Johnson Fight," *MPW*, July 16, 1910, 191; *MPW*, July 23, 1910, 201; "Save the Children!" *NY Tribune*, July 9.

87. "The Rochester Play Congress," *Survey*, July 2, 1910, 563.

88. "Morality and Film Censorship," *Nickelodeon*, January 7, 1911, 12.

89. "National Board of Censor of Moving Pictures," *NYT*, May 14, 1911; "National Censorship of Motion Pictures," *Survey*, July 1, 1911, 470.

90. Tevis, "Censoring the Five-Cent Drama," 70. Some members of the censorship board sought to censor prizefights. While Collier was issuing press statements tolerant of them, some civic groups that had representatives on the board were taking a stand against fights. The Juvenile Protective League and the Children's Aid Association criticized "the ridiculous practice of prohibiting prize fights . . . [while] showing pictures of prize fights" ("Moving Pictures in Indianapolis," *Survey*, July 23, 1910, 614).

91. Vachel Lindsay, *The Art of the Moving Picture* (New York: Liveright, 1915, 1970), 231. Apparently it was the interracial aspect of the film that Lindsay found insulting, as he published a poem celebrating the pugilistic glory of John L. Sullivan.

6. JACK JOHNSON FILMS

1. Jacqueline Najuma Stewart, *Migrating to the Movies: Cinema and Black Urban Modernity* (Berkeley: University of California Press, 2005).

2. W. W. Naughton, *Kings of the Queensberry Realm* (Chicago: Continental, 1902), 9. The poem "The Art of Self Defense" is attributed to the Australian poet Adam Lindsay Gordon.

3. Gordon Hendricks, *The Edison Motion Picture Myth* (1961), reprinted in *Origins of the American Film* (New York: Arno Press, 1972), 195.

4. Frank Lewis Dyer et al., *Edison, His Life and Inventions*, vol. 2 (New York: Harper, 1929), 543.

5. Francis Trevelyan Miller, *Thomas A. Edison: Benefactor of Mankind* (Chicago: J. C. Winston, 1931), 230.

6. Matthew Josephson, *Edison* (New York: McGraw-Hill, 1959), 393.

7. "No Prizefight on Vermont," *NYT*, August 3, 1909; "Boxed on Vermont; Dead," *NYT*, August 2, 1909.

8. *Edison Films*, July 1904, 29.

9. "Ruhlin & Maher in Fast Bout," *Gazette*, January 5, 1901, 7.

10. "Police Gazette Said Jeffries," *Gazette*, December 7, 1901, 10.

11. "Real Champion Gone," *Post*, August 11, 1910.

12. Jeffrey T. Sammons, *Beyond the Ring* (Urbana: University of Illinois Press, 1988), 14–15, 262; "The Negroes Good Fighters," *Freeman*, July 16, 1910.

The Canadian-born Dixon is identified as a "quadroon" in Denzil Batchelor, *Big Fight* (London: Phoenix House, 1954), 115–26.

13. "Fighters Draw Color Line," *Gazette*, December 3, 1904, 10.

14. "Colored Boxers Becoming Scarce," *Gazette*, November 3, 1906, 6.

15. "Joe Gans Cries Fraud but Admits He Faked," *Gazette*, March 10, 1906, 10; Peter Arnold, *History of Boxing* (Secaucus, NJ: Chartwell, 1985), 124–25; Nat Fleischer and Sam Andre, *A Pictorial History of Boxing* (New York: Citadel, 1959), 245–48.

16. "Almost a Lynching over Gans' Victory," *NYT*, September 5, 1906; "Race Riot over Prize Fight," *Trib*, September 4.

17. The Gans-Nelson film received "lots of attention" as part of a nickel show, according to the reporter who wrote "Women and Prize Fights," *MPW*, July 13, 1907, 374.

18. W. W. Naughton, "Colored Man Is Still Champion," *Richmond Planet*, October 23, 1909.

19. Editorial, *Baltimore Afro-American Ledger*, January 9, 1909. The *Afro-American Ledger* and *New York Age* did not accept theatrical advertisements, according to the theater critic Lester Walton (*New York Age*, October 14, 1914).

20. "Gans Says Moving Pictures Are Manipulated Unfairly," *New York Age*, October 25, 1906. (Thanks to Louise Spence for this reference.)

21. Ad in *Afro-American Ledger*, November 23, 1907.

22. Ad in *New Orleans Picayune*, November 26, 1906.

23. Battling Nelson, *Life, Battles and Career of Battling Nelson, Lightweight Champion of the World* (Hegewisch, IL: n.p., 1912), 158–60.

24. On October 11–17, 1908, the Baker Theater in Denver paired the *Gans-Nelson Fight* with an Uncle Tom company. Roger William Warren, "History of Motion Picture Exhibition in Denver 1896–1911" (master's thesis, University of Denver, 1960). An atavistic tale of blacks being beaten in the ring appears in Ernest Hemingway's "A Matter of Color" (1916). The narrator recollects that Joe Gans's first bout was fixed in such a way that "the smoke" was supposed to be backed up against a curtain and swatted on the head with a bat. *Hemingway in Michigan*, ed. Constance Cappel Montgomery (New York: Fleet, 1966), 47–49.

25. "Calciums' Glare Attracts Dane," *Trib*, September 11, 1908; *Nelson-Gans* ads in *MPW*, February 27, 1909, 236, and March 13, 299.

26. Randy Roberts, *Papa Jack: Jack Johnson and the Era of White Hopes* (New York: Free Press, 1983), 1–16. Unless noted otherwise, biographical information is from Roberts and from Geoffrey C. Ward, *Unforgivable Blackness: The Rise and Fall of Jack Johnson* (New York: Knopf, 2004).

27. "Champion Jeffries Sees No Logical Opponent," *Gazette*, October 8, 1904, 10; "Johnson, Negro Champion, Camps on Jeffries Trail," *Gazette*, November 5, 10.

28. Sam C. Austin, "Gans and Britt to Fight," *Gazette*, September 22, 1906, 10.

29. "Present Title Due to Manager," *Louisville Courier-Journal*, January 10, 1910; Rex Lardner, *The Legendary Champions* (New York: American Heritage

Press, 1972), 174; Maurice Golesworthy, *The Encyclopaedia of Boxing* (London: Haley, 1960), 85.

30. "Johnson Has Would-Be Champions on the Run," *Gazette*, December 8, 1906, 10.

31. "Three Judges for Boxing Matches," *NYT*, June 15, 1913. McIntosh discussed how motion pictures were affecting perceptions of the sport. "Even the moving pictures of a boxing bout give but one side of the battle. . . . As an experiment one time I had two picture machines rigged up to 'take' a bout at the stadium [in Australia]. One I placed at one side of the ring and the other directly opposite. It was surprising what a difference there was in the aspect of the bout as shown by the two films."

32. "Jack London Says Johnson Made a Noise Like a Lullaby with His Fists," *New York Herald*, December 27, 1908; Roberts, *Papa Jack*, 68; "Black Jack's Golden Smile," *Afro-American Ledger*, January 2, 1909; "Southern Negro is Heavyweight Champion of the World," *Richmond Planet*, January 2, 1909; Finis Farr, "Jeff, It's Up to You!" *American Heritage*, February 1964, 64–77. Tony van den Bergh tellingly misrepresents London as writing, "Wipe the golden smile off the nigger's face" (*The Jack Johnson Story* [London: Panther, 1956], 83).

The *Washington Post* embellished the legend of Johnson's playing to the movie camera: "He would throw Burns around into a position that would permit him to grin into the gaping mouth of the moving picture machine, and would then throw Burns off with one hand and smash him with the other, acting always for the camera" ("Wanderings of a Prize Ring Championship and the Result," July 3, 1910).

33. "Corbett Makes Known His Stand," *Trib*, January 3, 1909.

34. "The Caucasian's Plight," *Detroit Free Press*, in *New York Age*, January 14, 1909; Walt Mason, "The Black Peril," *Puck*, January 27, 1909; Albert Bushnell Hart and Herbert Ronald Ferleger, eds., *Theodore Roosevelt Cyclopedia* (New York: Roosevelt Memorial Association, 1941), 498, passim; " 'Bat' Sees President," *Post*, January 15, 1909.

35. Editorial, *Richmond Planet*, February 9, 1909. In 1906, Roosevelt discharged 167 African-American soldiers stationed at Brownsville, Texas, after the local white community charged one of them with the murder of a white bartender.

36. "The Johnson-Burns Contest," *Bioscope*, February 18, 1909, 11; "Gaumont's Big Scoop; £7,000 for the Johnson-Burns Fight," *Bioscope*, February 18, 16; "Popular Fight Pictures," *Billboard*, August 14, 13.

37. "Pictures of the Burns-Johnson Fight," *MPW*, January 2, 1909, 90; ad in *Billboard*, April 3, 1909, 32.

38. "Fight Fans See Pictures," *Trib*, March 22, 1909.

39. "Isman Seeks to Stop Moving Prize Fight Pictures," *NYT*, April 8; 1909.

40. "Fight Films in Iowa," *Nickelodeon*, January 1, 1909, 10.

41. "Burns Would Like to Be Slaughtered by Johnson," *Freeman*, January 9, 1909; "Johnson-Burns Fight Here," *NYT*, April 13.

42. Harry W. Jackson, "As the Fight Pictures Told the Story," *Freeman*, May 1, 1909.

43. "Three Judges for Boxing Matches."

44. Ad in *Richmond Planet*, January 30, 1909; "Popular Fight Pictures," 13.

45. *Freeman*, January 9, 1909; "Burns-Johnson Films," *Freeman*, February 20; Jackson, "As the Fight Pictures Told the Story."

46. "The Black Gladiator: Veni, Vidi, Vici—Jack Johnson," song by J. "Berni" Barborn. "Back Johnson Heavily," *Freeman*, January 23, 1909.

47. Juli Jones, "Dehomey in Peace," *Freeman*, October 23, 1909. Jones was the nom de plume of the Chicago-based theater manager and photographer William Foster, who turned to filmmaking in 1913. *Dehomey* was slang for the African American district, taken from the West African kingdom of Dahomey, as well as from the popular stage musical-comedy, *In Dahomey* (1903), the first Broadway musical to be written by African Americans and to feature a black cast.

48. Gregory A. Waller, "Another Audience: Black Moviegoing, 1907–1916," *Cinema Journal* 31, no. 2 (1992): 9, 23. "Movies Open in Dallas," *MPW*, March 23, 1907, 40, reported that a nickelodeon increased attendance by admitting black patrons and dividing the auditorium with a canvas wall. The chicken-wire anecdote comes from Christopher J. McKenna, "Early Movie Going in a Tri-Racial Community: Lumberton, North Carolina (1896–1940)," paper presented at the conference "American Cinema and Everyday Life," London, June 27, 2003. Lumbertonians in one instance were separated into African-, Euro-, and Native-American (Lumbee) seating sections cordoned off by chicken wire.

49. Sylvester Russell, "Eighth Annual Review," *Freeman*, January 9, 1909. "E. H. Morris Wins Color-Line Suit against Colonial Theater," *Defender*, June 11, 1910; "Will Boycott Theater," *Afro-American Ledger*, December 6, 1913.

50. *Freeman*, March 13, 1909; Sylvester Russell, "Musical and Dramatic Quarterly Review," *Defender*, April 9, 1910; "The Outlook for Colored Road Shows," *Freeman*, January 15, 1910.

51. *Washington Bee*, June 4, 1910; "Jacksonville's Pioneer Colored Theater," *Freeman*, December 23, 1911.

52. "Negroes Mobbed for Keeping Separate from Whites," *Defender*, March 4, 1911; "No 'Movies' for Race," *Defender*, May 23, 1914.

53. Mary Carbine, " 'The Finest Outside the Loop': Motion Picture Exhibition in Chicago's Black Metropolis, 1905–1928," *Camera Obscura* 23 (1990): 16–29; Stewart, *Migrating to the Movies*, 156.

54. *Freeman*, December 2, 1909; J. Hockley Smith, "Funeral of Robert T. Motts," *Defender*, July 15, 1911; *Variety Obituaries* (New York: Garland, 1988), s.v. "Colored Manager Dies" (July 15, 1911); "Another Pekin Theater," *Freeman*, January 30, 1909.

55. "The States Theater," *Defender*, August 9, 1913; "Foster Film Co.," *Defender*, August 30; "Former Pekin Star Makes Hit in Dayton," *Defender*, January 3, 1914; "One Large Evening," *New York Age*, April 9; Tony Langston,

"Lincoln Theater," *Defender*, May 9; "Peter P. Jones Heads Motion Picture Co.," *Defender*, June 13. See Jacqueline Stewart's extraordinary chapter on early African American filmmaking in *Migrating to the Movies*, 189–218.

56. On December 11, 1909, Jack Johnson wired George Kleine requesting a print of the Ketchel film. On December 27, he confirmed receiving one set of films (four reels). George Kleine Collection, Manuscripts Division, Library of Congress.

57. Sylvester Russell, "Musical and Dramatic," *Defender*, April 30, 1910.

58. Cary B. Lewis, "Champion Jack Johnson Makes Business Good along the Stroll," *Freeman*, July 16, 1910; "Chicago's Black Belt Bedlam was Good Natured," *Freeman*, July 9; "John Arthur Johnson Still Holds the Championship," *Chicago Broad Ax*, July 9; "Relatives Hear News in Theater," *Trib*, July 5; "Black Elite Honor Johnson," *Trib*, July 9.

59. "Jack Johnson Stops Moving Pictures of Wife's Funeral," *Defender*, September 21, 1912; "Johnson Stops Films," *Trib*, September 17; "Magnolia Theatre of Cincinnati," *Defender*, August 5, 1911; "Pekin Sold," *Defender*, July 26, 1913; "Opening of New Pekin Theatre," *Defender*, January 31, 1914. See also Mark W. Haller, "Policy Gambling, Entertainment, and the Emergence of Black Politics: Chicago from 1900 to 1940," *Journal of Social History* 24, no. 4 (1991): 719–40.

60. Sime. [Silverman], "Johnson-Ketchel Fight," in *Variety Film Reviews* (New York: Garland, 1983).

61. Lardner, *Legendary Champions*, 177; Roberts, *Papa Jack*, 84; Arnold, *History of Boxing*, 49, 127; Golesworthy, *Encyclopaedia of Boxing*, 82; William H. Wiggins, Jr., "Jack Johnson as Bad Nigger: The Folklore of His Life," *Black Scholar* (January 1971): 43–44. Wiggins lists several versions of the legend about Ketchel's teeth.

62. "Johnson-Ketchel," *MPW*, November 13, 1909, 678. J. W. Coffroth leased Kleine three prints of *Johnson-Ketchel* for seven months at $5,000 per print. Correspondence, October 1909, in George Kleine Collection.

63. John Sloan, October 29, 1909, in *John Sloan's New York Scene*, ed. Bruce St. John (New York: Harper & Row, 1965), 346.

64. Al-Tony Gilmore, *Bad Nigger! The National Impact of Jack Johnson* (Port Washington, NY: Kennikat Press, 1975); Roberts, *Papa Jack*, 69–70 ff.; Wiggins, "Jack Johnson," 4–19.

65. "Jeffries and Johnson Sign for Great Battle," *Courier-Journal*, October 31, 1909.

66. W. W. Naughton, "Colored Man is Still Champion," *Richmond Planet*, October 23, 1909.

67. "The Johnson-Ketchel Fight Pictures," *New York Sun*, in *Richmond Planet*, October 30, 1909.

68. "And May the Best Man Win!" *NYT*, November 1, 1909.

69. "Johnson-Ketchel Fight Films," *MPW*, December 18, 1909, 876–77.

70. "Moving Pictures of the Johnson-Ketchel Bout," *Freeman*, November 6, 1909.

71. Uncle Rad Kees, "Johnson Shows Physical Prowess of the Negro," *Freeman*, November 27, 1909. Similar skepticism was voiced by white reviewers. "If the two men had been accomplished actors they couldn't have devised anything half so good for moving pictures as the show that was put up" ("Right to the Jaw Puts Ketchel Out," *Trib*, October 17).

72. "Tex Rickard's Bid for Fight Accepted," *NYT*, December 3, 1909; "Rickard Gets Fight," *New York Tribune*, December 3; Lardner, *Legendary Champions*, 180.

73. "Can Jeffries Come Back?" *Afro-American Ledger*, January 15, 1910.

74. "Is Prize-Fighting Knocked Out?" *Literary Digest*, July 16, 1910, 85; Sammons, *Beyond the Ring*, 35.

75. "Corbett Says Black's Fear of White in Old Times Will Count on July 4," *Trib*, July 1, 1910.

76. James J. Jeffries, "The Need of an Athletic Awakening," *Physical Culture*, May 1909, 397–400; "Mental and Moral Training through Boxing," *Physical Culture*, August 1909, 153–57. The articles even had Jeffries advocating that boxing was a way to fight off "the Great White Plague" of tuberculosis. See also Jack London, "Johnson is Effervescent, While Jeffries Is Stolid," *Los Angeles Times*, June 28, 1910.

77. "The Psychology of the Prize Fight," *Current Literature*, July 1910, 57–58. See also "Intellectuality of the New Pugilism," *Current Opinion*, February 1913, 130–31. Rhett S. Jones, "Proving Blacks Inferior: 1870–1930," *Black World*, February 1971, 4–19; Steven J. Gould, *The Mismeasure of Man* (New York: Norton, 1981); Sammons, *Beyond the Ring*, 34.

78. "Booker Washington Meets Jack Johnson," *Afro-American Ledger*, August 21, 1909; "Now Jack!" *Afro-American Ledger*, March 12, 1910; Arthur R. Ashe, Jr., *A Hard Road to Glory* (New York: Warner, 1988), 38–41; Wiggins, "Jack Johnson," 44.

79. F. L. Goodspeed to William Howard Taft, May 9, 1910. Lapsley A. McAfee to Taft, May 10–11, 1910. *Papers of William H. Taft*, Library of Congress, microfilm ed., 1972; "Taft's Dates Mixed, Asks Son about Fight," *Examiner*, July 4, 1910.

80. Farr, "Jeff, It's Up to You!" 69; "Taking the Prize-Fight from 'Frisco," *Literary Digest*, June 25, 1910, 1249; "Gillet Now Opposes Bout," *NYT*, June 16; "California's Conversion," *Independent*, June 23, 1404–5.

81. Rex E. Beach, "Reno Now Center of the Universe," *Trib*, July 2, 1910; Farr, 72; Gilmore, *Bad Nigger*, 59; H.E.K., "The White Man's Real Hope Is that the Better Man Is Not Cheated," *Trib*, July 4.

82. "Pictures and Pugilism," *MPW*, December 18, 1909, 871.

83. Our Man about Town, "Fight Pictures," *MPW*, December 18, 1909, 876.

84. Edward B. Moss, "In the Ring for a Million," *Harper's Weekly*, May 14, 1910, 13; *Billboard*, May 8, 1909, 14; August 14.

85. *NYT*, December 3–5, 1909; "Pictures of the Jeffries-Johnson Fight," *MPW*, June 18, 1910, 1039.

86. "Why He Sold Pictures," *Jackson Clarion-Ledger,* July 14, 1910. Johnson told reporters:

> You always see the man who has the patents loses his money. If I had kept my interest I would have had to employ a large number of men to look after my interest. As it was I got $50,000 and a little bonus of $10–12,000 for my interest.
>
> Now, if I had kept my share of the pictures, by the time the other twenty-five or thirty of us had through cheating one another, I doubt if there would have been that much money left for me. So long as they are willing to manage [the films] and give me the money I was perfectly willing to accept it.

87. "Sidelights on Big Fight," *Trib,* July 2, 1910; "Fight Pictures Prohibited Here by Mayor," and "Fight Picture Men Threaten Litigation," *Examiner,* July 7; H.E.K., "Now Up to Jeff to Plan Battle," *Trib,* June 28; " 'Man about Town' on the Jeffries-Johnson Fight," *MPW,* July 16, 191. Rickard "had to sell out his picture rights to stage the show in Nevada," according to "Publicity Injures the Sport of Boxing," *Courier-Journal,* July 10.

88. *Jeffries on His Ranch* was distributed through the Motion Picture Sales and Distribution Company (and may have been a copy of the Miles Brothers film of the same name). Ads in *MPW,* June 4, 1910, 978, and June 18, 1039; *Clipper,* July 9, 531; *Billboard,* November 20, 1909.

89. "The Johnson-Jeffries Pictures," *Bioscope,* September 15, 1910, 9; John L. Sullivan, "Black before Picture Machine," *Trib,* July 1.

90. W. W. Naughton, "Jeffries Mastered," *Trib,* July 5, 1910; "The Jeffries-Johnson Pictures," *Nickelodeon,* June 17; K. S. Hover, "The Fight Picture Prospect," *Nickelodeon,* July 15, 1910, 31; "Is Prize-Fighting Knocked Out?" 84–85.

91. Rex E. Beach, "Johnson and Age Defeat Jeffries," *Trib,* July 5, 1910; "Record Crowd at Fight," *New York Tribune,* July 5.

92. Alfred Henry Lewis, "Johnson Fought Squarely," *Post,* July 5, 1910; *MPW,* July 9, 81.

93. Reported to me by Laurie Block during production of her documentary *Fit: Episodes in the History of the Body* (1991).

94. *MPW,* July 9, 1910, 80–81; "Pictures of the Jeffries-Johnson Fight," 1039.

95. Al Jolson, "The Fight at Reno," *Variety,* July 9, 1910, 4.

96. "Passing of Jeffries as a Fighter," *New York Tribune,* July 5, 1910. Nat Goodwin, a Jeffries backer, described the scene: "Imagine over sixteen thousand human beings filing slowly from a cemetery where departed heroes have been put away from earthly cares!" *Nat Goodwin's Book* (Boston: Badger, 1914), 192–96.

97. "Fight Pictures Arrive," *New York Tribune,* July 9, 1910; "At 'Stag' Houses Only," *New York Tribune,* July 11.

98. " 'Man about Town' on the Jeffries-Johnson Fight," 190; Roy Rosenzweig, *Eight Hours for What We Will* (Cambridge: Cambridge University Press, 1983), chapters 3, 6.

99. "Whites and Blacks in Many Riotous Battles," *New York Tribune,* July 5, 1910.

100. "Race Clash at Atlanta," *Courier-Journal,* July 5, 1910; "Ban on Negro Parade," *New York Tribune,* July 4; "Police on Guard in Richmond," *New York Tribune,* July 4; "Negro Dead after Riots," *New York Tribune,* July 6; "Fists Stir Up a Black Crowd," *Courier-Journal,* July 5; "Racial Bloodshed Follows Fight at Reno," *Arkansas Democrat,* July 5; Lester A. Walton, "Merit, Not Color, Won," *New York Age,* April 8, 1915.

101. Gilmore, *Bad Nigger,* 75–93; Lee Grieveson, *Policing Cinema* (Berkeley: University of California Press, 2004), 121–51; "Fight Pictures Prohibited Here by Mayor," 1.

102. At times, original sources refer to the *Jeffries-Johnson Fight.* Although the work was copyrighted as *Jeffries-Johnson World's Championship, Held at Reno, Nevada, July 4, 1910,* I use the most common title, *Johnson-Jeffries Fight,* throughout. This form also conforms to the practice of respecting the winner and champion by putting his name first.

103. Henry Warner Bowden, *Dictionary of American Religious Biography* (Westport, CT: Greenwood, 1977), 99–100; *New Catholic Encyclopedia,* vol. 3 (New York: McGraw-Hill, 1967), 638–39; Bert H. Davis, *Publicity Plans for Christian Endeavor* (Boston: International Society of Christian Endeavor, 1930).

104. "Fight Pictures," *Courier-Journal,* July 6, 1910; "Fuss over Fight Pictures," July 7; D. J. Price, "The Fight Pictures," letter to the editor, *New York Tribune,* July 11; "Fight Pictures Prohibited," *Examiner,* July 7; "Endeavorers Urged to Press for Peace," *NYT,* July 7, 1911.

105. *Spokesman Observer,* July 7, 1910, in *Theodore Roosevelt Papers,* microfilm ed.; Allen Sinclair Will, *Life of Cardinal Gibbons* (New York: Dutton, 1922), 802.

106. Theodore Roosevelt, "The Recent Prizefight," *Outlook,* July 16, 1910, 550–51.

107. Chopin, "Real Moving Pictures," *Examiner,* July 7, 1910; Chopin, "And Not a Friendly Port in Sight," *Examiner,* July 9. Winston Churchill acknowledged that "the British government itself [had] no power to suppress the films" ("Can't Bar Pictures," *Jackson Clarion-Ledger,* July 14).

108. *Washington Bee,* July 9, 1910; "To Bar Fight Pictures," *New York Tribune,* July 6; "Educational?" *Jackson Clarion-Ledger,* July 21; *MPW,* July 16, 191.

109. Jane Addams, "Social Control," *Crisis,* January 1911, 23; *Examiner,* July 9, 1910.

110. "Minister Denounces Nevada," *New York Tribune,* July 4, 1910; Robert T. Handy, *A Christian America* (New York: Oxford University Press, 1971), 126.

111. "The Johnson-Jeffries Fight," *St. Paul Appeal,* July 9, 1910; "The Independence Day Fight," *St. Paul Appeal,* July 16.

112. "On the Fight Pictures," *Freeman,* July 16, 1910.

113. *Defender,* July 30, 1910; *Planet,* August 6.

114. *Washington Bee,* July 16, 1910.

115. "Rev. G. E. Bevens' Opinion of Johnson's Victory," *Afro-American Ledger,* July 16, 1910; "Ministers Favor Fight Pictures," *Afro-American Ledger,* July 23.

116. "What a Folly," *Washington Bee,* July 9, 1910.

117. "Uncensored Fight Films," *New York Tribune,* July 6, 1910.

118. H. V. Andrews letter, *NYT,* July 13, 1910; Walter Storey, "Fight Pictures Weren't Censored," *NYT,* July 20.

119. "Patents Company Bulletin," *Nickelodeon,* July 15,1910, 42. Both Hammerstein's and the American Music Hall were "barred by MPPC because they showed the 'independent' *Nelson-Wolgast* views," *Variety,* July 9, 1910, 4.

120. " 'Man about Town' on the Jeffries-Johnson Fight," 190.

121. "The Fight Films," *Bioscope,* July 14, 1910, 3; "A Disgrace to the Profession," *Bioscope,* July 21, 1910, 52 (citing *Motion Picture News*); "Those Fight Pictures," *Moving Picture News,* September 30, 1911, 6; J.M.B., "On the Big Fight," *MPW,* July 16, 1910, 194.

122. "Fight Picture Consistency," *Nickelodeon,* July 15, 1910, 29; Arthur Young," "Can You Beat This for What Is Known as Gall?" *Puck,* August 10, 2; "Is Prize-Fighting Knocked Out?" 85; "Keith Bars Fight Films," *New York Tribune,* July 8; "Fight Picture Men Threaten Litigation," *Examiner,* July 7; "Film Men Rush to New York," *Examiner,* July 9; "Censors Pass on Reno Fight Views," *Trib,* July 11.

123. "Fight Film Men Will Bow to Law," *Trib,* July 8, 1910; "Picture Managers Will Not Buck Law," *Examiner,* July 9; Hover, "Fight Picture Prospect," 32.

124. "Ban against Fight Pictures," *Clipper,* July 16, 1910, 558; "No Bar to Johnson," *Post,* July 7.

125. "Chicagoans May See Fight Film," *Trib,* July 10, 1910; "Censors Pass on Reno Fight Views," July 9; "That Chicago Police Order," *Nickelodeon,* August 1, 59; "Censors Pass on Reno Fight Views."

126. "[Chicago C.O.P. Steward]," *Clipper,* July 30, 1910, 607; "Try to Lift Ban Off Fight Films," *Trib,* July 31; "Fight Picture Men Sue," *NYT,* July 31; "Suit in Fight Pictures Case against City of Chicago," *Clipper,* August 13, 651; "No Pictures for Chicago," *Clipper,* September 3, 725.

127. "Fight Picture Men Threaten Litigation;" " 'Man about Town' on the Jeffries-Johnson Fight," 191.

128. "Suburbs of City to Show Fight Pictures," *Examiner,* July 10, 1910.

129. "At 'Stag' Houses Only;" *MPW,* July 16, 201.

130. "Film Men Rush to New York."

131. Susan Courtney, *Hollywood Fantasies of Miscegenation: Spectacular Narratives of Gender and Race* (Princeton, NJ: Princeton University Press, 2004), 50–61.

132. "Jack Johnson Sees Jeffries Defeated," *NYT,* July 14, 1910; "Johnson Sees Fight Films," *Trib,* July 14.

133. "Weird Audience Sees Battle of Reno," *NYT,* July 17, 1910.

134. "Some Fight Pictures That Would Be Desirable," *Trib,* July 7, 1910; "Some Fight Pictures That We Would Permit," *Examiner,* July 8; "Real Moving Pictures;" H. F. Hoffman, "There's a Reason," *MPW,* August 20, 1910, 403.

135. Laurie Block pointed this out to me in conversation. See "There's a Reason," *Physical Culture,* October 1902; Harvey Green, *Fit for America* (Baltimore, MD: Johns Hopkins University Press, 1986), 309.

136. Ad in *MPW,* July 16, 1910, 220; "Reproduction of Jeffries-Johnson Fight," *Nickelodeon,* July 15, 42 (identifying the black boxer as Charles Diamond); *Variety,* July 16, 9.

137. "Fight Pictures Show a Laughable Fiasco," *New York Tribune,* July 10, 1910; "Fake Fight Pictures," *Clipper,* July 16, 555; "Fake Fight Pictures Stopped in Theatre," *NYT,* July 10; *Variety,* July 16, 9.

138. *MPW,* October 22, 1910, 956. This was probably the Chicago fake repackaged.

139. "More Jeffries-Johnson Pictures," *Clipper,* July 30, 1910, 602; Q. David Bowers, *Nickel Theatres and Their Music* (Vestal, NY: Vest Press, 1986), 100; Ann Lloyd, *The Illustrated History of the Cinema* (New York: Macmillan, 1986); *New York Tribune,* November 20, 1910.

140. "Fight Pictures Cause Riot," *Clipper,* July 16, 1910, 558; "Reno Fight Pictures at Riverview," *Courier-Journal,* August 29, 1910.

141. "Lantern Slides of the Fight," *MPW,* July 16, 1910, 175; *MPW,* July 30, 215; "Charged with Duping Fight Pictures," *Nickelodeon,* November 15, 1910, 285.

142. "Mr. Johnson Talks," *MPW,* August 20, 1910, 415. Parodies of the big fight included Kineto's *Grate Fight for the Championship* (in which a blackened chimney sweep and white-clad baker fight and exchange colors), *MPW,* August 6, 293. Both British and American short comedies repeatedly manifested a white fantasy about beating Jack Johnson: *Black and White* (Barker, 1910), *Great Fight at All-Sereno* (U.K., 1910), *The Great Black v. White Prize Fight* (Gaumont, 1910), *The Man to Beat Jack Johnson* (Gaumont, 1910), *The Man to Beat Jack Johnson* (Tyler, 1910), *The Night I Fought Jack Johnson* (Vitagraph, 1913), *Pimple Beats Jack Johnson* (Folly Films, U.K., 1914), *The White Hope on Championship* (Heron, U.K., 1914), and *Some White Hope* (Vitagraph, 1915). See Harvey Marc Zucker and Lawrence J. Babich, *Sports Films: A Complete Reference* (Jefferson, NC: McFarland, 1987).

Fiction films with race-related prizefight scenes in them included Nestor's *The Parson and the Bully* (with a "battle royal by four negroes") and *The Cowboy Pugilist* (featuring the unsubtly named White Hanson, a Jeffries-like son of a parson who becomes a reluctant fighter). Reviews in *MPW,* August 26, 1911, 574, and November 25, 640.

143. Ad in *Clipper,* August 6, 1910, 629.

144. "Keith Bars Fight Film," 4; H.E.K., "Now Up to Jeff to Plan Battle"; *Clipper,* July 16, 1910, 555; "The Johnson-Jeffries Fight," *Bioscope,* 9–11; "Havana Fight Films Barred from U.S.," *NYT,* April 16, 1915.

145. "Fight Pictures Fail to Attract," *NYT,* August 24, 1910; "A Fight Picture Frost," *Clipper,* September 3, 725.

146. "At 'Stag' Houses Only"; "Fight Pictures Liked by New York Audiences," *Clipper,* July 30, 1910, 603.

147. "First Fight Pictures Seen," *NYT,* July 17, 1910; "First Glimpse of the Jeffries-Johnson Pictures," *Clipper,* July 23, 583; "What the Pictures Show," *NYT,* July 19; "Fight Pictures at Meyerrose Park," *New York Age,* August 4, 1910; Lester A. Walton, "Music and the Stage," *New York Age,* August 11.

148. "Negro Teacher Sends Children to See Jeffries-Johnson Show," *Defender,* October 1, 1910; *New York Tribune,* July 8, 1910.

149. N. Barnett Dodson, "Johnson the Real Victor," *Afro-American Ledger,* July 16, 1910; Mildred Miller, "'The Nigger' Unmolested," *Defender,* December 10, 1910.

150. "Too Much Jack Johnson," *Richmond Planet,* August 13, 1910.

151. "The Johnson-Jeffries Pictures," *Bioscope;* "My View of Things," *Bioscope,* September 15, 11; *Wisconsin State Journal,* September 29—October 1, 1910, cited in Janet Staiger, "The Fuller Opera House: A Transition from Theater to Cinema" (unpublished MS, 1977); "Fight Pictures in Dublin," *NYT,* August 21, 1910; "Big Hit in Ireland," *Freeman,* September 3, 1910; [Johnson-Jeffries Fight Pictures still being shown in Paris], *MPW,* March 4, 1911, 486; "Jeffries-Johnson Fight," *Bioscope,* October 12, 1911, 143; "Fight Pictures in Ireland," *Clipper,* August 27, 1910, 662; "Berlin Sees Fight Films," *NYT,* September 17, 1911; "Berlin To See Fight Films," *NYT,* December 16, 1911.

152. "Among the Picture Theaters," *Nickelodeon,* August 1, 1910, 80; "Fight Pictures for Armory," *NYT,* August 27, 1910; "Petition Hughes to Bar Fight Pictures," *NYT,* August 28, 1910; "See Hughes on Fight Films," *NYT,* August 2, 1910; "Newport Sees Fight Films," *NYT,* August 9, 1910; "Mrs. Widener Entertains with Fight Pictures," *Nickelodeon,* September 1, 1910, 24.

153. Editorial, *Defender,* December 3, 1910; Roberts, *Papa Jack,* 118–20; *MPW,* March 4, 1911, 486.

7. JACK JOHNSON'S DECLINE

1. "Now Jack!" *Baltimore Afro-American Ledger,* March 12, 1910.

2. *Jack Johnson: Der Meister Boxer der Welt* (1911), 35 mm print, Nederlands Filmmuseum (my thanks to Nico de Klerk for supplying this film). Ads in *Bioscope,* August 31, 1911, 422, September 21, 1911, 604–5, and September 28, 1911, 698; *New York Tribune,* September 14, 1911; "Archbishop of Canterbury and Papers Ask Government to Stop Wells Fight," *New York Tribune,* September 20, 1911; "Those Fight Pictures," *Moving Picture News,* September 30, 1911, 6; "Our London Correspondent," *Moving Picture News,* October 28, 1911, 27; Randy Roberts, *Papa Jack: Jack Johnson and the Era of White Hopes* (New York: Free Press, 1983), 129.

3. "Langford vs. McVea," *MPW,* June 24, 1911, 1418; *Bioscope,* March 30, 1911, 72; "Which Will Fight Jack Johnson?" *Bioscope,* April 6, 1911, 36; *Bioscope,*

April 20, 1911, 118; Leon E. Johns, "The Largest Moving Picture Theater [Paris Hippodrome]," *Nickelodeon*, August 1, 1910, 94; Old Sport, "Zenith of Negro Sport," *Colored American Magazine*, May 1909, 295–300; Denzil Batchelor, *Big Fight* (London: Phoenix House, 1954), 115–16; Jack Johnson, *Mes combats*, (Paris: Pierre Lafitte, 1914).

4. *Freeman*, January 6, 1912.

5. "Articles Signed for Finish Fight," *Richmond Planet*, January 13, 1912.

6. *Las Vegas Optic*, February 13, 1912, cited in David J. Kammer, "TKO in Las Vegas: Boosterism and the Johnson-Flynn Fight," *New Mexico Historical Review*, October 1986, 301–18.

7. *Gazette*, July 27, 1912, 10; *New York Tribune*, July 5; Walter H. Eckersall, "Films Tell Tale of Rough Fight," *Trib*, July 20. An embellished recollection of *Wolgast-Rivers* casts it as a story of Trust thugs versus wily independents. The promoter Tom McCarey provided security to protect the camera. Although Trust "guerrilla" Bill Swanson and "his boys" came to the fight, the three cameras—run by Keystone operators and supervised by Mack Sennett himself—went unsmashed. (The alleged presence of Sennett and Keystone personnel is questionable, as the studio did not turn out its first California production until September 1912.) Fred J. Balshofer and Arthur C. Miller, *One Reel a Week* (Berkeley: University of California Press, 1967), 86–88.

8. Sam C. Austin, "Motion Picture Films Prove Jim Flynn Had No Chance," *Gazette*, August 3, 1912, 10; Jim Corbett, "Joe Jeannette Dubs Johnson a 'Moving Picture Fighter,'" *Freeman*, June 1, 1912. See also Raymond Wilson, "Another White Hope Bites the Dust: The Jack Johnson–Jim Flynn Heavyweight Fight in 1912," *Montana*, Winter 1979, 30–39.

9. "Against the Prize-Fight," *Literary Digest*, June 4, 1910, 1123; "Meant for Pugilist, Boxer Tells Cannon," *NYT*, May 18; "'Battler' Meets Speaker," *Post*, May 18; 61st Cong., 2nd sess., *Congressional Record* 45 (May 12, 1910): H 6185; "The Battle of the Giants," *Physical Culture*, July 1910, 2; *Prohibition of Interstate Transportation of Pictures and Descriptions of Prize Fights: Hearing before the Committee on Interstate and Foreign Commerce*, 61st Cong., 2nd sess., February 7, 1911, Statement of Walter I. Smith, 9–11.

10. 62nd Cong., 2nd sess., *Congressional Record* 48 (July 19, 1912): H 9305.

11. 62nd Cong., 2nd sess., *Congressional Record* 48 (December 11, 1912): H 502–4; "Johnson Weds," *Post*, December 4, 1912; "Bar Johnson Wedding Films," *Moving Picture News*, December 14, 1912.

12. 62nd Cong., 2nd sess., *Congressional Record* 45 (May 29–July 31, 1912): H 7408, 7501, 7887, passim; House Committee on Interstate and Foreign Commerce, H.R. 858, *Interstate Transportation of Pictures of Prize Fights*, June 8, 1912, 1–2. See also "Senate Ban," *Motography*, September 14, 1912, 205.

13. William A. Brady, *Fighting Man* (Indianapolis: Bobbs-Merrill, 1916), 195–96.

14. *Bioscope* February 9, 1911, 57; "The Shady Exclusive," *Bioscope*, June 13, 1912, 763.

15. Identifiable films include *Digger Stanley–Walsh Fight, Summers-Welsh Fight, Jim Driscoll versus Seaman Hayes, Summers-Britt, Hague-Langford Fight* (1909); *Welsh v. MacFarland, Welch and Daniels Fight, Joe Bowker versus Digger Stanley, Thomas versus Jim Sullivan, Stanley-Condon Contest, Jim Driscoll–Freddy Welsh, Nelson-Moran Fight* (1910); *Moir-Wells Fight, Jim Driscoll v. Spike Robson, Ian Hague v. William Chase* (1911); *Carpentier-Wells Fight* (1913); *Ritchie-Welsh Fight, Carpentier and Gunboat Smith, Jimmy Wilde vs. Joe Symonds* (1914); and *Jimmy Wilde vs. Tancy Lee* (1915). Rachel Low, *The History of the British Film* (London: Allen & Unwin, 1948), 149, argues that five films were particularly important: *Moir-Burns* (Urban, 1907), *Summers-Britt* (Urban, 1909), *Welsh-McFarland* (National Sporting Club, 1910), *Sullivan-Carpentier* (Warwick, 1912), and *Carpentier-Wells* (1913).

Frederick A. Talbot, *Moving Pictures: How They Are Made and Worked* (London: W. Heinemann, 1912), 122, summarized the British fight film's industrial and social status:

> A prize-fight between two famous champions provokes extraordinary energy on the part of the cinematographic artists. Fabulous prices are paid for exclusive rights to photograph the contest, and no expense is spared to secure a continuous record. In order to obtain adequate illumination of the ring, a battery of powerful electric lamps has to be set up, and the glare of tens of thousands of candle-power concentrated on the combatants. If the battle is short and sharp the results are disappointing both to the cinematographer and his public, but if it be long, requiring several hundred feet of film, he is happy. The prize-fight film, however, is meeting with considerable opposition, which should be welcomed as a healthy sign even by the film-producers themselves. The cinematography can surely do more elevating, profitable and entertaining work than the recording of a prize-fight. Furthermore, the result has not always paid the speculators concerned, and one or two more heavy losses in the field, combined with popular censorship, will result in the prize-fight being eliminated entirely from the category of "topical" films.

16. *Bioscope:* "The Best Fight Film Ever Taken," March 7, 1912, 710; "The Shady Exclusive," June 13, 1912, 763; [*Carpentier-Klaus*], July 11, 1912; "Big Fight Picture," July 18, 1912, 203; [*Wells-Carpentier*], June 19, 1913, 877; [*Carpentier-Wells*], July 3, 1913; Peter Arnold, *History of Boxing* (Secaucus, NJ: Chartwell, 1985), 130–32.

17. "More about the Champion," *Richmond Planet*, November 30, 1912; John Mitchell Jr., "What Does It Mean?" *Richmond Planet*, December 21; Lester Walton, "Jack Johnson a Menace," *New York Age*, October 24; "Why Indict the Whole Race?" *New York Age*, October 31; Booker T. Washington, "A Statement on Jack Johnson for the United Press Association," October 23, 1912, in *Booker T. Washington Papers* (Urbana: University of Illinois Press, 1981), 43–44, 75–76.

18. *Baltimore Afro-American Ledger,* January 4, 1913.

19. "Should Have Knocked Him Out," *Richmond Planet,* July 11, 1914; Lester A. Walton, "Johnson and Moran," *New York Age,* July 2; Gus Rhodes, "World Acclaims Jack Johnson," *Defender,* July 4; Brady, *Fighting Man,* 197–202; Roberts, *Papa Jack,* 191–95; Batchelor, *Big Fight,* 101–2. Only the NAACP offered a defense. Johnson's "unforgivable blackness" made him the center of "national disgust," it editorialized. In "white America," athletes and politicians were not "disqualified" because of moral shortcomings. "The Prize-fighter," *Crisis,* August 1914, 181.

20. "$1,000 a Day for Jess Willard," *Variety,* April 9, 1915, 4.

21. "Cowboy Wins Battle When Jack Weakens," *Trib,* April 6, 1915.

22. "Johnson-Willard Bout at Juarez," *NYT,* January 9, 1915; January 8, 1915.

23. While still at Biograph, Mack Sennett directed Fred Mace in *One-Round O'Brien,* released on July 4, 1912, to coincide with the Johnson-Flynn bout. See *AFI Catalog,* 1011; "Harry Herbert Frazee (1880–1929)," in *Concise Oxford Companion to American Theatre,* ed. Gerald Bordman (New York: Oxford University Press, 1987), 173; [L. Lawrence Weber], *Clipper,* March 13, 1897, 19; Anthony Slide, *The American Film Industry* (Westport, CT: Greenwood, 1986), 211–12; *Variety Obituaries* (New York: Garland, 1988), s.v. "Curley, Jack" (July 14, 1937), "Weber, L. Lawrence" (February 28, 1940), "Frazee, Harry" (June 12, 1929) and "Mace, Fred" (March 2, 1917). Frazee's notoriety came from his trading Babe Ruth to the New York Yankees.

24. *Variety,* March 25, 1915, 21; "Steamers to Cuba Crowded with Fight Fans," *NYT,* April 3, 1915.

25. "Sentiment of the Colored Press of the Country on the Johnson-Willard Championship Fight," *Richmond Planet,* April 25, 1915; Lester A. Walton, "Rumor of Frameup," *New York Age,* April 1.

26. "Battery of Movie Machines," *NYT,* April 6, 1915; "Pirate Films of Fight," April 9; "Johnson Put Off Again," April 10; "Fight Pictures in Cuba," April 15.

27. Ads and reviews in *MPW,* April 17, 1915, 332, 366; April 24, 1915, 653; May 1, 1915, 760; *Variety,* April 9, 1915, 4; *Motography,* April 24, 1915, 662.

28. Transcript of Record, Sup. Ct. of U.S., October term, 1915, no. 644 *[Weber v. Freed],* File No. 24927—New Jersey, filed Sept 28, 1915. U.S. National Archives and Records Administration, Washington, DC.

29. "Willard Victor," *NYT,* April 6, 1915.

30. "More about Jack Johnson," *Richmond Planet,* April 17, 1915.

31. Fred Dartnell, *"Seconds Out!"* (New York: Brentano's, 1924), 138. Sam McVey, Bat Masterson, and others discussed Johnson's faking his performance for the movies. See Lester A. Walton, "Fight Talk," *New York Age,* April 15, 1915; Walton, "Rumor of Frameup"; Al-Tony Gilmore, "Towards an Understanding of the Jack Johnson Confession," *Negro History Bulletin,* May 1973, 108–9.

32. "Willard Given Credit for Rescuing Boxing," *Detroit News,* April 18, 1915; "Sentiment of the Colored Press."

33. Gerald Early, *Tuxedo Junction* (New York: Ecco Press, 1989), 173.

34. Jim Nasium, "Color Line in the Squared Circle," *Afro-American Ledger,* January 30, 1909, 6 (reprinted from *Inquirer*).

35. "The Clansman," *Wichita Searchlight,* January 12, 1907; "Stop at Nothing to Prevent Performance of 'The Clansman,'" *Defender,* March 18, 1911; Al-Tony Gilmore, *Bad Nigger! The National Impact of Jack Johnson* (Port Washington, NY: Kennikat Press, 1975), 84; Roberts, *Papa Jack,* 113.

36. The *New York Age* reported with some satisfaction that white citizens of Augusta, Georgia, who had enacted a crowd scene were not told that their work would be edited into *The Nigger* as a depiction of a riotous, low-life mob. "Augusta Citizens Mad with Movie Company," *New York Age,* March 18, 1915; "William Farnum in 'The New Governor,'" *Variety,* March 25, 21; "Colored Men's Business League Protest," *New York Age,* May 20; "The Nigger—April Run in New Jersey," *New York Age,* May 27; ["Mystery of Morrow's Past"], *Afro-American Ledger,* July 31; Bordman, *Concise Oxford Companion to American Theatre,* 315, 377; Edward Sheldon, *The Nigger: An American Play in Three Acts* (New York: Macmillan, 1910).

37. See, for example, "Jack Johnson Loses," and "NAACP Fights 'Birth of a Nation,'" *Richmond Planet,* April 10, 1915.

38. "More about Jack Johnson," *Richmond Planet,* April 17, 1915.

39. "The Dirt of a Nation," *Defender,* June 5, 1915; "Protest against Birth of a Nation," *Afro-American Ledger,* August 7.

40. "Johnson-Jeffries Fight Pictures May Be Shown," *Defender,* September 4, 1915; "Council Inquiry Near on Permit for Fight Films," *Trib,* November 11, 1921; "Jeff-Johnson Fight Films Given Permit," *Trib,* November 12; Juli Jones Jr., "The Fight Pictures," *Defender,* December 10; Mae Tinee, "Where's the Thrill in Prize Fights?" *Trib,* November 25; *Defender,* January 21, 1922; "Fight Film," *Defender,* January 28.

41. "One Large Evening," *New York Age,* April 9, 1914; Lester A. Walton, "Ridiculing the Race," *New York Age,* April 23. The *Defender:* "'Hit the Nigger' New Film Insult," February 28, 1914; "Chicago Film Censor Board Purges 'Movies,'" April 18; "States Theatre Displays Vile Race Pictures," May 30.

42. Foster's films included *The Railroad Porter, The Butler, The Grafter and The Maid,* and *The Fall Guy,* 1913–1915; Jones made *The Troubles of Sambo and Dinah* (1914) and *50 Years of Freedom* (1915); Haynes made *Mandy's Choice, Uncle Remus Visits New York, Dandy Jim's Dream,* and the parade films *National Negro Business League, National Baptist Convention,* and *Odd Fellows Parade.*

43. *Defender* articles: "50 Years Freedom," September 25, 1915; "Lincoln Jubilee Motion Pictures a Success," October 2, 1915; Juli Jones Jr., "Moving Pictures Offer the Greatest Opportunity to the American Negro in History of the Race from Every Point of View," October 9, 1915.

44. "Federal Law Prevents Show of Willard Triumph," *Defender,* April 24, 1915; "Irritating, but It's All Right," *NYT,* April 17, 1915.

45. *NYT,* April 8, 1915; "Jack Johnson Will Not Get Cent from Moving Pictures," *Detroit News,* April 15; "No Fight Films for Ottawa," *MPW,* April 24,

596; Jack Johnson, *Jack Johnson is a Dandy* (New York: Chelsea House, 1969), 200–201; Jack Johnson, *In the Ring and Out* (London: Proteus, 1977), 157–58; *Variety Obituaries*, s.v. "Naylor, Rufe." "A Word about Jack Johnson," *Richmond Planet*, April 10, said that with "the motion picture syndicate" figuring to make $1,000,000, Johnson declined a buyout of $200,000.

46. "Showed the Fight Film," *MPW*, May 8, 1915, 939.

47. "Showed Barred Fight Film," *NYT*, April 12, 1916; "Barred Fight Films Leap U.S. Boundary," *NYT*, April 6, 10, and 15.

48. "Fight Films Not to Travel," *Motography*, September 28, 1912, 261; "Fight Pictures Barred," *NYT*, April 8, 1915.

49. "Collector Emmons Bars Fight Pictures," *Defender*, July 3, 1915; John H. Flanagan, "Lose Fight Film Case," *MPW*, September 11, 1915, 1866; *Kalisthenic Exhibition Co., Inc. v. Emmons* 225 Fed. 902 (1915); 229 Fed. 124 (1916).

50. "Havana Fight Films Barred," *NYT*, April 16, 1915; "No Films Can Enter New York," *Detroit News*, April 16; *Freeman*, April 17; "Uncle Sam Bars Prize Fight Films," *MPW*, April 17, 366; "Battle in Courts for Fight Films," *Detroit News*, April 27.

51. "Fight Films Might Be Shown in Ohio," *MPW*, May 1, 1915, 760; "To Test Fight Film Law," *MPW*, May 8, 952; W. Stephen Bush, "Arguments on Fight Films," *MPW*, May 15, 1049–50.

52. *Weber v. Freed*, 239 U.S. 325, 36 Sup. Ct. 131 (1915), 60 L. Ed. 308, Ann. Cas. 1916C, 317; 224 Fed. 355 (July 19, 1915); *Weber v. Freed*, Transcript of Record, National Archives and Records Administration, Washington, DC.

53. *Mutual Film Corporation v. Industrial Commission of Ohio*, No. 456, 236 U.S. 230; 35 Sup. Ct. 387; 59 L. Ed. 552 (1915). Also the previous ruling, *Mutual Film Co. v. Industrial Commission of Ohio, et al.; Mutual Film Corporation v. Same*, No. 205, No. 206; 215 Fed. 138 (1914). See also "U.S. Government Fights Entry of Films," *Defender*, December 11, 1915.

54. "Showed Barred Fight Film," *NYT*, April 12, 1916; "Plan to Show Pictures of Johnson-Willard Fight," *Defender*, April 15; "Fight Films Not Seized," *NYT*, April 15; "Fight Film Jury Disagrees," *NYT*, July 14; "Fight Films Again Barred," *NYT*, September 2; *MPW*, September 16, 1808; *AFI Catalog*, 1042; Gilmore, *Bad Nigger*, 147; Jeffrey T. Sammons, *Beyond the Ring* (Urbana: University of Illinois Press, 1988), 45; Terry Ramsaye, *A Million and One Nights* (1926; reprint, New York: Simon and Schuster, 1986), 694–98.

55. *Pantomimic Corp. v. Malone et al.* No. 141, 238 Fed. 135 (1916); Ralph O. Willguss, "Pictorial Representations of Prize Fights," *New York Law Review* 6 (1928), 7–9; "Fight Films Again Barred," 16.

56. Richard Koszarski, personal correspondence, August 11, 1989.

57. "Showed Barred Fight Film," 12; *Pantomimic Corp. v. Malone, Federal Reporter*, 136–37; Ramsaye, *Million and One Nights*, 696–97. See Gertrude Jobes, *Motion Picture Empire* (Hamden, CT: Archon, 1966), 120, for a spurious retelling of the event at Rouses Point.

58. George Plimpton, *Shadow Box* (New York: Putnam, 1977), cited in Roberts, *Papa Jack*, 227; Joyce Carol Oates, *On Boxing* (Garden City, NY: Doubleday,

1987). Other documentary treatments of the Johnson fight pictures include *Jack Johnson: Black Power in the Ring* (1979, WABC-TV, New York) and *Jack Johnson* (1982, Big Fights, Inc.).

59. Johnson appeared in the black-cast motion pictures *As the World Rolls On* (1921), *For His Mother's Sake* (1922), and *The Black Thunderbolt* (1922). Twenty minutes of outtakes from the Fox Movietone newsreel *[Jack Johnson's Jazz Band]* (December 21, 1929) are in the University of South Carolina Newsfilm Library, MVTN 4–669.

8. BOOTLEGGING

1. Lynde Denig, "Willard-Moran Contest Pictures," *MPW*, April 8, 1916, 283; Jolo., "Willard-Moran Fight," in *Variety Film Reviews* (New York: Garland, 1983); "Observations by Our Man about Town," *MPW*, April 15, 1916, 430, and April 8, 323; *American Film Institute Catalog of Motion Pictures Produced in the United States, Feature Films, 1911–1920* (Berkeley: University of California Press, 1988), 1042; Rex Lardner, *The Legendary Champions* (New York: American Heritage Press, 1972), 219; Nat Fleischer and Sam Andre, *A Pictorial History of Boxing* (New York: Citadel Press, 1959), 93.

2. Lardner, *Legendary Champions* 219–20; Steven A. Riess, "In the Ring and Out: Professional Boxing in New York, 1896–1920," *Sport in America: New Historical Perspectives*, ed. Donald Spivey (Westport, CT: Greenwood, 1985), 109–24.

3. "Willard the Most Unpopular Champ," *The Stars and Stripes*, July 26, 1918, 6; "The Screen," *NYT*, June 19, 1919.

4. "Motion Pictures to Standardize Boxing," *NYT*, October 6, 1917; "Famous Boxing Stars Help To Train Troops," *NYT*, November 5, 1917; "Fulton Knocks Out Moran," *NYT*, February 26, 1918; "Athletic Events Shown on Screen," *NYT*, December 9, 1917. *Boxing: Naval Aviation Physical Training Manual* (Annapolis: U.S. Naval Institute, 1943), 9; *Boxing: A Guide to the Manly Art of Self Defense* (New York: American Sports Publishing, 1922), 18–21.

5. Jeffrey T. Sammons, *Beyond the Ring* (Urbana: University of Illinois Press, 1988), 50. Mike Gibbons was the subject of the first "Selig Sport Service" series distributed by VLSE. Ad in *MPW*, May 27, 1916, 1520.

The U.S. National Archives and Records Administration's motion-picture holdings include military documentaries with boxing scenes, such as *The Making of a Man-o-Warsman* (1916–17), *Training Officers for Our National Army* (1917), *Physical and Bayonet Training* (1918), *Training Activities of the (83rd) Division, Camp Sherman, Ohio* (1917–18), *Post-Armistice Training, 5th Division* (1918–19), *Miscellaneous Athletic Activities in the A.E.F.* (1918–19), *Boxing Exhibition* (1919), *The Reawakening, Ford Educational Weekly* [boxing for wounded veterans] (1920), and *Activities of Reserve Officers Training Corps, Camp Jackson, Columbia, S.C., July 19, 1920.*

6. "No Bout Film for A.E.F.," *NYT*, July 20, 1919.

7. "Rights for Pictures Let," *NYT*, June 27, 1919.

8. "Ohio Bars Pictures of Fight," *NYT*, July 8, 1919; "Less than $500,000, Rickard Now Says," July 9.

9. Riess, "In the Ring and Out," 124.

10. "Dempsey to Jail If Mails Films," *Trib*, January 26, 1921; "To Test Law Prohibiting the Transporting of Fight Films," *NYT*, January 27; "Not to Show Fight Films," January 28. See Randy Roberts, *Jack Dempsey: The Manassa Mauler* (Urbana: University of Illinois, 2003).

11. Lardner, *Legendary Champions*, 228–31.

12. Description based on a continuity script in the copyright deposit record for Quimby's film. "Slow Pictures of Bout; Dempsey-Carpentier Bout First to Be Filmed This Way," *NYT*, June 27, 1921; "Suit over Fight Pictures," *NYT*, September 18, 1921 "Jury Excuses McLean," *NYT*, May 1, 1924. Baynes also co-founded the Kinograms newsreel service in 1919.

13. "July 2 Fight Described by Radiophone," *Wireless Age*, July 1921, 10; "Voice-Broadcasting the Stirring Progress of the 'Battle of the Century,'" *Wireless Age*, August 1921, 11–21. See Thomas H. White, "'Battle of the Century': The WJY Story," January 1, 2000, www.earlyradiohistory.us (accessed May 28, 2004).

14. Sam Taub, "Broadcasting Boosts Boxing," *Everlast Boxing Record* (New York: Everlast Sports, 1929), 65–66; Christopher H. Sterling and John M. Kittross, *Stay Tuned* (Belmont, CA: Wadsworth, 1978) 61, 78.

15. "Reformers in Drive to 'Clean Up' Jersey," *NYT*, July 5, 1921; "Carpentier Sees Movies of Fight," July 8; "Fight Film Shown at 44th Street Theatre," July 31.

16. Charles L. Mee, Jr., *The Ohio Gang: The World of Warren G. Harding* (New York: M. Evans, 1981), 138–40; Harry Newman, "Big Official on Visit to Jack's Camp," *Los Angeles Times*, May 25, 1921.

17. "Miss Stinson Faces Cross-Examination," *Post*, March 24, 1924; Philip Kinsley, "Senators Hear How Fight Film 'Played' Chicago," *Trib*, April 11.

18. "Way Seems Clear For Fight Pictures," *NYT*, July 28, 1921; "Quimby and Richard Are Fined for Transporting Fight Films to New York," *MPW*, August 6, 1921, 585; "Fight Film Fine Paid by Kearns," *NYT*, April 11, 1924. See also Harry M. Daugherty, with Thomas Dixon, *The Inside Story of the Harding Tragedy*, New York: Churchill, 1932.

19. The *Washington Post* covered the 1924 Senate investigation of Daugherty extensively, including these articles: "Fight Films Receipts Figured at $50,000," March 15; "Graft in Fight Film Charged by Quimby," March 16; "Daugherty Hearing Today Centers on Fight-Film Charge," March 17; passim. *New York Times* coverage of the Rickard trial includes "Rickard and Others Reported Indicted for Marketing Dempsey Fight Pictures," May 21, 1924; "Rickard Convicted in Fight Film Case," March 20, 1925; "Rickard Is Fined $7,000 in Film Plot," March 31, 1925; "Muma Loses Film Appeal," December 3, 1926; passim. Committee on Investigation of Attorney General, Select, Senate, *Investigation of Hon. Harry M. Daugherty, Formerly Attorney General of the U.S.*, vol. 1, 68th Cong., 1st sess., April 1–4, 1924.

20. Orr obituary, *Variety*, April 19, 1950, 63. Orr worked for Loews until his death.

21. "Rickard Fight Films Held Up in Chicago," *NYT*, August 19, 1921; "Calls Ettelson Overeager on Movie Opinion," *Trib*, November 22, 1921.

22. "Peanut Man Films Championship Fight," *Post*, July 28, 1921; " 'Great Fight' Film Injunction," *The Times*, July 29.

23. Gaston B. Means, in his bestseller *The Strange Death of President Harding* (New York: Guild, 1930), 215, listed the "privileges" taken by Daugherty's group as including "the exhibition of the Dempsey-Carpentier Fight Film pictures which netted us around seven or eight million dollars." Means, a federal agent in 1921, testified to Congress about Daugherty's corruption. However, Means was a lifelong criminal and con man and was convicted of extortion in the 1932 Lindbergh baby kidnapping case.

24. "Fight Film Shown at 44th Street Theatre"; "Rickard Arraigned in Chicago," *NYT*, August 19, 1921; "Tex Rickard is Fined $500," November 2; "$1,000 Fine for Fight Film Violation," November 3, 16; "Will See Fight Pictures," November 13; passim.

The cinematographer Fred Balshofer tells a convoluted anecdote about fight-picture racketeering. Balshofer claimed that scam artists, purporting to be agents of the governor of New York and Tex Rickard, approached him about filming the Dempsey-Carpentier bout. (His description suggests that William Orr might have been involved.) They would combine photography with animated boxing figures to create a film capable of evading the statute. They supplied Balshofer with an excerpt of the 1920 *Dempsey-Brennan Fight*. The bunco men sold phony stock certificates before disappearing. Fred J. Balshofer and Arthur C. Miller, *One Reel a Week* (Berkeley: University of California Press, 1967), 156–60.

Although using animation to evade the fight film law might sound implausible, Arnold Fanck's Berg- und Sportfilm GmbH released Leopold Blonder's animated short *Der Große Boxkampf Dempsey–Carpentier* (1921), now lost.

25. "Frederick C. Quimby Leaves Associated Exhibitors," *MPW*, October 30 1920, 1273; "Frederick Quimby Joins Universal," *MPW*, February 2, 1924, 417; Quimby obituary, *Variety*, September 22, 1965, 63. Gene Tunney starred in a Pathé serial, *The Fighting Marine* (1926).

There were two other exceptions to the rule that Hollywood players stayed out of boxing films. David O. Selznick entered the business by producing a short profile of the boxer Luis Firpo, *Will He Conquer Dempsey?* (1923), for his father's company. That same year, Universal shot "Milk Fund fight pictures" (Firpo v. McAuliffe at Yankee Stadium) for a charitable event. The studio head, Carl Laemmle, issued a statement saying that Universal would not release the films outside New York. Although "swamped with requests," he would pass up the "tempting money" of perhaps a million dollars. "Fight Film Restrictions," *NYT*, May 20, 1923.

26. "Title Bout Film Seized Here by U.S.," *Los Angeles Times*, July 18, 1923; "Movies of Battle Coming by Plane," *Post*, July 6; "Enjoins Police from Stopping Fight Pictures," *Trib*, September 1; "Freedom of the Screen," *NYT*, September 5.

27. "Slow Films Show Details of Fight," *NYT,* September 16, 1923; "Kearns Wants Films 'Doctored' for Champ," *Post,* September 16; "May Show Films of Dempsey-Firpo," *Hartford Courant,* October 14; "Arrest Starts Test of Fight Pictures," *Post,* November 7; Frank Smith, "Dempsey-Firpo Film Ends Knockdown Row," *Trib,* November 30; "Firpo Fight Film Seized," *Los Angeles Times,* February 2, 1924.

28. "Firpo Has Boxing Science of His Own," *NYT,* August 19, 1923; "In the Press Box with Baxter," *Post,* August 22.

29. Leon D. Britton made *The Official Motion Pictures of the Johnny Buff and Pancho Villa Fight* (Arista, 1922). He handled the *Firpo-Brennan Fight* (1923) and later claimed to have "been making fight pictures since the Dempsey-Willard bout." "New Incorporations," *NYT,* December 19, 1922; "New York Bidder Gets Bout Picture Rights," *NYT,* September 14, 1926; "Dempsey-Tunney Bout Movies Stolen," *Post,* February 9, 1927; "Seeks Ban on Tunney Film Showing," *NYT,* February 9, 1927; "Britton Buys Film Rights to Schmeling-Sharkey Bout," *Trib,* April 21, 1932; Leon Britton obituary, *Variety,* January 19, 1966, 75.

30. "Prize Fight Film Exhibited," *Trib,* January 23, 1927; "Tunney Will Review Title Fight Pictures," *Post,* July 3; "Last Showing of Dempsey Fight Pictures," *Los Angeles Times,* July 16; "Great Moments from Great Ring Fights" ad in *NYT,* March 30, 1924.

The Rise and Fall of Jack Dempsey (1928) was produced by Sam Hall, a sports editor and fight publicist. Hall's film was copyrighted by Simon Greiver [or Grevier], whose American Cinema Company had distributed duped prints of the first Dempsey-Tunney Fight in Illinois. See Juli Jones Jr., "The Fight Pictures," *Defender,* December 10, 1921; "Dempsey-Tunney Bout Movies Stolen, Claim," *Post,* February 9, 1927.

31. "Suit over Dempsey Film," *NYT,* August 9, 1927; "Starts Investigation into Fight Films," *NYT,* September 8; James Press. Dawson, "Bout Dispute Grows as Dempsey's Blows Escape Slow Movies," *NYT,* July 23; "Films of Bout Provide No Decision," *Post,* July 23.

32. *Post* coverage included "Rickard and His Boxers Face Trial over Films," September 29, 1927; "[G. B. Shaw] Sees Film," October 9; "Fight Films," October 13; "Showing Fight Film No Crime," October 15; "Prize Fight Films," October 18; "Fight Films Held Legal in N.Y.," October 21; "Prize-Fight Films," October 13, 1928. See also "Seizure of Fight Films," *Yale Law Journal* 37, no. 7 (May 1928): 992–93; "Exhibition and Advertisement of Prize Fight Films as Acts Effecting the Object of Conspiracy to Transport Films," *Virginia Law Review* 15, no. 3 (January 1929): 273–74; "Seizure of Fight Films Transported in Interstate Commerce," *Columbia Law Review* 29, no. 5 (May 1929): 677–78.

33. "Seize Owner of Tunney-Dempsey Fight Pictures," *Trib,* September 24, 1927; "Fight Films Go On as Inquiry Opens," *NYT,* October 11, 1927; "Indict Six for Plot to Ship Prize Fight Film," *Trib,* July 25, 1929; "Tuttle Is Balked Tracing Fight Film," *NYT,* October 8, 1927. Title card from 35 mm print at the Library of Congress, FEB 5059, AFI-Marshall Collection. The library holds several

different nitrate prints of the 1927 *Tunney-Dempsey Fight*. Only one (an incomplete version) has been preserved. The print has no Goodart credit on it, but it includes a certificate from the Ohio film censorship board, followed by a card reading "This print produced by the Columbus Industrial Film Co., Columbus, Ohio"—and is thus an example of one of the many bootleg copies.

34. "Fight Film Rivalry," *NYT*, October 9, 1927; "Acts to Clarify Law Fight Film Ban," *NYT*, October 12.

35. "Will Rogers Remarks," *Los Angeles Times*, September 30, 1927; "Fight Films Here," *NYT*, October 2; "Fight Film Shown," *NYT*, October 7; "Dempsey Fight Film Shown on Leviathan," *NYT*, October 18; ads in *Trib*, September 21–22; "N.Y. Sees Fight Pictures," *Trib*, October 8.

36. Felicia Pearson, "Moviegraphs," *Post*, November 6, 1927. In her debut column ("Movie Graph," November 21, 1926), Pearson alluded to the first Dempsey-Tunney fight and cheered that "America has invented the sport film." In 1927, Pearson was perhaps referencing the Pathé-Baby brand name to mean any in-home projector. The Pathé Baby was a 9.5 mm projector; she likely saw a 16 mm film print. If *Tunney-Dempsey II* circulated in 9.5 mm form, Pathé did not advertise it. By 1927 the 9.5 mm equipment was marketed as "Pathex" in the United States. Its 1926 catalog of titles for sale included *Boxing Form*, part of the "Grantland Rice Sportlight" series. The three-minute reels showed Tunney sparring with Corbett. Rice staged the event for cameras on a Manhattan rooftop in 1925, revisiting a mode of fight-picture production used thirty years earlier.

Thanks to 9.5 mm and Pathex experts William O'Farrell and Jerry Wagner. E-mail correspondence, September 6–7, 2006. See also Wagner's web site, www.pathex.com, and Grantland Rice, *The Tumult and the Shouting: My Life in Sport* (New York: Barnes, 1954), chapter 11.

37. "Fight Films," *St. Louis Post-Dispatch*, in *Trib*, October 10, 1927; "Moving Pictures of Prize Fights," *Trib*, April 1, 1925; "Fight over the Fight Films," *Literary Digest*, October 29, 1927, 16; Rolfe Humphries, "Fight Films," *New Republic*, November 2, 286–88; R. E. Sherwood, "The Silent Drama," *Life*, October 20, 30; "Film Bootlegging Next?" *NYT*, October 21. Pettijohn, quoted in "Boxing Enjoys Boon Year," *Hartford Courant*, December 26, 1926. Subsequent editorials included "Prize-Fight Films," *Post*, October 13, 1928; "Against Fight Screens," *Post*, December 2, 1928.

38. "N.Y. Sees Fight Pictures," *Trib*, October 8, 1927; "Film Witnesses Unable to Tell Jack from Gene," *Trib*, December 7.

39. Crafts erroneously charged that Daugherty had been "the attorney for Jack Dempsey when Dempsey was in trouble as a war slacker." "Censorship for Films Advocated," *Los Angeles Times*, May 10, 1922; "Charges Five Men Run Film Industry," *NYT*, May 12.

40. Alva Johnston, "Films Put on Ice for Fans Yet Unborn," *NYT*, October 24, 1926.

41. James P. Dawson, "Board to Support Film Ban Repeal," *NYT*, December 15, 1926; "Prize Fight Film Exhibited Here; Is Held Legal," *Trib*, January 23, 1927;

"Asks Fight Film Repeal," *NYT*, October 7; "Fight Films Held Legal in N.Y.," *Post*, October 21; "Legalizes Fight Films," *NYT*, October 25; "Fight Films Seized," *NYT*, November 2; "Celler Bill to Repeal Anti-Fight Film Law," *NYT*, December, 8; "A Sensible Repeal," *NYT*, January 20, 1928; "Moves to End Fight Film Ban," *NYT*, May 5, 1934; "Dempsey Here to Urge Repeal of Law Prohibiting Fight Films," *Post*, May 25, 1939; "Fight Films Shipment Ban Is Rescinded," *Post*, July 2, 1940; Sammons, *Beyond the Ring*, 87, 136–37.

Among the motion pictures copyrighted during the 1930s were: *Jack Sharkey–Max Schmeling* (1930), *Schmeling-Stribling* (1931), *Jack Sharkey–Mickey Walker* (1931), *Max Schmeling–Mickey Walker* (1932), *Tony Canzoneri–Billy Petrolle* (1932), *Primo Carnera vs. Ernie Schaaf* (1933), *Max Schmeling–Max Baer* (1933), *Jack Sharkey–Primo Carnera* (1933), *Jimmy McLarnin–Barney Ross* (1934), *Primo Carnera–Max Baer* (1934), *Barney Ross–Jimmy McLarnin* (1934), *Jack Dempsey–King Levinsky* (1935), *Max Baer–King Levinsky* (1935), *Tony Canzoneri–Lew Ambers* (1935), *Max Baer–James J. Braddock* (1935), *Max Baer–Joe Louis* (1935), *Joe Louis–Max Schmeling* (1936), *Joe Louis–Jack Sharkey* (1937), *Joe Louis–Tommy Farr* (1937), *Barney Ross–Henry Armstrong* (1938), *Joe Louis–Max Schmeling* (1938), *Melio Bettina–Billy Conn* (1939), *Henry Armstrong–Lou Ambers* (1939), *Max Baer–Lou Nova* (1939), and *Joe Louis–Tony Galento* (1939).

42. "Showing Fight Films Is Held to Be Legal," *NYT*, October 21, 1927; "Legalizes Fight Films," *NYT*, October 25, passim.

43. Fulton Brylawski to Register of Copyright, Library of Congress, August 3, 1928, in copyright deposit record for *World Heavyweight Championship Boxing Contest between Gene Tunney and Tom Heeney*. A letter in the 1921 deposit record for *Dempsey-Carpentier* (mistakenly addressed to the U.S. Patents Office) was authored by Fred C. Quimby. My thanks to Sam Brylawski for information on Fulton.

44. Otis C. Ferguson, "Pictures of the Joe Louis–Max Schmeling Fight," *New Republic*, July 8, 1936, 266; Jack Dietz obituary, *Variety*, February 12, 1969, 63; "Accused of Tax Evasion," *NYT*, September 17, 1942. The practice of filming boxing was so well established in the photographic industry by the thirties that Eastman Kodak, when announcing its new high-speed motion-picture film stock, could say "Prize fight pictures, taken under incandescent lights, will be better." "Kodak Develops New Speed Film," *Wall Street Journal*, February 6, 1931.

45. Charles J. McGuirk, "The Inside Story of the Fight Racket," *New McClure's*, November 1928, 18–21, 129–33; "Big Bill Duffy Dies," *NYT*, May 26, 1952; "Sue to Regain Film of Schmeling Fight," *NYT*, July 15, 1931; Senate Committee on Interstate Commerce, *Legalizing Transportation of Prize-Fight Films*, 76th Cong., 1st sess., May 25–26, 1939, 1–70.

46. "Life Story of Joe Louis: First Big Money," *NYT*, Nov 8, 1948.

47. "Fight Film Carrier Is Not Found," *NYT*, July 14, 1931.

48. "600 Prisoners Hail Lecturer Tunney," *NYT*, January 4, 1932; Nelson B. Bell, "Recent Fisticuffing Revives Problem of Widespread Exhibition of Fight

Films," *Post*, September 27, 1935; "This Morning with Shirley Povich," *Post*, May 22, 1939.

49. Testimony of M. C. Moore (Riverside Theater, Jacksonville, Florida), *Legalizing Transportation of Prize-Fight Films*, 1–70.

50. "Dempsey . . . Seeking to Have Federal Law Barring Shipping of Fight Films Changed," *Post*, May 26, 1939; "Fight Films Shipment Ban Is Rescinded," *Post*, July 2, 1940; *Divesting Prize-Fight Films of Their Character as Subjects of Interstate and Foreign Commerce*, H. Rept. 2348, May 30, 1940.

51. *Variety*, April 30, 1941, 16; *NYT*, May 2. No sepia or other tinting or toning is visible in the monochromatic version of *The Great American Broadcast* shown on the Fox Movie Channel (available on the gray market, DVD-R #MU-142, maymeadcompany.com, 2005). The sequence, however, artfully intercuts *Dempsey-Willard* footage and studio shots, with added sound effects (punches, bells, and crowd noise) aiding the continuity.

52. Clarence Muse, "What's Going On in Hollywood," *Chicago Defender*, January 6, 1940.

53. "Dempsey Fight Seen Again," *NYT*, November 17, 1939; "Dempsey-Willard Fight Films, 'Lost' for Many Years," *Post*, November 19.

54. "Louis Shows as Peer of All Heavies," *Hartford Courant*, January 22, 1944; "This Morning with Shirley Povich," *Post*, April 12; Arthur Daley, "Kings of the Ring," *NYT*, February 4; "Famous Ring Bouts Shown," *Los Angeles Times*, March 4. Henry Sonenshine sued Martin Lewis for using his 1927 footage of *Dempsey-Sharkey* and *Dempsey-Tunney* in *Kings of the Ring*. The films were clearly in the public domain, however, never having been copyrighted. "Dempsey Pictures Damage Suit Basis," *Los Angeles Times*, March 15.

55. Paul Zimmerman, "Sport Postscripts," *Los Angeles Times*, April 27, 1940; Leland Lewis obituary, *Variety*, September 29, 1943, 54.

56. Al Costello, "The Fight Racket," *Post*, December 19, 1943.

57. Eric Schaefer, *Bold! Daring! Shocking! True! A History of Exploitation Films, 1919–1959* (Durham, NC: Duke University Press, 1999); "Wages of Sin: David F. Friedman Interviewed by David Schute," *Film Comment*, July–August 1986, 32–48. Marion Post Walcott's Farm Securities Administration photograph (LC-USF34- 052508-D) of the "Rex Theatre for Colored People," taken in Leland, Mississippi in November 1939, reveals movie posters for the *Joe Louis–Bob Pastor Fight* (September 1939).

On Joe Louis, see Lauren Sklaroff, "Constructing G.I. Joe Louis: Cultural Solutions to the 'Negro Problem' During World War II," *Journal of American History* 89, no. 3 (2002): 958–83; Chris Mead, *Champion Joe Louis: Black Hero in White America* (New York: Scribner's, 1985); Lenwood G. Davis, ed. *Joe Louis: A Bibliography of Articles, Books, Pamphlets, Records, and Archival Materials*, (Westport, CT: Greenwood, 1983).

58. "This Morning With Shirley Povich," *Post*, June 19, 1939.

59. "Radio Men Regard Television as Ally," *NYT*, January 15, 1928.

60. Sammons, 130–83; "Television Covers a Prizefight," *NYT*, June 23, 1946.

61. Tim Brooks and Earle Marsh, *The Complete Directory to Prime Time Network TV Shows, 1946–Present* (New York: Ballantine, 1979), 81–82, 706–23.

62. Jack Gould, "Television Shown on Theatre Screen," *NYT*, Apr. 15, 1948; Leslie Bell, *Inside the Fight Game* (London: Rocklift, 1952); A. J. Liebling, *The Sweet Science* (New York: Viking, 1956). See Benjamin G. Rader, *In Its Own Image: How Television Has Transformed Sports* (New York: Free Press, 1984).

63. Peter Arnold, *History of Boxing* (Secaucus, NJ: Chartwell, 1985), 63–64; Robert Desnos, "Eroticism" (1923), in *The Shadow and Its Shadow: Surrealist Writings on Cinema*, ed. Paul Hammond (London: BFI, 1978), 122–23.

64. Martin Esslin, *Brecht: The Man and His Work* rev. ed. (New York: Norton, 1974), 31. Fritz Kortner's recitation of Brecht's "found poetry" about the death of Stanley Ketchel was taken from a boxing magazine: "Stanley Ketchel, famous for 4 real battles against Billie Papke and as the roughest fighter of all time. Shot from behind at the age of 23, on a smiling autumn day, sitting in front of his farm. Unbeaten." In 1927 Brecht completed his poem "*Gedenktafel für 12 Weltmeister*" *[Tablet to the Memory of 12 World Champions]*. See Klaus Völker, *Brecht: A Biography*, trans. John Nowell (New York: Seabury, 1978), 90–91; John Willett, *Art and Politics in the Weimar Period* (New York: Pantheon, 1978), 102–3; Willett, *The Weimar Years* (New York: Abbeville Press, 1984), 106–7; John M. Hoberman, *Sport and Political Ideology* (Austin: University of Texas Press, 1984), 9.

"Stanley Ketchel was 24 years old when he was fatally shot in the back by the common-law husband of the lady who was cooking his breakfast." John Lardner's lead for "Ketchel Was a Wild Man" (*True*, May 1954), became an often-quoted bit of prose poetry, perhaps linked in some way to Brecht's found poetry about the 1910 murder of Ketchel. The great writer and raconteur Dick Schaap spontaneously recited it to me during a conversation in 1994. Lardner's line is quoted in many sources, including: Red Smith, "A Lady Who Was wit' Ketchel," *NYT*, July 5, 1976; Tom Callahan, "Boxing's Allure," *Time*, June 27, 1988, 66; and in the book by Dick's son, Jeremy Schaap, *Cinderella Man: James Braddock, Max Baer, and the Greatest Upset in Boxing History* (Boston: Houghton Mifflin, 2005), 137.

65. "Figuratively Speaking," *NYT*, July 27, 1927.

Index

Ketchel, Stanley (*continued*)
  Johnson vs. Stanley Ketchell [*sic*]
  (film; 1909)
Ketchel-Thomas fight (1907), 340n40
Keystone, 250, 355n7
Kilbane, Johnny, 184
Kilpatrick, J. Reed, 284
Kilrain, Jake, 36
Kimball, Moses, 87
kinematograph, 71
kinetograph, 22; boxing and, 28; *Corbett
  and Courtney before the Kinetograph* filmed by, 34–39; early experiments with, 23–26, 24, 27–28; film
  capacity expanded, 29, 43–44; immobility of, 25; precinematic antecedents
  of, 26–28; profitability of, 53
Kinetographic Theatre, 40
Kineto, Ltd, 240, 353n142
kinetoscope, 3, 57; antipugilism bills
  concerning, 317n36; boxing and, 17,
  23, 28, 30; competing models,
  42–43; displacement of, 44, 45–46;
  popularity of, 35, 310n23; problems
  of, 315n5, 316n16; ringside photography for exhibition on, 56; rumored failure of, 65–67; running
  time of, 24–25; as verification in
  sports disputes, 74–77
Kinetoscope Company: as Edison subcontractor, 23, 29, 40; interfranchise
  competition and, 40–41, 43, 47; *Jeffries and Ruhlin Sparring Contest*
  (1901) and, 116–18; productions of,
  40–41, 41; sparring scenes by, 25;
  waning sales of, 47
Kinetoscope Exhibiting Company, 107;
  *Corbett and Courtney before the
  Kinetograph* produced by, 34–39;
  Corbett contract with, 54; as Edison
  subcontractor, 23, 29, 40, 44, 47, 53;
  feature-length films of, 33; financial
  backing of, 50–51; Fitzsimmons-
  Maher fight and, 56; incorporation
  of, 30; interfranchise competition
  and, 40–41, 43, 47; *Leonard-
  Cushing Fight* (1894) filmed by,

29–34, 31; letterhead of, 35, 35;
  licensing of, 53; Rector as director
  of, 47, 48, 65; sporting circle ties of,
  43; technological improvements demanded by, 43–44
Kings of the Ring (film; 1944), 285,
  366n54
kinodrome, 58, 136
Kipling, Rudyard, 21
Kiss, The (film; 1896), 25, 58
Klaus, Frank, 246
Klaw and Erlanger, 47
Kleine, George, 67, 178, 185, 209,
  210–11, 229
Kleine Optical Company, 118, 178,
  342n60
Kortner, Fritz, 289, 367n64
Krone, John ("Doc"), 182, 201, 204,
  218, 234

Laemmle, Carl, 183, 362n25
Laemmle Film Service, 183
Lahey, James W., 42
Laken, Jack, 286–87
Lambda Company, 44–45
Langford-Flynn Fight (film; 1910), 242
Langford-Ketchel Fight (film; 1910),
  182, 234
Langford-McVey fight (1911), 241
Langford, Sam, 183–84, 234, 240, 241,
  242
Langtry (Texas/Mexico frontier),
  56–57, 315n5
lantern slide shows, 79, 233–34
Lardner, John, 367n64
Lardner, Rex, 310n25
Last Round Ended in a Free Fight, The
  (film; 1903), 98
Latham, Gray, 3, 29, 44, 46, 50, 53, 56,
  60, 73, 313n63
Latham loop, 45
Latham, Otway, 29, 50, 53, 56, 73,
  313n63
Latham, Rector and Tilden. *See* Kine-
  toscope Exhibiting Company
Latham, Woodville, 29, 44, 312–13n54,
  313n63, 314n75

Text:	10/13 Aldus
Display:	Aldus
Compositor:	Binghamton Valley Composition
Indexer:	Kevin Millham
Printer and binder:	Thomson-Shore, Inc.